TRANSFORMING RUSSIA AND CHINA

TRANSFORMING
RUSSIA AND CHINA
Revolutionary Struggle in the Twentieth Century

William G. Rosenberg
and
Marilyn B. Young

New York   Oxford
OXFORD UNIVERSITY PRESS
1982

Copyright © 1982 by Oxford University Press, Inc.

Library of Congress Cataloging in Publication Data
Rosenberg, William G.
Transforming Russia and China.

Bibliography: p.
Includes index.
1. Soviet Union—History—1917–   . 2. China—
History—1900–   3. Communism—Soviet Union—
History. 4. Communism—China—History. I. Young,
Marilyn Blatt. II. Title.
DK266.R645   947.084   81–2306
ISBN 0–19–502965–8   AACR2
ISBN 0–19–502966–6 (pbk.)

Printing (last digit): 9 8 7 6 5 4 3 2 1

Printed in the United States of America

To
Sarah and Peter
and
Lauren and Michael

Preface
REVOLUTION AS PROCESS

> When I look at myself and everything
> I, Juan Without Anything only yesterday,
> and now Juan With Everything
> and today with everything,
> I look around, I look,
> I see myself and everything
> and I ask myself how it happened.

Nicolás Guillén

This book grew directly out of our experience teaching a course comparing the Russian and Chinese revolutions to diverse groups of students, many of whom were themselves engaging in American political life in a manner and to a degree unwitnessed for almost three decades. The historical vacuum in which they seemed to be operating, the crude historical analogies they were given to drawing, disturbed us. The lack of adequate teaching materials was a constant problem. No single volume drew together, in a usable analytic narrative, the exceptional complexities of theory and practice represented by the two major revolutions of the twentieth century. None focused in humanistic terms on what it was like, for millions of people, to live through these extraordinary transformations. What we wanted for our students, what we needed to do for ourselves, was to write a history of both revolutions that would capture the intimate meaning of Nicolás Guillén's poem. With considerable trepidation, we undertook this volume.

Given our students' political and social backgrounds, it is not surprising that "communism" meant merely Stalinist dictatorship or Maoist utopianism, or that communist revolution meant conspiracy, violence, and the overthrow of "legitimate" governments. Even democratic socialism was frequently dismissed, by the Left as inadequate, by the Right as illegitimate and radical, despite the dominant role of socialist parties in every major country of Western Europe. In our view, the fact that the United States alone, of all advanced industrial democracies, lacks both an influential socialist party and any perceptible socialist sympathies must be considered one of the great feats of cultivated political misunderstanding in modern history.

We will leave the issue of cultivated misunderstanding to those interested in exploring the American past. Before turning to Russia and China, however, a few words must be said more generally about conceptions and misconceptions of revolution.

Despite the Fourth of July, Patriots' Day, and the Bicentennial, or perhaps because of them, revolution has never had a very vivid place in the American imagination. It is seen as an event, specific and destructive, from which some societies recover (France), while others are permanently damaged (Russia, China, Cuba). Order, not change, is seen as normative and prescriptive; revolution occurs when social mechanisms necessary to stability break down, through disruption due to war, the failure of the system to meet the rising expectations of its people, the power lust of particular individuals, and so on.[1]

Apart from shortcomings in understanding revolution itself, such perspectives make it difficult to comprehend how societies function under "normal" conditions. They fail to appreciate, for example, the regular application of violence within established systems as a means of maintaining their institutions and values.[2] But the greatest difficulty is the implicit equation of social order with moral virtue, and the way such perspectives have developed as prescriptive and predictive components of government policy formation. Once one assumes that stasis, rather than change, is a normative and moral condition, one tinkers in the laboratory of political science for the precise mix of policies that will ensure the control of disruptive social elements.[3]

Also, by definition, a struggle for stability is largely a struggle to preserve that which already exists, whether it be political institutions or social values. And the desirability of such preservation must vary in relation to the benefits it bestows on one or another social group. Morality in social order, in other words, is a contingent set of values; and the very thrust of radical forces may be to challenge the moral prerogatives of established groups, governments, or institutions.

It is true, of course, that revolutions can conveniently be associated with a specific date on which sovereignty passed to the revolutionaries (1917, 1949). But in our understanding of the term, revolutions cannot be encompassed by that date. They are not simple coups d'état, in which power is passed from one sector of the ruling elite to another. Like history itself, revolutions must be examined as dynamic phenomena, as *process*, if they are to be fully understood.

The elements of mobilization that bring the revolutionary group to power are only part of what must be explored. Some insist that, once in power, revolution is to all intents and purposes over. What happens next is simply about how a new state uses its power to reshape the society. Yet both the Soviet Union and China were for a time ongoing revolutionary *societies*; and in both, the ability of the new revolutionary government to realize its impelling social vision was shaped by the way in which each had come to power, as well as the world in which each had to survive. Hence state power also meant the *possibility* of ongoing radical change. How, when, and in what form the possibilities opened by 1917 and 1949 were subsequently realized or aborted is an integral part of understanding revolution as a historical process.

We are not here especially concerned with the broader abstractions of underdevelopment, backwardness, or modernization that are often inferred by the terms "revolution" and "process," but rather that revolutions be perceived in terms of the unceasing dynamics of historical development. Most important, one must understand the ways in which various components of society relate to each other *over time* in order to appreciate revolutionary tasks or evaluate success and failure.[4]

We wish to emphasize that this book is not a general history of Russia and China in the twentieth century, but a study of their revolutionary development. Moreover, those who hope to find here a category of differences and similarities will be disappointed. We are not primarily interested in thematic comparisons, in chronicling the course of Sino-Soviet differences, or in examining the thick layer of arguments and polemics that have covered both interstate relations and the internal development of each society. Rather, our aim is to lay bare the principal historical features determining the development and outcome of these two great twentieth-century revolutions, and to analyze parallel developments within the specificity of Russian and Chinese historical contexts. Our study might even more properly be called a parallel history, rather than a strictly comparative one. What is important is how context structures development and how the efforts of replication or emulation on the one hand, and the implementation of theoretical abstractions on the other, are both circumscribed by the real conditions in which revolutionary development takes place.

Thus historical context dominates the chapters that follow. Our intention, in a phrase, is to see the revolutionary transformations of Russia and China as if from the inside out, as they occurred, and as they were perceived by those involved. We start with an inquiry into the basic characteristics of these contexts, investigating established institutions and value systems, and asking by whom, and for what reasons, they were considered immutable by established authorities. We then analyze the emergence of revolutionary situations, asking why and how these situations matured into revolutionary episodes. As readers will see, we lay heavy stress on the historical timing of these episodes and argue that in terms of subsequent revolutionary development there were paradoxical features in both the successes and failures of the Russian and Chinese Communist parties coming to power when they did. In neither case, moreover, do we believe that the outcome of these episodes could have been predicted, a characteristic that emphasizes the importance of historical circumstance and contingency. We then look in detail at the means by which the challenges of social context were addressed in both societies and analyze the ways in which revolutionary outcomes were structured. Finally, without trying to offer a new taxonomy of revolutionary change, we ask questions about the success and failure of Russian and Chinese revolutionary development and offer our judgments.

Our approach, in sum, is quite simple and straightforward. We want to learn about the broad similarities and differences in general developmental patterns between the two great revolutionary sequences of the twentieth century. Our ultimate goal, as direct as our method, is the simple one of historical consciousness and understanding. With "Juan Without Anything only yesterday" we ask ourselves "how it happened."

Ann Arbor   W.G.R.
New York   M.B.Y.
July 1981

ACKNOWLEDGMENTS

This book has been a collective effort in a number of ways. Our first acknowledgment must be to the students at The University of Michigan, and its Residential College, with whom its ideas and perspectives were first worked out. Intellectually challenging, morally passionate, tactically creative, they helped us learn as we tried to teach them.

Many colleagues and friends have read all or parts of the draft manuscript, and we are eager to express our thanks and appreciation. Charles Bright, Blanche Cook, Geoff Eley, Michael Geyer, Susan F. Harding, Carl Riskin, and Ronald G. Suny gave us the benefit of many useful and thoughtful observations, often from perspectives different than our own. We are particularly indebted to Thomas Bernstein, Stephen F. Cohen, James Peck, and Ernest P. Young for detailed, thorough critiques. Our work is better for their generous efforts.

Nancy Lane, our editor at Oxford University Press, has been patiently supportive throughout. Melanie Miller did a superb job of copyediting, which went beyond stylistic consistency to important matters of substance. We are grateful to the National Endowment for the Humanities for a generous grant in support of our work. Obviously this in no way associates the Endowment with our views.

Preparation of the volume was also supported by the Center for Russian and East European Studies at The University of Michigan. We thank with pleasure its successive directors, Deming Brown and Zvi Gitelman, and its able Administrative Assistant Darlene Breitner. We have been blessed by a superb typist in Jo Thomas, a Ph.D. candidate in political science, whose sharpness often saved us from errors and whose many abilities greatly facilitated our work.

Finally, we wish to say a word about mutual authorship, and its enormous rewards, if also occasional strains. Working and writing together was a remarkable experience. If only we could find a gracious way to thank each other, we would. Arguing, cajoling, criticizing, and always learning, we feel the volume is the result of our joint efforts in every way. We share prose, analysis, and responsibility throughout. In preparing both drafts and revisions, we worked separately and together, on our own and each other's pages and typewriters, in each of our kitchens, chastising and counseling our own and each other's children, who displayed unwarranted tolerance for our strewn papers, smoke, and loud voices. We owe a mutual and heartfelt debt to Ernie Young, whose clear intelligence has deepened our understanding of both Chinese and Russian revolutionary history. At moments of maximum stress, Elie Rosenberg was somehow able to sympathize with us both, absorbing rather than transmitting our petulance and frustration. Her equanimity, understanding, and continued friendship in the face of great provocation have been truly remarkable.

CONTENTS

A Note on
Transliteration and Pronunciation

In transliterating Chinese, we employ the *pinyin* system made standard by the People's Republic in 1979, with some exceptions: names romanized from the Cantonese, such as Chiang Kai-shek and Sun Yat-sen, retain their more common spelling; Kuomintang is preferred for the ease and familiarity of the acronym KMT; we use Peking, still the dateline of the *New York Times*, rather than Beijing, although we follow new usage referring to issues of the journal *Beijing Review* after 1979. *Pinyin* (literally, "to phoneticize") has now been widely adopted by writers and scholars, but virtually all books published in English prior to 1979 use the nineteenth-century Wade-Giles system. As an aid to translating between the two, we use both forms for proper nouns in our index.

Russian names, in general, are transliterated according to the Library of Congress system, again with several common exceptions like Trotsky and Alexander.

In pronouncing anglicized Chinese, the *x* is sounded halfway between *s* and *sh*; *q* sounds like "chee" in cheese; *z* is pronounced as in zebra and *zh* like the *j* in judge. In Russian, the sometimes formidable *shch* (as in Khrushchev) is simply like the *sh* and *ch* in fresh cheese. Russian in general is pronounced as it is written, although proper nouns have only one stressed syllable.

1

REVOLUTIONARY RUSSIA
AND THE DILEMMAS
OF SOCIAL DEMOCRACY

THE DYING VILLAGE

Early one morning in the spring of 1901 a young Russian doctor left the railroad station in the provincial town of Voronezh and headed into the countryside. He had been asked by a liberal regional journal to prepare a study on peasant welfare and was on his way to the village of Novo-Zhivotinnyi, a rural settlement some sixteen miles from town. The air was clear, but deep mud in the road made travel difficult, and by the time the doctor had reached the village, most of its inhabitants had long since trudged to the fields. He could see them from a distance, some struggling against the mire with simple wooden plows, others standing upright to no apparent purpose, their coarse grey tunics, rope belts, and cotton leg wrappings a literal symbol of their cultural and social distance from cosmopolitan Moscow and St. Petersburg.

The village itself was not a large one. According to the most recent census, it contained 664 persons divided into ninety-six households, a size some regarded as ideal for efficient production and economic self-sufficiency. It was also well situated, lying close to the Don river and less than two miles from a major, well-travelled highway. Its rough-hewn log huts, with their nondescript thatched roofs and decorated windows, had been built almost directly next to each other, giving the appearance of a strong, unbroken chain.

But appearances were deceptive. The closer the young doctor came, the more reality impressed itself. There were no trade establishments in the village, no inns or taverns, and none in the surrounding countryside. A small drinking-house, which had operated intermittently for several years, had recently closed; the only public places in the village other than the school and church were two tiny shops, each with a small supply of inexpensive goods. The huts themselves were small, cold, and poorly lit, their very proximity to one another an indication of the extreme insufficiency of the land. In all of Novo-Zhivotinnyi there were only two real beds; when the doctor had finished his inspection, he had found inadequate ventilation, poor sanitation, filth, and cockroaches in 90 percent of the dwellings.

It was clear from conversation that there was little the peasants felt they could do about this. Their task was to labor either on the small acreage owned collectively by the village or on fields rented from the old Count Venevitinov, whose great manor house could be seen in the distance. Just as they had done for decades, when they toiled as serfs and were the Count's personal property, they would soon redivide their land in fairness to each of the households, some now larger, some smaller; but there was little hope for betterment. Few households felt their strips would be adequate. None knew how to improve their yields. Less than a third of Novo-Zhivotinnyi's men could read or write, and this barely; only 6 of the village's 211 women. The school itself was really more of a nursery and had but 20 children. *Bez etogo nel'zia,* the peasants insisted: "It cannot be otherwise." The ways of God were as mysterious as the weather, his purpose as incomprehensible as a sudden summer thunderstorm. One prayed at the church or in front of the family icon and, just to be safe, left offerings of food at the small village cemetery, asking the dead to help with the weather. Nowhere in the village could the doctor find any concern for such basic agricultural problems as fertilization or crop diversification; none of the villagers talked to him about politics. "Such a horrible ignorance," he later wrote, "such a lack of understanding and unawareness of almost everything beyond the narrow confines of simple rural life, with its ageless prejudices and superstitions!"[1]

The doctor himself was soon to become a prominent member of Russia's leading liberal party, the Constitutional Democrats (Kadets), and eventually minister of agriculture under the Provisional Government in 1917. Already he was well respected in progressive circles as an activist and dedicated humanitarian, but his report on Novo-Zhivotinnyi, which he published under the title *The Dying Village*, caused a sensation. Many attacked the report for distorting Russia's rural condition and "subversively" encouraging criticism of the tsarist government. Others felt the doctor laid bare the root cause of Russia's "backwardness" and applauded his effort to generate social concern. But even here there were questions about the report's political implications.

Those critical of *The Dying Village* focused on the fact that Novo-Zhivotinnyi was not a "typical" village, but one which had received at the time of emancipation in 1861 a so-called beggarly allotment. This was a provision in the complicated reform act whereby serfs could escape huge redemption payments (in effect, mortgage payments) imposed on land transferred to them from their gentry landlords, with repayment provisions stretching over some forty years, in return for accepting free and clear a small portion of the land they had previously tilled, usually one-fourth. Some 6 percent of Russia's approximately fifty million peasants had accepted this provision in the 1860s, hoping to rent such additional land as they might need in the future. Like their brethren who assumed full allotments, they were forced to retain a communal structure (the *mir*) in their village and remained "tied" to the land not only by collective tax obligations, but by a provision granting village elders the sole responsibility for issuing the passports required for travel within Russia if they wanted to seek work someplace else or simply move. But unlike many other rural communities, some of which had managed to establish a modicum of prosperity (especially in regions where flax and other commercial crops were produced), those who accepted beggarly allotments were doomed to terrible privation. As the population increased (in the Novo-Zhivotinnyi region it had grown some 40 percent between 1860 and 1900), the desire for land rapidly became a desperate need, while material resources, and hence the means to procure new land, rapidly dwindled.

Critics of *The Dying Village* were right: Novo-Zhivotinnyi was not a typical village. Elsewhere peasants did acquire land, and in fact, held four times as much nonallotment land at the turn of the century as they had held in the early 1870s. Despite depressed prices on the world grain market, many villages produced for export; and if the countryside as a whole lived close enough to subsistence to be threatened with famine in the event of drought, as happened in 1891, prosperity in many places was still quite visible. When the Englishman Mackenzie Wallace visited the countryside in 1903, the villages he passed through "had not at all the look of dilapidation and misery which I expected. On the contrary, the houses were larger and better constructed than they used to be and each of them had a chimney! That was important, because formerly a large proportion of the peasantry had no such luxury, and allowed the smoke to find its exit by the open door."[2]

As those who applauded the report recognized, however, such "prosperity" was irrelevant to the doctor's arguments. Even peasants whose holdings had substantially increased after 1861 found themselves at the turn of the century hopelessly in debt, saddled with primitive methods of production, woefully deficient in draft animals, almost entirely without agricultural machinery, and totally without the wherewithal to improve their social and economic condition. By 1900 peasant arrears in redemption and tax obligations had grown to a staggering 119 percent of the annual assessment, forcing the government to defer and even cancel a portion of the debt! Even prosperous peasants usually pulled their wooden plows themselves, and if on the average their fields were almost twice as large as those in France or England, so was the Russian death rate. If chimneys represented progress, they also symbolized a desire for material betterment and economic security, conditions that the tsarist regime had never been able to provide. With its special focus on desperate, rather than ordinary need, *The Dying Village* only emphasized the government's ineptitude.

POPULIST STRATEGIES FOR CHANGE

It was precisely the political implications of this that troubled the report's most sympathetic readers. For those who feared peasant anger and worried about the possibility of revolution in Russia, Novo-Zhivotinnyi symbolized the pressing need for reform "from above." The tsar's resistance to even elementary civil liberties and limited representative government, much less to comprehensive land reform, seemed political suicide, at best, and was likely to bring to backward Russia the tumult and violence of massive social upheaval. For radical populists and others struggling to bring just such a revolution to Russia "from below," however, *The Dying Village* held another message. Rather than portending radical change, it reflected the isolation of the countryside and the problem of mobilizing even the poorest peasants into organized political action. If the hungry villagers of Novo-Zhivotinnyi were politically "dumb," how could even more prosperous peasants be organized to fight for social betterment? It was possible, of course, that peasant anger would erupt into social violence in the countryside, as had often happened in Russia's past. But without clear social and political objectives, it was just as likely that such an upheaval would be thoroughly crushed. The autocracy might then emerge even stronger, the cause of revolution and social justice set back once again.

Such had been the history of peasant radicalism in Russia for decades. In the immediate aftermath of emancipation, when its limitations were clear, a number of localities had taken their pitchforks and marched in the name of "land and freedom" against local authorities and landlords, only to be brutally repressed. In Bezdna, in the Kazan region, more than five thousand peasants battled tsarist troops, their cries of "Freedom! Freedom!" drowned in the agony of massive repression. Fifty-one died, scores were wounded and maimed.

Events like this made a deep impression on Russia's young and growing intelligentsia—bright and sensitive young men and women educated on principles of scientific method and humanistic tradition that traditional Russia regarded as irrelevant. In subsequent years, this populist movement intensified. The call for positive action became more strident. What student sensitive to the privileges of education and relative wealth could easily tolerate Russia's poverty, superstition, and "God-sent" political authoritarianism? The simplest sense of justice demanded a freer Russia, one more rationally ordered.

These feelings led to several different strategies for calling the peasants to action. One involved the organization of small revolutionary groups who would place themselves at the head of a peasant uprising, seize power, and act in the peasants' name to create a "socialist" Russia by force. In the 1860s, a group calling itself "Young Russia" spoke of the need to organize a "revolutionary party," and to "take the [tsarist] dictatorship into our own hands":

> The day will soon come when we will unfurl the great banner of the future, the red banner. And with a mighty cry of "Long Live the Russian Social and Democratic Republic!" we will storm the Winter Palace. . . . With full faith in ourselves and our forces, and in support of the people and the glorious future of Russia— which fate has ordained shall be the first country to realize the great cause of Socialism—we will cry "To Your Axes!", and then we will strike.[3]

Others followed Young Russia's lead at that time, immersing themselves in the radical writings of essayists like Chernyshevskii and Dobroliubov, organizing small radical bands, calling peasants "To axes!" But none seemed to penetrate the countryside and establish support or even significant contacts among the peasants they hoped to lead.

In the 1870s a second strategy emerged. Following Herzen and Lavrov, who stressed the need to move out among "the people," hundreds of students and young radicals went into the countryside to work with the peasants, propagandizing socialist values, and bringing peasants the truth about their own social oppression and the potential for radical change:

> Nothing like it had ever been seen before. . . . A powerful cry arose, calling living souls to the great work of redeeming the Fatherland and the human race. . . . They gave up their homes, their riches, honours and families. They threw themselves into the movement with a joy, an enthusiasm, a faith which one can feel only once in one's life. . . . It was not yet a political movement. Rather, it was like a religious movement, with all the infectious nature of such movements. Men were trying not just to reach a certain practical end, but also to satisfy a deeply felt duty, as an aspiration for moral perfection.[4]

Often dressed as peasants, and in any case shedding the obvious trappings of a privileged upbringing, the students spoke of love, of brotherhood, of truth and justice, in some cases explaining the perfidity of the tsarist government, elsewhere trying simply to establish bonds of mutual trust. But if they discovered firsthand the genuine want and deprivation of peasant life, they also discovered something else: a coarseness, a suspicion, and a striving on the part of some peasants to gain precisely the wealth and privilege that the students themselves were trying to overcome. "Socialism will be grand," a peasant shouted at one meeting. "We'll grab the land, I'll find myself a couple of hired hands, and then I can set myself up in a fine position."[5] Peasant suspicion also led to arrests; almost 300 people were turned over for trial, among them, the movement's most ardent and dedicated members. By 1875 this phase of the movement had been crushed. "Ethical" populism survived repression, however, and its commitments were perhaps even strengthened by the great trials of 1877, when scores of young radicals used the courtroom to proclaim their belief in social equality and the end of privilege. But a deep frustration and anger also survived. Some in the movement began to feel that the struggle had to be taken directly to tsarist officialdom, that it had to be "politicized" and moved from the villages to the offices of power. On January 24, 1878, the day the great "trial of the one hundred and ninety-three" ended, a young woman, Vera Zasulich, walked calmly into the office of the governor of St. Petersburg, General Trepov, and fired her revolver at point-blank range.

Zasulich's dramatic act signalled a new, terrorist political offensive, soon adopted deliberately by a new revolutionary group, calling itself the People's Will (*Narodnaia Volia*), and dedicated to shaking autocracy at its core. Russia had to be forced into political reforms; peasants had to be convinced by the revolutionary's resolute will that action was possible, that God's chosen ruler, the tsar, was fallible and vulnerable, that political freedom and social justice could be achieved. On March 1, 1881, this third populist strategy culminated in the assassination of Alexander II, the "Tsar-Emancipator," killed "to express the discontent of the people, the will of Russia to bring it to a new social system."[6] But rather than spark a massive revolutionary explosion, the terrorists' bomb brought only grief to the Russian countryside. "The Little Father is Dead! Long Live the Tsar!" And the relatively moderate government of Alexander II was succeeded by first the intractable reaction of Alexander III and then, in 1894, the more flexible, but still resolute reaction of Nicholas II, who would reign until 1917.

Russia thus entered a period of political quiescence. Radicals went underground or fled abroad, the government imposed still stricter controls on public life and upheld Russia's traditional, privilege-bound social order. For those still committed to radical change, the problem remained one of forging links between those willing to act against repression and injustice, and those in the city or countryside, like the peasants of Novo-Zhivotinnyi, who longed for change, but lived passively in squalor.

"MODERNIZING" RUSSIA

Meanwhile, as in China, where the strength of peasant tradition and economic insufficiency was similarly complemented by social privilege and authoritarian politics, the face of Russia was changing. The country's handful of major cities were becoming centers of manufacturing and commerce, spurred by new railroad construction, foreign investment capital, and the competitive social Darwinian ethos of the late nineteenth-century "imperial age," which layered industrial growth with expansionist notions of survival of the "fittest" and "most powerful." Alexander III and Nicholas II may have rejected the liberal capitalist premise on which this imperialist competition was based, but both were deeply concerned about the strength of Russia's empire; and both had advisors who clearly recognized the relationship between Russian might and the nation's industrial development.

The most prominent of these "modernizers" was Sergei Witte, whose career in many ways epitomizes the dilemma of those seeking to accelerate Western patterns of industrialization and growth in deeply traditional, agrarian societies. Pressing new ideas and methods, reformers face various impediments to change in terms of social structures and relations. They invariably clash with those attached to comfortable traditions, often becoming the scapegoats for individuals and groups unwilling to accept the consequences of changing social conditions. They are activists rather than ideologues; and they sometimes differ as well from those around them in social background and education. Their careers (and often their lives), consequently, depend in large measure on their ability to cultivate good relations with powerful officials who implicitly resent their efforts. Witte himself was a careful, outgoing man, who rose from the ranks of ticket seller on the Odessa Southwestern Railroad to become minister of finance. He pressed industrial development through government support of railroad building, the commercial "flywheel" of Russian economic growth, and by a series of liberal credit reforms, based on deficit state finance and protectionist tariffs. In the 1890s he secured extensive foreign loans from French money markets, increasing the Russian state debt to more than three billion rubles; in 1897 he led Russia onto the gold standard, a move encouraged in part by the desire to give Russia the same measure of national economic respectability enjoyed by the major European powers and Japan.

Witte's success is amply evidenced in statistics. Rail lines expanded from a mere 982 miles in 1861 to more than 17,000 miles by 1891; this figure doubled again in the 1890s, Russia's decade of great industrial expansion. Coal extraction increased from 763,200 tons in 1870 to more than 9.9 million tons in 1895 and almost 18 million by 1900, an increase that helped produce an average annual economic growth rate in these years of more than 8 percent. Oil production rose from 32,000 tons in 1870 to 6.9 million by 1895 and, again, almost doubled in the succeeding five years. A similar increase occurred with iron ore and the production of steel. In 1900 almost 2.4 million tons of iron and steel were produced, as compared to 1.1 million in 1895, 871,000 in 1890, and 261,000 in 1870. Most important in political terms, the number of Russia's industrial workers grew in corresponding fashion, from approximately 674,000 in heavy industry in 1865 to more than a million by 1890 and perhaps as many as 3 million by 1901. Of these, more than 1.6 million in some 18,729 enterprises were under the purview of the government's official factory inspectorate.

Although consistently underfunded and short of personnel, the very existence of the inspectorate indicated a degree of wariness about rapid industrial growth on the part of the tsarist regime, a wariness eventually reflected as well in Witte's removal from the post of minister of finance. Deficit financing and foreign loans meant heavy taxes and the maintenance of substantial grain exports, even when villages were hungry. In this way Russia maintained her credit abroad and could service her expanding debt. This meant squeezing the peasants in brutal fashion, exacting from villages like Novo-Zhivotinnyi every last available kopeck, every last *pud* of "surplus" grain.

Nonetheless, it was the workers, not the peasants, who most worried the tsar. In large factories and plants in industrial towns and neighborhoods, workers lived and worked closely together. Many had come only recently from the countryside, and kept close ties with their village. They sent home wages to help pay village taxes or returned to help with the harvest, which in some areas was a time in which factories simply shut down. But if poverty and discontent were endemic in the countryside, so were isolation and the inability to organize. In the cities, peasants-turned-workers could mobilize their discontent, focus their anger, and bring enormous political and economic power to bear simply by refusing to work. For most of the nineteenth century the tsarist regime had prided itself in avoiding the "workers problem"—the massive dislocation and political turmoil that had accompanied industrial development in Western Europe, particularly France. Discharged Russian workers simply returned to the countryside. Even "hereditary" proletarians seemed to preserve something of a village mentality, at least until the 1890s. Russia's first major strike did not occur until 1870. Despite wretched wages, long hours (officially reduced to eleven and one-half hours only in 1897 and then often ignored), high rents and other costs in factory housing, only a handful of strikes took place in the 1880s. It was not until after the famine of 1891–92, which brought large numbers of new workers into the factories, that Russia experienced anything that could be called a wave of strike activity.

But the potential for labor unrest grew with industrialization. So did the power of Russia's burgeoning proletariat. Even in a "backward," agrarian society a massive coal or steel shutdown, a textile stoppage, or a large-scale railroad strike could paralyze industry, interrupt the trade and export of grain, threaten government credit, and perhaps even bring the regime to its knees. On May 1, 1898, workers in St. Petersburg paraded for the first time with political banners, demanding civil liberties, the right to strike, and the right to form their own trade unions.

EARLY RUSSIAN MARXISM

If the tsarist regime recognized the workers' growing power, so did increasing numbers of young Russian radicals. Many despaired over the possibility of ever rousing the peasants; with the harsh and systematic repression that followed the assassination of Alexander II, even minimal efforts at bringing political pressure to bear seemed destined to fail. Alexander III believed deeply in Orthodoxy and the rectitude of Russia's autocratic traditions. Like his tutor and close advisor, Konstantin Pobedonostsev, he was convinced that democracy was a "lie," that order and progress in Russia depended on the monarch's will, that "constitution" was a "trite, deceitful, and accursed word."[7] And Nicholas II, although at first the object of hopes for liberal reforms, came to the throne in 1895 denouncing appeals for change as "senseless dreams," and declaring he would "maintain the principle of autocracy just as firmly and unflinchingly as did my unforgettable father." Hopes for reform "from above" thus seemed impossible; increasingly, the economic power of Russia's small but growing labor force seemed a better weapon for change than the genuine but amorphous discontent of her peasant masses.

In the early 1880s, a small group of radical Russian exiles in Geneva, soon to be known as the Liberation of Labor, began to consider seriously the workers' revolutionary potential. In the process, they studied the arguments and writings of Karl Marx and Frederich Engels. Marx was not a "discovery" for these refugees from Alexander III's police, nor was Marxism a "new" political philosophy. Several had read *Capital* shortly after its translation in 1872, and some had even studied it at the university, where Marxism was taught as an analysis of contemporary European economies. But like George Plekhanov, the neatly dressed, rather scholarly looking leader of the group, whose dignified bearing, small, neatly trimmed red beard, and expressive, penetrating eyes made a deep impression on close friends and casual visitors alike,[8] most accepted the materialist underpinnings of Marx's outlook while assuming his analysis as a whole was simply inappropriate to Russian conditions. The problem in Russia was not organizing workers but mobilizing peasants. Marx had stressed as much himself in a letter to Vera Zasulich in March 1881, arguing that the "rural community" rather than the urban proletariat remained "the mainspring of social regeneration" in Russia.[9]

Not only had the "rural community" proved its weakness in this regard, however, but so had terrorist efforts at calling peasants "To axes!" In explaining this failure, one could focus easily both on problems of peasant consciousness—with its religious fatalism and immobilizing servility—and on the ways in which life in the countryside and the processes of agrarian production, unlike those in industry, kept peasants "invested" in their labor and their crops, making mobilization difficult despite increasingly desperate circumstances.

Toiling in the fields tended to involve a personal commitment both to the land and to the product of one's labor. Nurturing crops to maturity seemed to hold intrinsic satisfactions, while struggling with one's own land, even if legal ownership lay elsewhere, seemed to induce an inherent attachment to property and place.

In the cities, however, no such attachment could occur. Those laboring in the mills or foundries worked long hours at tedious chores, with little satisfaction and even less pride in what they were producing. They returned at night to dingy apartments or factory barracks, for which they paid exorbitant rents; their principal amusement, even those with families, was getting drunk. Already in the 1870s workers on the average were spending almost an entire month's wages on alcohol each year. Russia was rapidly developing the highest per capita consumption rate in the world. Vice and crime accompanied heavy drinking, and, one can surmise, so did psychological depression. For many in the cities, it made little difference if their work was temporary or if they returned to their villages to celebrate the holidays or help with the harvest. While family ties were important for their own sake, and while peasants from the same villages tended to cluster together in the same factories, the work itself brought little reward. Industrial growth and expansion did not mean higher wages or better living conditions. Even when improvements were made, labor in the factories remained tedious and unpleasant, entirely devoid of any of the nurturent attributes that accompanied cultivation even in the poorest village.

It was unimportant to young Russian radicals that Marx had characterized this condition as one of workers' alienation or that he distinguished the separation of factory workers from the product of their labor as a special feature of the capitalist mode of production. It was true, of course, that most workers in Russian factories, like those in England and elsewhere, did not own their own tools, had nothing to say about the kind of goods they produced, and were paid a low wage, certainly one substantially less than the value of their output. "Surplus" value (profit) went to those who owned capital, whether in terms of the tools themselves or in terms of the financial investment that paid for the tools or built the plant initially. While these characteristics were undoubtedly accurate descriptive attributes of capitalist economic patterns in Russia and elsewhere, what impressed Russian radicals was not theory per se, but the way in which

Marx's analysis both explained the fundamentals of Russia's developing capitalistic order and offered within that explanation the promise of radical social and political change.

Marx was a deeply optimistic social critic, despite the squalor of his own living conditions and his family's misfortunes. He believed in the rationality of human behavior; he was convinced, in the best tradition of the European Enlightenment, that the human condition was both susceptible to improvement and moving in a progressive direction, necessarily and organically. Necessity derived from man's natural desire to be free from conditions of oppression, to lead a life of satisfaction and personal fulfillment. Where these conditions were denied, those experiencing oppression or exploitation would gradually become conscious of their condition and rationally begin to struggle toward the creation of a just social order.

Marx's task as historian and sociologist was to catalog the nature of exploitation and analyze the mechanism whereby oppressed social groups rectified the conditions of their oppression. In the circumstances of nineteenth-century European capitalism, oppression took the form of wage slavery, the increasing misery of workers, and the psychological dissatisfactions that came from monotonous work routines in which workers felt no sense of accomplishment or pride in what they produced. Naturally, these "contradictions" in the capitalist order would become increasingly "antagonistic" as industry expanded, as the number of workers increased, and as the degree of their misery deepened. And as antagonism intensified, rational workers would understand that the only thing they had to lose by revolting against their oppressors were the chains of their oppression.

Marx also argued that while these chains were determined by economic relationships, they were not entirely economic in nature, a view that struck real sympathy in both Russian and, later, Chinese readers. Related to economic patterns and the class relations that accompanied various modes of production were derivative "superstructures" that facilitated and justified these patterns. Capitalists anxious to squeeze the highest possible returns on their investments by keeping wage and other costs low, developed political "structures" that represented their interests and operated on such principles as "noninterference" in "economic" affairs. Thus "liberal" societies like Britain and the USA cherished a system of individual "civil liberties," which had the effect of preventing the state from interfering in an individual factory owner's exploitation of his workers. This "super-structure" of parliamentary government and "bourgeois rights" was not unimportant to the process of developing social justice, since its freedoms enabled workers to meet and organize together (by virtue, for example, of the right to assemble) and to awaken others to the reality of their exploited condition (through freedom of speech or freedom of the press). But sooner or later the laws by which a capitalist order preserved and perpetuated itself would have to be violated, since they defended and protected the capitalists' ability to exploit the work of others. Also, the achievement of social justice necessarily involved the redistribution of wealth, which meant the confiscation of property, expropriation of land, and transfer of the means of production (factories, tools) back to workers themselves. In effect, this meant the radical restructuring of bourgeois govern-ments, whose police and other coercive instruments were organized to defend property and the rights of private economic ownership. When states were no longer instruments of class coercion, since one social group no longer exploited or oppressed another, they would naturally "wither," their tasks being reduced simply to ordinary, utilitarian administration.

Thus optimism combined in Marx with a deep, thoroughgoing, and often intolerant radicalism; both were based on what appeared to be a careful, scientific analysis of the generalities of historical progress and the particularities of European capitalism. What excited Plekhanov and his comrades in the early Marxist Liberation of Labor group, however, and what began in the 1890s to draw increasing numbers of young Russian radicals to Marxist study circles in Moscow and St. Petersburg, was the realization that much of Marx's analysis might be applicable to Russia as well. Of course Russia remained essentially an agrarian society, and her overwhelming mass of people were peasants. But the heavy concentration of a relatively small proletariat in a few industrial and administrative centers meant the power of workers was focused; like rays through a prism, this concentration might make up in intensity what it lacked in magni-tude. Moreover, the implicit power of organized, mobilized workers was clearly more hopeful as a means to change in Russia than the sporadic and sullen anger of the peasants. Radicals living in cities and towns could certainly help in the process of worker organization more readily than they could by "going to the people" in the countryside. There was certainly no need to continue the dangerous terrorism of groups like the People's Will, since an organized, conscious proletariat could produce radical change organically without resort to such shock tactics as the assassination of Alexander II.

There were other advantages as well. Since the revolutionary potential of the proletariat intensified as industry expanded, Russia's Marxists found themselves supporting the same development goals as Nicholas's minister of finance, Sergei Witte. Articles encouraging Russian industrialization could even be published, despite their radical implications, because they corresponded so neatly with government policies. Also, since Russia lacked the elementary civil liberties that Western industrial societies enjoyed, and since these restrictions affected professional and bourgeois groups as much as they did the radicals, it was possible in this phase of the struggle to enjoy the help of bourgeois class enemies, whose respectability and whose "respectable protests" might achieve the "bourgeois" freedoms that radicals needed to facilitate worker mobilization. Once the bourgeoisie had completed *its* revolution and liberalized the tsarist autocratic order, the power of an organized, conscious proletariat could carry Russia past the exploitative socioeconomic patterns of a liberal, capitalist system into the social justice and economic equality of revolutionary socialism; in other words, the proletariat could move Russia in a radical way from liberal political democracy to a revolutionary, egalitarian social democracy.

LENIN AND THE PROBLEMS OF WORKER ACTIVISM

It was above all this promise of radical, thoroughgoing change that attracted a young, twenty-three-year-old attorney from the small Volga river town of Samara to the Marxist circles of St. Petersburg in 1893; it lay at the core of his Marxist commitment. Vladimir Ilich Ulianov —Lenin—was not by appearance, background, or profession what one might expect of a typical Russian radical. The second son of a highly respected school superintendent in Simbirsk province, whose earnest work at improving teaching methods and supervising school construction had won him the rank of actual state councilor in the tsarist civil service, Lenin had from childhood been a diligent, well-behaved student, studious and disciplined in his work, and always neatly dressed. The Ulianov household was apparently a warm and loving one, if also conservative and religious; although politics was expressly forbidden as a subject of family discussion, in favor, usually, of Turgenev, Pushkin, and the Russian literary classics, both Lenin and his brother Alexander were by all accounts consistently supported when politics radically changed their lives.

Political issues intruded early and in a dramatic fashion. In 1887 Lenin's older brother Alexander was arrested in St. Petersburg for conspiring to assassinate the tsar, a charge he readily admitted. By all accounts the arrest shocked the unsuspecting Ulianov family and profoundly affected Lenin, who loved and respected Alexander deeply. Despite his mother's appeals, Alexander refused to plead for mercy. He even took upon himself the primary responsibility for organizing the assassination attempt. In May 1887, he was hanged.

Lenin's response to this terrible event was not to withdraw into melancholy, despite the awful sadness that now gripped his family, but to plunge into political issues and read voraciously in the books and essays that Alexander had admired. As a young boy, Vladimir Ilich had spent his time with novels, while Alexander had devoured Chernyshevskii, Dobroliubov, and other radical writers. Now it was Lenin's turn. As if to redeem his lost brother's admiration, he began to study politics intensively, as if trying to absorb in a period of months more than three decades of populist teaching. Although a gold-medal gymnasium student, Lenin was soon expelled himself as a radical from the University of Kazan; it was only in response to his mother's desperate supplication that tsarist authorities finally permitted the future Bolshevik leader to complete his legal studies and take his exams.

This is not the place to discuss Lenin's subsequent commitment to radical populist thought, his particular admiration for Chernyshevskii, or even his attachment to Marxism, which developed strongly in the early 1890s after a close and careful reading of *Capital*. It is enough to say that, in all likelihood, Chernyshevskii influenced Lenin fully as much as Marx, that Lenin combined the populist's "subjective" radicalism with Marx's "objective," scientific analysis, and that Lenin himself never lost the impatient, passionate commitment, the tendency towards sweeping moral judgments, or even the intense hatred for liberals and liberal accommodationism that run throughout Chernyshevskii's writings:

There are musicians [Lenin later wrote] about whom it is said that they have perfect pitch; there are others about whom it can be said that they possess an absolute and perfect revolutionary feeling. Marx was such a man, and Chernyshevskii came very close to being such a man. To this day it is impossible to point out a single Russian revolutionary who understood and judged the cowardly, base, and treacherous nature of any form of liberalism with such profundity and insight as Chernyshevskii. . . . Before my acquaintance with Marx, Engels, and Plekhanov, it was Chernyshevskii who exerted the main overwhelming revolutionary influence on me—an influence which began with *What Is to Be Done?*. Chernyshevskii's greatest service lay in the fact that he . . . showed what the revolutionary must be like, what his rules must be, how he must go about attaining his goals, and by what methods and means he can bring about their realization.[10]

Methods and means now became crucial to Lenin. If he joined the small Marxist circles in St. Petersburg in 1893 fully armed with an understanding of the links between developing capitalism and the potential for revolutionary change in Russia, he also came wary of any radical tactics that might indirectly strengthen Russian liberals or the power of the autocracy.

Some of the groups Lenin found in St. Petersburg seemed to be doing just that. A small number of factory workers had organized themselves into various cells and set up a Central Workers' Circle to coordinate their activities. Following the pattern of an earlier Sunday School movement, the workers' focus was largely on education, although some of the participants saw clear connections between education and improved economic well-being. The problem here was that the workers' groups were giving the *appearance* of political conspiracy in connection with rather benign educational objectives. This appearance encouraged repression on the part of tsarist police, while not in any forceful way strengthening the workers politically.

Also in St. Petersburg were small groups of radical populists, essentially members of the radical intelligentsia who continued to adhere to the tenets of the old People's Will organization, which had assassinated the tsar. The *Narodovoltsy* hoped to rally urban workers in much the same way they had earlier tried to rouse the peasants, by agitating in favor of radical change. But here the problem of social distance between "leaders" and "led" remained much as it was when students went "to the people" in 1874: workers remained suspicious, often accusing populist agitators of getting them into trouble. "I listen to you and all the time I have the feeling that you want to get us mad," one worker was reported as saying. "We want you to give us the facts, and when we know everything and the time comes to get mad, we will get mad ourselves."[11]

Meanwhile, the Marxists (now generally calling themselves Social Democrats to distinguish their concern for social equality from the liberals emphasis on mere politics), largely under the leadership of future Mensheviks like Potresov, Dan, and Plekhanov, concentrated their efforts at "propagandizing" broadly among Petersburg workers, trying to build their confidence and their willingness to mobilize. They met with workers on Sundays and in the evenings and, while helping them to read and write, tried to raise broad political issues in a general, and often very indirect, fashion.

For Lenin and others, however, there was a real question whether a revolution could ever be organized by any of these "liberal" methods. Radicals might instead lose their radical commitments if they taught in "Sunday schools" for long periods of time. In the memoirs of Krupskaia, Lenin's future wife, there is an account of his first encounter with St. Petersburg Social Democrats early in 1894. One of the members was in the midst of a report on the "Committees to Combat Illiteracy," apparently praising these efforts to "prepare the working class for power," when Lenin, still a stranger, suddenly announced his appearance with a burst of laughter. "Well," he said sarcastically, "if anyone wants to save the Fatherland with Committees for Illiteracy, we won't stop him I am sure."[12]

But what were the alternatives? In 1895 a young Jewish radical, Iulii Martov, returned to St. Petersburg convinced that Marxists had to abandon the role of teachers and propagandists in favor of more direct agitation. Martov had had success among Jewish workers in Vilno, mobilizing them against their employers and leading a series of strikes. In 1894 he had helped edit a pamphlet called "On Agitation," which called for active Marxist participation in stirring up worker grievances. Dressed like a worker, he spent his time around the massive Putilov iron works, gathering information on worker grievances, passing out leaflets, and inciting strikes, trying at the same time to generate a clear, class-based political consciousness among the workers he met.

By all accounts, Martov had a profound impact on Lenin, whom he met in 1895. Lenin quickly joined his Union of Struggle for the Emancipation of the Working Class. Lenin himself was not inclined to put on workers' clothing, but Martov's conception of "agitation" was a neat bridge between populist calls "To axes!" and Social Democratic propagandizing. Focusing on workers' grievances and pulling strikes in a political direction was a way both of mobilizing the proletariat and bringing Russia's political system quickly to the point of crisis. It was a far cry from Committees on Illiteracy, and Lenin was quick to realize the potential role politically conscious workers and intellectuals could have in galvanizing worker militance.

The tsarist police, however, were no less quick. In 1894 and again in 1895, following a series of strikes and the appearance of various proclamations, police raids decimated all of the radical groups in St. Petersburg and virtually wiped out the remnants of the People's Will. Large numbers of workers' leaders themselves were arrested. When the Union of Struggle managed to put out additional proclamations claiming its work would continue, more raids followed. Martov and Lenin were both caught in this net; for Lenin it signalled the beginning of years of detention and exile that were not to end until April 1917.

In the aftermath of these arrests, two important aspects of the labor movement in Russia rapidly became apparent. One was the common and persistent bane of radical movements everywhere, a problem that each successive generation of militants tended (and tends) to ignore: if the political enemy is reasonably strong, repression works; as movement leaders are arrested or killed, they tend to bring down with them the most active of their supporters, weakening broad movement credibility. Thus in Russia after 1895, worker grievances and strikes continued, but associations between workers and Social Democratic groups virtually disappeared. The movement held high promise, but many workers felt it brought little but trouble.

The second problem was a gnawing realization on the part of Russian Marxists that workers in St. Petersburg and elsewhere simply did not seem to be moving on their own in a revolutionary direction, despite expanding numbers and persistent social and economic exploitation. In other words, the "inevitable" revolutionary solution to class antagonism, which Marx postulated would emerge from proletarian awareness of alienation and oppression, had not yet occurred in advanced capitalist societies like France, Germany, or England, and it did not seem to be occurring in Russia. From all indications, workers were far more interested in educating themselves, improving their living conditions, and in obtaining the perquisites and pleasures enjoyed by their bourgeois oppressors than they were in creating a radically new, conflict-free society. For the first time there appeared clearly an issue that would continue to cause serious problems for revolutionary Marxists everywhere: were the workers of the world really interested in uniting against their class enemies, or were they more ready, despite genuine exploitation and alienation, simply to try to improve themselves and carve out a somewhat larger share of bourgeois rewards within their own nation-state system, without radically changing its form or structure?

DEFINING THE TASKS OF REVOLUTIONARY MARXISM

While these events were occurring in Russia, a number of Marxists in Western Europe, especially in Germany, were increasingly coming to the conclusion that violent revolution was not an inevitable and necessary consequence of capitalist social relations. Prompted by the fact that conditions of alienation and exploitation simply did not seem to be leading to the type of explosion Marx had predicted, Eduard Bernstein and others began to reexamine Marx's writings and to revise his analysis in terms of changing historical conditions. Bernstein's "revisionism" argued in particular that Marx's notion of increasing proletarian misery was demonstrably wrong, as was the assertion that political consciousness was strictly and functionally related to class. There were a number of other important aspects to his critique, but the logical conclusion of each was that progress for workers did not necessarily have to come through revolution and that socialism might be obtained through peaceful, evolutionary means.

Some Russian Marxists, like the future conservative Peter Struve, were coming to similar conclusions; but whereas in Germany and elsewhere those in power seemed willing to accommodate Social Democrats to some extent and integrate their movement into the established political order, tsarist Russia held out no such evolutionary possibilities. The best revisionist Russian Marxists seemed likely to accomplish was some sort of tacit alliance with Russian liberals and mutual reinforcement in a common struggle to establish a constitutional, parliamentary order. Although a bitter opponent of the revisionist "heresy," Plekhanov himself argued for the necessity of achieving civil liberties in Russia as a vital goal of the socialist movement and welcomed liberal efforts in this regard. The arrests of movement leaders showed clearly that freedom of speech and assembly, the right to organize unions, and other liberal objectives were fundamental to realizing social as well as political democracy. In China, to young intellectuals and others, these ideas would also prove enormously attractive—the hallmarks of what seemed to be a progressive European movement for change.

Others took a different tack, hoping to reorient the movement around more specifically economic goals. The argument of men and women like S. N. Prokopovich and E. D. Kuskova was essentially that social democracy was failing in Russia because it seemed *too* "political" and worried workers and tsarist authorities alike with its agitation in favor of radical change. Instead, Social Democrats (formally organized as the Russian Social Democratic Labor Party in 1898) had to concentrate on achieving economic objectives: better wages, shorter working hours, better conditions. Such goals were obtainable by workers themselves through work stoppages and strikes; by lending support to these worker-based efforts, radical movement intellectuals could both bridge the social gap between movement leaders and ordinary proletarians and win worker confidence by helping achieve specific, much sought-for improvements. Once workers realized the enormous power they could obtain through organization, and once experience demonstrated that specific economic goals could be achieved, the labor movement, in close connection with active Social Democrats, would spontaneously come to the realization that this same power could be used to secure political change. In other words, if well-organized workers could take higher wages and better housing from a factory owner, they would soon realize they could use their power to take over the factory itself and also the government that supported and defended the owner. This, in any case, was the principal theme of a new clandestine Marxist journal, *Rabochaia Mysl'* ("Workers' Thought"), which began to appear in 1897.

These "revisionist" and "economist" tendencies were, however, anathema to militants like Lenin. Toward the end of his Siberian exile, in the closing months of 1899, the future Bolshevik leader began to formulate his response. Krupskaia's memoirs suggest how intensely the issues gripped him. He grew thin; he had difficulty sleeping; he corresponded passionately with Martov and Potresov; and he discussed the issues endlessly with Krupskaia and other friends. It is interesting that there were no unique circumstances that pressed Lenin to formulate his views, no Shanghai massacre or Long March, as in China, where ideological perspectives derived from special conditions. Rather, with Lenin, as with Martov, Plekhanov, Trotsky, and other early Russian Social Democrats, there was simply commitment: to ending social injustice and political oppression, to expropriating and redistributing wealth that a relative few held at the expense of many, and to obtaining the power necessary to achieve these objectives.

Liberal Western historians have concentrated on this "drive to power" and have generally used it to deprecate Lenin and his like-minded Social Democratic comrades. In a liberal order, the desire for power has immoral connotations, even among those who control and use a political order to their own advantage. Reluctance to assume the "heavy duties" of political responsibility is acceptable, but overt ambition is less so; those who "lust for power" bear all the stigma of Judeo-Christian sexual immorality.

But power for Lenin was the difference between endless talk about social oppression and the chance, actually, to improve social conditions. What angered him most as he surveyed the Social Democratic landscape at the turn of the century was the fragmentation in the movement and the apparent eagerness with which "revisionists" and "economists" seemed willing to work with, and thus in Lenin's view strengthen, oppressive social and political groups. Factory owners could respond to workers' economic demands rather easily, even if it meant diminishing their profits, if such rewards served to consolidate their class hegemony. Higher wages and shorter hours would "buy off" the workers, satisfy their ambitions at least for a time, and channel their potential power into "acceptable" or "legitimate" forms of protest that did not fundamentally threaten the existing order. Similarly the revisionist desire to work more closely with "the system" to achieve socialist objectives was also co-optive and misleading. If Wilhelmine Germany or Tsarist Russia could bring Social Democrats into their institutions, the movement would not be acquiring power, however many parliamentary seats it obtained, but surrendering it to those whose socioeconomic position the parliamentary apparatus served to support.

Thus Lenin responded to the movement's fragmentation by demanding organized class struggle for political control and resistance both to philosophizing and to seeking local, petty economic "victories":

> The real task of a revolutionary socialist party is not to draw up plans for refashioning society, not to preach to the capitalists and their hangers-on about improving the lot of the workers, not to hatch conspiracies, but to organize the class struggle of the proletariat, and to lead this struggle, the ultimate aim of which is the conquest of political power by the proletariat and the organization of a socialist society.[13]

And what, precisely, is "class struggle"?

> When the workers of a single factory or branch of industry struggle against their employer is this class struggle? No. This is only a weak beginning. The struggle of the workers becomes a class struggle only when the foremost representatives of the entire working class of the whole country are conscious of themselves as a single working class, and launch a struggle that is directed not against individual employers, but against the *entire class* of capitalists, and against the government which supports that class.[14]

Thus for Lenin, class struggle itself had to be the essence of the Social Democratic movement; and organizing and leading this struggle, "the ultimate aim of which is the conquest of political power by the proletariat and the establishment of a socialist society," had to be the "essence of the program common to all Social Democrats."[15]

The urgent first step in this direction was to organize a party organ that could direct Social Democrats all over Russia and end "narrow, amateurish local work."[16] Thus Lenin conceived of *Iskra* (*The Spark*), a newspaper that was to ignite the flames of social revolution in Russia not simply by militant phrasemaking or local worker agitation, but by welding the Social Democratic movement into a strong political organization, thus creating the means to turn the workers' spontaneous struggle against individual factory owners into "the struggle of the whole class, the struggle of a definite political *party* for definite political and socialist ideals."[17]

And what, for Lenin, were these ideals? Without embellishment, and also without any elaborate consideration of the methods of socialist government or economic organization, they were simply to abolish the division of society into classes, and thus all social and political inequality arising from that division. This was the meaning of social revolution. Securing political liberties was an important stage in revolutionary development, but "the real emancipation of the working class," Lenin wrote, "requires the abolition of private ownership of the means of production, their conversion into public property, and the replacement of capitalist production of commodities by the socialist organization of the production of articles by society as a whole, the means to assure full well-being and free, all-round development of all of its members."[18]

Thus, as the first issue of *Iskra* appeared in December 1900, the essential aspects of what would later be called "Leninism" were clearly formulated. Revolution in Russia required a strong, well-organized political party, capable of leading the workers' movement and converting its spontaneous energy into a coherent revolutionary force. The fragmentation of social democracy would be ended by energetic centralized direction; the tendency of both the Social Democratic movement and workers' discontent to be co-opted by liberal concessions would be thwarted by a revolutionary "vanguard," sensitive to the dangers and committed wholeheartedly to social revolution. Through agitation and propaganda, through energetic work on the streets and in the factories, this vanguard party would bring a true socialist consciousness to Russia's workers, galvanize their energy and anger, and lead them through revolution to an equalitarian socialist order. "What is to be done?" Lenin asked rhetorically in his famous pamphlet of 1902. His answer: create "a militant organization of revolutionists," a genuine "vanguard of the most revolutionary class," capable of developing a genuine Social Democratic consciousness.[19]

And what about Russia's peasants, the poor souls of villages like Novo-Zhivotinnyi? Lenin was well aware of the problem posed by the peasantry and the fact that a workers' revolution in agrarian

Russia implied the coming to power of what was still a tiny minority of the country's population. In *Iskra* and elsewhere he published several long essays calling for an alliance between poor peasants (particularly hired hands) and their proletarian comrades. "There exist two kinds of class antagonism in the modern Russian village," he wrote, the first between agricultural workers and wealthier peasants; the second between all peasants and the gentry. While the first antagonism was becoming acute, and would form the social basis for transforming the countryside after the revolution, the second was central to the revolution itself. Giving its support to *every* revolutionary movement against the tsarist state and social system, the Russian Social Democratic Labor party had to "inscribe on its banner *support* for the peasants, not by any means as a class of small proprietors or small farmers . . . but as allies in the revolutionary struggle against the survivals of serfdom in general and autocracy in particular."[20] Thus, with peasants as revolutionary allies rather than the spearhead of revolution itself (as the populists, organized after 1902 as the Socialist Revolutionary party, maintained), discontent in the countryside would help create the general conditions of a "revolutionary situation" while organized, conscious workers and their vanguard party carried Russia specifically to a new socialist order.

Above all for Lenin was a commitment to revolutionary struggle, the unifying thread of "Leninist" values and ideas, as Russian Social Democrats gathered in Brussels in 1903 for what proved to be the organizing congress of the Bolshevik party.[21]

THE REVOLUTION OF 1905

The Brussels congress took place against a background of increasing social and political unrest in Russia. The various pressures induced by a combination of rapid industrialization, peasant misery, liberal anger and tsarist intransigence built quickly at the beginning of the twentieth century, as if the changing calendar signified the need to modify traditional institutions and values. Poor harvests in 1897, 1898, and again in 1901 further extended peasant indebtedness and tax arrears, and led in 1902 to a series of violent disturbances, particularly in the Kharkov and Poltava regions. Even as tsarist troops brutally suppressed this unrest, it was clear that the nature of peasant land holding would have to be modified if the regime hoped to preserve any semblance of rural order. Belligerent peasants worried Russia's gentry and also prompted the growing corps of rural professional workers—agronomists, teachers, health-care workers, and the like—to press at various conferences and trade fairs for reform. This in turn led to the government's banning rural gatherings.

A similar dialectic unfolded in the cities. Between 1899 and 1903 a recession depressed real wages. While the number of strikes and strikers declined somewhat, there were unmistakable signs of growing worker discontent. A massive strike in Rostov in late 1902 turned into a forum of direct political protest in which even local authorities were reluctant to interfere; by late 1903, a wave of strikes had spread through virtually every town of the empire. At the same time, repressive violence against workers was in some ways much less effective than that applied against the peasantry since it agitated students and even members of the bourgeoisie, and almost invariably led to additional protests. In early 1901 an expelled student shot and killed the minister of education, N. P. Bogolepov; shortly afterwards, a rural statistician tried to assassinate the tsar's closest advisor, Konstantin Pobedonostsev. By 1902 a new populist terror organization was functioning, associated with the Socialist Revolutionaries. In April of that year, one of its members managed to enter the building of the Council of Ministers and fatally shoot the minister of the interior, D. S. Sipiagin. Terrorist violence bred further repression, which in turn brought additional protests. By 1903 the situation was such that Nicholas published an imperial manifesto vaguely promising reform.

What Nicholas said and what he did, however, were quite different. To replace Sipiagin he appointed an archreactionary, V. K. Plehve, who quickly applied even more brutal measures of repression. Deliberately fomenting hostility against the Jews as a means of "siphoning off" discontent, Plehve by 1904 was ready to engage Russia in a "splendid little war" against the Japanese as a means of smothering protest in patriotism. For a short time his strategy worked. The outbreak of hostilities initially muted social tensions, but the war itself soon began to go badly, and the increased strain on Russia's economy further aggravated the conditions of workers and peasants. In December 1904, as groups of prominent gentry and professional men gathered at "banquets" (to circumvent the prohibition on political assemblies) and began to formulate specific demands for political reforms, the Russian fortress at Port Arthur surrendered to the Japanese, dealing a staggering blow to the government's prestige. At the same time, discontent in St. Petersburg overflowed in a series of strikes, affecting thousands of workers. On Sunday, January 9, a massive demonstration began to march in an orderly and peaceful manner toward the Winter Palace, bearing a list of workers' grievances in a petition to the tsar. The demonstrators carried icons and portraits of Nicholas, but as they approached the palace, the nervous cordon of troops opened fire. Several hundred were wounded. When the smoke had cleared, more than 130 lay dead in the streets.

"Bloody Sunday" was the opening salvo of the Revolution of 1905, a series of events that culminated in the establishment of a limited form of parliamentary government (the Duma), a wide range of civil liberties (including the right to organize political parties and, for a brief time, the right to form trade unions), and a massive, bloody uprising in the city of Moscow in December, led in some measure by the Social Democrats. Then followed a brutal, thorough-going repression. In the spring of 1906, as the new parliament prepared to meet, a more liberal tsarist cabinet promulgated a constitution of sorts, the Fundamental Laws, and instituted a series of reforms designed to abolish redemption payments, free peasants from communes, and establish private peasant ownership of land. Nicholas and his advisors hoped these measures would both pacify the gentry and liberal bourgeoisie by increasing their participation in state affairs and create a new class of loyal, property-owning farmers to supplant dissident peasants. Severe restrictions were placed on the Duma's electoral base in 1907 after its initial membership had proved too radical; the peasant reforms proceeded at a pace some regarded as fatally deliberate. In essence, the 1905 revolution set the conditions under which tsarist Russia was to live out its last years.

This is not the place to discuss in detail the "dress rehearsal" for 1917, as Lenin and others called the Revolution of 1905, or even its influence in Asia, which was considerable. Several studies are available for those who want to pursue this question, including Trotsky's own valuable memoir-history.[22] Rather, for our purposes what is important is the way in which the events of these months are more broadly revealing in terms of revolutionary processes as a whole, and the manner in which this first revolution brought into focus in

Russia a range of dilemmas that radical movements everywhere sooner or later have to face.

The first point to be made is that Bloody Sunday triggered a massive outburst of popular indignation against the regime that cut completely across class lines. Professors, lawyers, students, factory owners, even many with substantial landed estates were simply appalled by what had occurred; in accord with ordinary workers and peasants they seemed to see the massacre as symptomatic of the need for change. "The events of January 9 have revealed Tsar Nicholas as the enemy and butcher of the people," the future conservative Peter Struve wrote in the journal *Liberation*, for example. "Yesterday there were divisions and parties. Today the Russian liberation movement must have one body and one soul, one unifying thought: retribution and freedom at all costs."[23] Even the tsar's own ministers described conditions as "grievous" and "unprecedented" while some 147 members of the Moscow provincial assembly of nobles voted on January 22 for a resolution calling for representative government.

"Bloody Sunday," in a word, was the spark that ignited the political consciousness of Russia's bourgeois social elements, to borrow Lenin's metaphor and use the term "bourgeois" rather loosely. Thus the revolutionary sequence began to unfold with potentially antagonistic social groups generally united in favor of change. From all sectors came appeals for civil liberties, the right to submit petitions, the right to assemble, and the panoply of freedoms associated with parliamentary rule. Professional unions of doctors, lawyers, teachers, and other groups organized even as labor unions themselves remained proscribed. By the late spring of 1905, a Union of Unions was formed to coordinate the press for change.

This press, however, remained focused almost entirely on *political* reforms. When the tsar responded in October with his Constitutional Manifesto, granting civil liberties and promising representative, parliamentary government, many in the nationwide "liberation movement" regarded the struggle as won. Thus there was a generalized respectability to the revolution's first phases, a respectability that helped radicals obtain the freedom they needed to organize for more fundamental social change. Analytically, the process reinforced the Marxist notion of "two-stage" revolutionary development, with the establishment of liberal bourgeois rule as a necessary step in the path to democratic socialism.

Second, however, it is important to realize that while bourgeois in terms of its political objectives, and respectable in terms of the social coalition that supported it, the revolution gained its *power* from the mass action of Russia's workers. The hundreds of thousands of industrial and factory workers who shut down their factories and took to the streets in the course of 1905 demonstrated without question their ability to bring Russia's urban economy to a sudden halt, thereby crippling tsarist authority. Peasant unrest in the countryside was also a factor, as was a spate of mutinous behavior in the army and fleet, most dramatically on the battleship *Potemkin*. But this was unorganized, uncoordinated, and, most important, not able directly to stop autocratic Russia from going about its business.

When railroad shop workers in St. Petersburg and Moscow went on strike in September, however, and when they were joined soon afterwards by masses of workers from all branches of industry in a general strike, the regime simply had to respond. "We began with a peaceful struggle for the improvement of working conditions" one workers' pamphlet declared in early October, "and we began the fight against one enemy: the owners. But we were met along the way by troops, police, and Cossacks . . . and we saw that another enemy confronted us—a fierce and terrible enemy—our government. Our peaceful economic struggle has led us straight on to that which some had previously wanted to avoid—to political struggle, to struggle with the autocracy."[24] In mid-October striking workers in St. Petersburg formed their own *Soviet* ("council") to coordinate their actions and to help each other where help was needed. Soviet delegates went to factories that were still working and appealed with considerable success for them to shut down. By the end of October the Soviet was a powerful institution whose elected leadership now included a number of prominent Social Democrats, including Leon Trotsky. In the view of some, if Nicholas did not quickly yield at least some of his power to the gentry and liberal bourgeoisie, the radicals might possibly destroy it altogether.

Thus the October Manifesto promising representative rule in Russia came only as a concession, wrung from the weakened grip of a still powerful enemy. The important point here is that accommodation was the result of necessity, not desire, and that the official commitment to change belied a powerful animosity. This had several important consequences for the revolutionary movement. On one hand, it rent almost immediately the broad social coalition that had striven throughout 1905 for reform. In the salons and drawing rooms of Moscow and St. Petersburg, the year's achievements were appropriately political and the revolution was over; in the factories and dormitories, where the principal bases of discontent were social and economic, the revolution at best was incomplete. This, in turn, emphasized the nature of class differentiation for many workers, and brought home clearly the limited benefits of political change. Social democracy acquired a more practical definition, and it is not too much to suggest that at precisely this juncture, liberal Russia lost in a fundamental way whatever possibilities existed for future mass support.

On the other hand, suspicions streamed two ways. Even the most progressive members of the gentry and the most liberal members of the urban bourgeoisie had reason to fear the demonstrable power of workers and peasants. Members of the liberal intelligentsia like Paul Miliukov, professor of history, chairman of the Union of Unions, leader of the new liberal Constitutional Democratic party, and future foreign minister, who in July had called workers and peasants to struggle "by any means possible," now recognized how little men like themselves could control "elemental mass forces," and how potentially destructive these forces could be to liberal institutions and values. Liberals thus grew wary not only of Russia's workers and peasants, but also of their "enthusiast" socialist leaders, still committed to revolution.

Finally, for workers and peasants, the revolution of 1905 revealed above all the dangers of partial victory. Having granted the concessions of October, the regime moved swiftly to reassert its power. When the Portsmouth peace agreement with Japan was approved, Nicholas immediately began to bring back loyal troops from the Far East. Dissident railroad workers were brutally "pacified" along the way, and by November 1905 the regime felt strong enough to strike out against the leaders of the St. Petersburg Soviet. Punitive battalions were also sent to the countryside. In early December, with an almost hopeless sense of desperation, the workers of Moscow went on strike to protect their leaders and their right to unions, as well as to press one final time for significant improvements in wages and working conditions. But by then the government was ready. The Moscow insurrection was fought as if it were a civil war, and there was no doubt whatsoever about the possible outcome, only about the numbers who would die. By January, workers' districts in Moscow and St. Petersburg were under martial law, as were the railroads and large sectors of the Russian countryside.

DILEMMAS OF SOCIAL DEMOCRACY

After 1905, the Social Democratic movement in Russia struggled to regroup and to come to grips with changing conditions. By the beginning of 1906, prominent party leaders like Lenin and Trotsky were again in exile or under arrest. The trade union movement itself had only a brief legal existence before it, too, succumbed in the main to tsarist repression. Between 1907 and the outbreak of the February revolution in 1917, both the labor and the Social Democratic movement in Russia led an underground existence.

There was, however, some Social Democratic representation in the Duma; the role of these deputies highlighted one additional dilemma that was to plague Russian social democracy throughout its existence, and which would also find reflection in the movement in China. The dilemma was, simply, how were radicals now to relate to the bourgeoisie—commercial elements, manufacturers, professionals, and others whose social interests seemed to confine their commitment to political liberties rather than fundamental changes in property relations or socioeconomic structures. Under conditions of tsarist repression (or in China, under conditions of extraterritoriality and the presence of imperial powers), who was the enemy, the class oppressor, or the political system against which even the liberal bourgeoisie was allied? The dangers of cooperating with bourgeois groups were painfully apparent in the aftermath of 1905: despite some concessions to workers in terms of wage and living conditions, as well as the start of significant changes in rural landholding designed particularly to benefit "strong" elements (relatively well-to-do) among the peasantry, the liberal-radical alliance in 1905 had not brought fundamental *social* change. Did cooperation necessarily lead, then, to a consolidation of the bourgeoisie and to the establishment of a political economy that would hinder the development of a socialist order? Did the tsar's concessions simply open to Russia's manufacturers and liberal gentry the opportunity to "co-opt" the labor movement and turn its power to their own advantage? Or was such cooperation necessary to building a genuine national liberation movement, one whose political objectives, at least initially, enjoyed some degree of respectability and support among all social elements, and hence some possibility of success?

Closely related was the question of using liberal institutions, even as the alliance with liberal and bourgeois social elements was broken. The danger Lenin and other radicals felt existed in terms of Bolshevik Duma representation was simply that workers would grow accustomed to liberal institutions and lose sight of their own social and political power. Sharing power even in this minimal way was also dangerously seductive to the representatives themselves; while Bolsheviks in the Duma made inflammatory speeches to dramatize their radicalism and their independence (as Khrushchev was to do more than fifty years later at the United Nations), the pressures to work within "the system" were very great. What was the cost, then, of the improvements in workers' well-being that came through such a mechanism? And did radical leaders like the Bolsheviks risk the danger of losing worker support if they refused to work for such improvements and struggled instead for further revolutionary confrontation, with all the dangers that implied?

This latter dilemma spoke in essence to what was to prove among the most critical issues of all in the Russian and Chinese revolutions, the relations between a vanguard party and its worker or peasant mass base. If a small, well-organized party was necessary, as Lenin and others maintained, to "bring revolutionary consciousness" to workers and poor peasants, to mobilize mass energies, and to lead the revolutionary struggle, there was an implicit danger of elitism and of leaders consequently losing the support of the led. In these circumstances there was also the danger that radical authoritarianism, struggling to maintain its support or its power, would become as repressive in its way as the system it fought to replace. This was the real concern of Menshevik Social Democrats like Martov and even Plekhanov about Lenin's vanguard conception; it lay at the heart of the Menshevik-Bolshevik split. If the party had to bring radical consciousness to workers from above, how could it be sure it genuinely represented proletarian interests? And how could the party maintain an organic tie to those for whose well-being it was fighting if masses of workers and poor peasants themselves disagreed with its objectives or its tactics?[25]

2

1917:
The Paradox of Victory

February 27, 1917, was a cold, clear day in Petrograd. By midmorning, huge crowds had gathered at the Putilov steel works and other major factories, prepared as they had the previous three days to march to the city's central squares. Colorful red banners billowed in the crisp air. Some said simply "Bread!" Others insisted "Down with the Tsar!" Along Nevskii and Liteinyi Prospekts, Petrograd's main boulevards, groups of people gathered in doorways and along the street, waiting expectantly to see what the day would bring. Some talked animatedly with each other and with passersby, arguing about the tsar and his advisors; others stood quietly, shuffling against the cold, occasionally shouting something at passing groups of soldiers.

From the beginning of the demonstrations on February 23, the reaction of the soldiers was on everyone's mind. General Khabalov, the garrison commander, warned against demonstrations; he would keep "strict order" in the capital. Placards appeared on the twenty-fourth and twenty-fifth demanding food; for the next two days, armed patrols roamed through the city. Several people were killed when mounted police opened fire on a demonstration in Znamenskaia Square, but as news of the attack spread, soldiers began to go out of

35

their way to show support for demonstrating workers. By Sunday, February 26, the city police had disappeared from the streets; late that afternoon, a company of the Pavlovskii Guard Regiment mutinied against their officers. Overnight, other units followed. By 9 A.M. on the twenty-seventh, reports reached members of the State Duma at the Tauride Palace that elements of the Volynskii and Litovskii regiment had declared themselves revolutionaries and that a number of officers had been killed. Shooting could be heard around the barracks. Groups of rebel soldiers were marching on the arsenals and mustering support from other units.

The scene at the Tauride Palace was chaotic. "The Government is paralyzed," Nicholas Rodzianko, the Duma president, telegraphed army headquarters on February 26. "The capital is in a state of anarchy. Transport service and the supply of food and fuel have been completely disrupted. General discontent is growing. . . . It is necessary that someone enjoying the nation's confidence be entrusted immediately with the task of forming a new government. There can be no delay. Procrastination is death!"[1] But the tsar's only response was to prorogue the Duma and State Council, suspending all official acts of both legislative houses for fear they might become points of organized opposition.

This staggered even the monarchy's strongest supporters. "Rescind your Imperial Ukaze," Rodzianko pleaded on the twenty-seventh. "The last bulwark of order has been eliminated! . . . Order the reconvening of the chambers."[2] Nicholas did not respond. Duma deputies and other government officials hurried from telephone to telephone seeking new information, hoping for new directives. None were forthcoming. The tsar seemed to think events in the city were not serious. In desperation, Rodzianko scheduled an unofficial meeting of State Duma members for 2 P.M. in the Polutsirkulnyi Hall.

At precisely this moment, in another wing of the same building, workers' and soldiers' delegates from scores of factories and garrison units were also coming together, hoping like the Duma deputies to give the city organization and direction. Led by a number of moderate socialists, some of whom had just been released from prison, the assembly here quickly formed a Provisional Executive Committee of the Petrograd Workers' Soviet. A formal first session of the Soviet was scheduled for 7 P.M. Emissaries were sent to gather delegates from factories throughout the city and to spread the word that workers themselves were organizing, just as they had in 1905. Whatever the course of events, the Soviet would at least provide Petrograd workers and soldiers with representative leadership.

From the night of February 27 onwards, consequently, the popular rebellion in Petrograd had its own headquarters, its own means of coordinating a defense of the city against loyalist troops if that were necessary, and its own legitimizing institution for revolutionary goals and aspirations, just as "privileged" Russia had the Duma. The political and psychological significance of this was enormous. While the State Duma met in an unauthorized session, ruminating over the legality of its convocation and wondering whether "the people would recognize a new government," if it should appoint one, workers' and soldiers' delegates were giving events a clear revolutionary focus and direction. Popular support for overthrowing the tsar's regime swept through the garrison and the city's working-class districts as news of the Soviet's formation spread through Petrograd. By the evening of February 27, as the Duma deputies struggled to organize a Temporary Committee to coordinate events and set up a new government, hundreds of workers and soldiers crowded into the first Soviet assembly down the hall:

> Standing on stools, their rifles in their hands, agitated and stuttering, straining all their powers to give a connected account of the messages entrusted to them . . . one after another the soldiers' delegates told of what had been happening in their companies. . . . "We had a meeting . . ." "They told us to say that we refuse to serve against the people any more, we're going to join with our brother workers, all united, to defend the people's cause. . . ." "Our general meeting told us to greet you. . . ." "Long live the revolution!" the delegate would add in a voice already completely wiped out by the throbbing roar of the meeting.[3]

Intense pressure for radical action touched even the most reluctant. As the Soviet session continued, the momentum for change seemed irreversible: "New groups kept pouring into the hall . . . Skobelev [took] the chair; in the midst of the hurly-burly and the general excitement he had neither a general plan of action nor control of the meeting itself, which proceeded noisily and quite chaotically. But this by no means prevented the Soviet from performing at this very first session its basic task, vital to the revolution—that of concentrating into one center all the ideological and organizational strength of the Petersburg democracy, with undisputed authority and a capacity for rapid and decisive action."[4]

Shortly afterwards, with the noise and commotion of the Soviet session clearly perceptible, the State Duma's Temporary Committee moved to organize a new regime, consulting frequently in the process with members of the Soviet's Executive Committee. Appeals were issued on February 28 to avoid bloodshed and protect property, and a joint Military Commission was established to direct the insurgent garrison. On March 1, Nicholas himself finally recognized the need to step aside. Several Duma deputies left to meet his train at Pskov and to secure a decree vesting power in the young tsarevich, hoping to maintain continuity with the monarchy through a regency sympathetic to liberal constitutionalism. By the time the deputies arrived, however, Nicholas had relinquished authority not to his son, a sickly boy he wished to protect, but to his brother Mikhail, who promptly refused to accept it. With a whimper, the 300-year-old Romanov dynasty came to an end. A cabinet of ten liberal ministers, appointed by the Temporary Duma Committee and acceptable to the Petrograd Soviet, assumed power as a Provisional Government.[5]

THE GOALS OF "ORDINARY" AND "PRIVILEGED" RUSSIA

News of "Revolution in Russia!" startled the world. For several months Western Europe had expected major changes in the Russian government. There was hope in some quarters that Nicholas might significantly increase the powers of the Duma, perhaps moving in the direction of a limited constitutional monarchy. The war was not going well on the eastern front. Monumental supply and transport problems were disrupting even essential material for the front; scarcities of food and fuel affected virtually every major city and town. The murder of the royal family's mystic confidant and advisor, Rasputin, in late 1916 by a small coterie of nobles, testified to the breadth of discontent. Massive strikes in January and early February had not so much disrupted production as called attention to the more than 200 percent increase in the cost of living since the beginning of the war and to the incompetence of Nicholas's ministers. When Paul Miliukov, the leader and principal spokesman of the liberal Constitutional Democratic party, rehearsed the government's shortcomings in a widely publicized speech to the Duma in November 1916, asking rhetorically "is this stupidity or is this treason?" many felt reforms were imminent. It was, as Rodzianko and others expressed it, "a question of the war, of victory, of Russia!"

But Miliukov and his liberal colleagues underestimated the tsar's intransigence, just as earlier, during the revolution of 1905, they had overestimated his willingness to accept parliamentary government and a rule of law. Nicholas only responded to pressure. Many have argued that the revolution in 1917 was largely, if not entirely, a consequence of the war; but the tsar's unwillingness to grant reforms even at a time of crisis like the winter of 1916–17 suggests the weakness of this view. The structural strains building in Russian society as a consequence of industrial growth and agrarian backwardness could only have been ameliorated, if at all, by a responsive and effective regime, something Nicholas and his advisors showed no inclination to create. Even Prime Minister Stolypin's rather conservative prewar effort at consolidating holdings of "strong" peasants and reducing tax and redemption obligations drew the wrath of Russia's gentry. Stolypin himself was assassinated by protofascist rightists. One need not stretch historical imagination too far to surmise the fate of a genuine liberal in the prime minister's office. In China, too, the monarchy under pressure would yield reforms whose full implications were then distorted by a powerful, entrenched gentry and bureaucracy. Autocrats are notoriously unwilling to accept the necessity of organic, structural change, since this itself necessarily vitiates autocratic power.

In these circumstances it was only a matter of time before the rebelliousness of alienated workers and poor peasants outran the government's capacity to respond, and Russia erupted again as it had in 1905. Some even argued for a renewal of the pre-1905 "Liberationist" coalition, when liberal professionals joined workers and even progressive bourgeois elements in demanding change. The masses' power had been demonstrated in 1905, however, and its fury frightened erstwhile social allies from the professions and liberal gentry. Serious contradictions consequently emerged not only between the goals of society and the regime on one hand, but also between the reformist ambitions of "privileged" Russia and the radical demands of workers and peasants on the other.

The outbreak of war certainly intensified these strains. The question of reform became clearly tied to the issue of military success. As problems at the front increased, liberals increasingly castigated the government for ineptitude, while its ability to suppress disorders decreased along with its credibility. In this sense one might rightly argue that revolution "stemmed" from the war. But just as likely is the possibility that the outbreak of hostilities muted popular dissidence and for a time, at least, presented the tsarist government with an unusually strong base of popular support, an unprecedented opportunity to institute change. If the war helped destroy the old regime, in other words, it also might have helped the regime ameliorate those fundamental antagonistic strains in Russian social relations, which themselves constituted the root cause of 1917.

This background helps explain the course of events in February, and it is crucial to understanding subsequent developments. What Russia experienced in 1917 was not really a single, unified revolutionary explosion; instead it was the culmination of several very different strands of dissidence, each of which was intrinsically complex, but each of which had its own social base, its own program for change, and after February, its own set of revolutionary institutions.

Russia's "Westernized" liberal professionals, the gentry, elements of the extensive state bureaucracy, and the small but economically significant commercial and manufacturing bourgeoisie joined in opposition to the old regime primarily because it could not prosecute the war effectively. No one in this group wanted revolution. "I have no desire to revolt," Duma President Rodzianko insisted in February, echoing the sentiments of upper-class Russia. "I am not a rebel. I have made no revolution and do not intend to make one. If it is here, it is because they would not listen to us."[6] Most also agreed with Vasili Maklakov, the liberal Kadet who felt ordinary Russians were not "ready" for liberal democracy, and who feared an "overdose" of freedom would lead to chaos.

This sector of society believed radical change was necessary, however, if Russia was to win the war. The bureaucracy had to be streamlined, decision-making decentralized, and persons brought into positions of responsibility who had genuine competence in the urgent tasks of production, supply, food distribution, and even military planning. Thus Duma leaders selected a respected leader of the national Zemstvo Union, Prince Lvov, to be head of the new Provisional regime. Lvov had close ties to local zemstvo personnel and past experience in national and city government administration, as well as in the Duma. There was no doubt, moreover, about what "privileged" social elements wanted from the war: a sound position politically for Russia in a postwar world (which meant for some control over Constantinople and the Dardanelles strait, and continued possession of the Baltic states of Latvia, Estonia, and Lithuania, and perhaps even Poland) and the opportunity for economic expansion. These goals were outlined quite clearly just before February by Paul Miliukov, the Provisional Government's new foreign minister, in *Vestnik Evropy* ("European Messenger"), a leading liberal journal. Constantinople in particular, as well as the Balkan states had to be liberated from the "heavy and bloody tyranny" of Ottoman rule in the name of Western values.[7] It was this group whose representatives occupied every cabinet chair in the new Provisional Government but one, that of Justice, held by the socialist Alexander Kerensky.

The new regime moved quickly to "clear the decks for victory." It decentralized state administration, bringing local people into the management of production, supply, and distribution problems at a local level. Early in March, a national grain monopoly was announced to alleviate food supply problems, requiring compulsory transfer of all marketable grain to the state at fixed 1916 rates. Shortly afterwards, the new government ordered the formation of a nationwide network of local food supply committees (charged with "administering the food supply and the organization of agricultural production within the framework of orders from Petrograd"); a similar network of land committees was also created (designed to accumulate factual data for subsequent reform and deal with specific local problems). Both sets of committees were to be composed of appointed and elected representatives, specifically including local soviet delegates. The new regime clearly desired to integrate Russian society as a whole in support of the war and build a new liberal order.

These goals also underlay an agreement between the Petrograd Society of Manufacturers and Petrograd workers early in March to establish an eight-hour working day, as well as the decision to decentralize administration in the crucial area of railroad transport by establishing authoritative workers' committees. In the broader area of national politics, the Provisional Government committed itself to holding power only until a Constituent (or constitutional) Assembly could be elected by national vote and to postpone major social reforms until the nation's elected representatives could express their wishes. Given the ad hoc way it came to power, the Provisional Government insisted it lacked "legal competence" to institute such fundamental reforms as the redistribution of land.

Quite a different perspective, however, dominated Russia's workers, soldiers, and peasants—the "democracy" in the terminology of 1917. The "ordinary people" were as variegated socially and politically as middle- and upper-class Russia, but similarities were more often significant than differences. Here revolution meant sweeping social reform, from the rectification of minor injustices, like regulations requiring soldiers to ride on streetcar running boards, to better living conditions and wages, lower prices, and, above all, land. On the war question there was at first little uniformity: scattered "Zimmerwaldists" opposed it, and no one wished to be sent to the front, but by and large the "democracy" initially saw fighting as a necessary evil. Certainly Russia had to defend itself.

As for civil liberties and representative government, these liberal institutions were certainly desirable, but "freedom" for most workers and peasants was freedom *from*, not freedom *for*: freedom from want and deprivation; freedom from hunger; freedom from debt and the insecurities of inadequate land and food; freedom from unhealthy living conditions, fines, sexual harassment; freedom from police repression and the anguish of frustrated hopes and ambitions. In the eyes of workers and peasants, these were *truly* democratic goals, far more important than whether elections took place according to this or that set of regulations.

INSTITUTIONAL DUALITIES

It was this sector of society which seized the opportunity in February 1917 to organize hundreds of factory committees, soldiers' councils, village meetings, and similar mass organizations, radically and spontaneously changing the institutional structure of Russian society. Railroad workers organized Provisional Line Committees on major roads in Petrograd and Moscow, announcing their intention to assume supervisory tasks in order to improve railroad operations. Scores of factory committees also organized, and in some places formed their own militias; soldiers met and threw out particularly obnoxious commanders, even as many regiments prepared to march in Petrograd in support of the Provisional regime and the Petrograd Soviet.

The formation of the Petrograd Soviet itself soon provided these mass, lower-level committees and councils with some national leadership, giving the "democracy," in effect, a powerful shadow government, one capable of exercising authority (since its orders were being obeyed) but not actually sharing "official state power," which was vested in the Provisional regime. Other soviets soon sprang up all over Russia to act as coordinating and leadership bodies for the huge number of local workers' or peasants' committees. Largely Socialist Revolutionary (SR) and Menshevik (in part because of heavier tsarist repression against the Bolsheviks), their representatives insisted Russia's new government was to be obeyed "only insofar as" its instructions did not conflict with mass interests or contradict the soviets' own orders and instructions.

Thus a pattern of dual power emerged in state affairs, one which lasted until the Bolsheviks came to power in October, and which historians have frequently pointed to as an inherently unstable political condition. Lenin described it as a situation of *kto-kogo* ("who shall rule whom"). By giving the liberal ministry official power while reserving for themselves the authority to validate government decrees, moderate socialist leaders in the soviets were attempting to balance social and political interests that were often irreconcilable. In the process, some argue, they encouraged disobedience and lawlessness. Coming to a great extent from the ranks of Russia's intelligentsia, many soviet executive committee members recognized these difficulties but at first refused to join the government (or take full power themselves) for several reasons. Few doubted socialist ministers would be bitterly opposed by Russia's middle and upper classes (its "bourgeoisie," to use the popular but simplifying designation of the time). Some feared the army would turn against the revolution. Others felt revolutionary gains had to be consolidated before the soviets could take power, which meant that the liberal bourgeoisie had to defuse the reactionary gentry and harness the army, prevent the creation of a military dictatorship, and accustom Russia as a whole to the rudiments of political democracy. Workers, peasants, and even soldiers also needed time to organize themselves and to develop a political consciousness appropriate to the moment, capable of avoiding anarchy and chaos. If civil war was to be avoided, and if Russia was to move peacefully toward socialism, avoiding authoritarianism of either right-wing "counterrevolutionaries" or left-wing "extremists," a Soviet regime could not take power prematurely.

It was unlikely such a balancing act could have worked even if the liberals themselves agreed to it, but Lvov, Miliukov, and other ministers were insistent on exercising "full plenitude of power" (as the new foreign minister put it redundantly) and pursued their own definition of national goals. These centered above all on the war. Workers' committees were at first welcomed, even encouraged, by the government as a means for peacefully resolving labor-management problems and increasing industrial productivity. Committees on the railroads, for example, were publicly applauded by Transport Minister Nekrasov as Russia's "best guarantee" for improving rail transport. Even soldiers' committees were tolerable if they lifted morale or otherwise strengthened a unit's ability to fight, and in the first weeks of the revolution, at least, this certainly seemed to be the case.

Yet the condition of dual power at the upper reaches of Russian state life was actually less important than another dualism emerging at this time, reflected in the very organization of the mass organizations themselves. The spontaneous formation of thousands of lower-level workers', peasants', and soldiers' committees represented a profound structural change in the organization of Russian society, one providing "ordinary" people with the institutional bases for taking control of their own affairs and the presumption that democracy meant both their right and their ability to do so. To many on the shop floor, socialist professionals and intellectuals in high-level soviet executive committees were more like the liberal ministers than the uneducated, common people they ostensibly represented.

Thus an even more profound dualism was developing, which reflected the deep social polarization between "we" and "they," and the corresponding, antagonistic social structures: mass committees and local councils on one hand, central state institutions on the other. On major substantive issues, moreover, those at the top in *both* the government and the Soviet Executive Committee seemed increasingly in agreement. At first the war was a divisive issue. The national Soviet leadership forcefully rejected any notion of fighting for "annexations or indemnities" and insisted only that Russia would fight "to defend the revolution." Foreign Minister Miliukov wanted control over Constantinople, and the government insisted on "war to complete victory." But Miliukov was forced to resign after massive demonstrations in favor of "revolutionary defensism" and "peace without annexations" in April; the cabinet was reorganized into a socialist-liberal coalition. Thereafter the liberals and moderate socialists pressed different programs, but both insisted on a rule of law; both insisted that major reforms, like the reorganization of land holdings or the nationalization of industry, be postponed until national elections for a Constituent Assembly and the formation of a popularly based regime; and both demanded that worker, peasant, and soldier committees not usurp state power or disobey the law.

LENIN'S RETURN AND THE APRIL THESES

But *whose* law were workers to obey? *Whose* state was to enjoy "full plenitude of power"? *Whose* welfare were the Provisional regime and Soviet leadership really pursuing in the name of "national" interest, by insisting the army continue to fight. To Lenin, who returned from exile on April 3, these questions had *unequivocal* answers. "The war unquestionably remains on Russia's part a predatory imperialist war, since the new government remains a capitalist government!" The moderate socialist leaders of the Petrograd Soviet were "selling out" workers' and soldiers' interests. The bourgeoisie was establishing *its* dictatorship over the revolution, pursuing *its* objectives, not those of ordinary Russians. These views did not, of course, reflect a new perspective on Lenin's part. What was remarkable, however, and what shocked not only moderate socialists in the Petrograd Soviet, but even some in his own party, was the tumultuous reception Lenin received when he arrived at the Finland station, and the boldness of his attack on the Provisional regime. The radical journalist Sukhanov recorded the scene:

> The throng in front of the Finland Station blocked the whole square, making movement impossible, and scarcely letting the trams through. . . . Motor cars throbbed. In two or three places the awesome silhouettes of armoured cars thrust up from the crowd. . . . Inside the station the crush was even greater—more delegations, more flags and sentries at every step. . . . The scene was extraordinarily impressive. "Delegates" were clinging to the outside of windows . . . banners hung across the platform at every step; triumphal arches had been set up, adorned with red and gold;

one's eyes were dazzled by every possible welcoming inscription and revolutionary slogan, while at the end of the platform, where the carriage was expected to stop, there was a band and a group of representatives of the central Bolshevik organizations, holding flowers. . . .

At long last the train arrived. A thunderous *Marseillaise* boomed forth on the platform, and shouts of welcome rang out. . . . The gloomy Chkheidze spoke . . . "Comrade Lenin, we welcome you to Russia in the name of the Petersburg Soviet and of the whole revolution. . . . But—we think that the principal task of the revolutionary democracy is now the defense of the revolution from any encroachments either from within or from without. We consider that what this goal requires not disunity, but the closing of the democratic ranks. We hope you will pursue these goals with us." Chkheidze stopped speaking. . . . But Lenin plainly knew exactly how to behave. He stood there as though nothing taking place had the slightest connection with him . . . and then, turning away from the Executive Committee delegation altogether, made this "reply":

"Dear Comrades, soldiers, sailors, and workers! I am happy to greet in your persons the victorious Russian revolution, and greet you as the vanguard of the world-wide proletarian army. . . . The piratical imperialist war is the beginning of civil war throughout Europe. . . . The hour is not far distant when . . . the people will turn their arms against their own capitalist exploiters. . . . Any day now, European capitalism may crash. The Russian revolution accomplished by you has prepared the way for a new epoch. Long live the world-wide Socialist revolution!" . . .

To another *Marseillaise*, and to the shouts of the throng of thousands, among the red-and-gold banners illuminated by the searchlight, Lenin went out . . . but the crowd absolutely refused to allow this. Lenin clambered on to the hood of a car, and had to make a speech.

". . . any part in shameful imperialist slaughter . . . lies and frauds . . . capitalist pirates . . ." . . . was what I could hear, squeezed in the doorway . . . Then I think Lenin had to change to an armoured car, and in it, preceded by the searchlight and accompanied by the band, flags, workers' detachments, army units, and an enormous crowd . . . [made his way] to the Bolshevik headquarters.[8]

Imperialist war as the beginning of civil war! A worldwide socialist revolution! Russian workers as the vanguard of a worldwide prole-

tarian army! Lenin clearly entered the Russian revolutionary scene
with a radically different perspective than the leaders of the Petrograd
Soviet. Within days he had formulated his views in a series of "April
Theses": since most workers "undoubtedly believed honestly in revolutionary defensism," it was necessary "with particular thoroughness,
persistence, and patience, to explain their error to them." The
"specific feature" of the current moment was that Russia was passing
from the first, bourgeois stage of revolution, to "the *second stage*,
which must place power in the hands of the proletariat and the
poorest section of the peasantry." The Provisional Government, a
capitalist, imperialist regime, could not be supported: "the utter
falsity of all its promises" had to be made clear.

To end the war, a "widespread campaign of fraternization" was
to be organized at the front. The police, the army, and the bureaucracy had to be abolished. Landed estates were to be seized, and all
land nationalized, to be redistributed by local peasants' soviets. Production and the distribution of products had to be brought immediately under the control of workers' soviets. At the same time,
Bolsheviks had to recognize that "in most of the soviets, our Party
is a minority against *a bloc of all* the petty-bourgeois opportunist
elements . . ." who have yielded to the influence of the bourgeoisie
and spread that influence among the proletariat. "The masses have
to be made to see that the Soviets of Workers' Deputies are the *only
possible* form of revolutionary government," while the Bolshevik
party itself was to bend every effort to gain control of the soviets.[9]

DEEPENING OF THE REVOLUTION

The import of Lenin's April Theses was immediately apparent. In a
single stroke, he identified the Bolshevik party with elemental mass
desires, translating a vague sense of what the revolution *ought* to be
in the minds of many workers, peasants, and soldiers, into a clear
political program. Already in the countryside, peasants were beginning to seize the lands of absent landlords, and disturbances were
spreading. Workers' committees were demanding a greater say in
factory operations. Angry voices could be heard on the government's
new food and fuel supply committees over the way in which scarce
necessities were being distributed. Lenin's political genius tapped

these feelings and even legitimized them by bringing the Bolsheviks as a party around to their support.

One can follow the subsequent political history of 1917 in some detail, but to understand its development, one must appreciate above all the way in which Lenin and the Bolsheviks recognized in April the basic, antagonistic, social cleavages of Russian life, and worked not to avoid conflict, as did the moderate Left and even the liberals, but to intensify its development. Social antagonism was the mechanism of further revolutionary change, the means by which Russian workers and poor peasants could eventually come to power themselves. But proletarians had to appreciate their own strength; they needed to be made aware and shown their "errors" with "particular thoroughness, persistence, and patience." This was the task of the vanguard party, the Leninist instrument capable of clarifying and articulating mass desires, and of moving the workers' and peasants' own institutions—the factory committees and local soviets—into the struggle for *social*, rather than merely *political*, democracy and onto the path of "proletarian dictatorship."

Here, however, was also the crux of the moderate socialists' resistance to Lenin: Russian workers were simply not ready to "dictate" their will, even in the sense of democratic political hegemony. The rights of other social classes had to be respected, even as they were changed, to avoid armed conflict and civil war. Particularly at this juncture, the Soviet Executive Committee insisted in April, with German armies capable of taking instant advantage of Russian weakness, "every rash step" was dangerous.

But the potential for "rash steps" abounded in 1917, and not only on the part of radicals. As already noted, the revolution's first crisis occurred over war aims, when the Kadet foreign minister, Miliukov, disregarded the soviets' strong feelings about annexations and indemnities and sent a note to the Allies implying Russia's attitudes on the war had not changed. Within forty-eight hours massive demonstrations filled the streets of Petrograd, appalling government and Petrograd Soviet leaders alike. On April 20 and 21, banners demanded "Down with the War!" and "Down with the Bourgeois Ministers"; but counterdemonstrations were quickly mounted, calling for "War to Complete Victory!" and castigating the Soviet.

Petrograd split into two camps, angry workers clashing with equally impassioned bourgeois elements. The Soviet called the situation "regrettable and disgraceful," disavowing any effort to seize power; the government insisted its policies were in Russia's best interests and blamed the disorders on "the primordial tendency to fulfill desires of individual groups . . . by direct action, bypassing legal avenues."[10] Miliukov, as noted, was soon forced to resign, and the government reorganized into a socialist-liberal coalition, with four Soviet representatives taking places as private citizens, rather than official delegates, beside the remaining liberals.

To some extent such an arrangement better aligned the government with the changing configuration of Russian social forces, but little was done to meet the growing press for social reforms. Meanwhile, it became increasingly clear that the really radical instruments for change were workers', peasants', and soldiers' committees—in the factories, in the villages, at the front. Under the impetus of these groups, the very structure of Russian society and life was being altered. When factory owners refused to meet workers' demands or threatened to close the gates, committees took over; railroad workers claimed that the lines were theirs; peasants on the government-sponsored land committees insisted the food problem could only be solved through the confiscation of gentry land, and when officials resisted, seized estates on their own. Columns describing "anarchy in the countryside" began to appear in Russian newspapers as early as April, accompanied by accounts of deserting soldiers rushing back to the village to "get their share." Supported by the Petrograd Soviet leadership, Lvov's Provisional regime still insisted it lacked the authority to implement major reforms on its own. But preparations for national Constituent Assembly elections "took time."

Delay, however, meant perpetuating bourgeois social relations. Lenin's indictment of the Provisional regime thus seemed increasingly warranted by workers and peasants desperately anxious for improvements in social welfare. The acquiescence of moderate socialists also seemed to substantiate Lenin's charges. By supporting the liberal regime, by insisting themselves on "order" and "due process," and by refusing to take power on their own, Mensheviks and others were themselves open to attack as "accommodationists," "appeasers," and "betrayers of the popular interest."

At the upper reaches of society and politics, the solution seemed to be to win the war with Germany as rapidly as possible and move toward a democratic, constitutional order. In May, preparations were begun for what would soon be known as "Kerensky's offensive," an effort to strike decisively at the Germans in conjunction with a push by Britain and France in the West. The offensive had actually been planned well before the February revolution; the coalition supported it as a means both of preserving Russia's place at the peace table and stopping what everyone in government regarded as the immediate cause of Russia's economic and social disintegration. War Minister Kerensky rushed to the front, bringing other Soviet spokesmen with him. "Forward, Comrades," he harangued the troops. "Forward to Liberty! . . . Forward to Death!"[11]

To the people in factories all over Russia, in the countryside at village gatherings, in army units, on the railroads, "Forward to Death!" seemed madness. Here a different solution made more sense: take control, take power for themselves. "Organize! Organize! Meet together, form committees, take control!" Yet precisely *this* seemed madness to liberals and others in the government, as well as to judicious well-educated Soviet leaders, to bourgeois groups like the Trade Industrialists, gentry leaders, the army's General Staff, and others. "Workers' control" was "anarchy." Russia was threatened with "chaos." The very notion of workers' control seemed insidious. Employers, government officials, and others felt their authority being undermined, their power circumscribed. "Those in power are always striving to become sole possessors of power," radicals responded. "Ruling groups always interpret every attempt by larger sectors of the population to subject them to some control as an encroachment on their rights. . . . Empty fears! Without control, there can be no confidence. . . . The bourgeoisie forgets where they got their power, they forget that the Provisional Government was created by the revolution. . . . The proletariat remembers this. Life has changed."[12]

Indeed, life *was* changing. The process of mobilization from below was bringing to ordinary Russians a new sense of power, a new sense of their ability to handle affairs. National authority was rapidly becoming remote. Whatever fear workers and peasants had for officialdom under the tsars was rapidly dissolving, replaced not by the general respect enjoyed by Western politicians, but by genuine disdain. Increasingly, workers and peasants referred to "our" people, using simply the Russian word *nash* ("ours"); increasingly, the coincidence of social, psychological, and political mobilization on the part of ordinary Russians intensified the antagonism of social relations and furthered social polarization.

In these circumstances, the political connotations of "class" in Russia rapidly became clear. Kadets and other liberals may have had little in common with many large landowners and manufacturers, but opposing workers' control or peasant land seizures and insisting on "full plenitude of power" for the Provisional Government meant identification as part of bourgeois or "privileged" Russia, regardless of actual social or economic circumstances. On the other hand, involvement in the growing network of local soviets or committees identified one as a member of the "democracy." The revolutionary process in Russia was simplifying the complexities of Russian life, as it was to do in China, blurring subtle social distinctions and even significant political differences. In the process, substantial political advantage went to those like Lenin, who recognized and used broad political characterizations, and who thus furthered Bolshevik identification with elemental mass desires.

Thus when Tsereteli and other moderate socialists addressed the first All-Russian Congress of Soviets in early June, pleading for unity and "an end to experiments dangerous to the revolution . . . which may lead to civil war," Lenin responded with clear battle lines: "Either we have an ordinary bourgeois government—in which case there is no need for any kind of soviet . . . and they can die an ignominious death—or we have a real government of soviets. There is no other way." And when rumors began to circulate about the Kerensky offensive in June, the Bolshevik Central Committee, over vociferous Soviet objections, called Petrograd workers into the streets: "Down with the ten capitalist ministers! . . . Abolish the 'orders' for soldiers and sailors! Hail workers' control and organization in industry! End the War! . . . Bread! Peace! Liberty!"[13] A similar display took place in Moscow in connection with elections to the city Duma, where Bolsheviks returned only 11 percent of the vote (compared to the 56 percent obtained by the peasant-oriented Socialist Revolutionaries—SRs), but showed themselves well organized and capable of dominating public rallies. And as the offensive, predictably, began to go badly, Lenin's party stood out sharply as supporters of radical change and of peace. In contrast, Mensheviks, SRs, and the moderate socialists still dominating national Soviet leadership in Petrograd were identified with military disaster and with the "bourgeois" orientation of the Provisional regime.

The anomalous position of the high Soviet leadership in these circumstances bespeaks the dilemmas of socialist moderates almost everywhere, and certainly in times of revolutionary change. Supporting land reform, nationalization of industry, and such radical social restructuring as workers' participation in industrial management, moderate socialists still recognized the validity of higher, nonpartisan national interests, treasured political democracy, and worried about militant resistance and civil war from those whose property or other rights were tread upon. Like the German revisionists scorned earlier by Lenin and other Marxist radicals (including Marx himself), the moderates joined. Russia's bourgeois government in a coalition designed to advance and protect popular interests; nonetheless, this move exposed them to the charges of co-optation and betrayal. Given the provisional nature of Russia's revolutionary government, it seemed possible that the moderates' dilemma could be resolved by national elections to a Constituent Assembly. But the war itself hampered election preparations, the liberal majority in the cabinet hoped openly for postponement, reforms were delayed, the military situation continued to deteriorate, shortages increased, and moderates remained open to threats and accusations from a deepening revolutionary radicalism. Open conflict was only a matter of time.

REVOLUTIONARY POLITICS: JULY TO OCTOBER

The explosion took place in three waves. The first occurred in early July, the second in August, and the last in ten October days "that shook the world." On July 3, Bolshevik machine-gunners from the Petrograd garrison led an armed assault on the government, hoping to radicalize the Soviet and force it to take full power. Lenin and the party leadership felt the effort was dangerous and premature, but reluctantly supported the soldiers who prepared it, demonstrating both their desire to stay closely allied with radical mass elements and the relative insecurity of their leadership positions. Lenin, however, was right. After three days of street fighting and demonstrations, the government and Soviet together suppressed the uprising, cracked down on the Bolsheviks, and indicated their intention of introducing stringent new measures, including the restoration of the death penalty, to enforce order and military discipline. Trotsky and others were arrested. Lenin went into hiding, charged with accepting German money and acting as a German agent.

Shortly afterwards, the Provisional Government was reorganized with Kerensky as both prime minister and minister of war, and the tough-minded General Kornilov as commander-in-chief. The new coalition expressed support for a program of reform drawn up by the Soviet Executive Committee on July 8, setting Constituent Assembly elections for the "very near future." But bourgeois Russia was moving rapidly to the right, and by early August, as General Kornilov presented the new regime with a rigorous program for restoring order, rumors began to circulate about the possibility of a military coup. At a meeting of State Duma members on July 19, reactionaries openly demanded the Soviet be "dissolved" and "all those dark forces sitting on the neck of the Provisional Government, and of which the Government is afraid, be destroyed."[14] In early August Kerensky convened a "State Conference" in Moscow to rally support for his regime, but right-wing forces welcomed Kornilov as a hero, and Russia's political cleavage intensified. Some on the Right appealed openly for Kornilov to take power.

Two weeks later Kornilov made his move, ostensibly to suppress an "imminent Bolshevik uprising." Kerensky himself encouraged the general, hoping to shore up his own authority, but Kornilov turned on the government as well, vowing to bring Russia "to a Constituent Assembly by means of victory over the enemy."[15] The mutiny was covered with ambiguity and confusion. It collapsed quickly as Petrograd workers rallied quickly to defend the capital and Kornilov's own troops refused to fight. But its aftermath was clear, and momentous for Russia's future.

Government authority all over Russia suddenly fell away, replaced only by increasingly radical local institutions like the village assembly (*skhod*), factory committees, and local workers' and soldiers' soviets. September elections in Moscow and Petrograd turned out moderate socialists and brought Bolshevik majorities for the first time. Trotsky and other party leaders were released from prison and elected to high Soviet positions.

Popular elections for city and town dumas in September also returned large Bolshevik delegations. Lenin's earlier charges of "collusion" and "betrayal" now seemed justified. Evidence suggests popular support for the Bolsheviks was increasing even before Kornilov's attempted coup, but in its aftermath, the party's political radicalism meshed more firmly than ever with a massive popular sense of grievance and elemental longings for social improvement embodied for many in the very word "revolution." By mid-September Lenin felt the time had come to take power. A startled Bolshevik Central Committee received a secret communique placing "armed insurrection as the order of the day," and the Bolshevik leader himself made his way back to Petrograd disguised as a locomotive fireman. Most important, the Kornilov episode prompted the formation of armed workers' committees in Moscow and Petrograd, militant revolutionary bands sympathetic to Bolshevik goals. With Trotsky as president of the Soviet in Petrograd, and other Bolsheviks in comparable places of popular authority, it seemed possible to coordinate an effective Red Guard from ad hoc factory militias and successfully lead a second revolution.

This coordination was essentially Trotsky's task. In mid-October he assumed control of a Central Military Revolutionary Committee in Petrograd, after the Bolshevik Central Committee voted ten to two in favor of insurrection, and began intensive preparations. Bolshevik intentions were certainly no secret. Specific plans to take power in conjunction with the Second All-Russian Congress of Soviets were splashed in Petrograd newspapers. At first Kerensky himself seemed to welcome the challenge, boldly insisting he would crush his enemies on the Left "once and for all." But wishes and realities were never farther apart. Nine months of revolutionary development had laid bare the essential cleavages of Russian life; the polarity between moderate liberal politics and mass institutions and aspirations was the Bolshevik path to power. On October 25, armed units led by Trotsky's Military Revolutionary Committee seized key points in Petrograd. Kerensky fled, hoping to rally loyalist troops, and the remaining ministers were arrested. Shortly afterward, Lenin announced that a Soviet government would replace the deposed Provisional regime.

PERSPECTIVES ON OCTOBER

One can hardly overestimate the October revolution's historical significance. The very concept of a "workers' and peasants' regime" staggered Western imaginations. "Human scum" is how an observer quoted in the New York *Times* referred to the Petrograd workers and Red Guards who brought the Bolsheviks to power: a "criminal element" that had to be dealt with harshly and whose tenure as Russia's "government" would obviously be brief. According to one report, Lenin and his comrades had set up an electrically operated guillotine in Petrograd, capable of lopping off more than 500 heads an hour.

But the international view of the outcome of October largely depended (and depends) on the social position of the viewer. To Clydeside workers in England, to mutinous French troops at Verdun, to Karl Liebkneckt and radical German workers in Berlin, to Chinese radicals in Peking and Shanghai, Bolshevism reflected the triumph of the oppressed, the power of the ordinary man and woman, the historically and socially powerless. Almost instantly, the heroism of Lenin and October became symbolic. The long shadow of mobilized Russian workers signalled the capabilities of ordinary people everywhere.

However tentative the Bolsheviks' power—and we will return in a moment to the importance of Bolshevik insecurity—the October revolution also seemed to justify brilliantly Lenin's concept of the "vanguard party" and hence his authority as a revolutionary strategist. Bolsheviks gained access to instruments of national government without exercising coercive authority—without, in other words, establishing a "base area" under their exclusive control—because party members identified themselves with powerful mass organizations and desires, crystallized those desires into coherent political goals, and mobilized dissidence into effective political action. These were precisely the tasks of the vanguard: to clarify political consciousness and "Organize! Organize! Organize!" Without the party, mass dissidence would have remained fractured and ineffective, capable at best of wringing concessions from reluctant elites (as in 1905), but not of taking state power in the name of proletarian dictatorship.

Moreover, the notion of "dictatorship" had moral as well as political and social foundations in 1917, since for the time, at least, the Bolsheviks were genuinely a "mass party," whose program and principles reflected mass aspirations. Like Rousseau's notion of the "general will," Bolshevik dictatorship theoretically promised to implement the general wishes of an overwhelming majority at the expense of a minority elite—the bourgeois/gentry social alliance. No national elections underlay the establishment of the first Soviet regime, and events would shortly prove that the SRs, rather than the Bolsheviks, enjoyed the general support of a majority of Russia's peasants. (Adapting quickly, however, the Bolsheviks promulgated the SR land program as their own.) But even SR sympathizers acknowledged that they had no more effective means of rule than the powerless governments of Lvov and Kerensky.

In an important sense, then, there is little meaning to the notion of Lenin "seizing power" or to describing October as a "coup d'état." At a time when the self-appointed Provisional Government could no longer enforce its will—it had lost its legitimacy in the eyes of overwhelming numbers of workers, peasants, and soldiers—Lenin emerged as a reflection of popular aspiration and said convincingly "we will govern in your interests." There were, perhaps, alternative outcomes to the revolutionary sequence that began in February. Early Constituent Assembly elections, an end to the war, liberal willingness to work closely with the Soviet and institute popular reforms despite the risk of civil war, even vascillation among Bolshevik leaders might have left events to run until the old Russian empire broke into smaller, self-governing units or until military authorities of some kind emerged to take control. What largely prevented this was Lenin's own towering, forceful personality—guiding and cajoling, articulating clear political objectives, simplifying the political complexities of 1917 into a "we-they" struggle that neatly corresponded to Russia's broad social cleavages and increasing social polarization. If Russia's general conditions of socioeconomic backwardness made revolutionary upheaval of some sort an inevitable consequence of pressures for industrial modernization, there was nothing necessary or inevitable about the Bolsheviks themselves coming to power. This in no small measure was Lenin's personal achievement.

BOLSHEVIK "DEMOCRACY"

Nor was there any certainty whatsoever about the Bolsheviks *staying* in power *after* October. Quite the contrary. Establishing a socialist government in the name of overthrowing world capitalism and crushing the imperialists, nationalizing Russian industry, expropriating gentry land, seizing property from the bourgeoisie, disavowing military obligations, international debts, and the World War itself—

such a panoply of goals could hardly evoke a greater array of anti-Bolshevik reaction. Even more so, critical problems of food supply and distribution, securing vital raw materials, maintaining production and employment, and even assuring an adequate supply of fuel for such essential utilities as electrical generating stations were now all tasks with which the Bolsheviks had to cope. Russia faced a bleak winter. Famine was possible; widespread hunger a certainty. With factories closing for lack of fuel or supplies, or because owners stopped making profits and simply shut down, unemployment among the Bolsheviks' most militant supporters was rapidly increasing. If the party failed adequately to defend itself against class or political opposition, or proved incapable of meeting urgent popular needs, there was little possibility that Soviet socialism would survive.

Urgent problems demanded radical solutions; they also seemed incapable of solution without help from workers abroad. In the first weeks after October the Bolsheviks decreed the "socialization" of industry and agriculture, officially ratifying the commandeering of private factories and estates, which many local soviets and committees had already been doing. But no one expected socialism could survive in one country alone, or successfully defend itself without imposing a great degree of centralized control and planning. "World revolution" was not merely ideological ambition. Unless the "workers of the world" could overthrow their own anti-Soviet bourgeois regimes (at least in Germany, France or England), Bolshevism might be crushed. Unless the wealth and resources of industrial Europe were available for overcoming Russia's own agrarian backwardness, socialism as Marxists conceived it could never be achieved. Unless the Bolsheviks could use their political skills to organize Russia's society and economy, the boney hand of hunger could choke the revolution more readily than imperial intervention.

More than anything else, it was this remarkable range of enemies —from Conservatives in the House of Commons and the Kaiser's advisors on the German Imperial Staff to the impersonal cruelty of hunger, cold, and the "armies" of "General Winter"—that structured Bolshevik policies once the party was in power, and led to what many within the party would soon regard as unacceptable methods and ideological compromise. The immediate pressing issue was the war. The Bolsheviks came to power promising to end the fighting, but many in the party worried that the German armies, strengthened by peace on the Eastern front, would crush any revolutionary outbreak on the part of German workers and destroy the possibility of a socialist Germany. Democratic forces in France might be defeated as well. Soviet Russia would then be permanently isolated and become easy prey to subsequent imperialist attack. Bukharin and others consequently wanted to take the revolution westward by force.

The Politburo as a whole, however, felt the best strategy was simply to stand firm, without active fighting, but also without a formal peace. This might at least keep the German troops in their trenches. "We vow to thee, brother workers of other countries," Trotsky declared, "that we shall stand our ground, but you, brothers, do not exhaust our strength, our patience. Hurry up, stop the slaughter yourselves, overthrow the bourgeoisie yourselves, take power into your own hands, and then we will be able to turn the whole globe into a workers' republic."[16]

"Neither war nor peace" was how the party's strategy was phrased; if less radical than many in the party might have liked, it at least gave Lenin's new government an aspect of uniqueness! Almost immediately, however, it failed. Faced with a barrage of Bolshevik antiwar propaganda, the danger of increased fraternization, and especially America's entry into the war, the German command quickly opened an offensive in the East, designed to bring the war with Russia to a rapid, victorious conclusion. Within weeks, German troops seized huge areas of the Ukraine and Belorussia; Petrograd itself was threatened, and early in February, government offices moved hastily to Moscow, adding a new dimension of chaos to Russia's hopelessly tangled state administration.

Lenin's alternatives now seemed exhausted, and he sued for peace. New German terms, presented at Brest-Litovsk, were devastating. The Ukraine and the Baltic states fell under German control, depriving Moscow of vast grain-producing areas and substantial manufacturing capacity. Some sixty-two million former Russian citizens were "lost" to the Bolshevik regime. Most important for some, Lenin's regime seemed to compromise its most fundamental principles, abandoning any effort to aid the workers' movement in Germany and Europe for a tentative domestic security. "This peace proclaims: All power to the bourgeoisie, all land to the landlords; all plants to the capitalists," the Left Bolshevik newspaper *Sotsial Demokrat* proclaimed bitterly in Moscow. "This peace proclaims:

ruin and death to the power of the soviets, ruin and death to the proletariat and its Red socialist army . . . it demands the servile silence of revolutionary Russia. . . . With all consciousness of its great historical mission, the working class must cry out: Never! Either death or victory! To Arms! Workers of the world, unite!"[17]

Death or victory! A clear-cut choice seemed to many radical Bolsheviks the only means of preserving party principles and revolutionary goals. Not so, however, to Lenin, whose powerful personality continued to dominate discussions in the Council of Peoples' Commissars and other high places. Lenin met constantly with this and other bodies. He listened to reports, argued, met with various delegations, pressed his views, even tried to settle differences with such oppositionists as the anarchist Nestor Makhno. Debates raged. Workers delegations and foreign visitors trooped to the Kremlin, amazed at Lenin's accessibility. A special form of Bolshevik "democracy" took hold, combining an increasingly ruthless suppression of party enemies with internal diversity and flexibility.

This paradoxical combination jars Western sensibilities, as of course it did those of liberals and others at the time. In China, too, the question of whether "tolerance" or "pluralism" had any meaning at all in a context of one-party rule would be raised after the Communists came to power in 1949. But the import of such early diversity within the party itself should not be underestimated, and its import does not lie simply in the contrast between Lenin's rule with what would come afterwards under Stalin. Many in the party opposed a flexible or pragmatic approach to the issues at hand. "Tolerance" challenged the authority of party officials even within their own local cells. Increasingly entrenched local "bosses," as their opponents called them, had little patience with critics of their decisions or power.

But Lenin insisted the party remain open, even as Brest-Litovsk was denounced as a "betrayer's peace," which added greatly to the ranks of the Left opposition both inside the party and out. Lenin at first hoped to establish a limited coalition regime, bringing left-wing SRs into the Council of People's Commissars under Bolshevik control. He also intended to crush Russia's bourgeoisie politically, but if possible, use their experience and expertise, and avoid pressing them into armed counterrevolution. In part for these reasons, in part because he may also have overestimated the party's support among the peasantry (he had consistently castigated the Provisional Government for not holding national elections), Lenin allowed balloting for the Constituent Assembly to proceed as scheduled in November. The result was a substantial majority for the SRs (although the Bolsheviks own support was extensive)[18] and a possible rallying point for anti-Bolshevik forces. Consequently, Lenin allowed the Assembly to meet only once, in early January, before Red Guards forcibly dispersed it, an event that demonstrated clearly the new regime's total disregard for civil liberties or tolerance outside party ranks. Now, however, organized opposition did intensify. Civil servants in Moscow and Petrograd went on strike. Zemstvo employees, historically a progressive "third element" in the countryside, refused to work in important welfare institutions unless civil liberties were restored. Managerial personnel and others with badly needed technological expertise prepared to emigrate. And in the Don region, remnants of the Russian Army officer corps, led by Generals Kornilov and Denikin and supported by Miliukov and the Kadets, worked to organize an anti-Bolshevik "Volunteer Army."

At the same time, there was little effective check on various workers' control or trade union organizations, who regarded October as "their" revolution and who moved rapidly on a local level to sequester whatever industries they saw fit. The question here was not one of support for Lenin but at what level and through which institutions important administrative decisions might be made. The party lacked at first a cohesive policy. Having come to power as the political expression of this social revolution, Bolsheviks now faced the enormously difficult task of molding elemental radicalism into political and administrative coherence without alienating proletarian supporters accustomed to autonomy. As Bolshevik commissars attempted to assert their control, popular opposition here became discernible as well.

But it was primarily the left SRs and militants within the party itself who pressed the new regime hardest after Brest-Litovsk, calling into question the very nature of the leadership's commitment to revolutionary goals and principles. Partly in response to these specific pressures, partly because in any revolutionary situation there is a tendency to seek extreme solutions for problems that are deeply embedded in complex historical circumstances, Lenin steered the party toward two momentous and fateful courses of action. Very soon after

October Lenin agreed to the formation of a secret Extraordinary Commission to Combat Counterrevolution, the *Cheka*. Headed by Felix Dzerzhinskii, a dedicated—some said fanatical—idealist, the Cheka at first seemed to operate with what most radicals undoubtedly regarded as ruthless but appropriate measures, arresting prominent anti-Bolsheviks and even undisciplined party supporters. There was great and wanton violence even in these initial steps, but terror as an instrument of power was not yet officially condoned. (It was, of course, also the case that violence had become broadly generalized in this period as a reflection of deeply rooted frustrations and jealousies, and as a means of settling countless petty grievances "in the name of revolutionary democracy.") After Brest-Litovsk, meanwhile, the Left SRs and others struck out forcefully and deliberately against the Bolsheviks. The former SR terrorist, Boris Savinkov, organized armed resistance in Kazan and Tambov along the Volga; workers supporting Mensheviks and local SRs struck several key industries in Moscow and Petrograd, particularly after the All-Russian Soviet Executive Committee expelled representatives of these parties from its membership and instructed local soviets to do the same. At the Fifth Soviet Congress in July, Left SRs assailed Lenin over Brest-Litovsk. They also castigated the Bolsheviks for organizing Committees of the Poor (*Kombedy*) to requisition grain from the peasants. The German ambassador, Count Mirbach, was assassinated in the hope that this would provoke the Germans into renewing hostilities. Shortly afterwards, other Left SR terrorists assassinated the head of the Petrograd Cheka, M. S. Uritsky, and tried to kill Lenin. The Bolshevik leader was shot in the chest and left shoulder.

Thereafter, the Bolshevik leadership unleashed a savage wave of "Red terror," theoretically rationalized as a defense against "White" terrorist opposition, that profoundly and permanently altered both the party's internal power alignments and the nature of the vanguard's relationship with its popular mass base. Within the party, power alignments changed because the authority of decision making bodies like the Party Congress, the Central Committee, and even the Politburo now became increasingly dependent for implementation on a police apparatus only nominally under their control. In these early months of Bolshevik rule, there was no question that Dzerzhinski would follow Lenin's and the party's directives; the

Cheka was wholly a party instrument. But there were no effective sanctions to prevent police terrorism from becoming the instrument of a small, willful clique.

The lack of sanctions equally affected party-mass relations. Cheka terror was wanton. All sorts of brutal personalities soon found employment in its ranks, including many who had served the tsar. Concentration camps (called precisely that) were organized in remote reaches of the Arctic. The omnipotence of local Cheka officials, the increasing practice of immediate executions without trial or firm proof of guilt, the notoriety of the camps, and the increasing use of Cheka repression even against dissident workers, particularly on the railroads, very quickly created a "second face" for the Bolsheviks among many Russians, one bearing little resemblance to the party's revolutionary goals and official ideological objectives. The practitioners of police control formed a world unto themselves. In terms of the disparities between principles, programs, party democracy, and the practical realities of power, the period after October would prove of crucial importance in determining Russia's ongoing revolutionary process.

WAR COMMUNISM AND THE SOCIAL ASPECTS OF CIVIL WAR

A disparity between principle and practice also emerged in the second momentous course of action adopted by the party in 1918, one that soon became closely related, in fact, to Cheka repression: the introduction of "War Communism." With civil war intensifying in South Russia and along the Volga, German troops cutting off desperately needed food material from the Ukraine and the Crimea, and militant leftists stinging party leaders with accusations of "betrayal" at Brest-Litovsk, Lenin and his comrades moved almost defensively into a series of measures designed to build socialism in Russia as rapidly as possible. In late June the Council of People's Commissars (*Sovnarkom*) ordered the nationalization of all large-scale industry (plants with capitalization over one million rubles), which officially transferred ownership to the state. Committees of the Poor were organized to confiscate "surplus grain" from wealthier *kulaks* and middle peasants; a centralized planning apparatus was set up under an All-Russian Economic Council, charged with coordinating production and resources, including labor. Some argued these measures were premature and potentially harmful in terms of generating additional internal opposition. Nationalization and planning required economic centralization, eliminating (often forcefully) the autonomy of workers' control organizations and even that of the unions. Increasingly, workers found themselves assigned to particular factories and subject to new codes of discipline, which were sometimes severely enforced. By 1919 and early 1920, the party in some areas had moved to the "militarization" of labor, replicating in industrial production and the railroads the principles of centralized control that were also the organizational basis of the new Red Army. But Left communists in the main welcomed War Communism as the proletarian dictatorship in practice, particularly in the countryside, where poor peasants moved against the "bourgeois" peasant mass. To them, social revolution was becoming socialist revolution, despite Russia's backwardness and the intensifying counterrevolution.

Yet the Bolshevik's beleaguered circumstances greatly affected the nature of Soviet socialism, just as the measures of War Communism were essentially a response to necessity, albeit ideologically derived. The imposition of communism from above required a prodigious use of force, available now through the rapidly expanding Cheka. Thus radical reform became inextricably associated with repression and coercion, despite heroic efforts simultaneously to mobilize propagandists and achieve party objectives through voluntary efforts. The important point here is that the measures of War Communism preceded the development of a receptive proletarian consciousness in Russia, just as the Bolsheviks' coming to power was conditioned by a proletarian radicalism, rather than any clear conception of what communism would involve. And this telescoping of historical development was itself the result of the party's need to defend itself, ideologically and militarily, from the onslaught of counterrevolutionary Whites, foreign interventionists, and militant leftists.

Mobilization against Whites and foreigners was relatively easy. Under the remarkable leadership of Leon Trotsky, the party molded various Red Guard detachments and Military-Revolutionary Committees into the nucleus of a Red Army. Most soldiers were volunteers, but Trotsky had little hesitation about using conscription, and even pressed former tsarist army officers into service when he needed their skills, sometimes by threats against their families. The Red

Army was largely effective, however, because its goals were clear. Kornilov, Denikin in South Russia, and Admiral Kolchak in Siberia collected all sorts of prominent reactionaries in their camps, despite the presence as well of progressive figures from among the Kadets and even some moderate socialists. Denikin himself, in particular, was quite moderate in his views. But supported to some extent at first by the Germans, and then with the end of the war by expeditionary forces from Britain, France, the United States and even Japan, the Whites were clearly fighting *against* the revolution, while the Red Army carried the banners of October. Peasants may have distrusted the Bolsheviks, but the Armed Forces of South Russia and Siberia represented the gentry; there was little question where most workers felt their loyalties must lie. "Fight to preserve our revolution! Fight to Defend it!" was far more powerful an appeal than "Great Russia, One and Indivisible!" (We will see in a later chapter how the Eighth Route Army in China was similarly able to mobilize popular support because of clear identification between military objectives and the party's general political goals.)

Revolutionary consciousness, in other words, was both successfully cultivated in Red Army ranks and vital to ultimate military victory. It was precisely in these terms, however, that the policies of War Communism began to appear ideologically weak, which precipitated opposition among those social groups from which the Bolsheviks expected support.

In the countryside, the requisitioning of grain from rich peasants and kulaks forced party cadre into decisions based on social status that were, in fact, very difficult to make. The *Kombedy* soon took to confiscating grain from whomever had it, and frequently these Committees of the Poor were composed more of hungry workers and scavenging officials than poor peasants. Against outsiders, moreover, village communities were generally closely knit. Requisitioning thus became more of an assault on the countryside as a whole than a policy based on careful class distinctions.

It also had serious economic and political consequences. Believing their crops were likely to be confiscated, peasants had little incentive to begin new plantings, despite their possession of newly seized gentry estates. In the winter of 1918–19, the already desperate food crisis grew worse. Some rural soviets began with party support to use gentry land for new, large-scale collective farms, hiring on peasants for wages and producing a crop entirely for the market. Several spectacular show farms were set up, but for the time being, the party lacked the necessary resources to press collectivization in a systematic or widespread way.

More important politically, peasant resistance increased to the point that in some places Bolsheviks faced regions where the peasants were as hostile as the Whites. The rebellion of "Greens," as it was called, spread rapidly in 1919, reaching its height in the movements of Makhno and Antonov, who led thousands of peasants into full-scale guerrilla war. The tenuous link between town and village threatened to break completely, with dire consequences for Russia's hungry urban population.

THE NATURE OF PROLETARIAN DICTATORSHIP

Mensheviks and other moderate socialists urged as a solution to the growing crisis that the measures of War Communism be relaxed, and that tradesmen, merchants, and others traditionally involved in grain distribution be allowed to function again, despite their bourgeois character. The wholesale nationalization of large industry also appeared premature, especially in areas where workers' committees had sequestered factories rather than wait for party directives. To some, nationalization meant simply the logical extension of committee activity in 1917, eliminating entirely any remnants of bourgeois control. But the result was a rapid increase of production difficulties, with new shutdowns, unemployment, and scarcities.

Leftists in the party at first castigated those who held these views, deriding the notion that socialist forms were being imposed prematurely on Soviet Russia and jeering suggestions that the party acquiesce to profit-oriented middlemen if this was necessary to survive the current crisis. Many were reluctant to accept another "Brest-Litovsk" by abandoning War Communism, despite their realization that the very black marketeers being shot by Cheka detachments were responsible for keeping thousands alive.

But the economic weakness of these policies only increased the arbitrariness of growing state and party bureaucracies, and intensified the need for coercion. Gradually, these developments began to dampen even the enthusiasm of militant leftists. Nationalized industries, state-administered trade, control over raw materials, food, fuel, and so on, expanded administrative bureaucracies in 1918 and 1919 at geometrical rates. State offices (and salaries) also provided a relatively secure haven for white-collar workers and other refugees from boarded factories, so much so that by one estimate, more food secured by food committees in 1919 went to feeding their own employees than supplying the general population. To supervise growing administrative ranks, the party established Control (supervisory) Commissions, headed in 1920 by a Central Control Commission, and set up a Workers' and Peasants' Inspectorate (*Rabkrin*) as a watchdog over party officials. "Control" organizations were not new institutions to Russia, but under the new regime in 1918 and 1919, their power—and often its arbitrary use—had few effective limits.

Thus, 1919 was a year of enormous contrasts in Soviet Russia. On the military front, the Red Army scored impressive victories, turning back Kolchak's Siberian armies in the summer and overrunning his capital, Omsk, by late October. A massive anti-Bolshevik offensive launched by Denikin's Armed Forces of South Russia was similarly turned back at Tula, some eighty miles from Moscow. By November, White forces everywhere were falling apart. British and French support in the South was withdrawn in the face of mounting problems at home; the Allied Expeditionary Force in Siberia, composed largely of American and Japanese troops around Vladivostok and along the Trans-Siberian Railroad, was rapidly pulling back to the safety of the Pacific coast port. The most serious military threat in early 1920, in fact, was from militant bands of peasants, whose antipathy towards the Bolsheviks was directly the result of War Communism.

Internally, however, as the peasant revolt indicated, conditions were rapidly disintegrating. Desperate economic circumstances for many ordinary workers made the radical hopes of 1917 seem like distant utopian dreams. Local party officials seemed puffed with arbitrary power, even to the extent of totally disregarding the expressed desires of local representative institutions like the soviets. Cheka and Red Guard detachments had by now almost fully circumscribed the autonomous powers of trade union and workers' control organizations, following party directives. Having come to power largely on the basis of these groups' support, the vanguard party had succeeded in less than two years in reasserting control "from above," a process often as arbitrary as it was brutal and one which, predictably, generated increasing dissidence from within its own ranks.

One group, the trade unionist opposition, protested most strongly the end of union autonomy and regarded state (party) control as a corruption of socialist goals. Led by the militant feminist Alexandra Kollontai and by Alexander Shliapnikov, Lenin's commissar of labor and an "old Bolshevik," members of this Workers' Opposition argued in some places that the proletarian dictatorship was becoming a *party* dictatorship, with all the potential for corruption that involved. "The masses are not blind," Kollontai wrote. "Whatever words the most popular leaders might use in order to conceal deviations from clear-cut class policy and the compromises made with peasants and world capitalism . . . the working masses feel a digression has begun. The workers may cherish an ardent affection and love for such persons as Lenin. . . . But when the masses feel that they and their class are not trusted, it is quite natural that they say, 'No, halt. We refuse to follow you blindly.' "[19]

The same was true for women. Bolshevik ranks during the revolution had been strengthened enormously by women identifying the party with commitment to female freedom and equality, as well as the end of Russian social and sexual discrimination. Through the newspaper *Rabotnitsa* ("Woman Worker") and the organization of the *Zhenotdel* ("women's section"), the link between the emancipation of women and the goals of the revolution as a whole was made explicit. Shortly after October, sexual discrimination was abolished by law, certainly one of the most progressive and radical changes introduced, at least officially, by the new revolutionary government, and an important reason for its broad appeal to radical women everywhere. But male prejudices were deep rooted and difficult to break. An antifeminist strain had long characterized such party leaders as Zinoviev and Rykov, who opposed separate efforts in this direction. Discriminatory attitudes began to appear in party activities, particularly at a local level, which threatened what Kollontai and others felt was a crucial element of the Bolsheviks' social alliance.

Others recognized the desirability of extensive party controls in this period but saw an arbitrary bureaucratism in the way decisions were reached and implemented. These Democratic Centralists felt the party was corrupting itself from within, abandoning any free flow of opinion in favor of directives from on high. Still greater democracy was urged *within* the party, even while many Democratic Centralists agreed that decisions once taken had to be uniformly obeyed.

Most important, worker and peasant resistance could not be denied, just as the radical measures of War Communism only exacerbated Soviet Russia's desperate economic circumstances. The uncertainties of personal survival in the winter of 1920–21 ironically balanced the increasing political security of the Bolshevik regime itself against its foreign and Russian civil war opponents. Most desperate of all was life in major cities and towns, particularly Petrograd, the Bolsheviks' revolutionary bastion. And in March 1921, with the final collapse of White opposition, the city exploded in massive resistance to the Bolsheviks.

KRONSTADT AND ITS AFTERMATH

The revolt centered at Kronstadt, twenty miles from the former tsarist capital and a major Baltic naval base. On March 2, dissident sailors seized the fortress demanding "land and bread" and declaring themselves for a Soviet government without the Bolsheviks. "The Communist Party has led the country into a hopeless position— because the party has become bureaucratized, has learned nothing, doesn't want to learn or listen to the voices of the masses . . . waves of uprisings of workers and peasants testify that their patience has come to an end. The uprising of toilers is near. The time has come to overthrow the commissarocracy. . . . We fight for the genuine power of the laboring people . . . the Third revolution of the toilers."[20]

Quickly, Trotsky and the Red Army mobilized to crush the rebellion and to reimpose order in Petrograd, much in sympathy with the Kronstadters. In a bloody assault that horrified even staunch Leninists with its brutality and its political implications, the fortress was subdued and the rebel sailors shot.

But the uprising emphasized for party leaders what many had already come to accept; revolution in Russia was historically timely in terms of bringing Bolsheviks to power, but a great leap forward into communism was clearly premature. Retreat was in order, even as victory was secure. Predictably in the eyes of Mensheviks and other socialist opponents, the party's political success had led not to close party-mass relations—a vanguard willingly and enthusiastically followed by a revolutionary mass—but to the isolation of Russia's new political elite and to a dictatorship *over* the proletariat, not a proletarian dictatorship.

The paradox of Bolshevik success thus lay not only in the explosion of mass dissidence and the cry for a "Third Workers' Revolution" just as victory in the massive civil war was finally secure, but also in the manner in which the party's coming to power reduced the political *necessity* for close mass support. Before October, Lenin and his supporters worked closely in mass organizations like the factory committees and soviets. They built a following by identifying with popular desires through participation and work. Party cadre provided leadership at a local level and helped shape the direction of political activity, as Lenin did nationally with the "April Theses," without "commandism" or authoritarianism. Such an alliance fit Lenin's conception of the appropriate role for a "vanguard party," but it was historical circumstance, not theory, that gave the party its opportunities and that allowed the forging of the popular alliance that brought Lenin to power. Of all parties and groups in the Russian political arena in 1917, only the Bolsheviks had both extensive popular support *and* the organizational wherewithal to translate this support into seizing state power. Had party leaders been "distant" or excessively bureaucratic in the summer and fall of 1917, the October revolution most likely would have failed.

Once in control of the state apparatus, however, the political necessity of mass support gave way to a need for control. Criticizing the Provisional Government could always draw an enthusiastic response from workers and peasants, but implementing policies of their own was bound to provoke resistance. Power after October rapidly became a defensive instrument, as well as a means of implementing social reform and of building Bolshevik socialism. And as such, its use led rapidly and naturally to authoritarianism, bureaucratism, and the conditions of political isolation that eventually produced Kronstadt.

Such isolation might have been overcome had the issues of revolutionary consciousness remained as clear in the minds of Bolshevik leaders as they had been in the early years of Russian social democracy. The limitations of peasant and even workers' understanding led Martov and others to stress the need to educate, to propagandize, and to teach. In principle Lenin agreed, although it was not the proletariat at large that concerned him so much as activist members of the party.

Efforts at maintaining revolutionary consciousness among party cadre—of assuring, in other words, close party-mass relations and a vigilant attitude toward careerism or bureaucratic indifference—were an important concern for some party leaders after October, but quite subordinate to the emergencies of the moment. Coming to power, in other words, seemed to obviate the *need* to worry about popular attitudes. Had the Bolsheviks been defeated and forced underground in 1917, as the Chinese Communists were to be in 1927 at Shanghai, it is possible the Bolsheviks, too, would have had a Long March and developed a leadership core relatively clear of careerists. As it was, the dialectics of rapid political achievement contained powerful corrupting tendencies.

These tendencies the party tried to meet head on at the Tenth Party Congress in 1921, held within days of the Kronstadt revolt. The major political theme at the Congress was party unity; the major issues of policy involved the end of War Communism and the introduction of a New Economic Policy (NEP).

Party unity involved accepting in large measure the substance of criticism from Workers' Opposition groups, recognizing the need to control arbitrary behavior, and restoring some greater degree of autonomy to local organizations. Centralist principles were strongly reaffirmed at the Congress, to the point of adopting a special secret resolution completely banning "factionalism." But party decisions were to be made only in "democratic" fashion, with "active participation of all members in the life of the party, in deciding questions, and in building the party organization," and "no violation" was to occur in the process of choosing officials through election by party members. Concessions were also made in the direction of free discussion and criticism.

Equally important, however, was the promise of radical change in economic and social policy. The NEP was finally to allow some measure of private trade, a concession to the problems of procurement and distribution that moderate socialists had been urging for three years. Requisitioning was abolished in the countryside, to be replaced by ordinary purchasing agreements and a fixed tax in kind, which would encourage peasants of all social strata to produce as much surplus grain as possible without fear of confiscation. Finally, major concessions were promised in industry. Efforts at centralization and planning would be replaced by a much freer market mechanism, strict labor regulations were to be relaxed, and "bourgeois" managers and experts were to be invited back, where appropriate, to salaried administrative positions. The party's immediate goal was now the recovery of agriculture and industry from seven devastating years of war and revolution, rather than the immediate construction of any new socialist order. Once Russia recovered and the international revolutionary situation became clear, questions of means and methods for industrial development and socialist construction could be reexamined.

Thus Russia's revolutionary seas subsided. While NEP was wrongly hailed in the West as a return to the "inevitable laws of capitalism," the Tenth Congress clearly signalled a major turning point in Soviet Russia's development. Lenin and the party's leadership was, in effect, recognizing and admitting its own ideological and practical failures, its own lack of omnipotence.

Paradoxically, at precisely this moment, almost 4,000 miles from Moscow, newly committed Communists in Canton, Shanghai, and Peking, looking at Russia in awe and admiration, determined to build a vanguard party in China capable of emulating what they regarded as Lenin's stunning success.

3

CHINA AND THE MEANINGS
OF RUSSIA'S REVOLUTION

IMPERIALISM

If one had asked a European Marxist early in the twentieth century where revolution was least likely to occur, the answer might well have been Russia, but China would not even have entered the list of the possible. Nor, before the nineteenth century, would many Chinese have entertained for a moment the notion of a system different from the one that for centuries had ruled the Celestial Empire in relative peace and prosperity. Within the Great Wall, a barrier to "barbarian" incursions as well as a symbol of the favored and flourishing civilization of the Middle Kingdom, incomparably superior in Chinese eyes to any on earth, a relatively stable and prosperous agrarian society functioned through small villages and local marketing networks. The Son of Heaven ruled over all. His Imperial state functioned through a remarkable bureaucracy, recruiting officials to govern on all levels by means of a sophisticated and socially restrictive examination system. The examinations tested, above all, one's knowledge of Confucius and the other great sages of China's past; these, in turn, formed a validating ideology for a state and social system whose very history seemed coincident with all civilized existence. Occasionally foreign visitors arrived in Peking, but always with appropriate tributes for those who ruled from the Forbidden City. Here one stood closest to heaven.

For centuries, the only serious threats to the Chinese state were the products of its own success: increasing pressures of a growing population on a finite amount of arable land. With little new land to exploit, the traditional economy reached the outer edge of growth at available levels of technology. Famines developed, rebellions occurred, dynasties changed. In China as elsewhere, economic hard times never fell on rich and poor alike. The dominant class, comprised of landlord families, one of whose members had usually passed the official examinations, was able to survive, even flourish, leaning harder on tenants for rent, collecting higher fees for a variety of essential services, and shifting the burden of taxation, when necessary, from their own shoulders to the peasantry.

All of this had happened in the past; many in China felt it might have gone on happening in much the same way had it not been for the growing intrusion of Western technology and commerce. The barbarians who arrived in the nineteenth century had remarkable strength. They could launch an Opium War for the "privilege" of selling a dangerous and debilitating drug after the Son of Heaven forbade them to do so; and they could win. They could land troops, seize cities, and seemingly come and go at will. The ability of ruling Manchus to resist was limited not simply by an inferior technology, but by their reluctance to risk their own hold on China's vast lands and people by mobilizing social elements—gentry or peasantry—that might themselves be difficult to control. Westerners clearly were not the only powerful group against whom resistance was possible, perhaps even likely. By the late nineteenth century there was considerable doubt among both Chinese and foreigners alike that a unified, traditional Chinese state could withstand much longer the multiple shocks of external aggression and continued internal rebellion.

In wars that directly involved China (and even those that did not, such as the Russo-Japanese War of 1905), China lost privileges fundamental to sovereignty. Foreigners could trade, travel, and proselytize anywhere in the Celestial Empire under the protection of their own flags. Foreign ships plied inland waterways; foreign money and technicians built and ran railways; foreigners set the rates through imposed agreements and supervised the collection of maritime customs, a vital source of revenue. Foreigners themselves, still, as always, "barbarians," lived and worked in enclaves of Chinese cities that they themselves administered. Port cities were held in "lease" by diverse powers; foreign troops were stationed in various places ostensibly to protect foreign nationals and commerce; even the external trade of some provinces in Chinese products was governed by treaty agreement. Each defeat brought with it a crippling burden of foreign debt, passed on to a peasantry already hard pressed. And worse seemed possible. Aware of the partition of Africa and of the loss of sovereignty suffered by India, Egypt, and Vietnam, Chinese feared they would be, in the metaphor of the day, "sliced like a melon" and parcelled out among the various countries that thus far merely fed on the periphery.

Western analysts, then and now, have debated how seriously imperialism actually disrupted the Chinese economy and social system.[1] There can be no debate, however, on how acutely Chinese of all classes felt the foreign threat and blamed the reigning Qing (Manchu) dynasty for its failure to meet it. In the late 1890s, North China was shaken by a vast popular antiforeign uprising only narrowly diverted from being aimed at the dynasty itself. Led by the Boxers, a secret society of mixed-class membership, the rebellion was finally suppressed by an allied expedition, whose ferocious and largely unnecessary pacification campaigns and direct humiliation of the central government increased the pressure for reform.

Russia's late nineteenth-century efforts at modernizing through industrialization were impelled by a fierce desire to catch up with and join the ranks of the predator nations; China's by an equally intense need to escape their depredations. Perhaps in part for this reason, even those Chinese who considered themselves revolutionaries were more concerned with political than social reform. News of the first Russian revolution of 1905 inspired few Chinese to a populist passion for the "people," despite China's evident social and economic inequities. While Russian students sought national meaning and transformation among Russia's peasants, Chinese students focused their energy on unifying all classes against the hated foreigner. An enormously popular pamphlet written in 1903 by a young Chinese student in Japan expressed the depth of passionate anti-imperialism of a student generation dedicated to mastering Western knowledge in order to drive the foreigners out of China:

Scholars: put down your brushes. Farmers: lay down your rakes. Traders: abandon your business. Artisans: put down your tools. Everyone, sharpen your knives, supply yourselves with bullets, swear an oath, and cry out. . . . If the Manchus help the foreigners kill us, then first kill all the Manchus. If those corrupt officials help the foreigners kill us, then first kill all the corrupt officials. . . . Forward and kill, forward and kill.[2]

Nor was this passion limited to an educated student group. In 1902, 160,000 peasants in North China, organized into village leagues by yet another secret society, rioted violently against the payment of indemnities to missionaries who had suffered damages during the Boxer Rebellion. Their slogan was unambiguous: "Sweep away the Qing, destroy the foreigners; when officials oppress, the people rebel."[3]

With each concession to foreign demands, with each loss of a war provoked by those powers, confidence waned in the regime's ability to defend China's sovereignty and protect its population. Humiliation engendered doubt; doubt bred fear and confusion, as the traditional institutions of stability began to crumble without clear alternatives to stand in their place. Even among those in the governing class itself, the sons of landlord gentry in or out of office, there was a growing conviction that the traditional social, political, and economic order that had sustained the Celestial Empire would have to be radically transformed if China was not to be sliced apart or fall into chaos.

BEFORE THE FALL: THE LIMITS OF QING REFORM

The Qing dynasty itself, meanwhile, fearful of its very tenuous hold on the loyalty of the vast population, introduced a series of reforms intended to strengthen the state through piecemeal introduction of Western institutions. What had made Europe, America, and Japan strong? Not Confucianism, clearly, but technical education. Consequently, the examination system, which for two millenia had governed the recruitment and regulation of government bureaucrats, was abolished. Henceforth, officials would be selected from modern schools with Western curricula and from among the ranks of those who had studied abroad.

What else? Some form of political participation on the part of the governed: in 1905 a mission to study Western-style constitutions was dispatched; sometime later, the government authorized the election of provincial assemblies and announced a plan for the staged implementation of constitutional government with a national assembly to be convened in 1914. Wide-ranging judicial and military reforms were undertaken; the imperial court made major efforts to eliminate opium smoking, repurchase railroads and mines lost to foreigners, and modernize frontier defenses in Tibet, Burma, Manchuria, and Indochina.

But instead of strengthening the dynasty, the reforms yielded revolution. Under the best of circumstances, piecemeal change would have been enormously difficult, as in Russia, in a social system that wove economic relations, social relations, ideology, and governance neatly together in a tight and intricate pattern. The need for change was hardly felt without crisis, and without reaction. The old examination system, for example, had superbly articulated an ideology of loyalty and order to the imperial state; to recruit the bureaucracy from the new schools was to enlist cadre for revolution, vigorous young men who rejected the dynasty and who increasingly believed that only a Western-style republican China could defend itself against the West. A New Army was formed, modeled on (and guided in part by) the Japanese. But New Army officers, drawn from the same social class as the students and new officials, resembled them as well in a desire for change that went far beyond anything the court had in mind. Provincial assemblies and local self-government councils, intended as instruments of gentry support for the dynasty, became instead vehicles for the politicization of the gentry as a class, a class conscious that its interests were not necessarily consonant with those of the Qing court.

Although it tried to keep in advance of the demands made upon it, the dynasty's modest successes were not enough to retain the loyalty even of the gentry; they were never intended to attract the support of the masses. To disaffected nationalist students in Japan, impatient New Army officers, merchants, and petty capitalists in the cities, overseas Chinese, and even conservative landowners gathering in provincial capitals to debate politics as they never had before, the Manchu dynasty—its successful sinification forgotten, its alien origins newly offensive—became the explanation of all current ills; its elimination became the clear solution.

Thus, what had long been a coherent and cohesive ruling social order began, in the first decade of the century, to fragment along social, political, and economic lines. In the cities, a growing "urban reformist elite," engaged in a variety of new professions and small industrial enterprises, agitated for the recovery of lost sovereign rights, for more thoroughgoing and rapid modernizing reforms. Members of this incipient urban bourgeoisie asserted themselves against both foreign and state encroachment. A process of class segmentation was underway, attenuating the links between conservative landowning rural gentry and their activist urban counterparts. The sons, and sometimes daughters, of both rural and urban elite, studying in Japan or Europe, went some steps further. Attracted by the personality and program of a well-known peasant-born, missionary educated doctor, Sun Yat-sen, who had been conspiring for almost all of his life to overthrow the Manchus, they joined his Revolutionary Alliance (the *Tongmenghui*) formed in 1905, and pledged themselves, sometimes in blood oaths, to the achievement of his Three People's Principles: national sovereignty, popular democracy, and economic equity.[4]

These developments brought a host of new contradictions. For the overwhelming majority of the population, foreign imperialism and the modernizing reforms intended to strengthen China against it meant only one thing: increased taxation. Often the link between reform and oppression was very direct indeed. In Hunan province, for example, tax revenues intended to support public granaries in times of famine were diverted to a movement for the recovery of railway rights from foreign powers. In one county of Henan province, the effort to raise taxes to support the reform program led to a tax rebellion of some 20,000 peasants armed and ready to march on the county seat. The move was harshly put down by yet another reform institution: the New Army, whose military leaders were increasingly powerful provincial figures and whose loyalty to the established order was increasingly uncertain.

In the face of popular unrest, the elite—urban reformist, military, or conservative gentry—could still unite. As in Russia, there was nothing so fearsome as a rebellious peasantry, angry to the point of self-destructiveness. Decades of bitterness could erupt overnight in a paroxysm of focused rage, leading not to significant change, which required organization, mobilization, and some specificity of objective, but to bitter and brutal local clashes. It was from educated Chinese society, rather, that pressure was directed on the government. Irreparable fissures began to open between the provincial elite and the dynastic powers in Peking. Greater provincial representation was demanded. The court, however, proved dilatory on the opening of a national parliament. Its plan for recovering lost railway rights from foreign powers was also contingent on the support of important provincial interests, which increasingly saw little reason to strengthen an archaic polity. Plots against the dynasty became rather common, particularly from Sun Yat-sen's revolutionary supporters in the Tongmenghui and from the officer corps of the New Army.

THE REVOLUTION OF 1911

On October 10, 1911, the discovery of one such conspiracy became the precipitating event in what came to be known as the Revolution of 1911. One by one the provinces, in decidedly unconnected and dissimilar ways, declared for revolution, and within three months of the October tenth incident, the dynasty had collapsed. An entirely new governmental apparatus was installed in Peking. Greeted with lyric enthusiasm by Lenin, among many others, the world's oldest empire had, as journalists of the day delighted in saying, become its newest republic.

Who had conducted the revolution? Indeed, who had won? Sun Yat-sen's revolutionary party was in charge of events in only one southern province. There a People's Army was recruited, incorporating secret-society members, revolutionary students, peasants, and urban workers. One hundred thousand strong, they forced a shift to the left in the city of Canton—only to disband and disperse when a new provincial government was organized. In three other provinces secret societies provided substantial military force, mobilizing heterogeneous urban and displaced rural elements without really representing their interests in clear or programmatic ways. Despite their importance in winning key provinces for the revolution, and despite their early leadership role in some reconstituted provincial governments, the societies were forced out of positions of authority in every case by the army, often with immense brutality. Provincial civil and military figures, some very recent recruits to the side of the revolution, acted quickly to restore "order."

Order thus meant political stability and, by implication, necessarily, the preservation of traditional social relations. Whatever impetus toward larger social change the revolution might have unleashed was thus quickly suppressed, most often in the name of national self-defense: foreign powers must not be given the slightest excuse to intervene. It was, after all, a revolution conducted in a painfully narrow arena, carefully watched by the powers who might well have acted quickly on the side of the Manchus if they thought their own interests were threatened. Conscious of the danger, revolutionary forces took care to reassure foreigners that this revolution, undertaken precisely in the hopes of reducing and ultimately eliminating the foreign presence, would not hurt them in any way—at least not yet. This paradoxical relationship between the revolution and the imperialist powers can be summarized in one symbolic image: rather than risk offense by seizing the trains, revolutionary troops marched alongside foreign-owned railroads on their way to battle. Some, like Sun Yat-sen, managed the contradiction by ignoring it. Surely a modern, industrialized republican China would be welcomed into the comity of nations by those who had so long condemned the "sick man of Asia." Surely, as future revolutionary leaders also imagined, the West welcomed those who paid the ultimate compliment of imitation.

Politically, 1911 *was* a revolution. Dynastic rule had been overthrown, the organization of popular sovereignty was made possible, and the forms of a "bourgeois revolution"—civil liberties, representative government, a rule of law—could begin to develop. But as in Russia, all of this had occurred in a country with a miniscule bourgeoisie, a fact of major importance to the subsequent revolutionary development of both societies. The fundamental structure of the economy and social system had begun to change, if only barely, and most observably in port cities. Rural China, like rural Russia, clung in the main to traditional methods and values, lacking any clear sense of alternatives. Although segments of the gentry were moving into new occupations, seeking new ways to develop the economy, the class as a whole still depended on skimming the surplus off a traditional agrarian economy where wealth and power remained rooted in the ownership of land. Peasants remained debt-ridden, impoverished, and ignorant. The social consequences of reform and revolution were hardly liberating. The new schools, far from fulfilling their promise of universal education, served instead to retool the old elite; the army, before and after the revolution praised as the salvation of the nation, was used only to suppress peasant revolts; the self-government movement augmented gentry power at the expense of both the central government and the peasantry. Political change, however great, however necessary a precondition for further transformation, was not (and never is) in itself equivalent to change in social relations, however strong the social forces of revolt.

The hope 1911 briefly held out to masses of Chinese, and the slow acceptance of its different reality, is perhaps best captured by the writer Lu Xun in a famous short story of the period, *The True Story of Ah Q*.[5] The hero is an impoverished laborer in a small town whose days consist of pick-up work, beatings, and flights of fantasy. Too poor to marry, Ah Q rests his self-esteem on "moral victories" snatched from scenes of utmost humiliation and on the abuse he in turn deals out to those unfortunates even lower on the social scale than he, namely women. Hearing rumors of revolution in 1911, the town is seized with fear, but Ah Q himself is strangely exhilarated: "Unable to contain himself for joy, he could not help shouting loudly: 'Rebellion! Rebellion!' " Members of the local gentry family approach him timidly and with respect, unsure what this revolution is about, or for whom. Ah Q lets his mind play with a vision of cleansing violence:

> Revolt? It would be fun. . . . A group of revolutionaries would come, all wearing white helmets and white armor, carrying swords, steel maces, bombs, foreign guns, double-edged knives with sharp points and spears with hooks. They would come to the Temple and call out, Ah Q! Come with us. And then I would go with them. . . . Then all those villagers . . . would kneel down and plead, Ah Q, spare our lives.

But to his dismay, reality is different. The local gentry, rather than being the enemies of the revolution, turn out to *be* the revolutionaries and will not let *him* join. For the ordinary people of the town, nothing significant changes: "The magistrate was still the highest official, it was only his title that had changed; and the successful provincial candidate had some post, while the head of the military was still the captain." Ah Q is jailed for a crime he did not commit; his cellmate is a poor farmer unable to pay back rent owed the local landowner by his grandfather. When asked why he has been arrested, Ah Q truthfully responds: "Because I wanted to revolt."

During the grotesque trial that follows, the tone of the story darkens until all that had been repulsive about Ah Q himself is subsumed in the much larger obscenity of his captors. Driven through town on the way to his execution, Ah Q looks out at the crowd gathering for the spectacle, watching him with the eyes of a wolf, "dull yet penetrating eyes that, having devoured his words, still seemed eager to devour something beyond his flesh and blood." The crowd is equally disappointed in Ah Q, a "ridiculous culprit . . . to pass through so many streets without singing a single line from an opera. They had followed him for nothing."

Neither traditional rebellion, though drawing support from some of its sources, nor structural social revolution, 1911 instead articulated the fragmentation of the Qing polity. Less a beginning than an end, the shape of republican China would now be carved out of a society still fundamentally anchored in its old social and economic structures, but lacking the coherent and legitimated institutional framework that had sustained imperial dynasties for centuries.

THE LIMITS OF POLITICAL REFORM UNDER THE REPUBLIC

After much negotiation, a new central government was organized under Yuan Shikai, a reformist official of the old dynasty, whose influence in and control over segments of the New Army made him a logical if not universally popular choice. The problems Yuan faced were precisely those the last dynasty had tried unsuccessfully to solve: national weakness and disunity in the face of foreign pressure. His solutions similarly resembled those of the court—a program of gradual reform firmly controlled by the central government. Yuan attempted to bring the military under firm civilian control, centralize state administration, reduce provincial power, and when their behavior seemed to work against unity and strength, abolish obstreperous republican institutions entirely. In the last alone was he successful. He could, using his own troops, dismiss the parliament and terrorize political associations like the Tongmenghui. But brute force, especially when others also have access to troops and arms, has its limits. Yuan rapidly lost the support of dominant social elements. The gentry reacted sharply against his policies of centralization, and neither repression nor appeals to foreign powers for support could make up for this loss. Ranking military figures jealously guarded their local power. Commercial figures found little significant assistance in trade and economic affairs. Students remained critical. Afraid of autonomous political movements and new rebellion, elite and peasant alike, Yuan's presidency became increasingly dictatorial; dictatorship soon devolved into the predatory chaos of regional warlord rule.

This, in turn, produced new dislocations. For centuries, central government officials operated in a system that worked to protect the population in general (and the power of the central government) from the danger of unchecked exploitation by local powerholders. The principle of avoidance, whereby officials were enjoined from holding office in their native districts, was intended to tie bureaucrats firmly to the central regime. At the same time, given the very thin layer of government under which the lowest official was responsible for as many as 200,000 people in his district, officials relied on local gentry for a variety of public welfare tasks. Local gentry could, and did, act as buffers between central government exactions and the peasantry at large. Moreover, between landlord and tenant, or large gentry landowner and small freeholder, there were reciprocal exchanges that, along with good harvests, helped to maintain stability in the countryside. In the last decade under the dynasty, local gentry power grew, in part as a result of the introduction of Western-style protoparliamentary reforms, in part as a logical consequence of the battering the central government had received in an unbroken string of defeats at the hands of foreign powers. Moreover, segments of the rural ruling class were beginning to form new coalitions in the cities, branch out to new enterprises, abandon or ignore that fabric of reciprocal exchange that, in good times, had greased the wheels of an inequitable system. Rather than collect rents themselves, absentee landlords farmed the task out to bailiffs, whose concern for tenant welfare was minimal at best. After the 1911 Revolution, direct control of taxes by provincial gentry became commonplace and, in the name of self-government, native-son office holders were the rule. In short, the balance between local power and central government, which had worked in the past to protect the rural masses from excessive exploitation by either, was now hopelessly eroded.

Political revolution spoke to none of these issues; strong-man government after the revolution was equally irrelevant. Those who participated in the Revolution of 1911 had expected unity, strength, and the recovery of Chinese sovereignty. Instead of unity, there was increasing division and shifting, local military confederations; instead of strength, there was renewed humiliation. The government in Peking, hostage to rival military cliques, lost all national legitimacy. Although it joined the Allied war effort against Germany, contributing thousands of laborers to that effort, China still remained defenseless against claims by its putative cobelligerents, especially Japan.

In contrast to Russia, moreover, China had no Social Democratic party armed with Marxist theory and supremely conscious of the revolutionary role mass mobilization could play in effecting change. No organized, coherent political group had the experience or theoretical base from which to analyze the nation's total social system and ask itself: what is to be done? Instead, it had a movement that expressed itself primarily in print, rather than action, and asked itself the question: who are we, and who shall we become? Literature, and particularly the periodical press, substituted for activist politics.

In 1915 the first issue of *New Youth* magazine appeared. Founded by Chen Duxiu, a thirty-five-year-old Shanghai intellectual, bitterly disillusioned with the results of the 1911 Revolution in which he had participated, it called for an unrelenting war against Chinese culture itself. Republican institutions were meaningless by themselves; only a thoroughgoing *cultural* revolution, one which incorporated the fundamental values of the West, could save China. The Chinese language itself had to be reformed and made the possession of the entire nation, not simply a handful of literati who spent a lifetime learning its ancient forms; the family system, with its binding relationships of strict hierarchy, age over youth, male over female, had to be radically changed. Science, genuine democracy, the release of individual creativity had to replace superstition, autocracy, and conformity. "I have only just realized that I have been living all these years in a place where for 4,000 years they have been eating human flesh . . . ," Lu Xun wrote, reflecting on Confucian morality and culture. "Perhaps there are still children who have not eaten men? Save the children!"[6]

New Youth proclaimed its goals boldly: "Our ideal new era and new society are to be honest, progressive, free, equal, creative, beautiful, kind, peaceful, full of universal love and mutual assistance, and pleasant labor; in short, happiness for the whole society. We hope that the hypocritical, the conservative, the negative . . . class-divided, conventional, ugly, vicious, warring, restless, idle, pessimistic elements, happiness for the few—all these phenomena will gradually diminish and disappear."[7] Within six months of the appearance of *New Youth*, some 400 new vernacular periodicals were in circulation, study groups proliferated, enthusiasts in the provinces besieged journals with articles. In the capital of Hunan province, one such enthusiast, a young peasant only recently demobilized from a brief stint in the army, felt the pull of this movement most strongly. The young Mao Zedong had spent months searching for a suitable school, one which he could afford and which taught through a new curriculum the means to useful education in a developing and progressive China. Unable to find what he wanted, Mao spent six months reading on his own in the Hunan provincial library, pausing from his labors only long enough at lunch to eat two rice cakes, until, still unsure of what he wanted to do, he enrolled as a student in Changsha Normal School. As what became known as the New Culture movement swept into Hunan, Mao responded by advertising in the papers for like-minded young men and women to join him for serious discussions, as well as physical exercise and mutual support.

It did not take much effort to observe how vigorously alive traditional institutions and their ideological expression remained. In 1918 a widow who had heroically attempted to serve Confucian virtue by killing herself was worshipped at a shrine after her ninth attempt succeeded. A professor at the Higher Normal College in Wuchang published an article mathematically proving that Heaven itself had ordained the subordination of women. One young woman reported that an abstract discussion of free-choice marriage with her father led him to denounce her as a "beast" who "could not be considered a human being." Young women who cut their hair, as a public declaration of their commitment to the modern world, were subject to extraordinary abuse. "To cut your hair," observed one of the heroines in Ba Jin's novel, *Family*, "does indeed require unlimited courage. When I walked to school a little while ago, I was followed by a number of students and young rogues who heaped jeers and insults on me." Her closest friend cannot bring herself to the decisive act: "I love my future, but I love my mother too."[8]

The movement had no program, no specific political expression. It was, in the words of its most knowledgeable historian, Chow Tse-tung, "a temporary coalition of intellectuals," united in their devotion to a set of supremely abstract ideas—liberalism, humanism, individualism, democracy, and science.[9] Speaking in the name of national transformation, the tiny Westernizing intellectual elite that comprised the New Culture movement seemed unaware of its inherent contradictions. The themes of New Culture literature were iconoclastic in the extreme. They spoke to, for, and of the cultural rebellion of a relatively small group of people. But the urban masses read, in growing numbers as literacy advanced, popular fiction of an entirely different order: stories that did not excoriate traditional values, but rather sought to remedy their abuses. Western-style love affairs always ended badly in these stories, while a tempered and moderate version of traditional family values triumphed. The radical rejection of traditional social morality celebrated in New Culture literature spoke no more intimately to the needs of the masses of Chinese than had the reformed schools and political institutions of the late Qing and early Republic. Reflecting years later on what his generation had produced, one participant in the movement argued that they never forged a "common language with the Chinese working people, and to the middle and lower ranks of the people they were almost 'foreigners.' " They had lived blindly in their own nation of "intellectual youth" and in the "stationary stores of Europeanized gentry."[10] Hu Shi, then a student at Peking University, recalled years later that there had been an agreement that "we should for twenty years not talk politics." Instead they would devote themselves to education and "build a political foundation by way of nonpolitical factors."[11] The warlords would be undermined by the spread of ideas and ideals. Unwilling to engage in politics, uninterested in social action, the New Culture movement might well have followed the path of more recent countercultural movements: gradual social acceptance of essentially symbolic shifts in styles of dress, behavior, and expression by a minority of intellectuals, while the underlying structures of society continued to determine ways of living and dying for the majority of the population.

MAY FOURTH

Two very different external events shifted the movement's course: the Bolshevik revolution and the Allied betrayal of China's legitimate claims at Versailles. For most Chinese caught up in the exhilirating abstractions of the New Culture movement, the Russian Revolution of 1917 caused hardly a ripple. But to Li Dazhao, professor of literature at Peking University and frequent contributor to *New Youth* magazine, it was the coming wave of world revolution, indeed of a new world civilization. Here was a nation that had thrown off the repressive past with one massive shrug of its shoulders. Gone were the churches, the nobility, the tsars, the timid liberals; Lenin had challenged and defeated both the imperialist West and Russia's domestic collaborators. But it took the events of the spring and summer of 1919 before others would see in it what Li did: "the dawn of freedom."[12]

Taking Woodrow Wilson's commitment of the Allies to the principle of self-determination seriously, Chinese, like colonial people elsewhere in Asia, greeted victory over Germany with enormous celebrations. Over 60,000 people marched in Peking, toppled the humiliating monument that Germany had forced China to erect after the Boxer affair, and sat back to confidently await the return of former German holdings to Chinese control. Instead news came that Japan, through secret conventions with both the Allies and the Peking government, would inherit them. The feeling of double betrayal—by the Allies and by their own government—was overwhelming. Beneath the mask of the West as teacher, was the reality of almost casual indifference to Chinese aspirations. "When the war ended," Li Dazhao wrote, "we had dreams about the victory of humanism and peace. . . . When we look . . . at the Paris Peace Conference . . . where have the freedom and rights of the small and weak peoples not been sacrificed to a few robber states?"[13]

On May 4, 1919, some three thousand people gathered in Peking to protest the signing of the Versailles Treaty. Forbidden to enter the foreign Legation Quarter, the peaceful mood of the crowd changed and, defying the police, several groups broke through the cordon toward the Foreign Ministry and the homes of the "three traitors," high government officials whose pro-Japanese sympathies were known and detested. After some spirited street fighting, during which two of the three officials were roughed up and their homes trashed, army troops arrived to finish the job Peking police seemed unwilling or unable to do. Following the arrest of thirty-two students and beating of countless others, the first of what was to become a series of huge demonstrations finally ended.

The move into the streets changed the nature of both the New Culture movement and its leaders. Politics could not be avoided for twenty years, or even twenty minutes. Shortly after his arrest for distributing leaflets, Chen Duxiu declared that world civilization had two primary sources—the study and the prison. Only these "provide the most lofty and sublime life."[14] Since Peking University itself served as a prison during the great summer demonstrations, most students could readily aspire to sublimity. But it was one thing to see the enemy as the whole weight of traditional Chinese society and to agitate for language and family reform; it was quite another to organize against specific government policy, urge and enforce a national boycott against Japanese goods, forge alliances with merchants and workers, and begin to understand the links between imperialism, warlord politics, and that same traditional society.

For a short time potential contradictions could be buried in an ecstasy of nationalism and countercultural liberation. "China after the May 4th incident," the poet Guo Moruo exulted, "seemed in my mind a lively and lovely young girl with a progressive manner: she simply appeared to be my sweetheart."[15] But it did not take long for them to emerge. The response of Shanghai workers to the boycott call, for example, had been gratifying to May Fourth leaders. When workers shut down foreign-owned factories, helped promote the use of Chinese goods, and so on, they were more than welcome. But when public utility workers tried to join, students and merchants dissuaded them, arguing that the extremely hostile attitude of the Shanghai foreign community would be dangerously exacerbated. It was Ah Q all over again. "Do you think for a moment that patriotism is confined to your classes only?" a spokesman for the workers demanded. And the answer was at best ambiguous.[16]

The nominal demands of the movement were eventually met. The offending pro-Japanese officials resigned, and Chinese delegates to Versailles were instructed not to sign the peace treaty. But the great strikes and demonstrations of the summer of 1919 had moved many of their participants well beyond such limited aims. A worker writing for a new Shanghai journal offers a hint of what was emerging. He is a man newly alive to himself, and he writes of a wave of revolution that has swept Russia and will consume China next.

> We are the masters of the wave. Let us occupy the houses we build! Let us eat the rice we grow. Let us wear the silk we spin and the clothes we sew. They must not be handed over to the good for nothings who live in them, eat and wear them without working. Let us take charge of the railways we build. Let us sail the ships we build. Let us take up the arms we cast. Let us occupy the factories. . . . They must not be handed over to the robber governments, to the robber capitalists who run them by force, sail them by force and occupy them by force.[17]

Inspired by Li Dazhao, students in Peking and elsewhere formed worker-education classes and began as well a first, tentative connection with the majority of China's population: the peasants. "Go to the villages," Li told them, "take up hoes and plows and become companions of the toiling peasants.... Those intellectuals who eat but do not work ought to be eliminated together with the capitalists."[18]

The most important aspect of May Fourth was this coming to social and political consciousness of tens of thousands of Chinese—and the beginnings of their search to realize themselves, individually and collectively.

THE APPEAL OF MARXISM-LENINISM

And it was also the May Fourth movement that, for the first time, turned the attention of politically active Chinese to the role workers and peasants could play in reshaping the nation.

By 1920, the political destruction of the old Empire was complete. Warlord armies controlled every province, and within each province local military satraps vied for power. One soldier in a minor warlord army described his activities: "Daily life was eating and drinking and watching executions."[19] To support all three, warlords taxed the population under their control mercilessly. In Sichuan there were twenty-six taxes on salt alone; in Gansu, there were taxes on kettles, stockings, pigs and pig by-products, doors, windows and, in case anything had been inadvertantly omitted, an "extraordinary tax"—for a grand total of forty-four. North China was parcelled out among three large and unstable warlord cliques, with Peking, still recognized internationally as the seat of "national" government, the prize. South China was similarly, and more finely, divided, and throughout the country civilian politics had become shamelessly corrupt and meaningless, though a national parliament continued to meet, as did some provincial assemblies.

For the gentry class, the only security lay in firm political ties with the local warlord. Small, less well connected landlords were often forced into bankruptcy, and in some areas a new class of landlords was emerging, their wealth built on civil or military service with a successful warlord rather than on ties to a central government apparatus. Lacking any particular reason to respect the old gentry social and political order, the rapacity of this new group was directed against all social classes without discrimination. Where the old social order did hold, its terms were increasingly attenuated. In all parts of the country, reciprocal, if unequal exchanges between tenant and landlord broke down. Traditional contracts were not renewed and tenants found themselves dependent on annual leases, under constant threat of eviction. Rents were raised and set at a fixed amount of the harvest (often as much as 70 percent to 80 percent) with no allowances made for bad harvests. Landlords no longer made contributions toward the purchase of agricultural tools, the expense of transporting grain to market, the cost of hiring people to watch the crop; gleaning rights were withdrawn, and new demands were made for direct service to the landlord and his family without compensation. Where tenancy was less of a problem, usury and the unfair burden of taxation took up the slack. Everywhere in rural China the tenuous balance that allowed for peasant subsistence within an inequitable but acceptable set of social and economic relations was breaking down. But peasants in China had been miserable before, and misery, contrary to the germ theory of revolution still popular in some quarters, does not breed revolution. Nor does the existence of new social groupings explain the revolutionary character of the 1920s. A small, concentrated, viciously exploited proletariat in the cities; a growing subclass of students and intellectuals with radical yearnings; and a nexus of Chinese capitalists impatient with their subordination to the imperialist powers made possible strategies and tactics undreamed of by earlier generations of Chinese rebels and revolutionaries. How to bring those possibilities to bear on the reality of warlord China was quite another matter.

Some Chinese were comfortable with taking a very long view of the situation. Hu Shi, prominent professor of philosophy at Peking University, argued firmly against his more impatient colleagues and students. Reform, not revolution, was the answer. "Reform means the reform of this or that system, of this or that idea, of this or that individual; it is reform by inches and drops."[20] The young people who had begun to gather in Li Dazhao's university office ("the Red Chamber") to discuss the Russian Revolution and the relevance of Marxism to China were deeply mistaken. The issue was not imperialism or capitalist exploitation, but China's cultural backwardness. America, progressive, capitalist, without serious class conflict, was China's best model; it was a living refutation of all Marxist assumptions. To move China toward the American example would require the slow, painful, education of the masses of people.

But to Li Dazhao, Hu Shi's reformism was anathema. Masses of people were drowning, and reform by inches and drops could not save them. "If the Romanovs had not been overthrown," Li wrote, "and the economic organization not reformed, no problems could have been solved. Now they are all being solved."[21] The basic outline of Marxist analysis had been available to Chinese, primarily in Japanese translation, for almost two decades. Its lack of appeal had much to do with the slow evolutionary path it implied for noncapitalist countries. Marxism, understood as a prescription for change in the industrial capitalist West, seemed irrelevant to China. But Lenin's Marxism was another matter. It offered an explanation of China's situation and, in Russia's practice, convincing proof of its immediate efficacy. China was poor and backward not as a result of the original sin of culture, but because imperialist powers worked hand in glove with a tiny ruling class to *keep* it poor and backward. Traditional culture was not rooted in the genes but in the basic structures of the society. It served particular interests and would be transformed only as those structures were transformed.

As theory, Marxism-Leninism was eminently suited to China's needs as perceived by its most politically active intelligentsia. It offered an explanation of oppression and a cure. Moreover it enabled Chinese to embrace the modern world without embracing the West.

If communism was the ultimate historical progression, then the scale of backward and advanced had been reversed: a China marching consciously toward communism would be, with Soviet Russia, in the vanguard, not the rear. It was no longer necessary to reject Chinese history and launch oneself on the uncertain seas of Westernization. Instead it was possible to read the past with entirely new eyes. In China's long tradition of heroic peasant rebellion, of a rich popular culture, of resistance to tyranny rather than acquiescence, one could find adequate sources of national pride. In 1918 Chen Duxiu had condemned the Boxer movement in the name of enlightenment. It was the "crystallization of all superstitions," a mindless obstacle to the "luminous path of science and atheism." Five years later he wrote on the subject again, this time as a member of the Communist party. The Boxers, Chen now argued, were a prelude to national revolution. Not the Boxers but the "culture of militarists, bureaucrats, disloyal merchants, university professors and journalists" who fawned on foreigners were the real enemy.[22]

The new Soviet regime in Russia offered more than just an example to be emulated. While the Western powers at Versailles were ignoring China's claims to recover lost rights, Lenin and his comrades voluntarily relinquished Russia's claims to special privilege. Proletarian internationalism, it seemed, was more than a distant hope.

REVOLUTIONARY ORGANIZATION

In July 1920 an international group of revolutionaries gathered in Moscow at the Second Congress of the Comintern to discuss the prospects for global revolution. It was not, at this date, Soviet national interests that governed the proceedings of the Comintern, but a shared belief in revolutionary theory and praxis that embraced all the delegates. The proletariat of the world *would* unite—it had to. Otherwise the victory of the first socialist revolution in world history might well be forfeit. Yet even to state it this way is to do an injustice to the dialectical understanding of the world most delegates shared. Revolution was to be along the broadest lines of unity—the working peoples of the entire world. The First World War had proven in blood that national boundaries served only ruling-class interests. With a secure base in the Soviet Union, the worldwide class struggle had a fair chance of success. And only by bringing down the enemies of Bolshevism in the advanced industrial nations could socialist Russia survive.

By 1920, however, the prospects for an early proletarian seizure of power in Europe were bleak. In the colonial world, on the other hand, matters were more promising. Lenin's analysis here was compelling: imperialism was the means by which the bourgeoisie of the West bought off crucial segments of the working class. This labor elite, corrupt and without class consciousness, would, like its masters, suffer from the loss of colonial possessions. Without these dependencies, the contradictions of Western capitalism would more quickly mature and the hopes of revolutionary change would increase proportionally. A *socialist* revolution in the colonial world was an absurd notion. Although these nations, with the help of the Soviet Union, would be able to avoid a capitalist stage in the development of their national economies, the bulk of their population was peasant, embedded in "bourgeois-capitalist relations." In such circumstances, Communists must support "bourgeois liberation movements," not indiscriminately to be sure, but "only when these movements are really revolutionary, when the representatives of these movements do not hinder us in training and organizing the peasants and the broad masses of the exploited in a revolutionary spirit."

Some of the delegates, those with direct rather than theoretical experience of the colonial world, disagreed profoundly with Lenin. M. N. Roy, the Indian delegate, was convinced that such a tolerant attitude toward the colonial bourgeoisie was dangerously off the mark. From the outset, he argued, leadership in the national liberation struggle must be "in the hands of a communist vanguard." Only thus could the revolutionary masses be prevented from "going astray." Communists must create an independent movement: independently organize the masses and independently seize power.

After vigorous debate, a compromise was reached that would govern Soviet policy toward independence movements in the colonial world. Distinctions would be made between revolutionary and reformist bourgeois nationalists. The latter, readily bought off by imperialism, were wholly unsuitable allies. Revolutionary nationalists, on the other hand, though their vision was limited to national independence rather than social revolution, were essential allies. The tactics Lenin had so successfully employed in the pursuit of the dictatorship of the proletariat in Russia were simply inappropriate in colonial conditions. A vanguard Communist party was a necessary, but absolutely insufficient, vehicle for revolution in the colonial world. Only in alliance with "revolutionary bourgeois nationalism" could such a party hope to move its people toward eventual membership in a socialist world. With this understanding, Comintern representatives travelled to China in search of both a vanguard and a revolutionary nationalist movement.[23]

The first proved an easier task. In Peking, the group of radicalized students and professors surrounding Li Dazhao eagerly responded to the advice brought by the Soviet Comintern representative, Grigorii Voitinskii. Chen Duxiu, who had fled to Shanghai after his brief stint in jail, organized a Marxist study group there, as did Mao Zedong, now director of a primary school and a part-time union organizer in Changsha. In July 1921, these and other Marxist study groups around the country joined to hold the first national meeting of the Communist Party of China (CCP) in Shanghai. Twelve delegates representing six branches (and a grand total of fifty-seven members) met in the French concession. Hindsight alone endows these twelve Chinese intellectuals with the glow of coming power. At the time they merited only the brief attention of the police.

The search for a suitable revolutionary nationalist group was more complicated. Some warlords professed progressive ideas, resented Western imperialism, and aspired to unify the country in the name of national independence and regeneration. Wu Peifu, in North China, was one. For a time, in return for Soviet aid against his rivals, Wu allowed the young CCP to organize railroad workers in areas under his control. But a more hopeful situation was developing in South China. Sun Yat-sen, pushed out of politics by Yuan Shikai, had been attempting to establish a power base in the South for years. Convinced of the necessity for a strong party organization, firmly led by himself, Sun sought the support of progressive warlords for a program that would eventually bring China both unity and sovereignty. Invited to organize a government in Canton by the warlord Chen Jiongming, Sun was elected "President of the Republic" in April 1921 as a first step toward winning international recognition and, ultimately, unity under his auspices.

At first Sun was indifferent to Soviet overtures. But when the warlord troops upon whom he relied proved untrustworthy and Western powers refused to aid him, Sun was far more receptive. By 1923, with the help of Soviet advisers, Sun had revitalized the Kuomintang (Nationalist party), a loose successor to the Tongmenghui. He had also begun to build an army, establishing Guongdong province as a fully secure base from which an expedition against Central and Northern warlords could be launched.

Sun was the very model of revolutionary bourgeois nationalist called for in Lenin's analysis. Uncorrupted by power, Sun also represented key class interests. His party could genuinely speak for that small group of Chinese capitalists that struggled against the constraint imposed by imperialism to develop a modern industrial economy. At the same time, rural landlords, suffering from the disorder of rival warloard exactions, constant warfare, the disruption of commerce, and the disintegration of any reasonable central government, saw in Sun's effort to rid China of warlords, their last best hope. To students and intellectuals the KMT offered not only a vision but a major role in the regeneration of China. The threefold task of national sovereignty, popular democracy, and economic equity were even more urgent now than they had been in 1911. The timetable Sun had developed by 1923 made their realization seem more real. First, there would be a period of military unification of the country; second a period of political "tutelage," during which the masses of peasants and workers would be instructed in the proper exercise of democratic political participation by cadres of his party; and finally constitutional democracy, prosperity, a New China.

To Sun's Nationalist party, the Soviet Union brought guns, money and expertise. To the Communist party it brought instead "the teachings of the classic writers and the propagandists, the ABC's of communism: to the ignorant, instruction about their condition; to the oppressed, class consciousness; and to the class conscious, the experience of the revolution."[24] The role of the vanguard party, at this stage in China's revolutionary development, was limited. To it fell the task of organizing workers and peasants, not independently, not even in a united front with the KMT, but in coalition with them. Communists had to join the KMT as individuals, work cooperatively with its leadership, and funnel all their energy into advancing its cause. Resistance to such a self-effacing and potentially self-destructive policy was considerable. The Comintern delegate to the Third CCP Congress in 1923 argued party discipline, but Li Dazhao and others supported the policy for more substantive reasons.

The very genesis of the Chinese communist movement, its passionate mix of nationalism and social revolution, its desperate awareness of the necessity for national unity as the ground upon which socialism must rest, made Comintern reasoning compelling. Those who shared Li Dazhao's understanding of China as a proletarian nation in a world of capitalists, saw the coalition not as a tactical maneuver, or even as a brief resting stop in a linear march toward socialism, but as a genuine national possibility. Perhaps the KMT could truly become what the Russians claimed it already was: a revolutionary alliance of all four major classes—peasants, workers, petty-bourgeoisie, and national bourgeoisie.

The CCP finally approved the policy by one vote and, on the basis of Li Dazhao's reassurance that its members would assiduously avoid building a divisive faction within his party, Sun Yat-sen invited Communists to join, appointing Li himself to the reorganized Central Committee of the KMT.

As has been the case in so many countries, Western and non-Western, Communists, their minds and hearts set with great clarity on a distant goal, now threw themselves into the immediate task of mobilizing the masses of the people on behalf of a movement they did not control, one that would at best tolerate that mobilization for its own purposes, at worst, repress it utterly. In the coming experience of national revolution, the Communists would learn that the "teachings of the classic writers and . . . propagandists" were not enough.

4

SHANGHAI:
The Paradox of Defeat

THE CONTRADICTIONS OF NATIONAL REVOLUTION

Efforts to understand the complexities of historical development often obscure the obvious. Comparative investigations reinforce this tendency. The emergence of the Chinese Communist party in the aftermath of the Russian Revolution under the tutelage of Moscow presses one to explore the manifold ambiguities in the Russia-China relationship, attaching special import to the role of individual Soviet advisors in Shanghai and Peking, the contrasting pressures from Comintern and Soviet foreign ministry representatives, and the tensions between Stalin and Trotsky over China after Lenin's death. Above all, one is tempted to view the way in which the communist movement developed in China as if it were overwhelmingly structured by, and intimately, conspiratorially, a part of, an international revolutionary organization and movement.[1] Yet precisely in exploring this crucial, formative period, the obvious is worth emphasizing: the Chinese Communist party's direction and development, from its clandestine founding in 1921 to its full participation in the national revolution of 1925–27, was shaped by the particular historical circumstance in which it had to operate. And the most important aspect of that circumstance, in dramatic contrast with Russia during the mobilization of the Bolshevik party before and even during 1917, was the absence of a viable, centralized state power.

In the summer of 1917, Lenin could argue passionately and persuasively that the task of the Bolsheviks was to seize the state through armed insurrection. Nothing less would do. Socialist Revolutionaries, Mensheviks, and the weak-willed in his own party had sunk "to the petty-bourgeois theory of 'reconciliation' of the classes by the 'state.' " They refused to see that the "state is an organ of domination of a definite class which *cannot* be reconciled with its antipode." State power had to be taken in the name of the proletariat: "The proletariat needs state power, the centralised organisation of force, the organisation of violence, both for the purpose of crushing the resistance of the exploiters and for the purpose of *guiding* the great mass of the population—the peasantry, the petty-bourgeoisie, the semi-proletarians—in the work of organising a socialist economy." Through the state apparatus, the proletariat, guided by the party, was "capable of assuming power and of leading the whole people to Socialism, of directing and organizing the new order, of being the teacher, guide and leader of all the toiling and exploited in the task of building up their social life *without the bourgeoisie and against the bourgeoisie.*"[2]

Yet in China, the party's task was almost precisely the reverse. In a country in which the state had been in a process of total disintegration for several decades or more, state power had to be *created* before it could be seized. The internationally recognized government in Peking had become by 1921 merely the prize of rival warlords. It lacked all domestic legitimacy. It was incapable of exercising a monopoly over the twin pillars of state power: coercion and taxation. Armed force was not only the prerogative of large and small warlords (over one thousand in number), who ruled virtually at will over their particular portions of an informally partitioned country, it was also exercised by larger landlords in the form of local militia. Civilian provincial government was entirely a creature of the reigning military power. Crucial national institutions, from the maritime customs to the administration of the salt tax, were controlled by foreign powers, whose financial assistance to favored warlord allies strengthened the centrifugal orbit in which China spun.

Before the Romanovs were overthrown, Li Dazhao had argued, no problems could be solved. In China there was not one Romanov to overthrow, but dozens.[8]

The reorganized Nationalist party, led until his death in 1925 by Sun Yat-sen, had to be the instrument of unification, of the building of a strong Chinese state. It and it alone seemed capable of attracting the necessary broad-based support. Particularistic groups, the Communists among them, would only exacerbate social tensions and political fragmentation if they tried on their own to make "armed insurrection the order of the day." Aided by the Soviet Union, a broad-based *national* revolutionary army could be trained to take the field against warlord troops, whose generals occasionally employed the language of national unity but whose practice destroyed it. Sun's ambition was not to frame yet another faction contending for an ever-shrinking set of resources but to forge an entirely new sort of army and party—patriotic, anti-imperialist, antiwarlord, and concerned with social justice. The Kuomintang (KMT) in power would bring order, stability, and the possibility of prosperity to a desperate country. It would unify China and reestablish a viable national state order, respected both internally by Chinese of all classes and as a member of the international community.

For Li Dazhao, Chen Duxiu, and their Communist comrades, consequently, the choice was rather straightforward: they could cooperate with the class enemy in the process of unification or sit the battle out altogether. It was, of course, no choice at all. Participation in the national revolution, led by a Nationalist organization they must ultimately either take over or defeat, seemed as much an objective necessity to Chinese Communists as Bolshevik participation in the overthrow of the Romanovs in February 1917, a revolution also led by moderate socialists and liberals.

But if Chinese Communists widely accepted the necessity of participating in a Nationalist revolution, the form of that participation was a matter of dispute from the outset. Sun's conditions were firm: an alliance between separate, equal organizations was simply unacceptable: Communists could join the national revolution only as a "bloc within" the KMT. The dilemma facing the Chinese was one familiar to non-Russian Communists then and later. To trust their own perceptions of the necessities of their situation or Moscow's? To pursue immediate domestic goals or behave as responsible members of an international revolutionary movement? Moscow spoke with the authority of practical success, but also with moral authority. Like their comrades elsewhere, Chinese Communists were committed to proletarian internationalism, and when the revolutionary authority of the Comintern was involved, resistance was difficult. M. N. Roy, admonishing the Chinese at a somewhat later date, stated the case sharply: "The Comintern determines the actions of its national sections not only on the basis of the appraisals of the internal conditions of any given country, but also from the point of view of the world situation. The CCP, as a member of the world proletarian party, must act in accordance."[4]

With the form of participation thus determined, the specific task of the Communists was also clear. For a national revolution to be successful in China, mass mobilization was essential; for mass mobilization to occur, peasants and workers had to find in it, through the cooperation and participation of the Communists, a solution to their own immediate and terrible needs. For the time being, then, the task of the vanguard party was to organize people into a struggle for the creation of a strong, independent Chinese state, one which could only be led by the Nationalists.

From this task, however, flowed a fundamental contradiction—one that would plague the Communist party until it was resolved in terror and repression: how to give mass movements enough benefits to maintain and sustain their commitment, without giving them so much that they threatened or alienated the urban and rural elite whose allegiance was also essential to the national revolution; in other words, how to satisfy the just demands of workers and peasants without driving the patriotic landlords, anti-imperialist businessmen, and antiwarlord army officers into the arms of the nearest protective warlord. In the actual experience of revolution, as will be shown, some Communists, especially those working in the peasant movement, began to get a sense of a different possibility: the melding of social revolution in the countryside with the Nationalist task, a way of making each a function of the other. A young rural activist in Hunan province, for example, not yet well read in Marxist classics and given to clear, straightforward arguments, began to perceive that national revolution *itself* required transformations going far beyond the military goal of eliminating the warlords or the political task of establishing central governmental power. "If you say 'Down with the warlords' and do not overthrow the rural feudal class," Mao Zedong argued, "you confuse the important and the unimportant, the root and the branch." In an "economically backward and semi-colonial country," he wrote, "the primary target of the revolution . . . is the rural, clannish feudal class (the landlord class)."[5] But for the time being the Communists were, of necessity, *in alliance* with segments of the very group Mao insisted should be their target. Based in the cities, without an independent armed force, constrained by the exigencies of their coalition politics, the possibilities partially glimpsed by Mao and others would open to the Chinese Communist party as a whole only in the aftermath of betrayal and defeat.

MOBILIZING AGAINST WARLORDS AND IMPERIALISTS

The immediate task facing both the Communists and the Nationalists was essentially military. First, Guangdong province had to be swept clean of warlord armies and secured as a firm base from which an expeditionary force could be launched to the North against the warlord forces of Zhao Hengti in Hunan, Sun Chuanfang, who dominated five rich provinces in the lower Yangzi, and the premier warlord of the North, Zhang Zuolin, who was firmly backed by the Japanese. It should have been a contradiction in terms for warlords to be able to join this revolution at all, but the Byzantine complexity of warlord factional politics was tempting. Why fight when you could manipulate? Gradually, as in the Revolution of 1911, political allegiance became a sufficient criterion for participation. Warlords betrayed by other warlords might now look to Sun and the National Revolutionary Army for aid and comfort. Thus, Zhao Hengti's bitter rival for power in Hunan and Hubei, Tang Shengzhi, declared for the revolution, was welcomed by the KMT, and had his troops appropriately redesignated as Nationalist units. In the North, politics also ruled. Zhang Zuolin's enemy, Feng Yuxiang, who proselytized his troops on the virtues of cleanliness and Christianity, agreed to cooperate with the National Revolutionary Army in return for Soviet military aid in his struggle against Zhang and Wu Peifu. (Wu had himself received Soviet aid in 1922 and 1923 when he briefly controlled the Peking government and sought a larger popular following. For a time, he allowed Communists free play in organizing workers on North China's railroads until their very success posed an intolerable threat, and then he brutally smashed the unions on February 7, 1923.)[6]

To many, however, the clear dangers of warlord manipulation still were remote. The Kuomintang was committed to Sun Yat-sen's Three Great Policies: alliance with the Soviet Union, allowing Communists to join the KMT, and working with mass movements against both imperialism and warlordism. Agreeing on an "alliance within," the CCP promptly took a leading role in KMT affairs. The new KMT party constitution was drafted by a committee that included Borodin, Mao Zedong, and Li Dazhao; three out of twenty-four members of the KMT Central Executive Committee were Communists; the KMT Organization Bureau was Communist dominated, as were the Peasant and Labor Bureaus. The new military academy, Whampoa, trained Communist and non-Communist officers alike. Many of its political instructors, including Zhou Enlai, were CCP members, and the head of its political affairs department was Liao Zhongkai, a leftist close to both Borodin and the leaders of the Communist party. The coalition clearly seemed to be paying off. If the conservative wing of the Kuomintang could be held in check and the Left progressively strengthened, Communists had reason to look forward to growing influence in a broadly based party whose aims were consonant with their own.

Although the immediate task may have been essentially military, both KMT and CCP leaders agreed on the necessity of broad popular mobilization against warlord control. Before it could become a secure base for further military operations, Guangdong province and its capital, Canton, had to be solidly organized for the revolution. Attention was focused on both workers and peasants, the former as the vanguard class, the latter as a vast reservoir of revolutionary energy. Slowly at first, and then with more concentrated effort as the Peasant Training Institute in Canton graduated more people, organizers fanned out to the countryside to persuade peasants that change was necessary, desirable, and, above all, possible. It was not an easy task.

In China, as decades before in Russia, intellectuals were to discover the inadequacy of their skills in the face of rural reality. Peng Pai, Communist son of a large local landlord in the Haifeng district of eastern Guangdong, began work among the peasants even before the alliance with the KMT was established. He began his organizing effort confidently by donning peasant dress and delivering, in what he thought to be an approximation of peasant language, a firm lecture on the necessities of anti-imperialism and national unity. The response was one of utter and complete indifference. He neither looked nor talked like a peasant, and his message, in its abstractions, attracted a small and rapidly dwindling crowd. Dropping all affectations, Peng drew better audiences when he demonstrated the modern magic of the phonograph or staged traditional market-day entertainment. But the real breakthrough came when he learned to listen to the peasants' articulation of *their* needs rather than lecture on what China required of them. Working closely with several young peasants, Peng organized a peasant union, the Red Hill Agricultural Association, which then established a variety of specific mutual-aid societies: a Parents' Burial Club (to help with onerous funeral expenses), a clinic, a school. Equally important, the union forged an agreement that no members would farm the land of a fellow member who had been evicted for inability to pay a higher rent. By winter of 1922, the association had 500 members, and, two months later, Peng was able to call a county congress that 60 delegates attended, representing some 20,000 families. Now the work of the union could expand. In addition to the agreement not to scab on evicted tenants, an arbitration department was formed that would deal with disputes between peasants as well as peasant complaints against landlords. Along every dimension the work of this department signified a radical reduction in the political and social system of control and patronage by which the local gentry controlled the lives of the peasant. Direct peasant arbitration of the major issues affecting their lives was a primary challenge to the power of the local elite at its most basic structural level.

Throughout 1923 the Red Hills Agricultural Association grew in numbers and visibility, mounting massive resistance to all non-traditional exactions by landlords. All the *excess* exploitation—short-term leases, lack of gleaning rights, rents collected years in advance, and so on—were protested. Landlord response was swift and characteristic. Organized as the Society for Maintaining Grain Production, they attacked peasant union offices with force and closed them down; Peng Pai, revered by Haifeng peasants as "Prince Peng," fled to Canton.[7]

The Haifeng peasant movement would soon reorganize. By 1925, working in close coordination with the Nationalist army, it provided invaluable aid to the KMT as sporadic campaigns against Guangdong warlords became a consolidated drive against them. The union had good local intelligence, an effective courier service, and ample supplies. Peng Pai had once again gone out into the countryside and managed to organize a force of peasant militia, which was able to capture the town of Haifeng and clear the way for the National Revolutionary Army, now led by Chiang Kai-shek. The KMT, at last, secured the entire province. But the first taste of landlord repression against "Prince Peng" and the union not only revealed its fundamental weakness, but highlighted the problematic relationship between pressures for social change and the movement for national reunification, which, in turn, posed special difficulties for the Communists. Either the peasants had themselves to be armed, or they had to have the might and power of Nationalist armed forces to protect them against landlord militias. The systematic arming and training of a peasant military force was, however, no part of Sun Yat-sen's Three Great Policies, while the commitment of KMT armed forces to the peasant cause, ultimately successful in Guangdong province, could not be counted upon.

For the Communists the question became one of strategy, as well as moral and political commitment. In its various operations, the peasant union had demonstrated its ability to perform some of the vital functions of a government. Should such unions therefore be understood as potential soviets? Should they become a pool, as some non-Communist leftists believed, from which "representatives" might be selected for guided participation in national government units organized from above by the KMT? Did their potential threat to the tenuous but necessary class alliances underlying the national unification movement as a whole dictate severe constraints on their operations? After all, to most Chinese Marxists in this period, the peasants remained what they had been to Russians, the social repository of backwardness, superstition, and political unconsciousness, however sharp and focused their social needs and grievances.

For the time being, however, these difficult issues were held in abeyance. Although Peng's work in eastern Guangdong was attracting the attention of both landlord and right-wing Nationalist enemies and left-wing Nationalist and Communist allies, it was the movement in the cities, combined with the military campaigns of the National Revolutionary Army that seemed, to both participants and observers alike, to be the real heart of the revolutionary matter. The task of mobilizing urban workers was made considerably easier for the Communists by the brutality with which the imperialist powers characteristically responded to a crisis. Early in May 1925, a striking worker was shot and killed by the Japanese foreman of a Japanese-owned textile mill in Shanghai. Two weeks later, on May 30, British policemen in the International Settlement fired into a crowd of peaceful demonstrators organized by the Communists to protest this murder, killing ten, and injuring and arresting many more. The event set off a wave of sympathy strikes and demonstrations, which were themselves attacked. In June a large sympathy demonstration in Canton was raked by British and French fire as it passed the international concessions, leaving fifty-two dead or dying in the streets, and over one hundred seriously wounded.

Suddenly a May Thirtieth movement emerged throughout major Chinese cities, a massive, intense response to this series of events by which foreign armed force, protecting foreign-owned industrial enterprises, not only repressed Chinese strikers on their own soil, but killed them with impunity. In Shanghai alone, 160,000 workers laid down their tools and struck; in Canton a general strike stopped the city and, spreading to Hong Kong, emptied that British colony of its Chinese work force, leaving foreigners devoid of servants and services of every kind. Workers formed armed pickets to patrol the coast and enforce a boycott of British goods; Chinese merchants and businessmen, working through their chambers of commerce, made major contributions to the strike funds, as did the Canton city government.[8]

Again, the alliance was not without acute strain. In some cities, the chambers curbed local boycott committees and discouraged sympathy strikes in Chinese-owned factories; in both Shanghai and Hong Kong, the May Thirtieth movement's demands (compensation for injured workers, improved working conditions, and a promise of change in the legal status of Chinese residents) met with both success and resistance. Yet, as in the case of the peasants' union, for the time being, the May Thirtieth movement had more significance in terms of renewed political activity than as a harbinger of intensified class antagonism. On a scale far larger than May Fourth, fully involving every segment of China's urban population, as May Fourth had not, this new movement was convincing proof of the strength, unity, and potential political power of China's organized workers.

For the Communist party, which played a major role in organizing the strikes and demonstrations, 1925 was thus a period of enormous growth. Only 1,000 strong on the eve of May Thirtieth, membership increased to 30,000 at the peak of strike activity in July 1926. The movement also served to confirm basic CCP theoretical principles. The Chinese working class had proven it was ready and able to respond to effective leadership, maintain solidarity under great pressure (the Hong Kong strike is among the longest in labor history anywhere, having lasted a full sixteen months), exercise quasi-judicial functions when necessary (as it had in disciplining scabs and helping to maintain order in Canton), and act on both political and more narrow economic fronts. Despite their relatively small numbers, Chinese workers, concentrated in a few large cities, had reached a stage of class consciousness which justified the party's confidence that, once the tasks of national unification—or of the bourgeois democratic revolution, as they were also now being described—had been fulfilled by the KMT, the vanguard party of the proletariat would indeed be able to lead China to socialism.

If the CCP took heart from the movement in the cities and in the countryside, its enemies could hardly be expected to display much enthusiasm. From the outset, conservative members of the KMT had disapproved of the alliance. They watched with growing trepidation as Communists assumed an ever more powerful role within the party and worked with great success to support its left wing. One indication of right-wing distress and the lengths to which it might go was the assassination of the leading KMT leftist, Liao Zhongkai, in August 1925. Organizing as the "Western Hills Group," the right-wing KMT then attempted to take over the party but were effectively outflanked by the KMT Left, in strong coalition with Communist members. At an emergency meeting of the Second Congress of the KMT in January 1926, where over 100 of the 256 delegates were Communists, a new Central Committee was elected, apparently consolidating Left dominance. Wang Jingwei, former anarchist, eloquent speaker, and political opportunist seeking safe waves to ride, led the party with Chiang Kai-shek, the "Red General," who had studied in Moscow and talked readily of the consonance between Sun's Three People's Principles and communism.

DILEMMAS OF THE "BLOC WITHIN"

By early spring of 1926, then, the CCP could view with considerable satisfaction its work in two major areas. Mass mobilization in both the countryside and the cities had advanced incredibly, winning real victories for peasant and labor union members and vastly increasing membership in the Communist party itself. Politically, Communist influence within the KMT was also stronger than anyone might have predicted at the start of the alliance.

In a third area, however, the Communists possessed no independent strength. The National Revolutionary Army, although it included Communists in its ranks and some sympathetic commanding officers, was controlled by Chiang. On March 20, 1926, the Red General moved with characteristic cunning and surprise. Claiming to have uncovered a Communist plot to have him kidnapped and sent to Russia, Chiang declared martial law in Canton, arrested a number of leading Communists and Soviet advisers, and, declaring his continuing faith in the alliance itself, established radical new constraints on Communist activities. Communists were to hand over a list of their membership, resign the chairmanship of all KMT bureaus, seek KMT permission for any separate activities, disband all separate organizations within the KMT, and desist from holding meetings. Nationalist party members were banned from joining the Communist party except with explicit permission; Communists could not hold more than one-third the seats on KMT executive committees at any level.

This was the danger M. N. Roy had warned against years earlier at the Second Congress of the Comintern. This was the fear expressed by Chinese who had resisted the alliance policy when it was first proposed and who continued to express doubts and hesitations. The bourgeoisie could not be trusted; it would turn against the revolution at the first opportunity. Now was thus the time, some thought, to get out and lead the revolution independently.

But Soviet advisors, more concerned than ever with maintaining the alliance in the light of a worsening international situation, were more sanguine. One stressed Chiang's "profuse" apologies over the whole incident and insisted that while he might be tempted to move against the Left, he could not possibly succeed, "for warmly received everywhere, the Left has substantial force. For Chiang to fight such a force is to seek self-extermination." Borodin's report was more realistic: "We could have seized power in Canton," he wrote, "but we could not have held it. We should have gone down in a sea of blood." Various Chinese proposals (to reorganize the alliance on the basis of two equal, separate organizations; to move to take over the KMT from within; or to wrest guarantees from Chiang before going on with the old alliance) were all rejected by Soviet representatives, and a summer plenum of the CCP voted instead to "expand and strengthen the force of workers and peasants," watch Chiang Kai-shek carefully, unite with the Left of the KMT, carefully avoid alienating the center, and isolate the Right. How this policy was to be carried out when the plenum itself acknowledged that the "armed center is now in power" was not specifically addressed.[9]

Caught in an alliance only partly of their own making, fearing they were approaching the shores of Borodin's sea of blood, it is still not surprising that the Communists agreed to continue to work within the KMT. Chiang's March coup was a warning. It was also an event that finally forced the Russians to back his National Revolutionary Army in a major move against the principal warlords who still controlled all but two southern provinces of China. Both the Soviet Union and the CCP would have preferred further deepening of the revolution in Guangdong and Guangxi to the dangers inherent in a superficial widening of its sphere. But to withdraw support from the penultimate effort against the twin goals of the national revolution—antiwarlordism and anti-imperialism—was impossible. Should the Expedition fail, otherwise sympathetic Nationalists might well blame the Communists. Should it succeed, the Communists would be excluded from enjoying its fruits. Finally, it was an opportunity, as yet unparalleled, to carry the message of the revolution to literally hundreds of millions of people. Communists active in areas under warlord control were constantly arrested, beaten, and executed. As part of a victorious Nationalist coalition, perhaps even once again a major factor within it, Communists could hope to shift the focus of the national revolution from politics to society itself.

THE NORTHERN EXPEDITION

The National Revolutionary Army (NRA), some of whose units had already begun to move north, officially launched the Northern Expedition in July 1926. Several southwestern warlords had already declared for the revolution. Their troops helped swell the NRA to about 100,000 men. Facing them were approximately 500,000 warlord troops in various fluctuating alliances. Of crucial importance was the uncertain loyalty of Feng Yuxiang, in control of a major portion of the Northwest. A western column of the NRA moved swiftly from Canton toward Hunan, and by October it had secured the central Yangzi valley and the key industrial tri-city complex of Wuhan. To the east, forces led by Chiang Kai-shek were victorious in Jiangxi, Fujian, Jiangsu, and Zhejiang. Securing these points, Chiang rested. The civilian wing of the KMT, dominated by the Left, had established a temporary capital in Wuhan and urged Chiang to continue to drive north toward Peking. Chiang, on the contrary, set up his headquarters independently in Nanchang, capital of Jiangxi province, and urged that Shanghai be secured before any further northern campaigns were made.

The polarization that Chiang had set off in March 1926 was thus, nine months later, fully articulated. At one level a struggle for control between the military and civilian wings of the KMT, it was as well a struggle over definition of the Nationalist party's very nature. With his conservative supporters and loyal military lieutenants, Chiang wanted, beyond personal wealth and power, a China free of the more rapacious warlords, in comfortable alliance with those who would cooperate, and the establishment of a unified national government that could command the respect of the imperialist powers and force renegotiation of the unequal treaties. The liberal left wing of the KMT, though hostile to both the concept and the reality of class struggle, was committed to far-reaching social change. But nationalism for this group had an absolute priority over social change. The large-scale mobilization of peasants and workers was welcome, but change must come only with a KMT-dominated national government, from the top down, and slowly. Class struggle was unnecessary, even harmful, dividing what might otherwise be a people united against foreign enemies and their domestic agents. The role of the Communists, given this split, was to strengthen the Left KMT in every way possible. In practice this meant both organizing *and* restraining the spontaneous mass movements of peasants and workers that had sprung up in the wake of the victorious NRA.

As advancing Nationalist armies fought their way through south-central China, however, the Northern Expedition began spontaneously to take on the shape of a social revolution. Rural China, as Mao reported some months later, rose "like a mighty storm, like a hurricane."[10] The movement was, in many places, peasant rebellion of the sort China had experienced throughout its history: seizure of landlord granaries, random beatings of "local bullies," and some confiscation of land. The realities of social and political power were not touched; in time the old order would invariably return. But this time peasant rebels were in contact with Communist organizers whose understanding of agrarian revolution, rather than rebellion, began to inform peasant actions. Peasant unions were organized whose duties and responsibilities meant, as they had earlier in Guangdong, a significant shift in the distribution of real power. Some of these unions were essentially gentry-dominated agricultural associations that changed their name to suit the times; some were newly organized but quickly dominated by traditional elements. Elsewhere, however, the unions were unlike anything Chinese peasants had participated in before. They became the local government in their area, jailing and executing exploiting landlords rather than simply depriving them of their hoard of grain; enforcing the KMT-endorsed rent reductions as well as the approved confiscation of temple, clan, warlord, and "evil landlord" holdings and distribution of them to tenants. They assumed, in short, many of the functions of state power, exercising them in their own interests. Political power, not a millenarian redress of grievances and inevitable return to the old system, was the goal.

When backed by sympathetic KMT military force and aided by Communist cadres, Chinese peasants stood up in ways that astonished their own leaders, terrified important segments of the Nationalist coalition, and caused grave concern to Soviet and Chinese Communists alike. There were two major connected problems. One was the way in which, in some counties, peasant unions had simply become the local government; the other was the failure of some unions to stay within approved KMT guidelines on confiscation. To the peasant, an exploiting landlord whose son served with the National Revolutionary Army was still an exploiting landlord. A small subordinate warlord who declared his undying allegiance to the national revolution was still an oppressive militarist. The *political* affiliation of these local powerholders was a matter of indifference to the peasant who suffered under them. To take social, economic, and political power *from* them, to exercise it directly in the interests of the majority of peasants is what the revolution had begun to mean.

Yet how could the Communists bolster the left wing of the KMT, retain the loyalty of former warlords like Tang Shengzhi, counter the pull of Chiang Kai-shek, and allow the agrarian revolution to follow the logic of its momentum? The enemy in the countryside had been defined in political, not social, terms: *evil* landlords, *local* bullies, *unpatriotic* warlords. If this continued unchecked, if a social rather than a political definition of the enemy was allowed to prevail, the alliance could not possibly be maintained. At an April 1927 meeting of the KMT Land Committee in Wuhan, one participant warned that the "army will not stand for redistribution of land unless it is undertaken by the government instead of the peasant masses." A subsequent meeting, struggling valiantly with the land problem, concluded: "Under present objective conditions only political confiscations are possible . . . the land of small landlords and revolutionary soldiers must all be protected. The basic solution to the land problem is beyond the capacity of the central conference to decide."[11]

In the cities, too, the mass movement, so necessary to the success of the Northern Expedition, threatened the alliance policy. Armed workers had served as pickets in advance of National Revolutionary Army units, sabotaged rail lines in warload territory, and otherwise acted to support the struggle. Once established in Wuhan, the Nationalist government ordered the disarming of workers and moderation of labor militancy. But in the cities, anti-imperialism, not Chinese capitalism, remained the target, and to this extent the contradiction between mass movement and political necessity took longer to develop. In January 1927 what began as a protest against the arrest and execution of seven Nationalist leaders by the British developed into a unified movement of the Hankow Chamber of Commerce and the Communist-led student, women's, and workers' unions to reclaim the British concession in the city for China. Under tremendous pressure from this display of collective militancy, the

British withdrew. A young "girl-soldier" described the scene: a dozen foreign warships anchored menacingly in the harbor, helpless as "the laborers, the students, soldiers, revolutionists, recovered that territory from the hands of the imperialists!" Delegates from Western revolutionary organizations addressed mass rallies on the importance of this victory and, listening to their speeches, "twenty thousand people standing on the open ground went mad, as if tomorrow the world revolution would be accomplished." A troop of Duncan dancers arrived: "At midnight a great crowd poured out like waves from a red-hot cauldron of blood. Everyone cried in admiration, 'It is great! Such a powerful revolutionary dance!' I saw it for the first time in my life, on the streets, in the bright moonlight."[12] Symbolically as well as actually, the recovery of the concession was an enormous victory for the Nationalists and yet another demonstration of the importance of mass mobilization.

Strengthened by this success, and by the defection of several key officials from Chiang Kai-shek's headquarters, the Left KMT-dominated Wuhan government felt strong enough in March of 1927 to denounce Chiang and sharply reduce his role in the party. But Wuhan could do nothing about his continuing control of a substantial portion of the NRA. Instead, they relied on the forces of Tang Shengzhi, ex-warlord and new patriot.

. For a time Wuhan, to foreign observers, seemed to be the center of the world revolution. An American reporter wrote lyrically of its air of total revolutionary dedication, the frequency of militant strikes and demonstrations, and the presence of revolutionary cadre from almost every country in the world. In the early spring of 1927, Vincent Sheean recalled, Hankow gave "the illusion of a highly organized social-revolutionary movement that might, at any moment, seize the machinery of production and proclaim the dictatorship of the proletariat."[13] In Changsha, Hunan province, foreigners complained that the city had "gone Red." Peasants travelled three days to reach a tenth anniversary celebration of the Russian revolution, and it took the procession over three hours to pass by Yale-in-China's hospital, where foreign doctors watched nervously. Everywhere unions were organized—among domestic servants as well as industrial workers. In Wuhan alone 200 new organizations were founded, and over 100 strikes called.[14]

However exhilarating the Duncan dancers or the sounds of

passionate tactical debate among the set of international revolution-aries in Chinese teahouses, the fact remained, however, that Wuhan was *not* a "highly organized social-revolutionary movement." It was a government with uncertain control over south-central China, anxious to avoid a complete break with Chiang Kai-shek, who remained in Nanchang, and attempting to make deals with Feng Yuxiang in the north in order to avoid the worst of all worlds—an alliance between Feng and Chiang against Wuhan. To this end, the mass movements, both urban and rural, would have to be restrained. Not only did they threaten to produce a total break with Chiang, they might well drive moderate and even liberal elements in the KMT into his arms. If the Communists were to continue working with the Left KMT, they must make sure a Left remained to work with; restraint on the part of the masses was essential. What is more surprising, perhaps, is the effort to keep Chiang Kai-shek within the fold as well. Chiang, Stalin advised the Chinese in early April, was, of course, a rightist, but "why drive away the right, when we have the majority and when the right listens to us?" Stalin was convinced that Chiang, despite his distaste for the revolution, "is leading the army and cannot do otherwise than lead it against the imperialists." Rather than oppose him, Chiang must be "squeezed out like a lemon and then flung away."[15]

THE SHANGHAI MASSACRE AND THE BLOODY SUMMER OF 1927

The most graphic and disastrous expression of the double bind the Communists faced was the problem of Shanghai. Controlled by the unregenerate warlord Sun Chuanfang, Shanghai, with its foreign and domestic financial resources, was the prize toward which Chiang Kai-shek now began to march in February 1927. Communist organiza-tion in the city was extensive, with a party membership of almost 3,000 and control over the Shanghai General Labor Union.

Local efforts to wrest Shanghai from warlord control were also underway. In mid-March the Communist-led Shanghai General Labor Union was able to call 600,000 workers out on strike and bring the city to a dead halt. Armed workers then fanned out through the city and took it in the name of the national revolution. Quickly organiz-ing a provisional municipal government, they turned to welcome Chiang Kai-shek and his troops into the city.

Fully aware of the danger of betrayal, the Communists nevertheless faithfully followed Comintern instructions. Workers' militia
were ordered to bury their weapons and avoid all provocation. Union
demands were held in check, Chiang was treated with respect, and,
in an atmosphere of increasing tension and foreboding, an open
break was avoided. Then, on the morning of April 12, Chiang struck,
ferociously, without warning. Every key union location was smashed,
sometimes with heavy fighting, sometimes against little resistance.
Protest demonstrations on the thirteenth were brutally attacked by
Chiang's troops and ruthlessly suppressed. And the repression spread.
In every city under Chiang's control, unions suddenly found themselves under assault. Labor associations were broken, leaders arrested,
and Communists hunted and killed in the street.

In the countryside, too, terror was unleashed. Everywhere the
Right was encouraged. No longer fearing the coercive power of a
National Revolutionary Army in apparent sympathy with peasant
demands, landlords and minor warlords (provided they were in
alliance with Chiang) now felt free to use their military force against
peasant unions with impunity. Appeals to Wuhan for troops to
protect the peasants were not answered. And when peasant unions
asked Wuhan for arms (Hubei's organized three million peasants,
for example, possessed a total of 700 revolvers), they were turned
down. Guns would be distributed only for defense against "bandits,"
not for "civil conflict within the village." "What can we do?" one
Hubei peasant leader protested bitterly. "The reactionaries recognize
no law; they kill us as they wish. But we must recognize law, for we
are a responsible union. Yet the law cannot help us and only forbids
us to help ourselves."[16]

Fleeing areas under Chiang's control, Communists from all over
China gathered for the Fifth Congress of the CCP in Wuhan in
late April, 1927, to assess the situation. In a sense, the choices facing
party members were not very different from those they had faced at
the party's founding six years before: social revolution now or later?
a united front within the KMT or independence? Alliance with class
enemies for nationalist aims or immediate confrontation? Comintern
advice was clear and sharp: maintain the alliance at all costs. Some
thought this should even be simpler now that the right wing had
shown its true colors. Everything must be bent to reassuring Wang
Jingwei, then head of the Wuhan government, of Communist loyalty

to the national revolution. At the same time, Chinese were advised to deepen the agrarian revolution that, it was declared, now "coincided with the national revolution." And, piling contradiction upon contradiction, the party was nevertheless to ensure that peasants did not go "too far." Land confiscation was to remain political, and the holdings of friends and relatives of Nationalist officers and small landlords were to be protected.[17]

Class consciousness, however, can be as powerful among the enemies of revolution as among revolutionaries themselves, even if not articulated as such. Whatever the resolutions of Comintern or Communist party congresses, warlord officers nominally in alliance with the Wuhan government also began now to draw their own conclusions. Should *they* ally with their class enemy or do the sensible thing and join Chiang Kai-shek? One after another they made their decisions, marked in the blood of Communists, labor, and peasant union leaders. In May one of Tang Shengzhi's subordinates switched to Chiang's side and, simultaneously, moved to crush labor and peasant organizations in and around Changsha city. Hundreds died and the Wuhan government did nothing. Outraged, the local Hunan CCP planned a march of hundreds of thousands on Changsha, only to be overruled by the Central Committee. Thousands of peasants, uninformed of the change in plans, marched to the gates of the city and were slaughtered. The CCP response was to form a joint investigating committee with the KMT and "notify all peasant and labor comrades of the province to be patient and wait for the government officials in order to avoid further friction." When the report was finally issued, it placed blame for the entire incident on the peasants themselves, who, it was charged, "have broken loose from control and precipitated a reign of terror upon the people."[18]

Compromises intended to reassure the KMT government in Wuhan that the Communists were not inciting the peasants led to more, not less, bloodshed until finally, in July of 1927, there were no choices left. From Moscow came shrill new instructions: halt dependence upon unreliable generals, and organize Communists, workers, and peasants into a reliable army led by trustworthy Nationalists. When he was shown the telegram, Wang Jingwei moved at once—but to Chiang Kai-shek. "The Communists propose to us to go together with the masses," he observed, "but where are the masses? Where are the highly praised forces of Shanghai workers or Kwangtung [Guangdong] or Hunan peasants? There are no such forces. You see, Chiang Kai-shek maintains himself quite strongly without the masses. To go with the masses means to go against the army. No, we had better go without the masses, but together with the army."[19] Feng Yuxiang came to a similar conclusion. The Communists and those in the KMT closely identified with them were everywhere on the run. The party could neither protect its own members nor those it had successfully organized. "They are killing people like chickens," a friend told one young left KMT activist when she came to Changsha seeking refuge—and then barred the door.[20] Unions, peasant and worker, women's associations, every expression of popular organization was brutally suppressed. Facing the forces of reaction in Russia after October 1917, the Bolsheviks had commanded a state apparatus, however rudimentary, and a rapidly forming Red Army. In China, however, Communists were simply eliminated from the state apparatus they had helped to shape, and the army was almost wholly in the hands of their enemies.

The repression of the women's movement was particularly thorough. Communist cadres had brought organization to the anger of peasants and workers, and to the 50 percent of both classes who were women. The women's unions challenged what Mao Zedong called the "patriarchal-feudal system" at its core. Holding out to women the promise of equality, the unions were almost inundated by the response. At the height of the national revolution, some one and half million women in ten provinces were members of women's associations. Their activity, however, challenged both revolutionary and counterrevolutionary forces. When women's associations began to protect runaway brides, peasant union males vigorously objected. In Hunan a thousand members of one peasant union sent their wives home in shame to their natal villages in a kind of sympathy boycott inspired by the divorce granted the wife of one of their members—leading to the nullification of the divorce decree.

Although potentially and at times actually divisive, the women's movement, in absolute numbers probably the largest in world history, added the force and resources of tens of thousands of women to the revolution. With the White terror, they were to die in like numbers. All women with bobbed hair, a symbol of liberation from feudal mores, were literally in danger of their lives. In Canton women were burned alive. In Hunan the ferocity aroused by the activity of these young women is reflected in the death of Wang Suchen, a vivid young cadre whose enthusiasm for enforcing reform in behalf of women had caused her organization some problems. Surrounded by soldiers, she was sexually humiliated and then hacked to pieces. In an orgy of hatred, soldiers fired seventeen shots into what was left of her body. The women's movement, like the agrarian revolution, challenged the deepest structures upon which the old order rested. It was repressed in precise correlation to the danger it posed. In the major cities of China, the hunt for women activists continued for three solid years.[21]

Meanwhile, still further instructions came from Moscow, where China seemed to have lost all concrete reality and become entirely symbolic of the struggle between Trotsky, who pressed for soviets free from KMT control, and Stalin, who maintained the Comintern line. The bloodshed of 1927 took place in China as Trotsky was becoming increasingly more isolated, until finally Stalin drove him into exile. It was as if Stalin's own power had to be secure before the Comintern line could be abandoned. Moscow's new strategy called for an end to the alliance. Communists were to conduct an expedition back toward Guangdong in order to recapture it as a base. In addition, rural insurrection was now to be encouraged in Hunan and Hubei with the goal of capturing central cities in each district through coordinated urban and rural action. Hearing these instructions, Mao, for one, was exhilarated, as if breaking with the KMT and encouraging mass insurrection would finally herald a Communist October in China.

But it was not October; it was the bloody summer of 1927, and the plan was a massive failure. Given the new situation in the countryside, peasants, not surprisingly, were cautious; secret society and bandit allies were unsteady. Central Committee instructions had little to do with the concrete military realities facing those who received them. In December, Canton was briefly captured, declared a commune, and as swiftly lost. Six hundred people died in three days; 5,700 in the following week. Everywhere Communists were faced with a magnitude of defeat for which nothing in their ideology or previous experience had prepared them. Finally disobeying Comintern and Central Committee orders, Mao and a small armed band retreated into the mountains, there to regroup and take stock.

SEEKING VIRTUE IN NECESSITY

The defeat of the Communists in 1927 is often seen as a direct result of bad advice, insisted upon by Stalin for his own nefarious ends. It is no doubt true that had the CCP broken with the KMT earlier, or had the original alliance been established on a basis of equality between the two parties, fewer Communists would have died in the bloodbath. But this does not speak to the issue of revolutionary victory, only survival. The classic statement of Soviet responsibility was made by Harold Isaacs, in his passionate indictment written only seven years after the event: "Moscow had imposed a formula which cancelled itself out: Victory was impossible without the agrarian revolution; victory was also impossible without the co-operation of the Left Kuomintang. But . . . under the leadership of the Left Kuomintang, it was impossible to have the agrarian revolution. Hence, on Moscow's terms, victory was impossible."[22] But Moscow did not set the terms of China's historical reality or of the theoretical framework within which both Chinese and Russians operated.

In Russia, a peasant revolution, moving on its own, uncontrolled and unguided by the Bolsheviks, had, in 1917 and 1918, expropriated the gentry class and destroyed its power. The Bolsheviks were free to welcome the social revolution in the countryside, validating it retrospectively; they were not burdened by the need to woo a class enemy like the gentry on nationalist grounds. Instead, spontaneous revolution in rural Russia left the Bolsheviks with an entirely different problem: how to establish their own political and economic controls.

In China, the power of the gentry class, despite a decade of warlord disruption and economic chaos, remained in place. However sincerely nationalistic, however outraged by both imperialists and warlords, the gentry as a class would not readily yield power. Faced with a choice between their class interests and the needs of the national revolution as defined by Communists and the non-Communist Left, the gentry acted for themselves. With respect to the peasantry, the Chinese Communist party also had a choice, most vividly expressed by Mao Zedong after his investigation of the Hunan peasant movement. "There are three alternatives. To march at their head and lead them; to trail behind them, gesticulating and criticizing; or to stand in their way and oppose them. Every Chinese is free to choose, but events will force you to make the choice quickly." A revolution, Mao insisted, "is an insurrection, an act of violence by which one class overthrows another. A rural revolution is a revolution by which the peasantry overthrows the power of the feudal landlord class."[23] By their actions, Russian peasants spared the Bolsheviks the necessity of leading a struggle to overthrow gentry power in the countryside. In the ensuing civil war, the Bolsheviks required only peasant neutrality, not mobilization. But the Chinese *did* have to choose; moreover, the choice they faced was hedged round by formidable barriers. Marching at the head of the peasants meant civil war, violent class struggle, and the fullest mobilization of the peasantry against the landlord class. The rural social revolution the Bolsheviks had more or less inherited would have to be *made* by the CCP. And it would be civil war and social revolution against a heavily armed class enemy, one which could in addition call upon concerned foreign powers to intervene. Finally, to lead the insurrection Mao described would have required locating the revolution in the countryside rather than the cities. It would have meant taking the peasantry as the main revolutionary force rather than seeing it as a useful adjunct. Nothing in the ABCs of communism looked toward such a conclusion. Urban based, the vanguard of the proletariat, the Chinese party welcomed the energy of insurrectionary peasants but rooted its vision in the cities. This urban view dictated a strategy that would place the national revolution in the forefront. Whatever the terms of the alliance with the KMT, such a strategy meant that the agrarian revolution had to be constrained, not encouraged.

The only possible alternative would have been for the CCP to lead the revolution itself, wedding social to national goals from the outset. For such a task, the CCP was both theoretically and practically unprepared—as were its Soviet advisors. From the rubble of 1927, some Communists, impelled by a praxis born almost entirely of necessity rather than theory, began to shape the dimensions of a new revolutionary pattern: it would be based in the countryside, not the cities; it would rely on its own judgments, drawn from experience, not Marxist-Leninist classics; and it would refuse, in practice, to subordinate the interest of China's revolution to those of an international movement directed by Moscow.

Had the Comintern's strategy worked, one can imagine a Chinese revolution rooted in the cities, with the party looking outward to the peasantry, harnessing its productive energies for national use, applying discipline when necessary, convinced in both theory and practice that the proletariat, embodied in the vanguard party, was the revolution. But in the aftermath of 1927, the course of China's revolutionary process shifted radically. Party members were plunged into the countryside, not to incorporate rural masses into the revolution, but to seek a safe hiding place among them. Perhaps alone among his contemporaries, certainly with a clarity they lacked, Mao understood that to be truly safe for revolutionaries, the countryside would have to *become* the revolution. From this paradoxical defeat would emerge China's unique path of revolutionary development.

5

VANGUARDS:
The Parties and Party-Mass
Relations in the 1930s

THE VANGUARD ISSUE

Shortly after the Shanghai massacre in the spring of 1927, the Eighth Plenary Session of the Comintern Executive Committee (ECCI) convened in Moscow. The events in China had been a principal topic of discussion for weeks, among both high party functionaries and ordinary workers. In some factories, in fact, the only way to assure good attendance at public party meetings was to schedule a report on China. Delegates arriving for the ECCI Plenum consequently expected a full-scale debate. The Shanghai debacle brought to the fore the whole question of Comintern strategy and tactics and, indeed, seemed to raise the very question of Soviet Russia's own ability to survive in an increasingly hostile world.

Much to the delegates' surprise, however, when they arrived at the Kremlin, they were ushered not into the large Andreev Hall, the tsar's former throne room that had been used for previous ECCI plenums, but to a small chamber off to the side. No visitors were allowed, and no notes could be taken. Stenograms of speeches had to be returned before delegates could receive permits to leave, and for the first time in Comintern history no published accounts of session discussions were permitted.[1]

Such secrecy had pervaded the Bolsheviks' own Central Committee meetings several weeks earlier, when China was also the major topic of concern. Stalin's famous "Theses on the Chinese Revolution" were officially part of the record at these meetings but were not read to Committee members. Instead they were published only afterwards in *Pravda,* and hence could be "unanimously adopted" by the Committee without the benefit of discussion.

At first glance such caution seems excessive, even with knowledge of the type of controls Stalin was soon to impose on Soviet politics. The "Theses" were unequivocal in their attack on Chiang Kai-shek and the Kuomintang Right, whom Stalin caustically identified as agents of imperialism. They insisted that Chiang's "coup" marked the "desertion of the national bourgeoisie" from the Chinese revolution and argued that the "principal source of strength for the revolutionary Kuomintang is the further development of the revolutionary movement of workers and peasants, and the strengthening of their mass organizations."[2]

But the issue was not really China; or to put the matter more precisely, the China question was of paramount importance because it reflected a more central concern: whether the Bolshevik party under Stalin was an appropriate and legitimate vanguard not only for the world revolutionary movement, but also for building socialism in Russia. To be sure, the response of Trotsky and others to Stalin's "Theses" struck at particular issues. Trotsky wanted the Chinese Communists to disengage entirely from the Kuomintang, establish its political and organizational independence ("precisely its lack of independence is the source of all the evils and all the mistakes"), and build worker and peasant soviets ("only the Soviets at a further development of the revolution can become the organs capable of really conducting the arming of the workers and the direction of these armed masses").[3] But the more important point, according to Trotsky, was that the Shanghai debacle resulted not simply from tactical errors but from the Bolshevik party's "bureaucratic style of leadership," its relentless "tailism" and lack of revolutionary commitment, its "apparatus-like" refusal to investigate the problems of the Chinese revolution and discuss the issues openly. In a word, the China question raised directly in Moscow the Bolshevik vanguard's right to rule.

In China, too, Shanghai explicitly raised the question of what the vanguard was and ought to be. To be a member of the CCP in 1927 was to face an entirely new range of problems. For many it meant a tense and confusing confrontation with a rural reality hardly guessed at. The distance between city and country in China could almost be measured in historic time, not geographic space. The issue was not poverty; that was familiar enough to party members of urban background. It was the social relations that stunned. "The worst part," a peasant told an American years later, was not the poor physical treatment but "not being able to talk back. In those days the landlords' word was law. They had their way. When it was really hot and they said it was not, we dared not say it was hot; when it was really cold and they said it wasn't, we dared not say it was cold. Whatever happened we had to listen to them. You could never finish telling of the abuse the landlords gave us."[4] What the landlords had was the power of definition, a power woven into the very fabric of peasant life whose toll cannot be fully measured by those who feel themselves able, to some degree, to define their own lives.

Yet the events of spring and summer, 1927, had decisively cut the Communists off from what they considered their appropriate mass base. Retreating to the countryside, what sort of vanguard would the Chinese party become? If it were not simply to await better conditions in a kind of internal exile, it would have to turn toward the people it found itself among, allowing itself to be shaped by them, becoming, as a result, a vanguard appropriate to its actual mass base.

Herein lay both promise and danger. It was not abstract theory alone that made the bulk of the CCP leadership wary of too great a dependence on the peasantry. As a political force, peasants were hampered by a range of objective conditions which made unlikely their effective participation as principals in the revolutionary process. Strong ties to lineage or clan caught poor peasants in a web of hierarchical loyalty that made organizing on the basis of class interest extraordinarily difficult. Moreover, the depth of subordination to landlord power; the narrowness of the peasant world and vision; the oppressive mixture of folk religion, superstition, and Confucian morality, which restricted options and movements, especially of women; the isolation from the cultural, political, and scientific passions that were transforming the city—all stood in sharp contrast to the emerging proletarian world to which the Communists had devoted most of their energy. Cut off from the cities, from the possibility of material aid from the Soviet Union, from access to the instruments of political power, the danger of devolving into traditional forms of peasant rebellion was real. The peasants, full of despair and anger, would respond to a leadership that offered immediate gain, but could they be mobilized for the long-range goal of fundamentally transforming society? Killing an oppressive landlord was a clear, comprehensible act. Working toward a change in the organization of the economy which would eliminate landlords as a class was an entirely different matter.

For most of the party's leadership, whatever other disagreements they might have, the shift of the revolution to the countryside was thus seen as regrettable, temporary, and full of risk. Li Lisan, soon to be removed as head of the party after his efforts to seize major cities had failed, noted with alarm the steady decline of working-class membership. "The Communist Party acknowledges that the peasantry is an ally of the revolution," Li conceded. However, "the peasantry is petty-bourgeois and cannot have correct ideas regarding socialism, . . . its conservatism is particularly strong, and . . . it lacks organizational ability." Only the proletariat, he warned, "can lead us onto the correct revolutionary road. Unless we proceed to correct the dangers involved in this peasant mentality, it may lead to a complete destruction of the Party."[5]

No orthodox urban party member can have been more critical of peasant weaknesses than Mao. But perhaps because of his peasant origins, he saw, as others did not, the particular strength and structural centrality of the peasantry. In an advanced industrial country, the proletariat might well hold the central place in making and sustaining the revolution; the proletariat, after all, could bring the whole of the economy to a grinding halt. But in a country like China, the linchpin was hardly China's two million industrial workers, but its five hundred million peasants. "There are those who say that the rampant savagery exercised by the compradors in the cities is altogether comparable to the rampant savagery of the landlord class in the countryside," Mao wrote. But compradors lived in concentrated locales, whereas landlords were everywhere—in every province, district, village. Moreover, China's proletariat did not yet "seek to destroy immediately the political position of the bourgeoisie."

Whatever their ultimate role, industrial workers at this point in the struggle had far more limited goals—such as the establishment of trade unions. Only the peasant movement combined political and economic struggle. When the peasants rise they "run into the political power of these village bullies, bad gentry, and landlords who have been crushing the peasants for several thousand years . . . and if they do not overthrow this political power which is crushing them, there can be no status for the peasants." If the peasants do not fight "in the villages to overthrow the privileges of the feudal-patriarchal land-lord class the power of the warlords and of imperialism can never be hurled down root and branch." Strikes and struggles in the cities were of course important, but only the peasants could attack the system "root and branch."

Investigating the peasant movement in Hunan in the winter of 1926–27, Mao "saw and heard of many strange things' of which he had hitherto been unaware. The peasant movement, he wrote, was a "colossal event" capable of sweeping "all the imperialists, warlords, corrupt officials, local tyrants and evil gentry into their graves." It attacked the very basis of privilege upon which the old society rested. The real objective of the revolution, Mao insisted, was to overthrow the "patriarchal-feudal class of local tyrants, evil gentry and lawless landlords [which] has formed the basis of autocratic government for thousands of years and is the cornerstone of imperialism, warlordism and corrupt officialdom." And this was precisely the goal and, briefly, the achievement of the Hunan peasant movement.[6]

Mao did not approach the peasantry as a romantic revolutionary, but rather as a passionate student of their condition and, equally important, as a teacher seeking to enable them to realize the birth of their power. A party that deeply understood their situation need not fear succumbing to a "peasant mentality" but could instead forge an alliance based on trust, mutual interest, and, ultimately, a shared vision. Defeat had placed the CCP in a position of odd advantage. Living within the reality of the overwhelming majority of the population, the party had the opportunity to redefine the nature of its mass base and, in consequence, shape a new relationship between vanguard and mass.

In Russia, by contrast, the paradox of victory in 1917 was that it brought to state power a party theoretically representative of the mass of Russia's workers and peasants but actually almost completely isolated from the peasant majority of the people. If the Bolsheviks had made good use of the peasant uprising, the peasants themselves had taken advantage of the revolution to withdraw from national tasks as defined by the Soviet state. Holding overwhelming economic power, they remained unresponsive to the demands of Bolshevik cadre. In the early days of the revolution, peasant neutrality was sufficient. By 1921, however, as we have seen, much more was required, and the Bolsheviks faced the formidable task of building a mass base in the countryside from a position of state power. The Chinese party came to the peasantry empty handed, seeking refuge, asking no sacrifice it was not itself ready to make, and offering its skills for a painful struggle against a common enemy. The Bolsheviks came empty handed as well, not as refugees but as authority, incapable of escaping the implications for the peasantry of its own power. To be in the Soviet vanguard meant to mobilize the masses for purposes of transforming Russia to fit the Bolsheviks' socialist vision: a strong, industrialized, secure, urban society; a countryside free of traditional social relations, superstitions, and backward means of production. These were goals that peasants might well fail to perceive as common.

NEP AND ITS CONTRADICTIONS

By 1927, at the time of the Comintern Executive Committee meeting after Shanghai, the nature of the Bolshevik vanguard and its tasks was hardly a new issue in Soviet politics. Trotsky's charge of "tailism" had been hurled across Bolshevik/Menshevik barricades for years, an epithet for those who refused to lead and who let events control the revolution's development. Lenin's very notion of a vanguard party had also provoked sharp debate. As the instrument of proletarian consciousness and will, as the sole vehicle through which society could shed itself of antagonistic, exploitative social relations and enter a new stage of social harmony and freedom, the party bore enormous historical responsibility. Its policies and strategies simply had to be correct. Otherwise, as Trotsky himself insisted in a memorable speech at the Thirteenth Party Congress in 1924, communist society itself was doomed, since the party was "the only historic instrument which the working class possesses for the solution of its fundamental tasks."[7] But how could one assure the party's "rightness"? If not through broad proletarian participation, as most Mensheviks insisted, at least by means of intense debate and discussion of all issues and alternatives by those sufficiently "conscious" to warrant party membership, according to Trotsky and also, to a great extent, Lenin as well. And this was precisely what Stalin was preventing. "It is an unheard of mistake to contend that a discussion of the problems of the Chinese revolution can injure our interests," Trotsky wrote. "If this were so, then not only the CPSU but every other party of the Communist International, including the Chinese, would have to abstain from any discussion."[8]

To be in the vanguard in the spring of 1927 was thus to confront Stalin's increasing heavy handedness in party affairs, and to face the paradox of accepting policies one might actually think were wrong because to oppose them would be to challenge Stalin's leadership and thus the party's legitimacy, which would weaken Russian and world revolutionary interests. The more wrong the policies and thus the greater the opposition, the more potential damage to the party and the greater indirect advantage to enemies of the revolution, a logical paradox from which there seemed no easy escape.

There were other contradictions as well. Building socialism meant constructing a society based on high technological achievement and material well-being, as well as the end of exploitation and antagonistic social relations. But Russia's revolution had not only taken place in an agrarian society, where the accumulation of investment capital for industrial development was very difficult without extremely high tax rates or foreign assistance, but also a society devastated by seven years of incredibly savage warfare and faced in the aftermath with enormous tasks of reconstruction. The winter of 1921–22 had brought the most brutal famine of a century. Conservative estimates suggest that more than three million persons died directly of starvation. The total number of deaths from related causes was undoubtedly more than three times that number. By 1927 agricultural production had barely regained 1913 levels. Industry continued to lag behind. Thus the very process of building a strong, industrially advanced socialism, much less the "socialism in one country" that Stalin had promised in 1924, seemed more a utopian fantasy than a socioeconomic possibility.

The very fact that Europe continued to be governed by bourgeois governments posed a further anomaly, since most Marxists expected either that the workers' revolution in Russia would spread quickly in Western Europe or that the capitalist world would mobilize to crush it. Indeed, for many in Russia the intrinsic importance of events in China had less to do with creating a better life for the Chinese than it did with engaging the bourgeois powers in continued struggle. China was a safe and distant front. But if the liberation struggle there collapsed, many feared it was only a matter of time before the West again turned its guns on the Soviet Union. Fascists in Italy and Germany repeatedly expressed the urge to do just that, as did the militant Right in England, France, and even America, while the workers' movements in these countries, if still ideologically radical, seemed to have lost their desire for full-fledged revolution, and at best were uncertain allies. Thus on the one hand, there was the paradox of Soviet Russia's very survival in the absence of international revolution, which implicitly challenged both the ideological underpinnings of Bolshevik rule and Stalin's claim to be a revolutionary Marxist; and on the other, the fear that unless world revolution occurred in the near future, even Russia's fledgling socialist order would be under attack, which implicitly justified protecting the party's (and Stalin's) power.

The New Economic Policy, meanwhile, compounded these problems for Russia's "vanguard," accentuating the contradictions of Soviet socialism. When Lenin announced the policy at the Tenth Party Congress in 1921, there was general understanding that it was a necessary but temporary expedient, a "breathing space" to allow agriculture and industry to recover. The NEP replaced requisitioning in the countryside with a tax in kind, as we have seen, that encouraged peasants to grow whatever they could beyond the tax amount and market it at a profit. Private trade—market relations—were also allowed as a means of facilitating distribution; in industry, extensive new regulations were introduced that, among other things, permitted factories in some sectors to return to private management. The purpose here was to facilitate industrial recovery in part by bringing back technical and managerial personnel whose skills were desperately needed. It was also hoped that the recovery of agriculture might begin to generate capital for investment, both through grain sales abroad and internal devices like the sales tax. Bolshevik planners could use this capital to further Russia's overall process of industrialization, at least until socialist revolutions in Western Europe freed surplus capital there for Russian needs.

Both as a breathing space, however, and as a means of laying the foundations for industrialization, the NEP was fundamentally at odds with socialist values and the concept of the vanguard. As a breathing space, it contradicted the ideological necessity of further revolutionary struggle, as well as the enthusiasm and energy of many party cadre. The vanguard, in effect, was being told to relax, although of course the matter was hardly put that way; Soviet Russia now needed to be administered, rather than led directly, or driven, toward socialism. Many of the most dedicated party members had been killed in the civil war, and there was little rank-and-file opposition to Lenin and the Congress's decision. But a breathing space clearly favored those in the party who had managerial talent rather than revolutionary commitment, a clear hegemony of "experts" over "Reds."

As a means of laying the foundations of industrialization, the NEP seemed dangerously dependent on the productivity of the peasants—a class whose deep attachment to traditional methods had helped keep Russian yields consistently low—and excessively liberal in the areas of management, trade, and consequently, also of pricing, which made centralized economic planning extremely difficult. More important for some, it also meant relying on a market system for the procurement of agricultural products and exchanging goods, which meant preserving the very system of bourgeois values (profit, individualism), leading to class antagonism and social exploitation, that the revolution had fought to erase. Thus Russia's peasants were seemingly being given a privileged position in a workers' state while the proletarians were being forced to submit to an essentially bourgeois social system.

To be sure, this was probably not the dominant perspective of Bolshevik rank and file. The Tenth Party Congress, which introduced the NEP, also resolved to purge the party of "non-communist elements," and perhaps a fourth of the party's 732,000 members lost their positions on charges of passivity, careerism, corruption, drunkenness, and failure to carry out party instructions.[9] But the more dedicated one was to socialist revolutionary goals, the greater the tension between administration and activism; while the more readily one could accommodate to such administrative organizations as Stalin's burgeoning Secretariat, the more likely the chance of party rewards and advancements.

In these circumstances it was only a matter of time before left-wing oppositional elements within the party again made their voices heard. Splinter groups like the Workers' Opposition under Kollontai and Shliapnikov, and the Democratic Centralists under Sapronov and Osinsky, which had sharply criticized the party in 1919 and 1920 for its bureaucratic and elitist politics ("which bind the wings of self-activity and the creativeness of the working class"), now began to disregard the strictures of the Tenth Congress against factionalism and lashed out at the party for "ignoring the decisions of our congresses on putting workers' democracy into practice."[10] The party Secretariat increasingly came under sharp attack, particularly after Stalin was appointed general secretary in 1922, and its functions of supervising local party organizations and both assigning and promoting party officials were consolidated under his control. Late in the winter of 1922 twenty-two prominent oppositionists sent a "Declaration of Protest" to Communists abroad; by the time of the Eleventh Party Congress in early April 1922, only 223 of a possible 523 votes could be mustered in favor of retaining the party's local control commissions, another supervisory agency soon to be firmly controlled by Stalin. (The commissions were retained, however, since only 89 votes were officially recorded as opposed.)

Even more troublesome was the criticism of the party's economic policies. By early 1923 the urgent objectives of the NEP in terms of agricultural recovery had largely been achieved, thanks in part to good weather and the relatively free trade and distribution system. But basic problems persisted: a shortage of capital for industrial investment, low productivity in the countryside, and such chronic difficulties as the relatively inelastic demand for industrial and manufactured goods on the part of the overwhelming majority of the population, which implied that rapid growth in this sector would be difficult to stimulate through the market place. There were also new problems. A lack of fuel compounded already serious weaknesses in railroad transport, and there was a desperate need for all sorts of raw materials. Scores of plants were forced to shut down, while others hurriedly sold off stocks and even equipment at very low prices in a desperate effort to raise capital. Unemployment was growing, while wage levels remained depressed, and the cost of food took most of a worker's paycheck.

In the summer and fall of 1922 the relative level of industrial and agricultural prices began to change, as recovery in the countryside made food more plentiful and the scarcity of depleted industrial stocks pushed goods prices higher. This "scissors" effect, as it became known, only defined the problem of investment capital in new terms.[11] Low agricultural prices were hardly an inducement to increasing production, and hence the possibility of overcoming capital shortages either through sales taxes or by squeezing peasants with high-priced manufactured goods was not very promising.

Under ordinary circumstances these problems might have been ameliorated by foreign loans, but Soviet Russia in 1923 was far from a welcome partner in the international financial community, even had party leaders been inclined to seek assistance. Some urged this course as a matter of practical necessity. It corresponded to overtures being made toward Germany and England to establish normal trade relations and could be distinguished ideologically as pragmatic state policy as opposed to the revolutionary goals of the party in the Comintern. But Lenin himself was now ill, having suffered a massive stroke in May 1922, and while he recovered partially in the fall, the party leadership clearly felt itself unable to take decisive action on this and other issues without his participation. Thus the criticism continued, intensifying in the summer of 1923 and climaxing late in the fall with a series of articles by Trotsky urging the adoption of a "new course."

With fiery eloquence, Trotsky focused directly on what had become the three central issues of Soviet revolutionary development in the 1920s: the problem of industrializing in an agrarian society without substantial outside assistance; the issue of party governance, which spoke to the question of how party policies might be modified; and the crucial question of the vanguard's relations with its mass base. The issues were closely related. Bureaucratism within the party (Trotsky's catchword for arrogance, careerism, and lack of concern for the relationship between revolutionary consciousness and successfully building a socialist society) was responsible for a passive approach to the problems of industrialization. Trotsky demanded "precise and decisive measures." The key to Soviet development lay not in breaking harmonious relations with the peasantry, but in careful planning and the successful "adaptation of Soviet industry to the peasant market, on one hand, and to the taxable capacity of the peasantry on the other, while preserving its character as *state*, that is, *socialist* industry." The principal weapon in the party's hands was the ability to regulate prices. By lowering the cost of necessary goods to the countryside and "educating the peasant" in the development of socialist attitudes, the party could induce greater agricultural productivity, absorb the profits that were now going increasingly to tradesmen and other middle-level entrepreneurs, and increase tax revenues. If especially favorable terms of trade were established, peasants might also be persuaded to join the growing network of relatively productive state and collective farms. Meanwhile, rank-and-file workers had to be drawn into industrial management once again, to assure efficient production and socialist progress. Above all, the party needed a "consciously *planned* approach to the market and to its economic tasks," which meant rational organization, careful consideration of the best uses for available capital, and serious efforts to develop the confidence, support, and revolutionary consciousness of workers and peasants.[12]

It was precisely here, however, that the party leadership was failing so badly. In the past months, according to Trotsky, it had been overcome with "insufferable traits: apparatus cliquism, bureaucratic smugness, and complete disdain for the party's thoughts, mood, or needs." Appointment had become a system, formalized hierarchy a growing way of life. The apparatus was stultifying revolutionary commitment and enthusiasm, cutting off the youth, depriving workers and lower-level cadre "of the feeling they are participating actively in the general work of the party," counterposing "a few thousand comrades, who form the leading cadres, to the rest of the mass whom they look upon only as an object of action." If this situation continued, the party would degenerate. The whole Soviet experiment would be threatened with collapse.

But how to change the party's direction? How to breathe revolutionary life back into the party's apparatus and regenerate the vanguard? This was Trotsky's dilemma and the problem of all oppositionists who accepted the notion that one "could only be right with the party, and through the party." Opposition factions were clearly proscribed as a threat to party unity and authority. Trotsky himself recognized such strictures as a necessary feature of transitional periods. Yet to avoid factions, "temporary groupings [had to be] avoided . . . [as well as] difference of opinion, for wherever there are two opinions, people inevitably group together." How, Trotsky asked rhetorically, could one avoid differences of opinion in a party of half a million: "That is the essential contradiction residing in the very situation of a party of proletarian dictatorship, a contradiction that cannot be escaped by purely formal measures alone."[13]

"Formal measures," however, were exactly what Stalin was ready to employ. Closely supported by Zinoviev and Kamenev, and skillfully hiding his personal animosity behind the screen of anonymous *Pravda* editorials, he began to unleash a virtual avalanche of vituperation against the one revolutionary Bolshevik who most assumed would succeed Lenin as leader of the party. Trotsky's "new course" was denounced in scathing terms: a "petty bourgeois deviation from Leninism," a "Bonapartist" attempt to place his own views above those of the party, "unconscionable oppositionism." In the middle of January 1924, Stalin, Kamenev, and Zinoviev presented the Thirteenth Party Conference with a resolution of censure. Skillfully and deliberately, Stalin had prepared the ground so that the outcome was never in doubt. Only three votes were recorded in Trotsky's defense. Without even waiting for the vote to be taken, Trotsky himself left the sessions to vacation and rest in the Caucasus. Then, within days, Lenin finally succumbed to the strokes and paralysis that had left him incapacitated for the better part of the preceding eighteen months. Unable even to return to Moscow for the funeral, Trotsky found himself hopelessly outflanked. The party apparatus, and hence Bolshevik power, was firmly in the hands of the man Lenin had described in his "Testament" as "unlikely to use it in a careful and appropriate fashion."[14]

Much has been written about the fateful collapse of Trotsky's position and his rapid exclusion from Bolshevik party ranks. The personal aspects of this process were filled with pathos; the sinister way in which Stalin used his power in the Secretariat to strip Trotsky of his post of commissar of war (January 1925), deprive him of his seat on the Central Committee (October 1926), and finally expel him from the party (November 1927) should have been ample warning that revolutionary commitment was by now a meaningless asset at the party's highest levels. Stalin used the posts assigned to him with great skill. As both general secretary and the dominant figure in the party's Organizational Bureau, he controlled the vital administrative center of party operations, handling personnel assignments, overseeing the propaganda and agitation (Agitprop) department, even preparing the agendas and documents for Politburo and Central Committee meetings. He was a careful and clever organizer. Assigning cadre to important party posts did not yet assure unswerving personal loyalty, but it clearly built a phalanx of support for Stalin's views on such important issues as party development (and the question of bureaucratization), placing priority on developing "socialism in one country," rather than international revolution, and suppressing "opposition," precisely the focal points of Trotsky's assault. When issues came to a vote in party conferences and congresses, it is hardly surprising that strong majorities stood behind Stalin.

Trotsky, moreover, was not the only prominent Bolshevik to be officially discredited as an oppositionist. The Fourteenth Congress in December 1925 also witnessed a fearsome attack on Kamenev and on Krupskaia, Lenin's widow, and the wholesale purge of Zinoviev's party organization in Leningrad. The issues here had ostensibly to do with party management and recruitment, but in fact Stalin's effort was to close in on his erstwhile allies and prominent rivals, consolidating his grip on the party apparatus. Zinoviev demanded the right to offer a "minority" report on party activities at the Congress, but he was loudly hooted down. "When Zinoviev is in the majority, he is for iron discipline," Mikoyan taunted, "but when he is in the minority . . . he opposes it." "We are against the creation of a Leader!" Kamenev shouted. But his plea was lost in a sea of angry Stalinist demonstrations, as the stenograms indicate.[15]

In comparative terms, however, what is significant is not Trotsky's personal drama or Stalin's ability to move forcefully against his own and Lenin's close associates, but the way in which this process reflected a fundamental change in the nature of the Bolshevik party vanguard at a critical moment of Soviet development. Western historians have spent a good deal of time arguing whether Stalin's politics stemmed directly from Leninism or were only facilitated by a Leninist disposition in this regard. Our own preference is for the latter interpretation, but the important issue is not the range of historical antecedents (which was broad), but the manner in which

Stalin's rule—increasingly personal, arbitrary, and authoritarian—dramatically increased Bolshevik isolation from rank-and-file workers and peasants *before* Soviet society had been mobilized to complete the necessary processes of agricultural reorganization and industrialization. By late 1927 the policies of NEP seemed to be failing. The problem of capital accumulation had become acute, industrial growth appeared stalled, the planning process was in shambles, and grain available for export (and hence the party's ability to buy foreign machinery) had dried up almost entirely. There were ominous rumors in the press, false and possibly contrived, about the dangers of a new foreign invasion, worrisome even to those who doubted their authenticity, given the general international dangers and the USSR's continued status as a pariah to the "civilized" West.[16] Procurements were critically low. There was even grave concern in the spring of 1928 whether Moscow and Leningrad could be stocked with adequate supplies of food.

The root of the problem remained in the countryside, or more precisely, in the party's relation to the peasants. Peasants were simply not marketing sufficient quantities of grain to meet the party's needs. There were various reasons for this, which will be discussed below, but the important point here is that the task of modernizing agricultural production still lay ahead in the Soviet Union, despite the fact that more than ten years had passed since the October revolution. The Soviet vanguard held state power in a country whose mass of rural inhabitants clung to traditional and outmoded ways. To Stalin and others, a "backward" peasantry remained an enemy of socialist progress. Industrialization seemed to require control over agricultural production and state regulation of rural social relations; it surely necessitated an increase in agrarian productivity, the mobilization of labor for industry, and the guarantee of an adequate food supply for the growing populations of industrial cities and towns. To complete Russia's social revolution with a minimum of political and social conflict thus required extraordinary care and, above all, a deep understanding of peasant outlooks and needs. At best peasants were suspicious of party authority; at worst, hostile. An alliance had yet to be forged, in other words, between the party and Soviet peasants so that party authority—the vanguard of Soviet socialist transformation—was at least respected, if not welcomed, and the peasantry, in the main, accepted party policies and objectives as their own.

RED POLITICAL POWER IN JIANGXI

In China, too, the peasantry remained the key to revolutionary development. Drawing on two years of experience in leading a remnant military force composed primarily of peasants and former bandits, Mao began to develop a political analysis of the specific state of the Chinese revolution, a set of military tactics and a mode of revolutionary practice developed out of the daily experience of his life. First, in the sparsely populated area of Jinggangshan, on the border between Hunan and Jiangxi, and later in the more substantial base established in southern Jiangxi Mao, working closely with another peasant-born leader, Zhu De, wrote a series of reports that began to outline an entirely new approach to revolution, one so close to the common sense of the situation that it is often hard to realize how outrageous much of it seemed at the time.

Mao started from China's very particular historical situation. The subjective forces of the revolution were indeed weak, he argued, but then so were the forces of the ruling class. The establishment of a separate area of "Red political power," in Mao's phrase, was possible only because China was not the direct colony of any imperialist power. In this, as opposed to those who bemoaned China's semicolonial position as rendering her weaker even than India, Mao saw strength. Imperialist competition, combined with the continuation of splits and wars between and among the new national government of Chiang Kai-shek and various warlords, meant that an independent political base could be carved out, sustained, and in time expanded.[17]

Central to Mao's approach was the development of a Red Army that would not, as in Russia, defend the revolution, but *make* it. Some comrades, Mao wrote, think the task of the army is "merely to fight. They do not understand that the Chinese Red Army is an armed body for carrying out the political tasks of the revolution." The army, he stressed, fought *in order* to educate, organize, and arm the masses as well as to help them establish revolutionary political power. "Without these objectives, fighting loses its meaning and the

Red Army loses the reason for its existence." To insure that political tasks were understood as primary, Mao established and defended against critics a system of party representatives within the army, from company level on up, whose task it was to supervise the soldiers' committees, guide mass-movement work, and serve as liaison to the party branch. An integral aspect of forging a fighting force that understood the revolution was to build into its practice a mode of social relations standing in stark contrast to the military experience of soldiers in warlord or Nationalist units. Everyone received the same pay; officers were forbidden to beat their men; soldiers were encouraged to hold meetings and speak their grievances. As a result, "newly captured soldiers in particular feel that our army and the Kuomintang army are worlds apart. . . . The very soldiers who had no courage in the White army yesterday are very brave in the Red Army today; such is the effect of democracy. The Red Army," Mao concluded, "is like a furnace in which all captured soldiers are transmuted the moment they come over." The weaknesses of a peasant army were as apparent to Mao as its strengths. Individualistic, undisciplined, enamored of quick victories, too easily discouraged by temporary setbacks, without constant political education, the Red Army might readily degenerate into a traditional rebel band. Indifferent to the constraints imposed by China's political economy, what peasants most wanted was absolute democracy, absolute equality. And yet to divide what little there was, without first thoroughly dismantling the traditional social and economic relations of rural life, would not only leave everyone poor, it would create no barrier against an eventual reproduction of the old system. The corrective to every weakness was education and more education. Party members and soldiers had to be brought to a sense of themselves as "instruments for carrying out the tasks of the revolution." Their struggle was to realize that *they themselves are makers of the revolution*" and not its "employees."[18]

But how was that struggle to proceed? On two major issues, military policy and land reform, Mao was distinctly at odds with various elements in the party. His approach was a kind of fine tuning to the actual social and political situation that existed at any given moment, rather than an overriding theoretical construct. Given the divided nature of the enemy, both domestic and imperialist, much was possible, even with an army of peasants, even without adequate arms, even without successful uprisings in the cities. What was necessary was the development of a new approach to guerrilla warfare —neither roving bands whose sole achievement was disruption nor fixed conventional warfare. The rules were relatively simple: when the enemy advanced, the Red Army must retreat, drawing the enemy further and further into territory whose peasantry had been organized and mobilized to support main force units. When the enemy halted, they must be vigorously harassed; when they sought to avoid battle, they could successfully be attacked, and finally when the enemy retreated, the Red Army should pursue. Gradually the area under Red Army control, and hence the revolution, would expand, not through the *capture* of territory, but through its political and military reorganization. Here was revolution in process. Marxists, Mao wrote, were not fortune tellers. He could not put a date on when a "high tide" of revolutionary action would finally sweep away the enemy, but, in a wonderful collage of metaphors, Mao urged his comrades to understand that "when I say that there will soon be a high tide of revolution in China, I am emphatically not speaking . . . of something illusory, unattainable and devoid of significance for action. It is like a ship far out at sea whose mast-head can already be seen from the shore; it is like the morning sun in the east whose shimmering rays are visible from a high mountain top; it is like a child about to be born moving restlessly in its mother's womb."[19]

Ironically, Mao's very success in the early Jiangxi years reinforced his critics' attacks. Some argued with Li Lisan that isolation from the cities would ultimately doom the revolution. Others, Zhou Enlai among them, insisted Mao was a "Right opportunist" whose poetic metaphors did not make up for his wrong ideas. In a stunning set of denunciatory clauses, Zhou criticized all those

who regard the seizure of one or several entire provinces as not an immediate but a distant goal; all those who are skeptical about occupying metropolitan centers and prefer to lead the Soviet regime and the Red Army toward remote areas; all those who . . . prefer to tie the hands of our armed comrades with such assignments as propaganda in the villages and raising funds for the army, forgetting that the principal mission of the Red Army is to destroy our enemy through combat; all those who still linger in a past stage for which gradual expansion of military action and a defensive and

conservative strategy were proper and who are consequently unwilling to move swiftly to deal a fatal blow to the enemy in the
non-Communist areas.[20]

Mao's response was sharp and clear. Of course the struggle in the
cities must continue, "but . . . it would also be wrong for any of our
Party members to fear the growth of peasant strength." The revolution would fail without proletarian leadership, which the party itself
offered, "but the revolution is never harmed if the peasant struggle
outstrips the forces of the workers." Indeed, if the urban movement
was to advance at all, the major thrust must be in the further development of "the struggle in the countryside, the establishment of Red
political power in small areas, and the creation and expansion of the
Red Army."[21]

In effect, Mao was developing throughout the Jiangxi years, along
with specific tactics, a long-term strategy for seizing power, one that
combined the administration and governing of territory with continued military struggle firmly rooted in a base area as secure as
possible. And his success, at first, was stunning. Operating in accordance with his rules, the Red Army defeated Chiang Kai-shek's first
"annihilation" campaign (launched in the winter of 1930). Facing a
force of 100,000, the 40,000 soldiers of the Red Army captured
10,000 men and 6,000 rifles. Almost a third of the captured soldiers
elected to remain with the Red Army, and they were welcomed.
Chiang's second campaign employed 200,000 troops and a small air-
force. These units, too, were torn apart, piece by piece, with 20,000
prisoners taken.

Land policy and military tactics were intimately linked. The
enemy could safely be drawn into Soviet territory, there to be decimated piecemeal, only if that territory was truly mobilized in support
of the guerrillas. The army had to rely on the population for intelligence, supplies, and recruits. The sort of "security" necessary could
not be imposed externally; it could only grow from the inside out.
But mobilization would succeed only if it dealt with the most immediate need of the people: land reform. In this area too, Mao's ideas
developed with his practice. Absolutely crucial to him was direct and
intimate knowledge of the actual situation in each village. Some
cadres, he noted, "like to make political pronouncements the moment
they arrive at a place." But the task of investigation was like "the

long months of pregnancy, and solving a problem to the day of birth." As soon as the army had made a village relatively safe from landlord or government armed forces, cadres must make the most minute, concrete investigation of the system of land tenure, usury, and other forms of exploitation as they existed in *that* village. No sacred Marxist text was of any use in this process. To change the world of the village, one had to know it in as much detail as the villagers themselves. Raw class differentiation was not enough: "Our chief method of investigation must be to dissect the different social classes, the ultimate purpose being to understand their interrelations, to arrive at a correct appraisal of class forces and then to formulate the correct tactics for the struggle, defining which classes constitute the main force in the revolutionary struggle, which classes are to be won over as allies and which . . . are to be overthrown."[22] Although there was much disagreement as to which specific groups were main force, ally or enemy, no one took issue with the method Mao had worked out for conducting land reform. As soon as an area had been secured, three committees were established, on all of which poor peasants and landless laborers served. First a confiscation committee would conduct a census and classify the population (landlord, rich, middle, poor, and landless peasants) and the size and quality of land holdings. Results were announced to the entire village and criticisms and corrections invited. A land committee, composed of government cadres, leaders of the poor peasant and farm laborers' unions, and representatives of families with sons in the Red Army, took charge of the actual distribution of land. Finally, inspection teams would investigate complaints and grievances and act to correct them. At every stage in the process (as well as in other aspects of local government), mass organizations of poor peasants and farm laborers took a major role, working closely with government personnel and experiencing, for the first time in their lives, the reality of political participation and power.

To be effective participation had to be voluntary, not forced. Written into the Agrarian Reform Law of 1931 was a recognition that confiscation and distribution, while clearly the "best method for destroying the entire system of agrarian feudalism," could not be achieved by violence and must not be attempted "even on orders coming from higher authorities." Indeed land reform was prohibited absolutely unless it had the "direct support of large masses of the peasantry. . . . Thus, if the majority of peasants desires it, they can be exempted from the principle of equal distribution."[23]

Most important to Mao was to "arouse the largest numbers of the masses in the shortest possible time and by the best methods." The policy of radical confiscation briefly practiced in Jinggangshan was not appropriate. The early capitulation of more prosperous peasants to the revolution was based not on support but fear, and at the first opportunity they would betray it, isolating poor peasants and weakening the revolution. In the absence of a nationwide revolutionary upsurge, surrounded by enemies, economic pressure on the base area would soon prove intolerable not only to the "intermediate class, but some day it will prove too much even for the workers, poor peasants and Red Army men."[24]

On this, as on military policy, Mao was severely challenged by a leadership group newly returned from Moscow—the Twenty-Eight Bolsheviks. Young, extremely competent in the Marxist classics, armed with external authority, Wang Ming and his cohorts found Mao's agrarian policy as conservative and unambitious as his military tactics. Not surprisingly, given, as we shall see, the antagonism between communists in the CPSU and Russia's peasants, by 1933 a much tougher stance toward rich peasants was instituted. Yet it was Mao who wrote the guidelines for the new classification that was ordered and in the course of it he extended his analysis of the nature of class in the countryside. The question was not so much one of straightforward ownership, but rather the forms of exploitation practiced within each village. Exploitation was the enemy, not a rigid formula that actually obscured village reality. In other words, no mere economic index of prosperity or poverty was sufficient for purposes of classification. The question was the source of income—if it derived from land rents or usury or if it involved the hiring of long-term laborers, it would be confiscated. Struggling against those who defined revolutionary purity in terms of a courageous indifference to the taking of life, Mao turned what might have been a campaign of terror against quite secondary enemies, into one that explored and rectified the results of earlier efforts at land reform. Had landlords and rich peasants, through intimidation or the exercise of traditional social privilege, managed to maintain their old positions? Had a new group of rich peasants emerged, composed of former middle peasants who benefitted from the abolition of rents and usury and were now in a position to exploit others? Verification committees were organized, criticism once more invited, and the masses mobilized for what was understood to be a war of attrition against the many faces of feudalism in the countryside. Under Mao's administration the "anti-rich peasant line" was transformed into a political weapon to further mobilize people. In the very midst of the battle against yet another Kuomintang annihilation campaign, teams were sent out to investigate the land situation in each locality, to correct abuses, to draw upon the anger of those who were still (or again) the most exploited, and to arouse in the peasantry a new commitment to the revolution at the same time that the party demonstrated its commitment to a new order in the countryside.

Above all, Mao constantly stressed not just the work itself but the style in which it was done. Over and over again, he exhorted cadres against bureaucratic leadership, against commandism, against going by the book: "There are obviously some comrades . . . who are content to leave things as they are, who do not seek to understand anything thoroughly and are groundlessly optimistic, and they spread the fallacy that 'this is proletarian.' They eat their fill and sit dozing in their offices all day long without ever moving a step and going out among the masses to investigate. Whenever they open their mouths, their platitudes make people sick."[25] Precise, personal investigation required cadre to leave their offices and listen to people; it was both the substance and the method of the vanguard's central task.

Investigation was more than a matter of census taking and classification. The closest possible attention had to be paid to the *immediate* interests of the people. Cadres preferred to talk about expanding the army, collecting taxes, dealing with transport problems, and so on. But what really mattered was solving the "problems facing the masses—food, shelter and clothing, fuel, rice, cooking oil and salt, sickness and hygiene, and marriage." In some townships, local officials could hardly get anyone at all to attend a meeting; in others, 80 percent of the young people (men and women) had joined the army. How come? In one, bureaucratic leadership was everywhere apparent; in others, the local government knew precisely what troubled people and worked to correct it. If fire burned down a peasant's house, the township government raised money for its repair; if several people were discovered to be actually starving, immediate grants of grain were forthcoming. "The women," Mao wrote, "want to learn ploughing and harrowing. Whom can we get to teach them? . . . The wooden bridge over there is too narrow and people may fall off. Should we not repair it? Many people suffer from boils and other ailments. What are we going to do about it?" Everything needed to be known, discussed, acted upon, and the results checked. "We should convince the masses that we represent their interests, that our lives are intimately bound up with theirs. We should help them to proceed from these things to an understanding of the higher tasks we have put forward, the tasks of revolutionary war, so that they will support the revolution and spread it throughout the country, respond to our political appeals and fight to the end for victory in the revolution." It was in this sense that a true Communist, as Mao understood it, created out of the materials at hand "favorable new situations through struggle." In what was literally the final analysis, victory depended upon the support of the masses; to win that support, "we must be with them."[26]

Although he retained some control over the administration of land reform policy, Mao's leadership role in this and the crucial realm of military tactics was successfully reduced by Wang Ming and his allies. Given the record of success against the first three of Chiang's extermination campaign, there was understandable reluctance to continue to fight in a manner that implied weakness rather than strength. Why draw the enemy into your territory when you could stand up and fight him at the gates—indeed perhaps carry the fight into his territory? Employing conventional tactics of positional warfare, the Red Army under Zhou Enlai's leadership defeated a Kuomintang army now 500,000 strong in a campaign that lasted from January 1932 through February of the following year. Some base areas were lost to the Nationalists, but the central Jiangxi zone remained intact, and Mao did not regain control over the military. Indeed, by January 1934 his role was reduced to the strictly honorary one of president of the Chinese Soviet Republic.[27]

SYMBOLISM AND SUBSTANCE IN THE LONG MARCH

While the Soviet Republic declared war against Japan after the Manchurian incident of 1931, Chiang turned his attention exclusively to what he perceived was his main enemy: the Communists. Late in the summer of 1933 he launched what proved to be his final campaign against the Jiangxi Soviet. Combining a rigorous economic blockade with a system of blockhouses that circled the base area in an ever-tightening noose, an army one million strong pressed inexorably forward. With an overconfidence born of their success in employing conventional warfare the year before, the 100,000 troops of the Red Army attempted to fight on Chiang's terms. Mao's insistence that only a reversion to guerrilla warfare could save any of the base area was firmly overruled.

Backed by the Comintern's military adviser, Otto Braun (Li De), who berated Mao and Zhu De for their ignorance of military matters, Zhou Enlai, Bo Gu, and those of the Twenty-eight Bolsheviks who had not left for Moscow to observe the battle in greater comfort, led the Red Army into a series of pitched battles and disastrous defeats. By June 1934 the base area was reduced to a few counties, and the decision was finally taken to break through the blockade and run for it. In early October the survivors left on a march whose final destination was not set. Approximately 90,000 people (only 35 of them women) began the journey, 6,000 survived it. They marched 6,000 miles, for 370 days, averaging a military engagement per day; they crossed eighteen mountain ranges, climbed five permanently snow-capped mountains, crossed twenty-four rivers, captured sixty-two towns, and broke through the armies of no less than ten different provincial warlords. In Jiangxi they left behind 20,000 wounded, wives, children, and families, and small groups of guerrillas who would continue to fight. The wounded were sent home, as soon as they recovered, with a promise of fifty dollars per year for as long as funds held out. And the remaining men, aided by peasants, became, as one of them said later, "like wild men, living and fighting by instinct."[28]

Although it began as a headlong retreat, after a crucial conference at which Mao regained much of his lost power, the Long March became something far more purposive. At Zunyi the policies pursued in the last year of the Soviet were severely criticized, Mao's leadership affirmed, and the organization of the March streamlined. As one historian has put it, the retreating forces now behaved "like a provisional government on the road." In so doing, they both conceptually and in practice kept alive the revolutionary situation.

In memoirs, opera, film, novels, short stories, art, poetry, and dance the Long March has been celebrated almost from the very moment of its completion. To be a revolutionary means to be able not just to survive but to celebrate that survival as a foretaste of ultimate victory. Mao's poem, written shortly after he had led his remnant army through the last of the enemy blockades, rings with triumph, not exhaustion: "High on the crest of Liupan Mountain, our banners billow in the west wind."[29] Like the others, Mao had lost comrades and family members, had left his children behind, knowing he would probably never see them again. "We have received," he wrote, "an extremely great historical punishment."[30]

What is so extraordinary about the Long March is its perfect melding of real and symbolic. It was an epic, at times almost unbearably heroic. Those who survived it, those who heard its exploits, possessed as part of their immediate lives the very stuff of China's best-loved traditional tales of courage and daring. Take just one example. By May of 1935, the Red Army had reached the shores of the Dadu River, a roaring torrent whose three possible crossings were all heavily guarded. Known to every soldier from the historical *Romance of the Three Kingdoms*, the river resonated as well with even more appropriate echoes. Here, exactly seventy-two years earlier, the peasant army of the Taiping rebel Shi Dakai was decisively defeated. On moonless nights, local legend ran, "you can still hear the spirits of our Taiping dead wailing at the Dadu River crossing and over the town where they were slaughtered. They will wail until they are avenged." Repeat history, Chiang Kai-shek urged the warlord armies allied with him, by destroying the Red Army at the Dadu River as the Taiping Army under Shi Dakai was destroyed. Instead, Shi Dakai was at last avenged. In the face of an enemy machine gun unit, over an iron suspension bridge whose planking had been set ablaze, men "ran through the flames and threw their grenades in the midst of the enemy. . . . The bridge became a mass of running men with rifles ready, tramping out the flames as they ran." After the crossing, Zhu De addressed the assembled troops. Recalling Shi Dakai's fate, he drew a new, revolutionary moral. "Heroism," he told them, "is an ancient concept. In the past, individual heroes arose above the masses. The Red Army embodies a new concept of heroism. We create mass heroes of the revolution . . . who are willing to die for the revolution or live and fight until our people and country are liberated."[31]

In a report to party activists two months after their arrival in northern Shaanxi, Mao summarized the meaning of the March for the revolution:

> The Long March is the first of its kind in the annals of history, . . .
> it is a manifesto, a propaganda force, a seeding machine. Since Pan
> Ku divided the heavens from the earth and the Three Sovereigns
> and Five Emperors reigned, has history ever witnessed a long march
> such as ours? For twelve months we were under daily reconais-
> sance and bombing from the skies by scores of planes, while on
> land we were encircled and pursued, obstructed and intercepted
> by a huge force of several hundred thousand men . . . yet by using
> our two legs we swept across a distance of more than twenty thou-
> sand *li* through the length and breadth of eleven provinces. Let us
> ask, has history ever known a long march to equal ours? No, never.

But the March meant more than survival. It was as well a manifesto: "It has proclaimed to the world that the Red Army is an army of heroes, while the imperialists and their running dogs, Chiang Kai-shek and his like, are impotent." And it was a propaganda force, announcing to some "200 million people in eleven provinces that the road of the Red Army is their only road to liberation. Without the Long March, how could the broad masses have learned so quickly about the existence of the great truth which the Red Army em- bodies?" Finally, it was a seeding machine, sowing seeds through eleven provinces that "will sprout, leaf, blossom, and bear fruit, and will yield a harvest in the future."[32]

What is significant in Mao's assessment of the Long March is not its factual accuracy. Whether the March had indeed been a seeding machine and manifesto to 200 million people in eleven provinces is less interesting than Mao's ability to transform what might have been experienced as defeat into what could be used positively, as revolutionary mythology. Once again Mao was able to make virtue out of necessity, possibility out of weakness. There is an element of cult-making here, but it is not the cult of an individual, omnipotent, personal leader as was becoming the case in Soviet Rus- sia. Rather it is the cult of an armed party, of *collective* invincibility.

BUILDING A NEW BASE IN SHAANXI

Although one knows it didn't happen that way, one sometimes has the image of all 6,000 survivors throwing themselves down exhausted among the welcoming impoverished peasants of northern Shaanxi and then rising as a single powerful body to build once more a revolutionary base. In fact, the Red Army entered a region with a long history of struggle, starting with a small Marxist study group established in 1919. The area itself was among the poorest in the entire country, where for decades a balance of terror among bandits, warlord armies, landlord militia, and, in time, Red troops had existed. It was an armed and starving province, where famine—as much the result of political collapse as natural disasters—had killed no less than one-third of the population between 1928 and 1933. Many of those who had neither starved to death nor managed to migrate sold what they could—wives, children, and land—and clung to bare subsistence as tenant farmers or landless laborers.

The history of the Communist movement in Shaanxi recapitulates, in another key, the successes and failures in the South.[33] Until 1927 the party's commitment to the united front with the Nationalists severely limited the possibility of full mobilization for the revolution. The breakdown of the alliance exposed Shaanxi Communists to the fate of their comrades throughout China and with much the same result—flight to more remote parts of the province, and death for those who could not escape. As in Central and South China, strains developed between those who were committed as deeply to a theory of revolution as to revolution itself; between those, in other words, who insisted on the necessity of basing further revolutionary activity in urban areas (largely an abstract notion in the context of rural Shaanxi) and those who insisted on *acting* in the countryside.

In the wilder regions of northern Shaanxi, where remnant Communist forces were able to establish primitive bases, they experienced many of the same problems that beset Communist peasant policy from Peng Pai in the 1920s to Mao before the evacuation of the Jiangxi Soviet. Clan and lineage ties, though less powerful than in the South, still worked against the peasants' consciousness of themselves as a class. And even when this obstacle could be overcome, centuries of deference prevented their behaving as a "class for itself." The tendency was to receive reforms—whether confiscated land or rent and interest reduction—as benevolence from some new form of secret society rather than as the result of their own actions and efforts. A pervasive lack of military security made for a reasonable reluctance to join the guerrillas or, having joined, to remain if things got too rough.

Not surprisingly (except to those who assume Mao invented revolutionary warfare as an abstract exercise), local solutions in Shaanxi resembled those taken in Jiangxi. As the guerrillas moved toward agrarian revolution, as they proved more able to provide military security so that peasants could enjoy the fruits of that revolution, their strength grew enormously. By mid-1935, Communists controlled twenty-two counties in the Shaanxi-Gansu border area and were able to establish a Soviet government. Before the arrival of the Long Marchers, then, a government apparatus able to compete with Nationalist-affiliated warlord power holders was already functioning.

Two important conclusions emerge from even this brief treatment of the movement in Shaanxi. First, the common sense of Mao's approach to revolution in the countryside should now be clear. Like Mao, local cadres in Shaanxi had adapted to specific Chinese circumstances and, within that context, kept alive the possibility of a genuine social revolution. Secondly, the success of the Shaanxi movement occurred before the Japanese had raised, in brutal form, the issue of national survival. Peasants rallied to the revolution in Shaanxi not because of nationalism, but because it was *their* revolution.

ASSAULTING BACKWARDNESS IN RUSSIA

It was precisely these features of common sense and peasant commitment that were lacking in the great social transformation begun by Stalin and the CPSU in 1929. Stalin's heavy-handedness had brought into positions of responsibility not persons of special sensitivity but precisely the opposite. Forbidding discussion of the issues had the effect of discouraging those in power from identifying with the masses they ruled. Close alliances of the revolutionary period were being destroyed, even between Bolsheviks and workers; a political context was emerging in which any effort at wholesale social change could not help but throw the party into pitched battle against millions of its countrymen. In terms of industrialization and Russia's fundamental needs for social (and socialist) transformation, the mid-1920s had been a critical moment of need and opportunity. Party-mass relations might have been cultivated to a point where, with a careful and responsive agrarian policy, the Soviet Union could have moved steadily toward advanced industrial development. Efforts might have been spent either in positive mobilization of the peas-antry, as in China, or in a more careful and systematic pricing system designed both to increase marketings and to press peasants voluntarily to join collectives. Instead, Stalin mobilized the party, first against his own opponents, and then, secure, against the countryside.

In terms of the Soviet Union's immediate economic needs in 1928, this separation of vanguard party from the peasant sector of its mass base was felt most directly in the area of grain procurement. Agricultural production had regained prewar levels around 1925, and the recovery of livestock was also reasonably good.[34] But according to available statistics, the rate of increase dropped in 1926 and 1927 and, more important, the share of marketed grain and other food-stuffs fell precipitously below 1913 levels.[35] By 1928 the party had virtually no reserves. Some 250,000 tons of wheat had to be imported. Rationing of bread began, followed shortly by sugar, tea, meat, and other staples. Private retail food stores were closed. Measures were soon taken as well to stop local grain traffic in the countryside, in-cluding the manning of roadblocks by the militia and forceable con-fiscation. But these were rather easily circumvented by the peasantry. While hostility toward state authorities increased in the villages, the supply of essential foodstuffs did not.[36]

The reasons behind the growing crisis were complex. Marketable surpluses had historically come from larger estates, which were seized and divided during the years of revolution and civil war. Production, consequently, was relatively inefficient, and since manufactured goods were in short supply, there was little incentive to market grain that could otherwise be locally consumed. Some peasants also undoubt-edly feared higher taxes.

But much of the reason lay in the party's inability to penetrate village society, gain peasant confidence, and overcome the crisis of a market economy in which peasants were failing to meet the state's increasing demand for agricultural products. Evidence from the one party archive available to Western scholars suggests very strongly that mass work of *any* sort was generally unattractive to party cadre in the NEP period, even in the cities. It was "trench work" at a time when approbation and advancement came from above, when appointment mattered more than real achievement.[37] And if mobilizing workers was unattractive, work in the villages was "utterly neglected," according to "Papa" Kalinin, the only Politburo member with a peasant background. Newspapers and party propaganda stressed the need to gain peasant cooperation, but the party-state remained an alien, outside authority, concerned above all with procurement, tax collection, and political control.[38]

There was also what Viacheslav Molotov, one of Stalin's closest associates and in 1930, chairman of the Council of People's Commissars, called the "colossal stupidities" of pricing policies.[39] The evidence suggests that after 1925–26, the ratio of procurement prices to the real costs of production in the countryside began to drop, so that by 1926–27, as Jerzy Karcz has demonstrated, sales to the state resulted in substantial losses to the average peasant, and even larger losses to high-cost producers. In 1927, prices of private traders on the grain market exceeded state procurement prices by as much as 70 percent for oats and more than 50 percent for rye and barley.[40]

These problems simply had to be overcome to meet the demands of urban areas for foodstuffs and the requirements of rapid industrial development, but it was a matter of perspective and choice whether peasant "backwardness" was the enemy to be assaulted, or a bureaucratized party insensitive to rural conditions and indifferent to the quality of its relations with rural society. Most party leaders regarded agricultural marketings as a principal source of industrial capital; all recognized the need to improve technology in the countryside; and all saw the importance of food and other agrarian products in sustaining rapid growth in the urban work force, providing exports needed to purchase foreign industrial machinery, and supplying raw materials for clothing and other essential goods. One obvious solution, therefore, was for the party itself to gain control over the harvest and arrange its distribution to meet state needs.

This was already being done to a limited extent through the system of state and collective farms (*sovkhozy* and *kolkhozy*), where the party, in effect, hired peasants into collectives (with favorable wages or other inducements) and used the grain produced either for export or to supply the cities, subtracting, of course, a share for local needs. Some statistics suggested that it was precisely these state and collective farms that in 1926 and 1927 were producing the largest proportion of marketed grain. Many in the party urged that this network of collectives be rapidly expanded in the countryside, but others, including Stalin, remained cautious. Repeatedly they invoked Lenin's strictures against hurrying the peasants into new forms of agrarian production. Collectivization by fiat ran the grave risk of further alienating the countryside, which in turn could result in a further reduction of available grain. Well into 1928 Stalin himself warned against "implanting" collectives by force from above, hoping shortages could be overcome through more favorable terms of trade. He thus sided with Bukharin and other economic "gradualists" who supported expanding state and collective farms only insofar as peasants could be persuaded in some way to join.

In one important respect, however, there was growing ambiguity in Stalin's position: increasingly, he singled out the small stratum of relatively well-off peasants, the kulaks, as objects of special scorn, as if all difficulties in the party's relations with the countryside could be laid at their doorstep. While he publicly insisted as late as the Fifteenth Party Congress in November 1927 that even kulaks could not be dealt with by force, that "those comrades are mistaken who believe we can and should do away with the kulaks by fiat, by the GPU," it seems clear that the complexities of the countryside were being simplified in his mind in such a way as to find both a "Marxist" explanation for the problems of grain procurement (the "bourgeois" stratum was "wrecking" the party's efforts at building socialism) and a "clear" social group against which to launch his attack. Had Stalin known the countryside well, the limits of such "clarity" would have been apparent; as it was, his rhetoric encouraged even well-to-do peasants to work hard and produce as much in the way of surplus as they could, while privately he prepared to attack them broadside, a duplicity even poorer peasants would soon find quite objectionable. If important social differentiations existed in the countryside, so did common aspirations for prosperity and collective village loyalties, as Teodor Shanin and others have demonstrated.[41]

Thus when Stalin issued orders a scant two weeks after the Fifteenth Congress for the application of "extraordinary measures" against the kulaks, including the forced requisition of grain that the

Congress itself had just rejected, local party officials returning from Moscow may well have been "thunderstruck" by the contradiction, as Roy Medvedev suggests, but the effect on many peasants themselves was even more hopelessly confusing.[42] In January 1928, Stalin issued a further order, threatening party officials with dire consequences if grain procurements were not drastically increased. Forced requisitioning began on a massive scale. The peasants now realized, however, that the more they produced, the greater the danger they could be labeled as kulaks and enemies of the regime, and the more likely the fruits of their labor would be seized.

Consequently, 1928 was a year of drift in Soviet Russia. It was also one of fear, precisely at the moment firm leadership from the vanguard party was most needed. Popular attitudes can never be measured accurately in this period, nor can the precise degree of social stratification in the countryside. It is undoubtedly true, as R. W. Davies has recently argued, that petty capitalist activities were extensive within a small group of some half-million households, less than 2 percent of the total; perhaps it was even proper for those so involved to be designated a "kulak class," although here there is much dispute.[43] In practical terms, however, it was virtually impossible to apply such categories with precision or to label peasant behavior as "petty capitalist" in ways that made sense even to those seeking to conduct their affairs in accordance with state directives. It is hard to imagine, in fact, how the party could have created a greater degree of suspicion and distrust among the overwhelming mass of Russia's rural inhabitants had it set out to do so deliberately. In his novel *Virgin Soil Upturned*, Mikhail Sholokhov using the voice of Yakov Lukich, captures the peasants' predicament brilliantly:

> I returned [from the Red Army] in 1920 . . . to a bare hut. Ever since, I've worked day and night. . . . I began to listen to the agricultural inspectors, started a proper rotation of crops, and looked after my land as though it was a sick wife. My corn is the finest in the village, and I get the best harvest. I treated my crops chemically, and took steps to keep the snow on my fields. I sowed the spring seed immediately after ploughing, without any spring tilling, and my sown fallow was always the first. In a word, I became a scientific farmer, and I've had a letter of praise from the District Agricultural Department. . . .
> During the first years I sowed five hectares, then, as I got on, I

bent my back to it even more. I sowed twelve, then twenty, and even thirty, think of that! I worked, and my son and his wife. I only hired a laborer a couple of times at the busiest season. What was the Soviet government's order in those years? "Sow as much as you can!" And I sowed until my back almost broke, by the true Christ! And now . . . my friend, believe me I'm afraid. I'm afraid that because of my thirty hectares they'll drag me through the needle's eye, and call me a kulak! The Chairman of our Soviet, the Red Partisan comrade Razmiotov, he was the one who led me into this. "Sow!" he used to say; "sow the maximum you can, Yakov Lukich; help the Soviet regime, it badly needs grain. . . ." Now I think his "maximum" will get my legs tied up to my neck, God help me![44]

Then, as abruptly as he had called for massive requisitioning, Stalin changed directions once again. Peasant resistance to confiscation was now judged even more dangerous than "implanting" new forms of social organization "from above." Directives consequently came down to selected grain regions urging rapid increases in the total land area under collective farm control. Yet how much, and by what means, still remained unclear.

At precisely this time, in the late spring and early summer of 1929, Stalin and his closest associates, particularly Molotov and Kaganovich, also decided formally to adopt the "optimal variant" of the First Five-Year Plan, offered by the State Planning Commission (Gosplan) to direct economic development for the period 1929–34. As Gosplan explained in the introduction to its project, however, the optimal variant assumed that there would be no serious failure in the harvest over the next five years, that Soviet foreign trade would expand (largely through the export of agrarian surpluses), and that other qualitative improvements in the economy would occur, such as an improvement in crop yields and a reduction in the costs of production. The deteriorating situation in the countryside must consequently have seemed to Moscow as a threat not only to political and social stability but to the party's optimal goals for industrial development.

Thus the circumstances of peasant resistance, food shortages, feelings of political insecurity and national weakness, and specific plans for rapid industrial development all came together in the summer and fall of 1929, as Soviet Russia prepared to mark the twelfth anniversary of the October Revolution. Underlying all was the commitment to building a strong, industrialized, socialist society, a commitment that signified for many the very meaning of October on the world historical stage. And on November 7, just as the capitalist West began its crash into the throes of the Great Depression, Stalin announced triumphantly that the Union of Socialist Soviet Republics, for its part, had begun a Great Turn—the massive creation of state and collective farms "with all the resources and means at our command," a rapid move "full steam ahead along the path of industrialization towards socialism, finally leaving behind Russia's age-old backwardness." The Soviet Union was going to become "a country of metal, a country of machines, a country of tractors," Stalin insisted. "When we have put the USSR in an automobile and the peasant on a tractor . . . we shall see which countries are 'backward' and which are 'advanced.' "[45] So Lenin's successor formally launched one of the most awesome social transformations in all history.

Our retrospective knowledge of what was to follow tends to blind us to the genuine enthusiasm and deep excitement that these goals evoked among many Communists and others, yet without a sense of this enthusiasm, what followed is impossible to understand. In early December 1929, for instance, a congress of "shock brigades" called for the fulfillment of the Five-Year Plan in four years, a goal soon adopted by the party leadership. It is possible, of course, that the "shock workers" acted on instructions, but more likely, as many memoirs testify, they felt a genuine, revolutionary commitment. Wheels began to turn, the pace began to quicken, fueled as if magically by its own momentum. To be sure, economists and engineers were worried; professors, planners, and technicians cautioned against an optimism based on socialist enthusiasm rather than social reality. But to many in the party and elsewhere, it must have seemed that "they"—the "bourgeois professionals," the intellectuals, and the upper-crust remnants of Russia's old order—still doubted what workers could actually accomplish if they committed themselves to the task.

Soon "bourgeois" professors were being forced out of technical institutes, skeptical writers and poets told to "shut up." Full-scale "cultural revolution" was underway. But socioeconomic realities had a way of imposing strictures of their own, just as Marx had always insisted. Russia's leap toward full industrialization began with the

misplaced hope that collectivized agriculture might provide something like a third of the state's capital needs "in the course of the
next three or four years." Planned targets for the First Five-Year Plan
were adjusted accordingly. But neat figures at the top bore little
relation to the practical tasks of local committees. Receiving orders
to collectivize, and often promised premiums if the rate of collectivization exceeded district norms, local cadre were faced with the
enormous problem of sorting out which land and which particular
sectors of rural society should be organized into collective farms,
securing resources necessary for the change, setting up appropriate
administrative organizations, and fighting angry, desperate peasant
resistance. Meanwhile, ordinary grain procurement had to continue,
either through taxation or through outright seizure. An impossibly
fine line had to be drawn between ordinary (middle) peasants subject to "routine" repressive measures (requisitioning, taxation),
kulaks subject to extraordinary measures (special tax and procurement levies, payments in advance, forced loans), and those poorer
and "economically weak" peasants (*bedniaks*), who were to be
pressed into collectives "with all the resources and means" at the
party's command.[46]

The herculean task of transforming rural Russia would have
posed immense difficulties even to a party with close ties to the
peasantry, but the weakness of the Bolshevik vanguard in this regard
made chaos inevitable. "He will drown the countryside in blood!"
Bukharin muttered in an unguarded moment; Krupskaia tried to add
Lenin's voice to other opponents, insisting he felt "it was madness
to believe that collectivization could be decided and dictated from
above."[47] But the greater this anxiety, the more Stalin displayed his
hostility to this "new, dangerous Rightist opposition," and the more
obsessional he became. The kulaks, redefined as a powerful and
dangerous enemy, were no longer to be treated simply with "extraordinary measures" but physically liquidated as a class, their
possessions seized, their land turned into collectives.[48] State security
forces were consequently mobilized for a massive "kulak resettlement
campaign," an appalling euphemism for forced deportation to remote
regions of Siberia or, for those lucky enough, attachment to industrial
labor batallions.

In the villages, this only further wrecked whatever efforts there
still were to proceed in a rational way. The distinctions between

different peasant strata in a particular area were often impossible to draw, yet collectives had to be organized. And if avoiding the label "kulak" now became virtually a matter of life and death to the peasants, who witnessed and reacted to the party's assault with loathing and horror, "ferreting them out" and "fulfilling party directives" became a matter of great urgency to local party officials, desperate to preserve their authority and their positions. "Achieve 100 percent in two days or turn in your party card!" "Down with Right-wing Deviationists!" Those who failed were quickly replaced by younger, more eager comrades; those who opposed the process altogether were soon stigmatized as "wreckers" and overwhelmed by a mass of new recruits to the party's ranks, anxious to seize the moment of revolutionary opportunity and advancement. Fittingly, *Pravda* editorials and party proclamations adopted military metaphor ("To the Grain Front!" "Victory in the Fight for Grain!"), honing the elements of conflict. In the fall and winter of 1929–30, the Soviet countryside erupted in civil war.

Even if one grants the urgency of full-scale industrialization, and the necessity both of changing rural social relations and modernizing agrarian production, the Soviet party's assault on the peasantry was a great and, above all, unnecessary tragedy—a frantic, improvised response to threatening circumstances that undoubtedly remained within the party's control. Stalin may have believed that state management of agricultural surpluses was a necessary component of rapid industrial development, but even strong adherents of obtaining this surplus through collectivization had in mind the expansion of state farms through investments and price adjustments, not by making collective farms, in Jerzy Karcz's felicitous phrase, instruments of collection rather than of collective work.[49] There is good evidence, in fact, that forced draft collectivization not only contributed little to the capitalization of Russian industry in the First Five-Year Plan, but may actually have turned the countryside into a net user of capital, doing serious damage to agrarian production and making the real tasks of industrial development much more difficult than they had to be.[50] The issue is still under debate, but at the very least, the net contribution of collectivized agriculture was far smaller than the party leadership maintained, and undoubtedly far smaller than would have been the case without the party's massive assault on the peasants. Most important, the transformation of Soviet Russia from a "backward" agrarian society to a complex, "modern" industrial nation would have meant in any case the eventual destruction of traditional peasant society, as it has everywhere. If for Mao rural backwardness was a problem, for Stalin it was the enemy, as were, consequently, the peasants.

TO BE IN THE VANGUARD

To be a member of the vanguard in the midst of this monumental upheaval was undoubtedly to experience a variety of contradictory feelings. The dialectics of progress through conflict was frightening in reality, even if, for some, theoretically pervasive; but for many the struggle itself was what communism was about. The immediate dangers were real. It seemed incredible that the party could survive the peasants' massive resistance. When entire villages began to burn their fields and slaughter their livestock to prevent their seizure, urgent shortages of food also threatened to precipitate widespread unrest among workers. There were also confusing orders from Moscow and "adventurism" on the part of many lesser officials who drove brutally toward 100 percent collectivization without regard for the immediate human or economic consequence. Achievement took on symbolic meaning through lies and empty statistics. In March 1930, Stalin himself warned local officials against becoming "dizzy with success" and demanded a halt to "excesses"; but while collectivization slowed markedly for a time (and collectives were dismantled in many places), there was no reversing direction.[51]

Russia *was* changing. The stunning decision to abandon all restraints in favor of rapid, "forced draft" industrialization, to adopt the optimal target figures for the First Five-Year Plan and then to try to achieve them in four years, to begin the massive collectivization of agriculture forcefully "from above"—all this *had* ended the obvious drift of NEP, as opponents and enthusiasts alike recognized, and set Soviet Russia on a course of industrial and social change historically unprecedented in its scale, its tempo, and the unnecessary horrors that accompanied it. Looking backward, one sights the truly heroic achievements of workers at massive construction complexes like the Magnitogorsk iron works, described with such poignancy by the American John Scott, and visualizes with awe a nation doubling its gross industrial production in four and a half years, almost tripling its supply of electricity, and increasing its output of iron ore, pig iron, coal, and oil by twice or more the levels of 1928. Russia's labor force doubled, as peasants driven from the countryside struggled on meager rations to build unfamiliar structures, use strange machinery, and construct a blast furnace, a plant, or a whole town that became in some important way "theirs." "Magnitogorsk in 1933," Scott writes, "a quarter of a million souls—communists, kulaks, foreigners, Tartars, convicted saboteurs and a mass of blue-eyed Russian peasants —making the biggest steel combinat in Europe in the middle of the barren Ural steppe. Money was spent like water, men froze, hungered, and suffered, but the construction work went on with a disregard for individuals and a mass heroism seldom paralleled in history."[52] One realizes the excitement of such momentous change, and understands what pulled Scott and thousands of other Westerners to leave the gloom and suffering of the capitalist Depression for the excitement and suffering of socialist growth.

And then one turns toward the countryside, to the horrendous brutality of "liquidating" kulaks, to the agony of the villages. A traditional way of life was being destroyed, not through evolutionary necessity or careful mobilization, but deliberately, mercilessly, and without convincing economic reason. Collectivization *was* securing party control over the harvest, but if the decision to collectivize was largely a response to critical procurement problems, the short-run benefits rapidly gave way to long-run—some would even argue permanent—damage. Strikingly, the procurement crisis returned. Marketings increased by as much as 20 percent between 1927–28 and 1931–32, but much of this was in the form of feed grain and irreplaceable meat, surrendered because livestock herds were being killed. Grave shortages continued and then grew even more severe. Gross production fell precipitously after 1931, yields declined, and staggering losses occurred in the procurement process itself, as the tonnage collected in many places far exceeded storage or distribution capacity, and much of it rotted away.[53]

With the heroism of "impossible" achievement thus came a new and momentous suffering. Hunger returned to the countryside, as well as the town, accompanied by "compulsory deliveries," a new and lasting form of requisitioning. Scenes of terrifying malnutrition and mortality, especially among children, accompanied reports of expensive new equipment rusting in the fields, delivered before it could be properly used, wasted in the compulsion to move ahead with an ever increasing tempo. Many urged caution; some, at great risk, insisted policies be changed. But for them, Stalin had an answer:

No comrades, the pace must not be slackened! On the contrary, we must quicken it as much as is within our powers and possibilities. This we must do to meet . . . our obligations to the workers and peasants of the USSR . . . and the world.

To slacken the pace would mean to lag behind; and those who lag behind are beaten. The history of Russia is one of ceaseless beating. She was beaten by the Mongol Khans, she was beaten by the Turkish Beys, she was beaten by Swedish feudal lords, she was beaten by Polish-Lithuanian pans, she was beaten by Anglo-French capitalists, she was beaten by Japanese barons, she was beaten by all—for her backwardness. For military backwardness, for cultural backwardness, for political backwardness, for industrial backwardness, for agricultural backwardness. She was beaten because to beat her was profitable, and went unpunished. . . .

We are fifty to one hundred years behind the advanced countries. We must make good this lag in ten years. Either we do, or they crush us![54]

But if the pace could not be slackened, neither could the peasants' fury: "They killed oxen, sheep, pigs, even cows; they slaughtered animals kept for breeding. In two nights the cattle in our village were reduced by half. . . . 'Kill, it's not ours now!' 'Kill, they'll take it from you if you don't!' 'Kill, you'll never taste meat in the collectives!' "[55] In response, party cadre were equally murderous: "They are slaughtering the livestock, those bastards! They'll choke themselves on meat, rather than hand the animals over to the collective farm. I say we hold a meeting, pass a resolution, and ask permission to shoot those found deliberately slaughtering. . . . Shoot them, I say! Whose permission do we need? The Peoples' Court can't do it, can it? Kill off some of those who have slaughtered cows in calf, and the rest will come to their senses. We must act with utmost severity!"[56]

"Utmost severity," however, was clearly not enough. It was as if, in Stalin's mind, the backward peasant, resisting change, became the defender of backwardness. Earlier attention to degrees of poverty, ignorance, class differentiations, virtually disappeared. Whole villages resisted; whole villages soon found themselves totally without food, forced to board up windows and doors, and trek as beggars to the towns. The fortunate got rations and work, perhaps as laborers on a construction project; if not, "they wandered through the mean and dusty streets, dragging bloodless, swollen legs, feeling out each passer-by with dog-like begging eyes."[57] Perhaps as many as ten million persons—several million households—were deported in this period under articles of a criminal code that made resistance equivalent to sedition and speaking out against collectivization equal to agitation against the regime.[58] In 1932, as foodstuffs accounted for almost one quarter of the value of all exports, massive famine swept through the middle and lower Volga regions, the Kuban and north Caucasus, and the Ukraine, the consequence of policy, not circumstance. It was the "most terrible and destructive famine" the Ukrainian people had ever experienced, one writer noted: "The peasants ate dogs, horses, rotten potatoes, the bark of trees, grass—anything they could find. Incidents of cannibalism were not uncommon. . . . And no matter what they did, they went on dying, dying, dying. They died singly and in families. They died everywhere—in yards, on streetcars and on trains. There was no one to bury these victims of the Stalinist famine."[59]

ENEMIES OF THE PEOPLE

Controlling food was a powerful weapon, but other coercive instruments were needed as well. Massive collectivization and forced draft industrialization involved compulsory mass mobilization on an unprecedented scale. Abandoning what many felt was the Leninist course of education and persuasion, the party vanguard faced the staggering task of forcing tens of millions to follow policies they rejected.

One obvious weapon to be developed for this process was the GPU, the state security police spawned from the civil war Cheka, and subsequently to be known by a whole series of equally sinister initials (OGPU, NKVD, MVD, KGB). By later standards, the activities of the GPU were relatively innocuous throughout the 1920s. Its responsibilities included combatting espionage and counterrevolution, policing the borders, guarding rail and water transport, fighting banditry, and staffing the special *kontsentratsionnye lagery* ("concentration camps") set up to house hardened criminals and political prisoners. The most notorious of these was on the Solovetskii Islands near the Arctic circle, which probably held in the mid-twenties from six to seven thousand prisoners. Solzhenitsyn's brilliant description of these camps is testimony enough to their horrors, but the fact remains that NEP was a period of relative calm in this area, even for members of former opposition parties. In matters of penal policy for nonpoliticals, it was even remarkably progressive.[60]

All of this changed drastically with the decision to collectivize. Reorganized into what were, in effect, fully armed military divisions, the OGPU was assigned responsibility first for grain confiscations and then for driving kulaks and other peasants off the land. Relocation centers had to be set up, camps and transport organized, and prisoners taken and supervised. Rapidly, the police burgeoned into a powerful apparatus, vast in scale, unlimited in power. Huge construction projects (like the infamous White Sea Canal) were begun under OGPU direction; by 1934, the OGPU was responsible for a significant share of lumber, coal, iron ore, and other heavy industrial production. The physical agony of slave labor under OGPU supervision was matched only by the mental torment of dissident intellectuals and "politicals," who found themselves suddenly arrested in 1929 and 1930 for "counterrevolutionary" objections to Stalin's policies and other forms of "subversion."

The arrests began in dramatic style. A group of engineers from the Don coal region were put on public trial in Moscow, accused of "wrecking." Specific charges included purchasing "unnecessary" equipment abroad and maintaining "criminal" ties with undesirable "bourgeois" elements. Four of the fifty-three defendants were acquitted, but there were several "confessions," and five were shot. The rest received sentences ranging from four to ten years.

The public nature of the trial, the vagueness of the charges, the confessions, and especially the executions were sinister indications of the real motive behind the arrests, which was to reintroduce terror as a means of making potentially recalcitrant social groups more pliant and to dissipate real or imagined resistance to Stalin's party policies. "Wrecking" as a capital crime could be applied to just about anything; to be sure its uses were truly unlimited, Stalin pressed into service the famous "analogy" provision of the Soviet penal code, which made any behavior a crime if it was merely analogous to specifically proscribed acts. Thereafter the show trials expanded. A number of leading Ukrainian intellectuals were charged with harboring secret ties with Poland, a clear warning to potential dissidents among the Soviet Union's national minorities; in 1930 Stalin announced the discovery of a subversive organization called the "Toiling Peasant Party," headed by a number of prominent agronomists who feared collectivization was pushing Russian agriculture to the verge of collapse. Eight prominent industrial engineers were brought to trial in November and December 1930 as members of a counterrevolutionary "Industrial party," including two members of Gosplan and the chairman of the Scientific and Technical Section of the Supreme Economic Council; in March 1931 there was a major trial of former Mensheviks, including V. G. Groman, a member of the Gosplan presidium. Here ties with anti-Soviet elements abroad were stressed. The defendants were, in effect, tried as traitors. All received long sentences and disappeared into the camps.

To be sure, there were precedents for what Stalin was doing. Terror had been an effective weapon during the civil war when the party also faced problems of mobilization and control; few could deny that collectivization was a time of genuine crisis. "Revolutionary legality is for us a problem which is 99 percent political," the prominent jurist Evgenii Pashukanis declared in 1930; courts, like the police, were an appropriate weapon.[61]

But terror now had a distinctly new aspect. Those being tried were not counterrevolutionaries but, at worst, merely critics of Stalin's policies. Many were effective and dedicated state employees. Menshevism was an absurd political libel, so were charges of close ties to foreign elements. There was no real evidence in the trials that any "wrecking" activities were deliberate; while some incidence of sabotage undoubtedly occurred, it was clearly not committed by the prominent officials brought to public trial. Their very removal, in fact, deprived the party of desperately needed talent.

It was also obvious that the very extent of the crisis was in no small measure attributable to the precipitous, careless, and arbitrary way in which party policies were being formulated and implemented; to the rampaging "enthusiasts" at lower levels anxious to please the "bosses" at the top; to the sheer irrationality of specific decisions even in terms of the overall goal of rapid collectivization and industrial growth. Most important, the very lack of reliable data, the contradictory statistics and instructions, made confusion inevitable and arbitrary behavior a necessary part of *any* policy implementation. For many in the party it was this aspect of Stalin's "revolutionary legality" that caused genuine concern, rather than any special moral repugnance. To commit oneself seriously to the success of the "great change" was virtually to require sharp criticism of party tactics.

Increasing numbers of dedicated Bolsheviks consequently began to express their concern. In late 1930 the first secretary of the party's Transcaucasian Committee spoke out against neglect of worker and peasant needs, and the "feudal and seignorial behavior" of some local officials. S. I. Syrtsov, chairman of the RSFSR Sovnarkom and Central Committee candidate, echoed these views, but both soon found themselves accused of forming a "rightist-leftist bloc," the label's absurdity testifying to the paradox of their position.[62] Shortly afterwards, a petition began to circulate among high-ranking party officials calling for Stalin's removal, framed by M. N. Riutin, an official in the Central Committee apparatus, and head of a Moscow district committee. Riutin's memorandum sharply criticized the implementation of collectivization policies and, according to Bukharin, attacked Stalin as the "evil genius of the Russian Revolution, motivated by a personal desire for power and revenge, who was bringing the Revolution to the verge of ruin."[63] Responding fiercely, Stalin demanded that Riutin be shot, along with those who had disseminated the memorandum, but this time the Politburo disagreed and resorted merely to expulsions from the party. Opposition grew particularly in Leningrad. Many here still smarted from Stalin's assault on Zinoviev and his supporters in 1925, and gathered strength behind efforts to replace Stalin with S. M. Kirov, the popular city committee chairman. By late 1932 and early 1933, at the height of what was rapidly becoming the most horrifying famine any nation in history had ever inflicted upon itself, cadre throughout the party's ranks undoubtedly felt Stalin had to be replaced.

Still, the Leader pressed forward, fixated on impossible output goals, seemingly oblivious to the chaotic and destructive aspects of Soviet Russia's "Great Change." (The Russian word *Vozhd'* ["leader"] was now consistently used in *Pravda* as a synonym for Stalin.) Rarely leaving Moscow, never inclined to tour the countryside and gain some appreciation of the real situation, Stalin lauded the heroics of "socialist construction" and measured success in statistics. National income had lept from 24.4 billion rubles in 1927–28 to 45.5 billion in 1932, pig iron from 3.3 million tons to 6.2, hard coal production from 35.4 tons to 64.3, the total number of workers in the labor force from 11.3 million to 22.8, some 7 million workers over the plan. The output of machinery of all kinds increased four-fold, the production of large-scale industry as a whole grew by 118 percent. The increase came at the expense of light industry and con-sumer goods, of course, but for the time being, this was of little moment. So were the countless number of lives lost on the industrial battlegrounds. Both a high rate of investment and the priority as-signed to heavy industry were continued in the Second Five-Year Plan, introduced in 1933.[64]

Indeed, by late 1933 the immediate crisis seemed to be passing. The massive shifts of population and resources had created monu-mental new problems in transport, and goods of all sorts were in preciously short supply; but the industrial foundations of Stalinist socialism were being laid, without the much feared Western (or Japanese) incursions. By February 1934, Stalin felt sufficiently con-fident to bring ranking party officials together again for the first All-Union Party Congress in four years, the Congress of Victors. One can only conjecture what his thoughts might have been as he looked out over the more than 1,900 delegates, or how he might have felt to learn that in balloting for the Central Committee, he received fewer votes than any other candidate! S. M. Kirov, with only three votes against him, emerged as the party's most trusted and popular figure.[65]

Nine months later, Kirov was dead, killed by the assassin Nikolaev. Evidence of Stalin's complicity is circumstantial, but there are few political murders in which the circumstances are more compelling. Within days, Kirov's personal bodyguard had died in an automobile "accident" while being brought by the secret police for questioning (he was the only injury); within weeks, the Leningrad apparatus itself was devastated. Kirov's death gave Stalin precisely the reason he needed to begin a wholesale purge. Who in Leningrad allowed such lax security and why? Who had failed in their responsibility for protecting the party? Who was weak and lacked sufficient vigilance to prevent counterrevolutionary terrorists from penetrating the party apparatus? Where else had subversives penetrated? How long had they masqueraded? After "intense investigation," Nikolaev was found to be a supporter of Zinoviev and an "agent" of foreign sources. Soon Zinoviev and Kamenev themselves were directly implicated, and later

Trotsky as well. The extent of conspiracy within the party appeared to be vast.

To be in the vanguard in 1935 and to remain an honest, committed Bolshevik like Evgeniia Ginzburg, whose memoirs *Into the Whirlwind* depict this period in stunning fashion, was thus to face a truly paralyzing set of dilemmas. The possibility that the enormous difficulties of collectivization and industrialization were in part the consequence of deliberate subversion could not be overlooked. At best one might argue that party officials had not done enough to avoid miscalculations and minimize the excessive brutality, but was this the result of error or indifference, or was it calculated? Stalin now called for absolute vigilance. Party cards were to be turned in and reissued only to the absolutely loyal. Errors were to be freely admitted in self-criticism sessions, and party members judged on the extent to which even errors and indifference constituted "oppositionism" and perhaps, by analogy, support for the party's enemies. Arrests at various levels began to occur. Startling rumors about this or that comrade being an "enemy agent" began to circulate. Confessions soon appeared, tensions grew. Hard-working comrades of unquestionable integrity were dragged off by the police, but did this mean that even more errors were being made, or had the police also been infiltrated by subversives, as they appeared to have been in Leningrad? On the other hand, to protest that a comrade had been falsely accused was itself a dangerous attack on the party; if the person arrested suddenly confessed, defenders were "guilty" either of allying with traitors or of insufficient "vigilance" themselves.

Eisenstein's films became "worthless, vicious," Mandelstam's poetry "decadent," Shostakovich's *Lady Macbeth* an "ungainly, muddled flood of sounds," publicly condemned in *Pravda* against a backdrop of letters from terrified artists and writers demanding death for subversives, wreckers, and spies. The literary depiction of socialist reality as it was gave way to a "socialist realist" idealism, describing a fantasy world of what should be. Party officials became awesome critics. "Just before the Theater of Meyerhold was shut down, Kaganovich came to a performance. . . . As was to be expected, Kaganovich did not like the play. Stalin's faithful comrade in arms left almost in the middle. Meyerhold, who was in his sixties then, ran out into the street after Kaganovich. Kaganovich and his retinue got in the car and drove off. Meyerhold ran after the car, and ran until he fell."[66] The great theater director was soon arrested and killed.

The nightmare of Stalin's high purges is by now familiar history, but the extent of the carnage both within and outside the party between 1936 and 1939 remains staggering. In the summer of 1936 Zinoviev, Kamenev, Smirnov, and others went on public trial as the Trotskyite-Zinoviev United Center, amidst an orchestration of public calls for vengeance. "Shoot these rotten agents of the German Gestapo," Khristian Rakovskii pleaded in *Pravda* shortly before his own execution; indeed, secret police cellars began to run with blood. Within weeks of the United Center trial, "Trotskyites" and "Zinovievites" were arrested by the thousands, sucked into the whirlwind, as Ginzburg describes so poignantly, with no means to resist.[67] Piatakov, Radek, and leading Comintern officials went on trial in January 1937 (as the Anti-Soviet Trotskyite Center); early in 1938, Bukharin, Rykov, and nineteeen others were tried as the Anti-Soviet Bloc of Rightists and Trotskyites. Virtually every close friend and associate of Lenin during the years of struggle and revolution found himself fighting to survive. Stalin's executioners swept in all directions. The ranks of every conceivable "tendency," "inclination," "grouping," or "bloc" were decimated virtually beyond belief.

Yet "virtually" is an important modifier. The fact is that the accusations *were* widely believed, inside Soviet Russia and abroad. The American Ambassador Joseph Davies saw the trials as unravelling a vast German effort against the party and Russia's security. So did Winston Churchill. And indeed, Hitler for years had strained to launch such a fusillade against the Bolshevik leadership, striking the very core of what he called the "insidious Communist scum."

The vanguard fell in Russia, however, not from Nazi or White Guard attack, or the strength of bourgeois counterrevolutionaries, but because its power had become concentrated without check or qualification in the hands of persons oblivious to socialist consciousness and morality, totally ruthless in their attachment to power, indifferent to suffering, and able in an awesome, frightening way to effect their will. Socialist commitment to working with and through the masses was lost in the impulse to command. Need became habit, reinforced by an ever-expanding *apparat*; bureaucratic authoritarianism itself became a magnet for obedient, frightened careerists anxious to secure their status. In the process, worker and peasant welfare became distant abstractions for a transmogrified party, itself and its power isolated from the ordinary course of human affairs. The awful tragedy of socialist construction under Stalin lay in the *needless* costs, the millions who died in the countryside *after* the battle to collectivize had already been won (a battle itself unnecessary in the forms Stalin adopted) and the millions more who died in the purges and camps because of an insatiable desire to control, to dominate, and to identify and destroy "enemies." Of the 1,966 delegates to the Congress of Victors in 1934, only 59 returned to the Eighteenth Congress in 1939. Of the 139 members and candidate members elected to the 1934 Central Committee, only 24 returned. By official decree, 98 had been found guilty of "treason" and shot. Thus the vanguard itself succumbed in Stalin's revolution from above, replaced by a totally new elite cadre, trained and raised in the Stalinist mold.

To be sure, Russia *had* been transformed. National income had again doubled under the Second Five-Year Plan. Gross industrial production, at 43,300 million rubles in 1932, lept to 95,500 million by 1937; electricity output grew from 13.4 billion kilowatt hours to 36.2; pig iron from 6.2 million tons to 14.5; steel from 5.9 to 17.7.[68] But however substantial the successes of Stalinist industrialization— and they were, indeed, historically unprecedented in tempo and sheer magnitude—the unspeakable costs of the 1930s clearly prevented socialist Russia from becoming as strong as it might have, even in terms of Stalinist economic objectives. In the Leader's own misperception of freedom and rationality, revolutionary Russia lost both, tainting forever the genuine and heroic accomplishments of Soviet socialist transformation. The contradictions are staggering. At precisely the time that Russians everywhere lived in dreadful fear of a midnight rap on the door, the world's first socialist nation pulled itself exhausted into the community of "advanced" industrial societies; as millions shuddered and froze in the agony of arctic labor camps, the economic foundations for a developed, technologically sophisticated socialism were laid; as the vanguard of vanguards lapsed into barbarism, Russia itself would never again be beaten for its backwardness.

6

GREAT PATRIOTIC STRUGGLES: The Soviet Union and China in World War II

"Nationalism," Chalmers Johnson writes in his book *Revolutionary Change*, "remains the fundamental organizational principle of the peoples of the world, and no set of alternative values—least of all that of 'proletarian internationalism'—has even begun to challenge it."[1] Nationalism acted in China as a principal ideological underpinning to Communist mobilization of peasants against the Japanese, Johnson argues; in the USSR, the emergence of Stalin's autocratic politics and his single-minded concentration in the 1930s on building Russian national strength have been seen as more closely paralleling the efforts of Ivan the Terrible or Peter the Great than Lenin. Mao, and possibly Stalin as well, were no less radical in their personal commitments, the argument runs; but their success lay in popular allegiance to nationalist goals and values, rather than revolutionary precepts.

The problem with this argument—"endlessly and accurately repeated," according to Johnson—is not that nationalist values were unimportant in the Russian and Chinese revolutionary experience, but that the compelling appeal of social reform is obscured. Studies by Gillin and others on China have shown convincingly that however important the struggle against Japan may have been in some

167

areas and for some social groups in mobilizing support for the CCP, the commitment to radical land reform and the social transformation of the countryside remained the principal source of Communist strength.[2] This is not to diminish the importance of nationalism in either popular consciousness, particularly for some social strata, or the party's own sense of national identity. But it is to argue that the role of nationalism and nationalistic values must be understood in terms of their relationship to the goals of revolutionary social change, not as generalized "agents of political mobilization." To accept Johnson's argument is to reduce the historic importance of both Soviet Russia and China as revolutionary societies and to deemphasize the degree to which popular support for the CPSU and the CCP—and hence their political legitimacy—turned at crucial points of the revolutionary process on commitments to radical change. Nationalist values undoubtedly played an important role in structuring Russian and Chinese development. The question is: how did these values affect and transform revolutionary commitments?

THE UNITED FRONT IN CHINA

In China, at a strategic level, there was no contradiction at all between nationalism and social revolution for the Communists. No important gains in the struggle to transform the country could be realized so long as China remained dominated, in whole or part, by foreign imperialists. By 1936, the imperialist threat was direct, military, and growing in strength. With Japanese control over Manchuria consolidated by 1932, the danger to North China became paramount. Despite considerable pressure from a noncommunist nationalist movement and the deep dissatisfaction of powerful warlords whose territory had been overtaken or was endangered by the Japanese, Chiang Kai-shek continued to insist that the primary enemy China faced was not Japan, but the pockets of Communist power that continued to challenge his authority. Compromise with the Japanese was far less threatening to his power than the risks involved in a struggle against them, which would, of necessity, involve mass mobilization and extensive cooperation with Mao, Zhou Enlai, and their followers. Chiang had successfully reaped the benefits of that route in the 1920s, but there was no certainty he could repeat the performance. For the Communists, of course, without mass mobilization through revolutionary action, genuine resistance to Japan was impossible; without a successful movement to expel the Japanese, the gains of the revolution were forfeit. There was no choice at this strategic level.

Tactics, however, were something else again. Effective resistance required the widest possible coalition of forces. Yet the very agrarian policies that had resulted in such rapid growth for the Communists alienated significant sectors of the population and made a united front against Japan difficult, if not impossible. How could the Communists continue to present themselves as agents of radical rural transformation if they could not, at the same time, attack the gentry base of Nationalist strength?

There was local tension in Shaanxi as well. The successes of the movement there were limited in both scope and ambition. Isolated from larger national currents, Communist partisans were vulnerable to parochialism, degeneration into simply another, relatively more egalitarian, secret society. By some peasants, indeed, they were known (and admired) as the "Soviet clan"; many sought their favor and protection with no clear sense of the movement's larger goals. The Long Marchers brought with them the most varied revolutionary experience: direct participation in a coalition government that, albeit briefly, had pretensions to national power; hard lessons learned through defeat in both urban and rural China; contacts, however problematic, with the world's first and only socialist power; a tempering through hardship that rivalled the history of any revolutionary movement in the world; and, perhaps above all, an absolute determination to challenge the government of Chiang Kai-shek for state power. Tensions between newcomers and those who had struggled to secure the very base to which they had fled marked these early years of what has become known as the Yanan period, and were exacerbated by the problem confronting the Communists with respect to the struggle against Japan.

Simply put, the question was which took precedence: civil war against the KMT or national war against Japan? Moscow, as in the past, had an unequivocal answer. However sincerely internationalist Soviet policy toward China might have been originally, it had quickly become a dependent variable of the necessities of "socialism in one country." By 1935, in the interests of protecting socialism in the USSR (and coincidentally, of course, Stalin's regime), Communist parties throughout the world were deeply engaged in the establishment and maintenance of united front governments, whose relevance to the needs for social change in any particular country were often obscure. In China there was no near hope of Communist victory. In the meantime it was crucial to the Soviet Union that the government of Chiang Kai-shek be induced to resist Japan rather than reach a compromise that would free Japan to turn against Russia. This dictated, once again, a policy of alliance with the Nationalists. To this end, the first appeal for a united front between the Chinese Communists and Chiang came not from Yanan, but from Moscow. Issued in the summer of 1935, it was not even known to its putative proponents until November. Mao's report on the united front the following month made no mention of the earlier Comintern manifesto, and on the specific issue of allying with Chiang it was firmly negative.

Within the Chinese party there was considerable (and understandable) resistance to the very concept of a united front, much less one that included Chiang himself. Mao characterized (and perhaps caricatured) the opposition as those who believed that the "forces of revolution must be pure, absolutely pure, and the road of the revolution must be straight, absolutely straight." The national bourgeoisie and warlords were viewed by the opposition as "entirely and eternally counter-revolutionary"; no concessions should be made to rich peasants; intellectuals were "three-day revolutionaries whom it is dangerous to recruit." In sum, "the united front is an opportunist tactic." But, Mao argued, like everything else, "revolution always follows a tortuous road."[3]

According to Mao, the road allows for many detours. The united front would include "those who are interested only in the national revolution and not in the agrarian revolution, and even, if they so desire, those who may oppose Japanese imperialism . . . though they are not opposed to the European and U.S. imperialists." The government of the Soviet area would be transformed and renamed, from a "workers' and peasants' republic" to a "people's republic" representing the entire nation—with the exception of the "landlord and comprador classes, the lackeys of imperialism" and the "camp of traitors" led by Chiang Kai-shek. Concessions must be made to rich peasants and even small landlords, and the agrarian revolution must be significantly modified. The revolution, at this stage, remained bourgeois-democratic, not socialist. China, Mao insisted, was not Russia. "The change in the revolution will come later. In the future the democratic revolution will inevitably be transformed into a socialist revolution." But that change would not be soon.[4]

What Mao had to argue most vigorously against was the vivid and bitter memory of his listeners. Dealing with their fear and anger directly, he urged them to look at the essential difference in the current situation:

> Now we have a strong Communist Party and a strong Red Army and we also have the base areas of the Red Army. . . . The national united front will live and grow as long as the Communist Party and the Red Army live and grow. Such is the leading role of the Communist Party and the Red Army in the national united front. The Communists are no longer political infants and are able to take care of themselves and to handle relations with their allies.[5]

On the issue of Chiang's inclusion, however, Mao remained adamant. Pressure from Stalin perhaps, combined with an independent assessment of the value of Chiang to a truly national united front led to a shift in policy by May of 1936, and in December the issue was joined in a spectacular way. Enraged at the refusal of his warlord ally, Zhang Xueliang, to vigorously pursue the battle against the Communists, Chiang Kai-shek flew to Xian to personally press his case. Zhang, who had been pushed out of his territory by the Japanese, not only refused to comply with Chiang's wishes but arrested him and telegraphed the glad news to Yanan.

At an emergency meeting of 300 activists in the late afternoon of December 13, Mao voiced the passionate desire of all who had survived Chiang's butchery in Shanghai, his five annihilation campaigns, his ruthless, unrelenting pursuit of the Long Marchers: "Since April 12, 1927, Chiang has owed us a blood debt as high as a mountain. Now it is time to liquidate the blood debt." He proposed a public trial "by the people of the whole country."[6] Instead Zhou Enlai flew to Xian and successfully negotiated for Chiang's release. It was a logical, if dispassionate, outcome of the crisis. For whatever Chiang's blood debt to the Communists, he, like Sun Yat-sen before him, was a necessary, even crucial, figure in the formation of a nationwide united front. Zhang Xueliang had kidnapped him in order to force his hand on the issue of resisting Japan and seems to have had no intention of turning Chiang over to the Communists for a show trial. The alliance system Chiang Kai-shek had worked out with various warlords may have been thin, but he remained central to it. Abandon him and the country might well disintegrate again into multiple civil war just at the moment of maximum Japanese pressure.

There remained important choices to be made, even within the general framework of a united front that included Chiang Kai-shek, and on these Mao's differences with Moscow and its most loyal Chinese representative, Wang Ming, held significant implications for both the immediate situation and the future. Mao's outline of the united front stressed the importance of an independent territorial base, a Red Army, and the leading role of the Communist party. These alone guaranteed that a renewed united front would not result in another April twelfth; they must never be compromised. For Wang Ming, as for Stalin, maintaining the front was paramount; anything could be compromised. Moreover, Mao's confidence in the efficacy of a rural strategy struck Wang Ming as frankly ludicrous, as it did others in the party whose dedication to a more orthodox version of Marxism-Leninism remained unshaken. The great attraction of the united front was that it once more opened the cities of China to the Communist party. At last the vanguard could return to the home of its natural mass base. The "stable and longlasting cooperation" with the KMT that both Wang Ming and the Comintern urged was intended to extend well beyond the end of the Sino-Japanese war. Should it require the dissolution of the Communists' independent base and army, so be it. Like Mao, Wang Ming believed the stage of the revolution remained bourgeois-democratic, not socialist. Unlike Mao, however, he saw the KMT, despite its sorry record, as its leader. The Communist party's role remained subordinate and supportive.

The actual terms of the united front represented a compromise between what the KMT wanted (to which Wang Ming was ready to agree) and the maximum concessions Yanan would make. Both the land revolution (insofar as it involved confiscation) and armed insurrection against the KMT would end. The Red Army would be renamed the Eighth Route Army and would function in cooperation with KMT forces against the Japanese. It would not, however, be dissolved or fragmented; nor would it accept KMT officers. The Shaanxi Soviet would also be renamed as a Special Border Region with provisions for universal suffrage and democratic elections. In return, the Nationalist government promised an end to the civil war and the blockade of Communist areas; democratic rights within its territory; subsidies to the Eighth Route and reformed New Fourth Armies; a united struggle against Japan; and a serious effort to improve the lot of workers and peasants in the area it governed.

Wang Ming, under the slogan "everything for the united front," left Yanan for Wuhan, insisting that the fate of the entire nation rested on the successful defense of that city. Mao, in secure control of the party, army, and government organization in the northwest, graciously agreed that Wuhan was important. But, suspecting it would fall, he continued to plan on the expansion and strengthening of rear-area bases.

However different this united front was from the disastrous "bloc within" pursued a decade earlier, the switch from all-out struggle against the KMT to alliance was not easy. Men wept as they removed the Red Army insignia from their military caps and replaced it with the Eighth Route Army designation. For a time, guerrillas holed up in the remnant mountain bases of southeast China were not even aware that a truce in the civil war had been declared. Constantly embattled, units that had been left behind in Jiangxi found it hard to imagine the armies they had been fighting were now their allies. Chen Yi, later foreign minister of the People's Republic of China, described what life had been like for those fighting in southern Jiangxi:

> Towards dawn
> Our men wake early
> Dew-drenched clothes and bedding even in summer
>   are cold;
> In the trees cicadas shrill;
> Grass clings to our uniforms.
>
> Towards noon
> Bellies rumble with hunger;
> Three months we have been cut off from supplies;
> We can count the grains of rice left in our bags;
> Our meal is a mess of herbs.

But in August 1937 this world turned over:

> After ten years' war
> KMT and Communists collaborate again.
> On recalling past fallen comrades
> Tears of grief stain my sleeves.[7]

That the switch in policy was accomplished with reluctance, but without active resistance, is due only in part to party discipline. More important was the conception of a unified and independent China shared by all party members, their willingness to participate in a halt to the civil war if it would facilitate victory over Japan. This was not patriotism in the usual sense of the term, but a nationalist commitment to the achievement of a strong, sovereign China, free to choose its own destiny, a commitment shared by Chinese of various classes or class strata and one that the Communists could honor.

In contrast to Russia's situation during World War I, the Chinese Communists were exempt from concern over the success or failure of revolutions in other countries. Whatever complexity the united front involved, there was no thought that it compromised revolutionary movements elsewhere in the world, as so many had felt Brest-Litovsk did. Indeed, insofar as it strengthened the Soviet Union against the possibility of attack by Japan, the united front made a positive contribution to the world revolution.

And yet, the united front policy still raised questions in a Chinese context that had disturbed the sleep of many Bolsheviks in the early 1920s: how did one keep a revolution honest? what guidelines insured that necessary compromises did not become opportunistic betrayals? What seems, in retrospect, to have been essential was the attainment of meaningful independence and the courage to take vast risks without losing sight of the ultimate goal or acting in such a way as to preclude reaching that goal for the sake of a short-term gain. What was required was the capacity to see the world in dialectical terms, understanding the way in which every action shaped future possibilities.

REVOLUTIONARY VIRTUE IN MILITARY NECESSITY

The task of making the united front work required not only the cooperation of the KMT but also the clearest possible understanding by all party members of precisely what it involved. Throughout the early years of the front, Mao, in essays for party publications, lectures at Central Committee meetings, and interviews with foreign journalists, tried to instruct the membership on its opportunities, its necessities, and its dangers. Clarity as to the purposes of the front would enable the Communists to avoid "capitulationism" on the one hand, "adventurism" on the other. Absolutely central was the maintenance of party independence: "There is no doubt that independence within the united front is relative and not absolute. . . . But this relative independence must not be denied; ideologically, politically and organizationally, each party must have its relative independence, that is, relative freedom."[8]

Cooperation with the KMT focused on specific tasks; it also allowed for enormous flexibility, and responsiveness to shifting political circumstances and class forces. The tactical goal of the party was to move the KMT to a policy of total resistance, not to accommodate to the partial resistance it had so far mounted. The KMT had to be brought to understand that without mass mobilization there was no hope of successfully resisting Japan. A united front of two parties, as such, was hopeless: "So far, the united front has in fact been confined to the two parties, while the masses of the workers, peasants, soldiers and urban petty bourgeoisie and a large number of other patriots have not yet been aroused, called into action, organized or armed." Clinging to "autocracy and suppression," Chiang's government "has estranged itself from the people, the army from the masses, and the military command from the rank and file."[9] The "war of partial resistance advocated by the KMT," Mao conceded, "also constitutes a national war and is revolutionary in character to a certain extent," but it could never defeat Japan. "We stand for a national revolutionary war in the full sense, a war in which the entire people are mobilized, in other words, total resistance. . . . Herein lies the difference in principle between the stand of the Communist Party and the present stand of the Kuomintang. . . . If Communists forget this difference in principle, they will be unable to guide the War of Resistance correctly, they will be powerless to overcome the Kuomintang's one-sidedness, and they will debase themselves to the point of abandoning their principles and reduce their Party to the level of the Kuomintang."[10]

The mobilization Mao urged was political. For a time, after the opening of full-scale hostilities with Japan, it was the "enemy's gun-fire and the bombs dropped by enemy aeroplanes that brought news of the war to the great majority of the people." It was a kind of mobilization, of course, "but it was done for us by the enemy, we did not do it ourselves." Now that must be turned around: "The mobilization of the common people throughout the country will create a vast sea in which to drown the enemy." The army and people must understand "why the war must be fought and how it concerns them." The aim of the War of Resistance was to "drive out Japanese imperialism and build a new China of freedom and equality." "Our job," Mao instructed students at the Yanan Association for the Study of the War of Resistance, "is not to recite our political programme to the people, for nobody will listen to such recitations; we must link the political mobilization for the war with developments in the war and with the life of the soldiers and the people, and make it a con-tinuous movement." How? "By word of mouth, by leaflets and bulle-tins, by newspapers, books and pamphlets, through plays and films, through schools, through the mass organizations and through our cadres."[11]

As for the difficult relationship between the class and national struggle, it was clear that during the war "everything must be sub-ordinated to the interests of resistance." Yet classes and class struggle "are facts. . . . We do not deny the class struggle, *we adjust it.*"[12] The central question was "will the proletariat lead the bourgeoisie in the united front, or the bourgeoisie the proletariat? Will the Kuomintang draw over the Communist Party, or the Communist Party the Kuomintang?" Everyone knew how those questions had been answered in 1927. This time out, there was cause for optimism; perhaps, ten years after Stalin's original instructions, Chiang could be squeezed like a lemon.

Through its effort to fulfill the terms of the agreement with Chiang, through its overwhelming dedication to total resistance against the Japanese, the CCP made good its claim to represent the interests of all nationalistic Chinese. Opening itself to an influx of anti-Japanese nationalists of all classes, Yanan itself became a school for people's war. Thousands of patriotic students and intellectuals made their way through Japanese and puppet army lines to join the cause. By 1942, Yanan boasted twenty full-time schools, whose task it was to train Communists and non-Communists alike in the political and military skills necessary for leadership in the resistance. Schools were divided into party and united front institutions of which, in the latter category, Kangda (Anti-Japanese Military and Political University) was the best known. Over 100,000 young people were trained there, gaining basic military knowledge and, for most, their first direct study of Marxism.

Out of necessity, a broad range of virtues was forged. Students dug their own class and living rooms out of the loess soil (over 170 caves in one particularly strenuous two-week period); local peasants, Red Army soldiers, students, and intellectuals from outside the border region mixed in the same class and learned from each other; production campaigns rendered the school almost entirely self-sufficient in food grain. "The work," one student wrote later, "was not heavy, but it was a stern test to the majority of the young students who had never worked with a pick before. After a day of work, we were all sweaty and our two hands were studded with blisters. . . . However, it was precisely such labor which steeled and educated us and transformed our way of thinking."[13]

The pledge to universal suffrage was kept. Local government officials were chosen, with party members restricted to no more than one-third of the possible posts. Industrial policy was equally restrained. All "unnecessary strikes" were to be avoided and laws that encouraged the management of various enterprises by the workers themselves were repealed. Instead, "the workers are advised not to press demands beyond the capacity of the enterprise. In non-Soviet districts, though we support the improvement of the living conditions of the workers, we similarly do not willfully intensify the anticapitalistic struggle. . . . The *joint interests* of capitalists and workers are built on the foundation of struggle against imperialism."[14] Peasant mobilization was to be directed specifically at "feudal exploitation," and the interests of such rural capitalist forces as existed were to be not merely protected, but encouraged. Tax policy, for example, was directed at making it more profitable for landowners and rich peasants to invest in industry rather than continue to put surplus funds into various forms of usury or the amassing of large lots of land that would have to be farmed by long-term hired labor.[15]

WAR WITH JAPAN

From 1937 to 1941, Yanan policy was firmly focused on the creation of "good government" along lines that had wide appeal within the Border Region and, as word of it filtered out, for Chinese everywhere. However, on the KMT side, the united front was dictated in the first instance by entirely opportunistic political and military considerations. A growing non-Communist "national salvation movement" combined with Zhang Xueliang's dramatic actions in Xian had given Chiang Kai-shek very little room for maneuver. Although he paid for his brief mutiny with a lifetime under house arrest, Zhang had forced the Generalissimo to a stance of resistance against Japan from which it would be difficult to retreat. But he made concessions grudgingly, violated the cease fire agreement with regularity, and stalled on making those reforms in army, government, and social policy that were the prerequisites of "total resistance."

Japan initiated all-out war against China in July 1937. Peking fell virtually without a fight, and the major coastal cities followed in quick succession. Driven further and further from its urban base, Chiang Kai-shek's government finally holed up in Chongqing, the remote capital of Sichuan province. Confident that the United States would be drawn into the war, Chiang's dedication to cooperation with Yanan faded rapidly. Shortly after Pearl Harbor, with all of China's major cities and railroad lines occupied by Japan (whose army conducted a "three-alls" campaign of utter brutality in the countryside—"burn all, kill all, loot all"), Chiang stretched the united front to the breaking point. In the southeast, the New Fourth Army was almost wiped out in a surprise attack by Chiang's forces, and in the northwest Chiang added to Japanese pressure by strengthening his blockade of Communist base areas. With the United States now committed to defend "free China," Chiang had only to offer nominal loyalty to the united front, sufficient to convince both Americans and patriotic Chinese that he was not sabotaging the war effort for personal political reasons.

ZHENGFENG

Meanwhile, military reverses shrank the region under direct Communist control to almost half its former size. This time there was really no place to run. Instead of cutting losses and consolidating what remained, however, Mao was now in sufficient control of party policy to launch a kind of internal Long March, a choice he probably would have made in 1934 had he had the power. The *zhengfeng* ("rectification") movement, which began in 1942 at the height of military pressure on Yanan, was an extraordinary revitalization movement, directed at reforming the party (grown from 40,000 in 1937 to perhaps as much as 800,000 by 1942) and its relationship to the people. Instead of retreat, Mao insisted on upping the revolutionary ante, confident that mass mobilization was the only possible response to Yanan's crisis and convinced that only a renewed party could inspire and maintain that mobilization.

What was to be undertaken was a direct confrontation with tensions that had been present in Yanan from the very first: between local cadres whose experience was rooted in land reform and who operated at district levels, and the new cadres, working on a regional level, who had only limited experience of village life and peasant expectations; between a decentralized, fairly rudimentary administrative system and one that, stressing efficiency and stability, preferred clear lines of authority and top-down implementation; between the struggle of local peasants to regain at best secure subsistence and the revolutionary vision of Communist organizers who looked to the creation of a proletarian world in which all that the peasants clung to would be cheerfully tossed aside. There was tension too between the Communist promise, and premise, of equality for women and the ferocious hold of patriarchy on the peasants of North China; between the non-Marxist abstract nationalism of much of Yanan's student and professional population and the peasants' need to see in the most graphic terms what concrete links existed between victory over Japan and their ability to survive on the land.

With *zhengfeng*, the party, as one historian put it, "went to school."[16] For two years, small groups in every unit of government, education, and the military engaged in the most intense discussion, debate, criticism, and self-criticism. Their curriculum consisted of eighteen documents, only four of Soviet origin (which led a Russian observer to bemoan the "anti-Soviet" nature of the entire campaign). *Zhengfeng* was a declaration of maturity and independence. The work of Chinese revolutionaries, supplemented by foreign classics, was sufficient to educate cadres of the kind this revolution required.

The same methodology and some of the same material were used in nonparty study sessions. Every aspect of life in the base areas was examined, from the position of women to the role of art and literature. Mao, lecturing at length on the widest variety of subjects, returned to the role he perhaps always held in highest esteem, that of teacher. And the discussions yielded immediate, practical results.

A campaign for "crack troops and simple administration," for example, shifted the focus of government work down to the village levels. Administrative personnel in Yanan itself were radically reduced and cadres were sent to the villages to work directly with local peasant activists. There was an equally important move to decentralize education. Schools were to become the direct servants of the village population, their curricula shaped by the known needs of local peasants rather than some universal conception of what they should need. Economically, the push was toward a "guerrilla model" of development in which the practice of one brigade, the 359th, was widely propagandized as a model for emulation. The brigade had been assigned a barren tract of mountain land in the winter of 1939–40. It lacked everything—tools, houses, and adequate food. Under their commander, Wang Zhen, the soldiers of the brigade foraged for wood which they sold to local villagers in exchange for grain. As for tools, they used whatever they could find; for example, once a young soldier had discovered an abandoned temple bell. "It was," Wang Zhen recalled, "too heavy to bring down and I don't know how it even got up there. Liu dug a big hole underneath and smelted it on the spot and we found some blacksmiths who were willing to teach our men how to make tools from the 2,000 lbs. of iron we got from the bell." By 1944, the brigade had reclaimed thousands of acres and expanded its activities from agriculture to light industry. Like some of the schools in Yanan, the brigade was virtually self-sufficient in food production.[17]

The 359th was a model for both civilians and the military. The lessons it taught about the fullest utilization of all resources, human and material, working cooperatively and inventively, could be applied anywhere. As important, the 359th, by growing its own food, reduced the burden of military support on the civilian population. The hope was that *all* the institutions of government could at least contribute to the production of food and other necessary goods so as to relieve the strains of the KMT-Japanese blockade. Of equal importance, the production campaign insisted upon the high value of manual labor for everyone, intellectual or soldier, bureaucrat or teacher.

With *zhengfeng* also came a renewed stress on implementing the united front policy of double reduction (rent and interest) that had been introduced in 1937 with the end of outright confiscation and redistribution of land. The importance of double reduction is sometimes denied because it would seem to assume the existence of widespread tenancy, which did not in fact prevail in North China. But double reduction went far beyond simple controls on the amount of rent and interest extracted from the peasantry. It was, instead, a way to significantly transfer wealth within villages without resorting to outright and widespread confiscation, which the united front prohibited. Cadres were directed to lead the villagers in a struggle which the peasants themselves had to conduct to correct abuses they themselves identified. Landlords and, to a lesser extent, rich peasants were to "settle accounts" with those they had exploited. The profit gained from usurious debts or underpaid hired labor was to be repaid, and in many cases this required that landlords sell their land, a neat reversal of the usual order of things. In some districts, neither rent nor interest was the issue so much as the obligatory unpaid labor poor peasant owners were forced to supply local landlords. What mattered was the careful identification of the almost infinite variety of ways in which the poor were exploited, followed by direct action to end that exploitation. In case after case, "rent reduction" quickly moved beyond its limited goal and, through one means or another, led to a redistribution of village wealth. The policy was thus far more radical than its mild title would lead one to believe, and the KMT accordingly argued that it was a violation of front policy. Looking closely at the object of some 1,782 "struggle" movements conducted in the base area in one two-year period, Suzanne Pepper concluded that the focus of the overwhelming majority was on "local tyrants and corruption," the arbitrary use of political power and social position by landlords, rich peasants, and on occasion, middle peasants as well. Working through associations of poor peasants and hired laborers, cadres sent down to the villages from Yanan sought to break that traditional power, lead peasants in the direct redress of grievances through their own actions, and mobilize their energy for the defense of the "fruits" of their struggle.[18]

The practical changes wrought by *zhengfeng* are inseparable from their theoretical assumptions. The movement was all of a piece, and it is misleading to separate out its elements. Like the Long March, it was "a manifesto, a propaganda force, and a seeding machine."[19] Mao's discussion of the role of art and literature in the revolution was as major a component as the reforms in education or the reactivation of double reduction. Central to the whole was the articulation of the "mass line" as both a style of work and a first principle for understanding what the work was about. "Our comrades must understand," Mao insisted, "that we do not study Marxism-Leninism because it is pleasing to the eye, or because it has some mystical value, like the doctrines of the Taoist priests. . . . Marxism-Leninism has no beauty, nor has it any mystical value. It is only extremely useful." And further, "abstract Marxism" did not exist, but only "concrete Marxism," Marxism "that has taken on a national form." Nothing would come easily. "The intellectuals must identify themselves with the masses and must serve the masses. This process may, in fact it definitely will, produce much suffering and friction." And what was to be the manner of service? "All correct leadership is from the masses, to the masses." Mao wrote.

> Take the ideas of the masses (scattered and unsystematic) and concentrate them (through study turn them into concentrated and systematic ideas), then go to the masses and propagate and explain these ideas until the masses embrace them as their own, hold fast to them and translate them into action, and test the correctness of these ideas in such action. Then once again concentrate ideas from the masses and once again take them to the masses so that the ideas are persevered in and carried through. And so on, over and over again in an endless spiral, with the ideas becoming more correct, more vital, and richer each time.[20]

For Mao, as opposed to many in the party, the hundreds of millions of China's peasants were not just a source of energy available to implement policies laid down from above, but were *themselves* the source of both leaders and ideas; there must be an exchange between party and mass in which both were teachers, both students. However difficult, what Mao sought was a reconciliation between the very useful *ideas* of Marxism-Leninism, including the vanguard party, and the realities of China.

"MODERN" MEN AND WOMEN IN YANAN

One standard interpretation of Communist victory in 1949 is that it was essentially a gift of the Japanese. The argument is run in many different ways, some more, some less sophisticated, but basically the idea is that, through no fault of their own, the Nationalists were the main losers as a result of Japanese attack. City based, the government had to withdraw inland and became cut off from its normal sources of finance, talent, and the skills of reformist professionals and intellectuals, dependent instead on a reactionary rural landlord class whose interests it feared to disrupt. Recognized internationally as the government of China, defeat at the hands of Japan redounded more against Chiang Kai-shek than against the Communists. Free of national responsibility, Mao could relax and fight insignificant guerrilla skirmishes unburdened by the need to maintain large conventional armies, a complex financial structure, and a functioning government apparatus. The Communists were thus released to seize the banner of nationalism and run for glory, millions of outraged peasants joining them out of sheer patriotism. The very brutality of the Japanese effort benefitted the Communists, making it easy for them to attract support, allowing them to move into a situation of social anarchy ("power vacuum") and build from the ground up. The bias inherent in this view should be clear: the only way to explain a Communist victory ("take-over," "seizure of power") is that in any given social setting, it momentarily appears to be the lesser of two evils. The Communists didn't win, the KMT lost. Thus, the Japanese invasion was just one of those lucky breaks for Mao and his comrades.

But the Japanese invasion did not occur in a vacuum. The relevant question is why the Nationalists responded to its challenge so differently from the Communists. Obviously the answer lies in understanding the internal differences between the two Chinese groups; the mere fact of Japanese devastation explains nothing. Why did Chinese in Communist areas fight back? Why did those in nominally Nationalist areas appear indifferent? The Japanese themselves were amazed at the extent to which Chinese villagers were often ready to cooperate with their forces without coercion. For a fee, peasants would dig trenches, help build fortifications, and so on. What really surprised the Japanese was the way peasants often fled the approach not of Japanese but of Chinese Nationalist troops, refusing to sell them supplies, leaving the wounded to bleed to death. To many Chinese in non-Communist areas, the conflict was just another warlord battle, only this time one of the contending armies was foreign based. Yet Communist troops, even after the change in designation, were welcomed, given gifts, and supplied, often with considerable difficulty, with clothes, food, and shelter. One source records the reaction of an old woman to the appearance of Eighth Route troops: "Right! Right! I know! I know! You are the southern army, the Eighth Route army . . . the good army that doesn't harm people or do evil things. You are the Red Army."[21] When Nationalist troops withdrew in the face of advancing Japanese, they frequently pursued their own version of a "three-all" policy—looting, raping, ravaging as they went. Advancing or retreating, the Eighth Route and New Fourth Armies were something new on the Chinese scene: soldiers who seemed truly to act on the notion that the people, in Chen Yi's phrase, were their "second parents."[22] Every bit of supplies was paid for; the penalty for abusing local women was death; every effort was made to leave people better off than they had found them. An American military intelligence report describes the Eighth Route's practice succinctly. After describing the KMT as a coalition of "reactionary militarists, bankers, capitalists and landlords," the author (basing his observations on material gathered between 1937 and 1941) remarked that wherever the Eighth Route went "its retinue of propagandists, social and economic workers, school teachers, etc., immediately started organizing and training the peasant masses for resistance through guerrilla warfare. Their central idea in all these efforts was that the social and economic level of the peasants had to be improved in order to maintain morale and to instill among the people a will to resist the Japanese and support their own armies."[23]

In terms of civil rule, a painful but useful comparison can be made by looking at how each side responded to the devastating famine and drought that affected large areas of China in 1942–43. The province of Henan was particularly hard hit. Two American journalists traveling through the province estimated that some two or three million people had died of starvation:

The quick and the dead confused us. . . . The people were slicing bark from elm trees, grinding it to eat as food. Some were tearing up the roots of the new wheat; in other villages people were living on pounded peanut husks or refuse. Refugees on the road had been seen madly cramming soil into their mouths to fill their bellies.[24]

According to an American embassy report, the famine was "man-made" and would not exist "if it were not for the war and its background in Honan [Henan] of brutal and oppressive treatment of farmers by their government and army."[25] Yet despite the famine, forced military conscription continued, as did the recruitment of thousands for unpaid transport labor.

And there was more. The greatest problem Henanese faced was the continued taxation, despite drought or famine. "Stop the taxes," Theodore White was told, "we can suffer the famine, but we cannot bear the taxes."[26] In Communist base areas, every effort was bent toward making the army self-sufficient in grain; in Henan, peasants were required to help feed armies in neighboring provinces, where 400,000 troops were employed in blockading the Communists rather than fighting the Japanese. Henan's tax burden actually *increased* in the famine years. The rates, based on estimates of a normal rather than actual crop yield, amounted to 30 to 50 percent of the harvest and had to be paid in wheat. "And as the farmer does not devote all of his land to wheat, . . . the percentage of this crop which he must turn over is much higher," John Service reported to the American embassy.[27]

Service's report lists other abuses: more grain was collected than was necessary, as officers drew rations for fictitious troops, selling the difference at a profit; collections were made by local officials "who are themselves the gentry and landlords, and who often see that they, and their friends do not suffer too heavily. . . . The poorer farmer sees a larger proportion of his grain taken—just as he sees his sons, rather than those of the . . . landlord taken for the army."[28] By July 1942, 1,000 refugees a day were leaving the province, increasing the burden on those who could not move, and still the grain collection program was enforced. "In many districts the entire crop was insufficient to meet the demands of the collectors. There were gestures of agrarian protest: all weak, scattered and ineffectual. Apparently, in a few places, troops were used against the people. But generally the people, failing in their peaceful protests, watched their grain being taken and then, with no hope of surviving the coming winter, killed ther animals, sold their tools and few effects (at greatly reduced prices) and took to the road."[29]

Ten Mile Inn Village in Shanxi province also suffered from drought and war. Located in one of the Communist base areas, it met the disaster with a series of campaigns designed to relieve the immediate situation and mobilize for the future. In the words of its foreign chroniclers, the famine itself became the occasion for strengthening and extending the participation of peasants in their own governance. "It was in the course of combatting [the famine] that the newly formed peasant union established itself as the village's most powerful mass organization." The first effort, "Digging Out the Landlord's Hidden Grain," successfully discouraged hoarding and arranged for appropriate distribution to the hungry. Taxes were collected, but they were levied proportionally among the richest families, while the remaining 70 percent of the population was, for the first time, tax-free. "Gone was the need to borrow at seeding time when grain prices were highest and to repay at harvest time when they were lowest. By this simple but sweeping reform, the cycle of peasant debt was frontally assaulted."[30] Even so, there was suffering. Reforms eased, they could not eliminate, the effects of natural disaster. But the contrast to Henan was searingly apparent to all those who knew of it.

The final chapter on Henan was written in 1944, when some 60,000 Japanese troops smashed through the defenses of Nationalist General Tang Enbo, one of Chiang's staunchest allies and commander of no less than 500,000 troops. Instead of rallying to the aid of Tang's army in the face of the national enemy, Henanese peasants turned against it, disarming some 50,000 troops before they were stopped. In Communist areas the consonance between the welfare of the people and the struggle against Japan was as nearly complete as it was antagonistic in KMT-held territory.

What is difficult to convey about the Communist base areas is what life there felt like to people whose knowledge of China's possibilities was drawn entirely from their experience with the Chongqing government. John Service, China-born and intensely connected to the country, admitted his own reluctance to be impressed. "The feeling is that things cannot possibly be as good as they have been pictured, and that there must be a 'catch' somewhere." The group he travelled with, equally determined to resist being swept away, all came to the same conclusion: "that we have come into a different country and are meeting a different people." Service described the lack of formality, the simplicity of dress, and the absence of secret police, of beggars, of desperate poverty—all of which marked Chongqing. He pointed to the sense of mission, the presence, among all classes, of high political consciousness, and the shock of seeing coolies reading the newspaper. In a report on the top leadership, Service, whose ordinary tone was wry and refreshingly skeptical, used unrestrained italics to communicate his enthusiasm: one's first impression of the leaders as a group was their *"youth,"* then of their *"physical vigor"*; they were *"well-rounded,"* men of *"strong conviction,"* full of *"sincerity, loyalty and determination."* They possessed, in full measure, *"assurance,"* *"pride"* and *"self-confidence."* Personally courageous, realistic, practical, capable of self-criticism, objective, scientific, modern, adaptable, willing to change, orderly, logical, straightforward, frank, unpretentious, honest, incorruptible, efficient, they were remarkably unvengeful given their recent history. "It is not surprising," Service concluded, "that they have favorably impressed most or all of the Americans who have met them during the last seven years: their manners, habits of thought, and direct handling of problems seem more American than Oriental."[31] Indeed, journalists constantly commented, with manifestly unconscious racism, on how un-Chinese these Chinese were. Agnes Smedley was repeatedly told that they were "not Chinese, but new men," "modern men, men much like themselves."[32]

Perhaps, if Kuomintang China had been less corrupt, had its streets not been filled with beggars, prostitutes, refugees like vast running sores, the contrast would not have been as stark. What is more significant than the ambiance of Yanan, or even the personal qualities of its leaders, is the policies pursued both in North and Central China. One of Service's most interesting reports concerns the recovery of the New Fourth Army's strength and power behind Japanese lines. Stable base areas had been created in east Zhejiang and south and west Hubei with a total population, taxed solely by the Communists, of approximately 30 million people. In great detail, Service traced how this force, which "started from almost nothing," grew "as it went along, out of the people." It was, he stressed, "an orphan, without any powerful, well-established government with large resources behind it. It has had to supply itself entirely."[33] KMT troops also operated in the area, well supplied by the central government. Instead of increasing, however, these forces steadily disintegrated. They had fought no offensive battles against the Japanese and could not withstand a concerted Japanese attack, whereas the Communist New Fourth had increased in strength and successfully withstood repeated Japanese attack. How come?

First, according to the New Fourth's acting commander Chen Yi, it was necessary to win people's confidence by establishing military security. Next, intensive propaganda efforts were made to explain the anti-Japanese struggle and win popular support. "This is followed," Chen went on, "by the creation of mass organizations of the people . . . farmers, youth, women, militia, and so on" that are encouraged to direct their energy against the enemy *but also* "to interest themselves in their own problems." Democratic governments were elected, from village level up, and once established, campaigns for rent and interest reduction introduced. Great moderation was exercised "to avoid driving the landlords away and into the Japanese camp." Where landlord strength was extremely strong, "the Communists move slowly by strengthening the organization of the people until they gain control by democratic methods."[34] Self-reliance by the New Fourth troops and the elimination of official corruption reduced the overall tax burden on the people, and what remained was assessed on a progressive basis. There was no forced conscription. Every effort was made to take special care of the families of those who volunteered for the army. Important as these discrete programs was the

practical demonstration of the unity of the army and the people. The army takes as one of its major tasks the protection of the people (to the degree that this often determines its military operations). It takes positive measures to prevent enemy interference with the sowing and harvest. It actually assists, when possible, in farm work. When and where able, its troops produce a part of their own needs. It avoids any sort of arbitrary demands on the people, pays for what it takes, and replaces breakage or damage. It helps the people cope with disasters. . . . In times of poor crops it reduces its own rations to the level of subsistence of the people. It continually harps on the idea that the army and the people are "one family."[35]

Perhaps, Service winds up his report, Chen Yi was exaggerating. Yet "the fact remains that the Communists have been successful in winning the support of the people in the areas in which they operate, while the Kuomintang has not. General Chen laughingly says that the Communists should thank the KMT for coming into the same areas, because they have provided the people with a basis for comparison."[36]

One American journalist, anguishing over the battles he had witnessed, in which the individual bravery of Nationalist soldiers won them only the most painful and untended deaths, also struggled to understand the comparison:

> So I began my search backward from the battlefield for the reasons why reinforcements failed to arrive on time, why the peasants acted as guides to the Japanese and why orders were frequently disobeyed or ignored. I found that reinforcements never could arrive on time because of the state of the railways, the dearth of roads and the lack of transportation; that peasants acted as guides for the Japanese because they did not see or believe that their individual fortunes were bound up with the outcome of the war; that division commanders often ignored orders because, like feudal lords, they were afraid if they lost their troops they would no longer be commanders. So back from the battlefield, my pursuit of knowledge led me to government to society and its forces.[37]

Why so many contemporary historians of the Chinese revolution have resisted making a similar search is puzzling. The war the KMT fought was a product of the society it had created; the same is true for the Communists.

BOURGEOIS EUROPE AND SOCIALIST RUSSIA

So, too, in all of its manifestations, was the war waged by the Soviet Union against Hitler's Germany a product of the society Russia had become at the end of the 1930s. Most historians see this struggle as bearing no relation whatsoever to the Russian revolutionary process. Domestically, as we have shown, the manner in which Stalin's vanguard fulfilled the original goals of revolutionary change distorted them beyond recognition. The old Bolshevik vanguard itself largely disappeared. Yet internationally, even as Stalin's practices internally were reaching their most criminal proportions, the Soviet Union retained validity as a revolutionary state and vitality for those who sought revolutionary transformation in their own countries. Just as much of the meaning of 1917 lay in the sheer fact that it had occurred, the revolutionary character of Soviet Russia's "Great Change" under Stalin stemmed in large measure from the fact that it occurred outside the global capitalist system. Thus the question of its ability to survive the onslaught on capitalism's "highest phase"— fascist Germany—encompassed for many the future of communist revolutionary movements everywhere.

Moreover, one must distinguish between rhetorical and working creeds.[38] However Stalin brutalized Soviet Russia, remolding the revolution and the party to his own design, the goal of Soviet social transformation never was to establish that nation's "rightful place" among the European bourgeois powers; nor was Russia's new order ever intended to venerate wealth, champion individualism, or applaud the "fittest" for their capacity to survive. Whatever the working values of Stalinist authoritarianism, the *rhetorical* creed underlying industrialization described instead the creation of a totally new social order, one in which new wealth was shared, privilege abolished, and the means of production, as well as its fruits, the property of all. A strong Soviet Russia would not only shed the vulnerability of backwardness, but would demonstrate the unlimited potential of socialist economic and social organization to all nations of the world, exploiters and exploited alike. Planning would replace the uncertainties of market relations; a controlled economy would guarantee social welfare and security in contrast to the unemployment, poverty, and anguish of workers under capitalism. Russia's new national greatness, in other words, and consequently Soviet nationalism, lay in her differences with bourgeois Europe and the West and not, as before 1917, in her similarities.

A new Soviet Russian nationalism was thus inherent in the very triumph of Bolshevism, despite the party's early proletarian internationalism, creating a tension that remained acute throughout the 1920s. The very survival of a revolutionary communist state after the defeat in 1919 and 1920 of workers' uprisings all over Europe, and despite French, British, Japanese, and American intervention during the civil war with the Whites, was a genuine ideological anomaly. The necessity of revolution in the powerful bourgeois states of Western Europe as a means of protecting and advancing communist Russia was contradicted by the necessity of reaching some form of accommodation with them should revolution not occur. In this one can appreciate the popular appeal of Stalin's insistence on building "socialism in one country," whatever its actual motivation. The very necessity of Russia's defense touched nationalist impulses, even among those who abhorred Bolshevik rule; for many within the party, there was real comfort in the thought that Soviet power might not, after all, be dependent on foreign workers. Of course, as Stalin constantly reminded his country, this would require herculean efforts, unstinting commitment, and the ruthless suppression of any opposition. Adventurous internationalism could seriously threaten Russia's own security, just as divisions within the party could only lead to weakness. With prodigious (if unconscious) political acumen, Stalin was making Bolshevik revolutionary objectives and the building of Soviet socialism compatible with nationalist goals, a crucial and (for many in the international communist movement) fateful identification.

Thus the struggle to industrialize—to lift Russia from her many varieties of backwardness, in Stalin's rhetoric—was in important respects a patriotic struggle, and identified as such by the Bolshevik party leadership. And the more desperate the struggle in the early 1930s, the more Stalin and his lieutenants felt the necessity to protect Soviet socialism by reaching some new accommodation with the foreign bourgeois enemy. Hitler's coming to power in 1933 compounded this need enormously. Stalin may well have compromised German communism by regarding moderate Social Democrats, rather than the fascists, as the principal enemy in the last years of the Weimar republic, as many have argued; undoubtedly he hoped at first that the Nazis would continue and possibly expand Russo-German trade. The ideological content of bourgeois governments was far less important than their practical policies, and for Stalin perhaps even entirely without significance, something many in the West did not understand. But the Nazis were a direct and overt danger. Hitler was unstinting in his attack on Bolshevik "scum." Within days after taking power, he had virtually all leading Communists put in concentration camps (first organized, in fact, for this purpose); in his first major foreign policy statements, he reiterated his arguments about "living space" and the need to "push to the East" with a new and shocking vehemence.[39]

It is hard for Western students to appreciate in retrospect how frightening the emergence of German fascism was for many Soviet citizens or how vulnerable their chaotic, outcast, communist order seemed to be. The ideology of international class conflict reinforced desolate memories of the First World War, and would likely have brought ordinary Russians to a state of high tension in the midst of the First and Second Five-Year Plans even without the daily announcement that one or another trusted party official was actually a foreign agent. The irrationality of Stalin's domestic terror tends to eclipse the increasing and terrifying danger of massive war; if Stalin's urgency now seems politically contrived, the course of international events rapidly invested ruthlessness and chicanery with at least some aura of vision. Soviet power simply had to grow, and grow quickly.

Propelled by necessity, Stalin began to seek new accommodations with the European democracies. He appointed the urbane Maksim Litvinov foreign minister (well-travelled, married to an English-woman, fluent in several languages, and congenial and charming to Londoners and Americans), announced Russia's desire to join the League of Nations, opened negotiations with France and Czechoslovakia for treaties of mutual assistance, and actively cultivated support and diplomatic recognition in Washington. Unofficially, he ordered the Comintern to drop its opposition to socialist moderates and moved to create united fronts in Europe as he had in China, with varying configurations and degrees of success. The Seventh Comintern Congress in the summer of 1935 saw the new line become general policy, but even before, in July 1934, a unity pact was signed between Communists and socialists in France, and left-wing coalitions scored impressive victories in local elections. In 1936, as Hitler's troops audaciously reoccupied the Rhineland, effectively destroying the last defensive sanctions of the Versailles treaty, Leon Blum's Popular Front government took power in France. At the same time, the new Comintern strategy pursued a republican alliance in Spain to fight Franco, while in England and America, Stalin's supporters worked assiduously to strengthen ties with organized labor and to cultivate more favorable diplomatic contacts. Stalin's famous "democratic"

Constitution of 1936, perhaps the best example of Soviet rhetorical creed in this period, was specially designed to assist this campaign. It had absolutely no domestic relevance.

Still the bourgeois governments kept their distance. The French General Staff balked at undertaking the substantive military discussions necessary to give teeth to the Franco-Russian pact, despite Moscow's urging; Blum himself worried about doing anything that might further alienate France from conservative Britain, which continued to regard Stalin with the utmost suspicion. There was no formal Western intervention in Spain, despite Mussolini's involvement and Franco's use of the Luftwaffe; nor did London, Paris, or Washington react in any significant way when Hitler and Mussolini announced the Anti-Comintern pact, tying Italy, Germany, and Japan. One can only conjecture how different the response might have been had the pact been directed against England or America.

Subsequent months brought even greater concern, and one must appreciate the urgency with which Soviet Russia viewed a successful Chinese front against Japan in this context. The Italian invasion of Ethiopia and the League of Nations' almost total acquiescence suggested forcefully that little would be done if the Soviet Union itself was invaded; Hitler's annexation of Austria in the spring of 1938 to "prevent a bloody communist uprising" seemed to make mockery of any defense against fascism based on traditional notions of territorial integrity. In this sense, Neville Chamberlain's dramatic capitulation at Munich was only the logical extension of what many in Moscow regarded as studied Western indifference to Russia's fate. Despite the Russo-Czech agreements, Stalin was not even informed about the course of the negotiations, much less invited to send his diplomatic representatives.

If one approaches these events from a Western perspective, they each have a logical explanation. In France, the profascist Right was itself a powerful deterrent to closer ties with the USSR; the threat of a military coup or civil war, as in Spain, was more pressing for many than the likelihood of a German invasion, particularly considering the size and reputed strength of the French army, thought to be the best in Europe. Stalin's brutal purge of Marshal Tukhachevskii and other high-ranking officers in 1937–38 had destroyed the Red Army's best talent. The Soviet Union's own official *History of the Great Patriotic War* notes that "nearly half of all regimental commanders were subjected to repression, almost all brigade and division commanders, all corps commanders and troop commanders of military districts, members of military councils, and chiefs of the political directorates of the districts, the majority of the political workers of corps, divisions, and brigades, some one third of all regimental commissars, and many instructors at higher and intermediate military educational institutes."[40] Although the extent of the carnage may not have been fully known, the Red Army was clearly crippled, hardly an attractive military ally. Many foreign ministry officials in France and England regarded Poland as a far more promising and trustworthy Eastern power. Chamberlain in particular belittled Stalin's protests over Munich. "I must confess to the most profound distrust of Russia," the British prime minister wrote in his diary shortly afterwards. "I have no belief whatever in her ability to maintain an effective offensive even if she wanted to. And I distrust her motives, which seem to me to have little connection with our ideas of liberty, and to be concerned only with getting everyone else by the ears."[41]

From Moscow, however, the view was quite different. It may well be, as some Western scholars have argued, that ideology no longer played any role whatsoever in Stalin's attitudes or actions, that his only serious motivation involved *realpolitik*. But it had to be hard for many thoughtful Russians, party members or not, to see Western behavior as anything but the coalescence of bourgeois powers behind German as opposed to Soviet interests. Hitler clearly wanted living space to the East. The increasing shrillness of his attacks, coupled with his palpable intention of actually carrying through the insane designs of *Mein Kampf*, seemed to indicate clearly that "peace in our time" for Europe would be gained at Russia's expense.

THE NAZI-SOVIET PACT AND THE OUTBREAK OF WAR

In August 1939, Stalin himself, in a stunning *volte-face*, reached agreement with Hitler, achieving what some have suggested may have been an acceptable alternative all along.[42] The Molotov-Ribbentrop pact staggered an incredulous West. In its scope and implication, no act of modern diplomacy was more shocking or more momentous; in its effect on European and American Communists, nothing else Stalin might have done could have so shattered popular sympathy and potential support. The "scum of the earth" greeted the "bloody assassin of the workers" in David Low's famous cartoon. All pretense of Soviet internationalist ideology seemed to evaporate. Europe readied for war. Within ten days Hitler's troops invaded Poland, and the Second World War had begun. By prearrangement with Berlin, the Red Army moved into the Baltic states and eastern Poland, up to the borders Russia had held before the Treaty of Brest-Litovsk.

In retrospect, the pact represents not so much the end of internationalist ideology, as specifically and idiosyncratically defined by Stalin and his coterie of party lieutenants, but the primacy, once again, of concerns for his and Soviet Russia's immediate survival. As nationalist impulses again fused with conceptions of an outcast socialist state under siege, Stalin retreated to the self-determined necessity of reaching an accommodation with Hitler because Germany seemed to promise him a greater advantage than alliance with the "bourgeois democracies," however contradictory this might have seemed to the rhetorical goals of Soviet socialism or to the Communist and "fascist" prisoners dying in German and Russian camps.

Yet in the late 1930s, in contrast to the period of revolution and civil war, the USSR was an outcast state even for many socialists in the West because Stalinist necessity had become a self-determined phenomenon, a pernicious and self-perpetuating perspective pervading and corrupting socialist revolutionary development. At first glance, one of the most surprising aspects of the Molotov-Ribbentrop pact seems to be how little Stalin used the opportunities it afforded, at such great moral cost, to build up Soviet defenses against Hitler's possible betrayal. A simple understanding of Nazi diplomacy made such a betrayal more than likely, but Stalin clung with an increasingly irrational tenacity to the notion that the pact was sacrosanct, that nothing should be done to give Hitler the idea that the USSR might itself break the alliance, and that evidence about Hitler's real intentions was somehow part of an elaborate Western scheme to force Russia and Germany into a war of attrition. To be sure, defense and military production intensified under the Third Five-Year Plan (prepared in 1937–38, and formally ratified at the Eighteenth Party Congress in 1939). Work began on sophisticated new weaponry, including the Yak-1, MiG3, and Pe-2 airplanes, the famous T-34 tank, and the "Katusha" rocket launchers, which would play such important roles in Russia's eventual victory. In June 1940, the government also forbade workers to quit their jobs or move voluntarily from one enterprise to another. Drastic penalties were imposed for lateness, including long prison terms. New defense plant construction was begun well away from the Western border. While most strategic production remained in vulnerable areas (especially around Moscow and Leningrad, and in the Central Industrial Region to the south), the costs of moving these industries was staggering, and doing so would have drastically interfered with production. It made reasonable sense to concentrate resources and build on strength, especially if one suspected an invasion in the near future.

But Stalin did not allow for any such suspicions, and industry stayed where it was largely because Stalin convinced himself that Russia's borders were secure. He acted as if war was only an abstract possibility, as if the Nazi-Soviet pact guaranteed Soviet (and his) security for years. Production lagged under the Third Five-Year Plan, even in crucial industrial areas. Output figures for pig-iron and oil showed little increase in 1940 over 1938; steel production rose only to 18.3 million tons, compared with 18 million in 1938 and 17.7 million in 1937. Meanwhile, troops along the border were left in exposed and dangerously concentrated positions. Commanders were refused permission to put their units into defensive alignments or on military alert. Little effort was made to assure an adequate supply of equipment or spare parts, or even to contemplate the possibility that Soviet armies might be forced to retreat. Good fortifications with superb secondary defense capabilities were dismantled along the old Soviet-Polish and Baltic borders since Stalin could foresee no possibility for their use. In the aftermath of the horrendous military purges, few dared disagree. Those who did were instantly stifled. Airplanes and other vital military equipment were consequently left exposed. Even as late as mid-June 1941, as German ships were being hastily withdrawn from Murmansk and other ports and rumors of war filled the air, infantry and artillery divisions remained in peacetime deployment, understaffed, stripped of essential equipment, virtually locked up in concentrated encampments, uncoordinated and ill-prepared for battle. Although an invasion was clearly imminent, Stalin still refused to accept the now frantic pleas of front-line commanders. Tens of thousands died in the first weeks of war because of what Marshal Romanovskii himself later called these criminal blunders.[43]

With a second, closer look, however, Stalin's failures in the crucial twenty-one months between the pact and the beginning of war are not quite so surprising. The real costs to Soviet security were rooted in his corruption of the party and of Russia's revolutionary process. In industry, production lagged not because of capacity, but because a pervasive fear had permeated industrial production at all levels: repression had made the country "feverish." In the words of the Soviet historian Nekrich, it had "introduced fear and uncertainty, fettered initiative. Managers of enterprises were replaced one after another. The new people coming into managerial positions in the economy often did not possess the necessary experience and knowledge. The atmosphere of spy-mania, artificially created by J. V. Stalin, strengthened suspicion and opened doors for ambitious men and lick-spittles, for unprincipled people and careerists, for self-seekers and slanderers."[44] In the army itself, Stalin's senseless killing off of competent and proven commanders left lesser and often incompetent people in control. The brief and largely unsuccessful effort to expand Soviet territory during the so-called "Winter War" with Finland in 1940 showed these deficiencies glaringly, and may well have prompted Hitler to advance his own invasion timetable.

The irony and tragedy here was not only that Hitler's own murderous intentions were real, but that loyal and committed Communists who perceived the fundamental antagonisms in Nazi-Soviet relations were powerless to affect the course of events. One such person was Richard Sorge, who worked for Soviet intelligence in the German embassy in Japan. In 1938 Sorge's wife was arrested in Moscow and disappeared. His close associate, Karl Ramm, was called from Shanghai and shot. Sorge himself may also have been called back from Japan, according to some reports, but refused to go, suspecting, perhaps, the real nature of "wrecking."[45] Deeply committed to his work and his cause, Sorge began to learn of German preparations and passed an enormous amount of vital information back to Moscow. In the late spring of 1941, he was able to report the exact timing of the German attack, as well as to provide detailed information on its size, its main points of assault, and its operational plans. Stalin filed this material away. According to one account, he wrote on it "for the archives."[46]

Other warnings were similarly disregarded. Military attachés and Soviet embassy officials in Berlin and Paris heard frequent rumors of the attack; American agents learned of "Barbarossa," the German plan, in details similar to Sorge's. Roosevelt passed them along through the Soviet Ambassador in Washington, Konstantin Umanskii; other warnings came from Churchill. Stalin simply refused to accept their validity. So absolute had his own personal will become, it was as if he dared not admit he could be challenged; so threatening were the actual realities of challenge that he acted as if any concession to fallibility would be a fatal sign of weakness. It was as if Stalin distrusted the power and commitment of industrialized Russia itself, achieved so recently at such cost.

THE GREAT PATRIOTIC STRUGGLE

When the war finally broke on Soviet soil, on June 22, 1941, Stalin at first, stunningly, withdrew to his dacha, and then, after an incredible period of isolation lasting from June 23 to July 2 (during which the dazed heads of the ministries and armed forces desperately waited for direction), he emerged to speak to his country as the head of a traditional national state in crisis, not as the leader of an internationalist or socialist society based on powerful, supranational class affiliations. Russian "comrades" became "brothers and sisters"; the war itself became the "Great Patriotic Struggle for the Fatherland," even as three million German soldiers crossed the frontier to "deliver civilization from the deadly Bolshevik peril." A new national anthem was introduced; controls on the Orthodox church were relaxed; national heroes in the war against Napoleon were alluded to and glorified.

In important ways, however, Stalin badly underestimated his own people, just as he denied the commitment of men like Sorge or the loyalty and honesty of the hundreds of thousands he allowed to perish in the 1930s. There were significant defections to be sure. Villages in the western Ukraine and elsewhere greeted the Germans as liberators, with the traditional welcoming bread and salt. People in the Baltic states, only recently reincorporated into the Russian state system, genuinely welcomed the opportunities for "independence" under the German Reich. Poorly trained units surrendered quickly; enormous confusion in the chain of command led companies and divisions to disintegrate, sometimes in battle, sometimes not. The "idiotic disposition" of some frontier armies, as Soviet deployment has been properly described, opened the center of Russia's lines to four deadly "battles of annihilation," clearing the way for a rapid and extensive German advance.[47]

But something far more significant also soon began to take place in the bloodied forests and swamps of Western Russia. Attacked savagely and without mercy, raw Soviet recruits began to regroup, to form new units, to fight back. Retreating, the Red Army scorched its own installations, burned houses to deny the enemy shelter, drove off livestock, and slaughtered what had to be left behind. To Germans accustomed to "civilized" resistance as in France, the Red Army's tenacity was extraordinary, as was its

> profligacy in battle. First, exultation: the Germans counted heads, measured the miles of their advance, compared it with their achievements in the West, and concluded that victory was around the corner. Then, disbelief: such reckless expenditure could not go on, the Russians *must* be bluffing, in a matter of days they would exhaust themselves. Then, a certain haunting disquiet: the endless, aimless succession of counterattacks, the eagerness to trade ten Russian lives for one German, the vastness of the territory, and its bleak horizon.[48]

For many in the West, the explanation had to lie in the ruthlessness of NKVD battalions repressing their own men or, as the standard Western history of the war puts it, the "primitive" mentality of the Red Army soldier, "who believed what he was told, and [whose] emotions were an easy target for the race hatred preached by the commissar. Many of the troops were primitive and some were barbaric, and chivalry or the niceties of established rules of war meant nothing to them."[49] But to committed Communists, as well as many others, the notion of "chivalry and niceties of established rules of war" in the face of SS atrocities and German occupation policies was precisely what was degenerate about capitalist Europe, reflected in the Nazi invasion.

The Germans themselves were more perceptive. They recognized they were meeting not only an enemy of extraordinary resilience, but one of dedication and commitment as well. "Now, for once, our troops are compelled to fight according to their combat manuals," Chief of Staff Halder wrote in his diary. "In Poland and the West they could take liberties, but here they cannot get away with it."[50]

"In spite of the distances we were advancing," a captain in the Eighteenth Panzer Division noted further, "there was no feeling, as there had been in France, of entry into a defeated nation. Instead there was resistance, always resistance, however hopeless. A single gun, a group of men with rifles . . . once a chap ran out of a cottage by the roadside with a grenade in each hand."[51] Behind *this* was clearly much more than the NKVD.

But what, exactly? A fury at the Germans' own atrocities? A sense of desperation? A stirring of national pride? All, perhaps, and more, as the bloody struggle continued and intensified. Smolensk fell, on the road to Moscow, but with incredible tenacity Soviet troops held southeast of the city, and after four weeks of furious battle recaptured the town of Yelnia, the first 100 square miles or so of territory to be reconquered from Hitler's legions. German casualties in the first ten weeks of fighting numbered 440,000, including 94,000 killed—four times the figure for France.[52] Leningrad, surrounded, refused to surrender. Moscow, its defenses reinforced, determined also to hold.

On a cold, overcast November 7, the twenty-fourth anniversary of the revolution, Stalin spoke in Red Square. In one of his most memorable and dramatic speeches of the war, he synthesized the diverse and diffuse strains of Soviet resistance—physical, emotional, psychological—into a new Soviet national perspective. Thousands of the assembled troops were about to leave for the front. Millions more listened on the radio. In the distance, one could hear the constant rumble of guns. Overhead, Soviet fighter planes flew protective cover. The time had come, Stalin said, for Soviet Russia to realize the fruits of years of heroic building and hurl back the fascist invaders. The revolution had survived many ordeals, and it could survive this one:

> In 1918 . . . three quarters of our country was in the hands of foreign interventionists. We had no allies, no Red Army . . . no food, no arms, no equipment. . . . Yet we organized the Red Army, and turned our nation into a military camp. Lenin's great spirit inspired us. . . . Now our position is far better. We are richer in industry, in food and raw materials. We have allies, and the support of occupied nations in Europe. We have a fine army and navy . . . and no serious shortages of food, arms, or equipment. . . . Lenin's spirit can inspire us in our struggle now as it did 23 years ago. . . .
> Comrades, men of the Red Army and Navy, officers and

political workers, men and women partisans! The whole world is looking on you as the power capable of destroying the German robber hordes! The enslaved peoples of Europe are looking on you as their liberators. . . . Be worthy of this great mission! The war you are waging is a war of liberation, a just war. May you be inspired in this war by the heroic figures of our great ancestors, Alexander Nevsky, Dmitri Donskoi, Minin and Pozharsky, Alexander Suvarov, Mikhail Kutuzov! May you be blest by the great victorious banner of Lenin! Death to the German invaders! Long live our glorious nation, its freedom and independence. Under the banner of Lenin—onward to victory![53]

Thus, Stalin tied the Soviet regime and its achievements inextricably to Russia's national past. From all accounts, his speech made an enormous impression. The symbolism of celebrating the revolution's anniversary under German guns, of refusing to evacuate Moscow, of defending Russia against an enemy convinced that communism in any form was perfidious and the Slavs themselves an inferior race, was hardly lost on a nation whose historic sense was keenly tuned to past invasions. The Red Army and its victory would vindicate the years of struggle to build a powerful, industrialized state.

RUSSIA'S STAGGERING VICTORY

This is not the place to review in detail the momentous sequence of events by which Soviet Russia reversed the course of German expansionism and emerged from her "backwardness" to defeat the most powerful nation in European history. The story is simply too complex. One also stands in danger of trivializing the horrendous suffering involved if events are displayed like a Saturday night late movie. Still, several important points must be made about the Great Patriotic Struggle in terms of the way it gave meaning both to previous and subsequent phases of Soviet development.

First, shortly after Stalin's speech, Russian lines tightened on the outskirts of Moscow. "Operation Typhoon," as the German command tagged their offensive, sputtered to a halt, hampered by cold, overextended supply lines, and relentless Soviet resistance. Russians suffered as well as the Germans from the especially harsh winter, but threw their energies into a dramatic counteroffensive, aware that their country and much of the world would appreciate the meaning of saving Moscow. Within days, Hitler's troops were retreating for the first time in the war. The myth of Nazi invincibility had been broken, and broken by Soviet troops fighting alone.

Moscow was a "defensive victory," but succeeding weeks brought similar gains, obtained at enormous cost. By the end of December, as America entered the war after the Japanese attack on Pearl Harbor, German casualties in the East approached 800,000 men, including almost as many dead as the United States would suffer through the entire war. Soviet losses were well over a million. Some 2,000 towns had been destroyed and over 70,000 villages almost totally obliterated. Equipment and production losses were virtually incalculable, as the fighting raged meter by meter over Soviet soil. Perhaps as many as twenty-five million were homeless. But as 1942 began to unfold, Soviet strength gradually increased as Germany's weakened. Klin, Kalinin, Volokolamsk, Mozhaisk, Kaluga, and Tolstoi's village of Iasnaia Poliana were all retaken. Fresh troops and new matériel came from industries relocated beyond the Urals. An ice highway was built across Lake Ladoga to relieve beleaguered Leningrad. By late spring of 1942, the USSR had more tanks, field guns, and mortars in place than the Germans, and almost as many aircraft. By the fall, troop strength was roughly equal.[54]

None of this weakened German determination or reduced the fighting. Nazi troops in May 1942 were still only ninety miles from Moscow, where haggard citizens lived on near starvation rations, as in Leningrad; in the Crimea, the German Eleventh Army under Field Marshal von Manstein began driving on Kerch and Sevastopol, which finally fell after a heroic resistance in mid-July. (Sevastopol was occupied after a bitter nine-month siege, during which most of the city's inhabitants lived in underground caves and shelters. In the last days, defenders wore gas masks to ward off the unbearable stench of thousands of dead bodies rotting in the July heat.) In August, the Germans struck toward Stalingrad, a strategically vital city on the Volga, with almost 300,000 men entering the outskirts of the city early in September after bitter fighting. On one day more than 600 German aircraft bombed Stalingrad, and by the middle of September Soviet troops were giving ground house by house. Holding the city meant protecting the vital Volga River supply line, preventing an attack from the north on Caucasian oil fields, and simply refusing to surrender Stalin's city. Everyone possible was pressed into the city's defense.

One must recognize in these facts that 1942 represented the hardest and most bitter fighting of the war, and that Soviet Russia—communist Russia—resisted the Germans almost entirely on its own. The scale of fighting on the Eastern front was almost beyond comprehension, and certainly beyond the understanding now of most Westerners. In comparison, every other war theater in 1942 pales in significance. For many in the Soviet Union, the very momentousness of the struggle fused Russian nationalism with the "banners of Lenin and Stalin" in a way no rational experience or achievement could ever have done. Put another way, the war gave legitimacy to the Soviet regime by identifying it with Russia's historical past in a way its rhetorical commitment to socialist values had never been able to do.

This is not to suggest that the horrors of the thirties were forgotten. Indeed, Stalin's murderous irrationality persisted. Ordering Russian troops "not to surrender an inch of our land," he had thousands of army personnel shot for "disloyalty" with a ruthlessness staggering even by Stalinist standards. Tens of thousands were also lost because Stalin personally rejected appeals that troops be allowed to rest and regroup; whole divisions were surrounded and forced to surrender because he refused to allow retreat. Red Army POWs lucky or clever enough to escape from the Germans found themselves arrested by the NKVD as "dangerous elements" or "suspected enemy agents." As before, Stalin himself continued to underestimate the loyalty and commitment even of heroic and dedicated Communists, while the sybaritic excesses of many Stalinist sycophants staggered and depressed both Russians and foreigners alike.[55]

Nor is it to maintain that the Allied campaign in North Africa, pitting Rommel against Montgomery, did not worry the German high command or threaten the Axis with direct attack on its "soft underbelly," as Churchill liked to phrase it. The loss of colonies in Egypt and Libya and the mandate possession of Palestine would have closed the Suez Canal, weakened British links with its empire in the East, and undoubtedly threatened Russia as well, in addition to cutting off vital European oil resources. Also, large numbers of German troops were being kept in the West to defend against a possible Allied landing in Europe, a situation that helped the

Russians enormously. But none of this would have mattered in 1942 had the Russians collapsed like the French and allowed Hitler to use his overwhelming military superiority in other theaters. The entire course of the war would have altered. Victory, if possible at all, could have come only from staggering Western loss of life, twenty, maybe thirty times greater than actually occurred.

This staggering cost *was*, however, being paid by the Russians, now fighting, in Stalin's explicit rhetoric, in the name both of traditional Russian greatness and the October Revolution. In November 1942, with the "pride of the German army" poised at Stalingrad, the Red Army launched a counterattack under Generals Rokossovsky, Vatutin, and Eremenko. Once called Tsaritsyn, the city's new name symbolically meshed the revolutionary and the traditional, and so, more importantly, did the outcome of the battle. By late January an encirclement was complete; in February, Field Marshal von Paulus was forced to surrender his entire remaining army. With Stalingrad utterly ruined but secure, Russia could hardly lose the war. Supply lines remained intact, the Ural industrial region and Caucasus oil beyond German reach. Terrifying battles lay ahead, particularly at Kursk, which would prove to be the greatest armor engagement of the war and would finally demonstrate the strength of Russian industry and technology in the victory of Russian tanks over Nazi panzers. But by early summer of 1943, the question in Moscow was "when" Russia would win, not "if."

Lend Lease, of course, played a role in supplying the Russians in this time, as did the limited Murmansk convoys, running from Britain. Some 1.2 million tons of supplies were shipped in 1942, most coming into the USSR through Iran and the Caspian. This figure increased fourfold in 1943 and by 1944, reached a level of almost 6 million tons. But however valuable, Lend Lease was, in important ways, after the fact of Soviet resistance and relatively unimportant in terms of reversing the German advance. Western supplies increased as the Russian position improved; Russia was most isolated during the months of its greatest need. In September 1942, in fact, as Soviet troops were beginning their desperate street-by-street defense of Stalingrad, Churchill suspended the Murmansk convoys because of "exceptionally high losses" (in one case, convoy PQ 17 in July, twenty-three of thirty-four ships had been sunk) and because ships

were needed to assemble troops and supplies from America, pre-
paratory to an Allied invasion of Europe. Stalin responded caustically,
calling Churchill's arguments "wholly unconvincing," but the matter
was beyond his control.

"Wholly unconvincing" was, however, an accurate reflection of
Stalin's increasing skepticism about the extent and nature of Western
commitments in the war. Having himself aligned with Germany in
1939 expecting in part, no doubt, that Germany and France might
exhaust themselves militarily in Europe, Stalin now undoubtedly
worried that Churchill and Roosevelt would do the same to him.
Speculation aside, the fact was that 1942 in the East was very nearly
a war of attrition.

The crucial issue was the opening of a second front in Western
Europe, the focal point of almost all wartime diplomacy until the
Allies actually landed in June 1944. Again, volumes can be (and have
been) written on this issue, but the important point for our purposes
is that the lack of a second front very much reinforced Stalin's
suspicions about relations between communist Russia and the capitalist West, even if these categories of analysis were rarely displayed.
The essential facts on the second front are these: in the spring of
1942, Roosevelt and particularly Churchill gave assurances to Stalin
through Molotov that a second front would be opened in Western
Europe sometime in 1942, "probably September," but shortly afterwards scrapped the plan as unacceptably risky. (The Allied command
had in mind General Marshall's "Operation Sledgehammer," a
landing at Brest or Cherbourg.) Churchill communicated the decision to postpone the landing to Stalin indirectly, in a communique
of July 18 indicating that supply convoys would soon be dropped:
"Besides affecting the food supplies by which we live, our war effort
would be crippled, and above all, the great convoys of American
troops . . . would be prevented, and the building up of a really strong
second front in 1943 rendered impossible."[56] Stalin was thus dealt
a double blow at a critical moment for Soviet Russia. He responded
angrily, pointing out that "no major task can be carried out in
wartime without risk or losses," and complaining that he "never
imagined the British government would deny us delivery of war
materials precisely now, when the Soviet Union is badly in need of
them in view of the grave situation on the Soviet-German front. . . . I

state most emphatically," he continued, "that the Soviet government cannot tolerate a second front in Europe being postponed until 1943."[57]

Stalin may also have felt that Churchill was taking advantage of his own willingness to be "accommodating," since shortly before he had agreed to the British government's urgent request that forty Boston bombers being sent by Roosevelt to Russia be diverted to British troops in Egypt. Churchill thanked Stalin several times for his "generous response," but such generosity could also be interpreted as a sign of political weakness, contributing to the tough British line on the convoy issue and the second front.[58] Stalin certainly did not wish to appear weak; clearly from this moment on his attitude toward the West stiffened dramatically. Churchill travelled to the Soviet Union shortly afterwards in an attempt to improve relations, and briefly restarted the convoys, but Stalin now doubted Allied intentions to launch a second front in 1943, and said so directly.[59] Viewed from Moscow, the Anglo-American reluctance to risk casualties could only mean that Russian losses were preferable, however much they weakened the Soviet Union. At the moment of Russia's greatest military crisis—a crisis that tested a ten-year effort to make the USSR a great world power—the Russian leader and his close associates, especially Molotov, may have felt doubly challenged by the specter of future East-West confrontations.

A third point that must be made is that when the D-Day landings finally came in June 1944, the Red Army was already driving the last German troops from Soviet soil. The spring of 1944 saw the recapture of Sevastopol and the Crimea, as well as Odessa and most of the Ukraine. On April 2 the Red Army entered Rumania. In May armies of the first and fourth Ukrainian fronts crossed the Dniester near the Czech border, and the battle began for Belorussia and the Baltic States. Soviet troop strength now exceeded 6,500,000 men, more than the British, Free French, and American forces combined. By early July Red troops were at the Polish border, and by August, entered German territory in the Baltic region near Königsberg. Bucharest, in Rumania, fell on August 31; Sofia, the Bulgarian capital, two weeks later. The fighting was incredibly fierce, but the German retreat was steady and irreversible.

In these circumstances, the Allied landing in Normandy may

have seemed to many in Moscow a necessity not so much for military reasons, although these were rarely discounted entirely, but to prevent Soviet Russia from moving into Germany entirely on her own. "The whole world knows that the Second Front in Western Europe was opened only when it was quite obvious that the Red Army, supported by the anti-fascist movement could liberate occupied Europe single-handed," the official six-volume Soviet history of World War II reports.[60] And while this is clearly an exaggeration, Patton's famous dash across France and Churchill's growing consternation about the likely postwar political configuration as a result of Russian advances indicate the Western offensive was hardly devoid of political considerations. In any event, if one can understand Western fears about the Red Army's "liberation" of Europe (and the final realization, as Churchill clearly understood, of early Comintern goals in this regard), one can also appreciate how Western depreciation of Soviet success at the very moment of victory could only intensify Russia's sense of distance from her erstwhile allies. Justified or not, the USSR remained a pariah in the European community, despite its role in freeing Western society from the demonic fascist creature of its own invention.

It is tempting for Western students to seek explanations for the Soviet Union's victory in extra-Soviet terms—confusion within German military circles; tactical weakness of early invasion strategy, which split the German army into three groups; brutal occupation measures, which thoroughly alienated potential supporters among dissident Soviet nationalities; aid from the Allies; the evocation of the Russian national past and a return to old traditions—almost anything, in fact, other than the achievements of the Soviet Union itself. Viewing Russia in 1940, and considering the traumas of collectivization, industrialization, and the purges, many in the West expected Russian soldiers to walk away from the trenches in the event of a war, just as they had in 1917, a concern likely shared by Stalin himself.

But if the cost of Soviet Russia's transformation in the 1930s was staggering in human terms, if there were deep structural deficiencies in Soviet industrial organization, if the countryside reeled in the aftermath of collectivization, and if agricultural productivity (if not the state's share of production) was set back for years, still the ultimate test of their regime for millions of Russians lay in the war. Under the "banner of Lenin," in a sense made tangible by military victory, the USSR had not, in the end, been beaten for her backwardness. Thus for millions of Soviet citizens, party supporters or not, the victory over Germany tended to validate the sacrifices of communist transformation—indeed, made sense, as something *had* to, of what to many seemed to be (and in many ways *was*) without reason. Russian nationalism and communism fused together in the crucible of Red Army success; for many in the Soviet Union, legions of dissidents notwithstanding, and for many thousands in national liberation movements elsewhere, October and Russia's subsequent radical transformation was precisely what made the Soviet Union a great historical model. Victory was treated rhetorically as vindication of revolutionary creed.

Finally, and in some ways most important, although Soviet Russia emerged victorious from the war, it was devastated beyond description. Between 7,500,000 and 10,000,000 Russian soldiers died in the fighting, perhaps as many as 15,000,000 civilians. In contrast, German battle deaths stood at approximately 3,500,000, while the United States, Britain, and France each lost less than 300,000. The utter destruction of more than 100,000 towns and villages posed staggering reconstruction costs, as did the need to rebuild industry in the Western provinces and transfer the economy as a whole onto a peacetime footing. Demobilization alone involved herculean tasks of social and economic integration.

But achieving the unachievable and demonstrating herculean power was what Stalin insisted his leadership was about. The cult of personality now took historic justification and was renewed with a vengeance. And if military victory could be misinterpreted as a triumph of Stalinist government, one can hardly be surprised that in the occupied countries of Eastern Europe, in the face of renewed East-West antagonism and in the absence of alternative guarantees of Russian security, reconstruction was imposed from Moscow on a Stalinist model. Spreading this system westward by force served Stalin as if it were a drive for international revolution in the years after 1917: security against a hostile, international capitalist order, assistance in economic recovery and reconstruction, and the destruction of capitalist regimes. From the Kremlin, the "iron curtain" was

Stalinist Russia's—and hence communist Russia's—new line of defense. Many despised Stalin's corruption of revolutionary values; others rejected them outright. But through the war and its victory, the ideological premises of Marxism-Leninism became for the Soviet Union as a whole the acceptable language for understanding international antagonisms and expressing deeply felt nationalist commitments.

7

SOCIALIST ROADS
AND THE VARIETIES OF RECOVERY

DEFINING THE TASKS OF SOVIET RECONSTRUCTION

On February 9, 1946, Joseph Stalin strode briskly onto the stage of the Bolshoi Theater in Moscow to address a meeting of Supreme Soviet electors. He was greeted by a thunderous ovation lasting several minutes, no doubt heartfelt on the part of many in the hall who saw their *Vozhd'* ("leader") as a great military hero and a man of remarkable vision. It was Stalin, many now insisted, who had understood the fascist danger even before Hitler came to power. Almost single-handedly, others proclaimed, he had led Russia through collectivization and industrialization, building the Soviet Union's industrial might. Of course the Man of Steel had an iron hand. No doubt he moved ruthlessly against oppositionists, and no doubt the police were often excessive in their vigilance. But whatever mistakes had been made, many delegates believed, whatever suffering the country had endured in building its strength—and who could deny the suffering!—victory over the fascist invaders had clearly proved the wisdom of Stalin's leadership. Who would have thought a country like Russia, scorned as backward by *all* the European powers, could have developed by herself the strength and will to defeat the greatest military power in European history! Who, indeed, but Stalin!

Besides, some delegates must have thought as the applause rang down, Russia's hardships were over. The tensions of the 1930s had given way early in the war to a new spirit of comradeship and relaxation. Comrades no longer seemed so concerned about politics. Russia had a new national anthem, Britain and especially the United States were spoken of as allies, and priests had even appeared on occasion to conduct services among Red Army troops. Soon prisoners-of-war would be coming home. Families would be reunited, the harmonious spirit of victory carried to the massive tasks of reconstruction. Surely, despite the difficulties of rebuilding, Russia's socialist road would now be a smooth one. The Soviet Union would begin to enjoy the fruits of past labor and hardship. Perhaps these were the issues Comrade Stalin intended to address.

They were, the delegates soon learned, but not in the way many must have anticipated. From the moment Stalin began his address with a curt "Comrades!" it was apparent a new period of struggle had begun. "It would be a mistake to think," Stalin declared, "that the Second World War developed accidentally, as the result of mistakes by this or that governmental figure. . . . In fact, the war occurred as the inevitable result of the development of world economic and political forces based on contemporary monopolistic capitalism." These destructive, competitive forces still existed. The necessary alliance of Soviet Russia with "the United States, Great Britain, and other freedom-loving states" had not altered these fundamental patterns of world historical development.

What, then, of the Allied victory? It was of course true, Stalin continued, that the victory was a joint one, but this "truth" was "too general," and it was necessary to be "more concrete." What, specifically, did the victory mean about "the development of the internal forces of our country?" First of all, it meant the "triumph of our Soviet *social* system." In the West, this system had been disparaged repeatedly as a "risky experiment," a "house of cards," supported and sustained only by the secret police. "Now we can say that the war has completely disproved these assertions of the Western press. The war has shown that the Soviet social system is a truly national structure, sprung from the heart of the people." More than that, "the war has proven that the Soviet social system is a better form of social organization than any non-Soviet social structure."

Second, "our victory signifies the triumph of our Soviet *state* system." Here again, leading figures in the foreign press had "often spoken of the artificiality" of Russia's Soviet regime and its likely fragmentation in the pattern of the old Austro-Hungarian empire. The war belied this assertion, too. The victory of the Red Army proved the value of the Soviet regime and affirmed its competency and strength. ("Under the leadership of Comrade Stalin!" someone shouted from the floor, leading to a prolonged, standing ovation, lasting many minutes.)

Therefore, Stalin continued as the applause died away, it would be a dangerous mistake to think in terms of modifying Russia's social and political system. More so, it would be a dangerous mistake to abandon the Soviet road to modernization, which had accomplished such an extraordinary transformation of the country in thirteen short years, "from backwardness to the leading ranks, from an agrarian nation to industrialization." There could be no doubt that the policies and methods of industrial development and collectivization had been correct, and must be continued.

More, in fact, than simply "continued." In the near future rationing would come to an end (stormy, prolonged applause); prices of consumer goods would be lowered and more would become available (again, stormy applause). At the same time, however, the party intended not simply to stop at reconstruction, but "to organize a new, mighty, upward surge in the economy, which would make possible an increased level of industrialization, to a point twice the pre-war level . . . 50 million tons of iron annually (prolonged applause), 60 million tons of steel (prolonged applause) up to 500 tons of coal (prolonged applause) and 60 million tons of oil (prolonged applause). . . . This will take at least three five-year plans, if not more. But it can be done, and we must do it! (Stormy applause.)"[1]

Thus Stalin personally defined the Soviet Union's road to recovery. It would, of course, be a socialist road, but more importantly, a Stalinist road, since all distinctions between these two very different forms of social and political organization no longer had any practical meaning in the Soviet party leadership's political consciousness. By arguing that the war had vindicated the process of Soviet social transformation in the 1930s, Stalin and others could refuse to differentiate the truly remarkable accomplishments of industrial growth and development from the truly horrendous brutality, irrationality, and social destruction that were their unnecessary accompaniment. And in recovering from the war, the Soviet Union was not to have one without the other.

THE CULT OF PERSONALITY

This tragic and fateful aspect of the Soviet revolutionary experience simply must be understood in order to grasp fully the nature of developed Stalinist socialism and the manner in which it corrupted the very essence of revolutionary social relations, precisely what Communists in China and elsewhere were struggling at this very time to achieve. As we have seen, industrial development in the 1930s had been a mix of planning, expediency, hesitation, retreat, commitment, and heroic achievement, organized as a struggle against real and imagined enemies, and alloyed with blood. What emerged was a highly structured sociopolitical system institutionalizing not an ability to respond rationally and carefully to real social need but the willingness to adapt to systemic irrationality, in which real and imagined social needs were dealt with fitfully, even spasmodically, without careful, planned consideration of costs and alternatives. Under Stalin, knowledge itself became suspect. Access to vital information for planning and "scientific economic management" was restricted at best to a highly privileged official elite, more concerned with coercion, control, and survival than socialist values. Stalinism institutionalized suspicion and doubt, not commitment and conviction; fear, not security; the promise of betterment, not the enjoyment of life. And above all, after the war, Stalinism meant an awesome trembling before a single individual, apotheosized in victory, whose will had replaced Marx's masses in motion as the accepted explanation of historical process. If for some Communists outside the Soviet Union, Stalin retained an heroic aura as a "true figure of the masses," committed in all ways to their welfare, it was only because they were not yet aware of what Stalin had really become.

And what *had* Stalin become? "All Wise Leader and Teacher," the posters proclaimed; the "Luminous Star" whose radiance brought "unlimited happiness to the Soviet people" according to the popular journal, *Ogonek*, which replaced its traditional New Year's star with Stalin's visage. A recluse, who never visited a collective farm, who sped through Moscow in a cavalcade of identical Stalin Factory automobiles at breakneck speed to a spartan country dacha with four safely identical bedrooms on a highway no one else was permitted to use. "Dear Father, Genius Teacher, Savior of the Fatherland," Khrushchev wrote on Stalin's Seventieth Birthday; "Teacher and Friend of Mankind and of the Chinese People" (Mao Zedong); "Great Leader of Progressive Humanity" (Malenkov); "Inspirer and Organizer of all our Victories" (Kosygin); "Genius combined with simplicity and modesty, with extraordinary personal charm, with consideration and paternal concern for all" (Beria); a man who had ordered countless staunch supporters killed and his own relatives thrown into prison, whose first son died disgraced and ignored as a prisoner-of-war, and whose second son became the Air Force commander of the Moscow Military district at the age of thirty-one despite an incapacitating alcoholism that prevented him from flying. A "Lover of Children," who had never met five of his own eight grandchildren, and who seemed to enjoy the extreme discomfiture of his "comrades-in-arms." In 1949, he arrested without apparent reason the wife of Viacheslav Molotov, his closest collaborator, most faithful supporter, and then foreign minister. For years she languished in a camp in northern Kazakhstan, her whereabouts unknown even to her prominent husband. The wife of Poskrebyshev, Stalin's powerful private secretary, was also arrested, and so was the wife of Soviet President Kalinin, who continued nonetheless to receive the credentials of foreign dignitaries in formal state ceremonies.

Stalin's books, slogans, and portraits were everywhere. More than 130 photographs and paintings adorned the Kazan railroad station alone. There were 1,500,000 "first edition" copies of his *Economic Problems of Socialism* published, and still the citizens of Moscow scrambled for copies. When the Volga-Don Canal was opened with the passage of the vessel *Joseph Stalin*, an enormous copper Stalin gazed over the proceedings, constructed from thirty-six tons of a metal so scarce that the Great Leader himself had to order its release from industrial use. "If only Stalin knew," grumbled housewives when they found empty shelves in the stores; when orders speeding up production were received in the factory, workers accepted them with "Stalin knows!" Millions of school children sang songs of praise several times a day. His awesome presence was everywhere. "One day I was walking down the Arbat," Boris Slutsky later wrote, "when God passed by in five automobiles."[2]

All this was the totally unnecessary consequence of necessary historical and political circumstance. In the very Leninist notion of a vanguard party, of course, there were strong tendencies toward centralization, tendencies that the historical conditions of revolution and civil war validated in practice. The necessities of administrative order, even authoritarianism, in the chaotic conditions of popular upheaval clearly facilitated the development of a highly bureaucratized party-state in which the elements of initiative, revolutionary commitment, and responsiveness to mass interests were naturally challenged by careerism and power-mongering, as well as the willingness to take (and give) orders. Centralization was also implicit in socialist planning. While an effective and judicious planning mechanism required careful attention to social and economic realities, to the subjective characteristics of attitude and mood as well as to the objective conditions of resource supply and distribution, planning also worked, however less well, as commandism from above, particularly in conditions of frightening scarcity. In a society accustomed to three centuries of autocratic rule, moreover, commandism was hardly a new phenomenon, even if its uses were now revolutionary.

Both systemic and historical pressures thus infused grave dangers into the Russian revolutionary process, and imposed on Bolsheviks an extraordinary task: to resist them and head off tendencies toward personal, arbitrary rule or else to establish institutional mechanisms within the party and state that would prevent those so inclined from fulfilling their ambitions. In this, Lenin and other "old Bolsheviks" clearly failed. Despotism remained an immanent possibility. And in Stalin, historical and systemic pressures coincided with a personality who not only did not turn them aside, but who craved personal power, and whose very commitment to the revolutionary movement had strong cultic aspects to begin with.

Freedom, Engels wrote in *Anti-Dühring*, paraphrasing Hegel, is the appreciation of necessity. But as Mao and other Chinese revolutionary Marxists came to realize, and as many Russians understood too late, freedom is also the *transformation* of necessity and involves the recognition of dangers in historical circumstances, as well as of the opportunity to shape their development.

THE SOCIAL CONSEQUENCES OF HIGH STALINISM, 1946–1953

The heaviest burden of Soviet reconstruction after the war fell on the countryside, just as in the 1930s. Without substantial funds from abroad for rebuilding, the costs both for reconstruction and for Stalin's ambitious new industrial objectives had to be squeezed from savings or taxes (minus, of course, the spoils of war, taken in massive quantities from Eastern Europe as a result of military victory). The possibility of aid from the West virtually disappeared after the United States turned down Stalin's request in January 1945 for a six billion dollar loan, and Lend Lease was abruptly terminated in May. (In August, Stalin resubmitted a loan request for one billion dollars, but this was somehow "lost.")[3] Through a currency "reform" in 1947, the government effectively absorbed the vast bulk of personal savings simply by issuing new currency at a 1 : 10 ratio while maintaining constant prices. Bonds were also reduced to a third of their original asset value and converted to a lower interest rate. Since cash hordes were largely held by peasants (and since savings accounts under 3,000 rubles, held largely by urban workers, were excepted), the "reform" was essentially a measure of simple confiscation, falling (like past confiscatory measures) largely on the countryside.

It was in terms of agricultural production, however, that the burden of reconstruction proved most onerous. The Stalinist model, after all, had "proven" Russia's ability to generate investment capital through collectivization and the intensification of peasant labor. Low procurement prices allowed the government to market essential foodstuffs at substantial "profits." The regulation of commodity prices (as well as those for feed, machinery, and other agricultural necessities) could generate additional state revenues (through an indirect "turnover" tax), and so could strict control over wages, particularly for state farm workers. During the war, these and other controls were considerably relaxed in the countryside, as part of an effort both to build morale and increase productivity, and to allow local authorities flexibility in responding to radically changing local conditions and needs. Peasants expanded cultivation of private plots to meet their immediate needs. Often they took land not otherwise being used by the collective farms (analogous, in part, to American

Victory Gardens). Substantial leeway was allowed in marketing procedures to encourage the supply of additional foodstuffs above and beyond those taken and distributed according to a strict system of rationing.

Shortly after his February ninth speech, however, Stalin moved to eliminate these "abuses." An order "Liquidating Violations of the Kolkhoz Statute" again imposed strict limits on the amount of land available for private cultivation and announced the confiscation of all livestock holdings above the small numbers fixed in the Kolkhoz Statute of 1939. Procurement prices for obligatory deliveries were reduced (along, however, with some retail prices), but the price differential for many items was increased to as much as 95 percent (producers being paid 5 percent of the price charged to consumers).[4] In some places, the cost of transporting obligatory deliveries to the collection point was actually *greater* than the price received for the goods! Meanwhile, tax rates were increased for goods of all sorts, particularly agricultural produce from private plots. Within a short period of time, peasants in some areas were cutting down fruit trees and killing off livestock to avoid tax obligations, just as they had in the early 1930s. In some places, private plots were abandoned entirely, while throughout the countryside, real wages paid to agrarian workers rapidly declined. According to one estimate, the *average* cash income from collective farm labor during the 1948–50 period was such that twenty days' work was required to buy a bottle of vodka, forty days for a kilogram of butter.[5]

In 1949–50, new reforms were introduced, amalgamating smaller collective farms (*kolkhozy*) and expanding greatly the area and work force controlled by single collective farm administrations. Giant "agro-towns" were mentioned in the press, replicating the gigantism of the early Soviet period, in which bigness seemed to promise solutions to problems of low productivity and efficiency. In effect, Stalin was remolding collective farms into state farm units (where workers received wages) without the accompanying wage bill, a change that increased the remoteness of farm administration, further depressed collective farm incomes, and from all evidence, contributed even more to a deterioration of peasant morale.

For all this, agricultural production *did* increase in postwar Russia, and more important, the state's share of rural production, coupled with the intensification of domestic industrial labor, outright confiscation of vital industrial machinery, and extraordinarily favorable terms of trade forced on the new satellite states of Eastern Europe, was more than sufficient to finance reconstruction and to increase industrial output substantially. Soviet Russia *was* recovering from the war, and her industrial and military strength were moving her rapidly into superpower status, even as the slave labor population of Stalin's camps swelled to perhaps as many as thirteen million persons.

But in continued contrast to China, the costs remained the isolation of the party from ordinary citizens, a fiercesome and brutal authoritarianism, generalized popular discontent, and continued depression in the level of material welfare, imposed only in part by the truly staggering tasks of reconstruction. Ruthless political controls led to ever stronger and more corrupt "mutual protection societies" between managerial personnel and local officials, designed to keep production within safe limits (and thus avoid inviting unobtainable new goals as targets were "racheted" upwards in the future); incentives remained limited; innovation was still extremely difficult, impossible if it involved overt borrowing from the West. All social sectors suffered from insufficient and shoddy goods, the faulty allocation of scarce resources, and resultant waste. The planning mechanism remained in disarray. A new five-year plan, supposed to begin in 1951, was simply ignored.

In these circumstances there not only emerged full blown what Milovan Djilas and others have aptly termed a "new class of socialist owners," monopolistic in its control over the means of production and self-serving in the way it utilized this control to advance its own power and well-being, but also a social context that held little place for creativity or imagination, however genuine one's loyalty to the USSR. Commitment to social democracy was dangerous, free thinking out of the question. Intellectuals became "superfluous," just as they had been when the Russian revolutionary movement began. To some, Stalin's willingness to issue pronunciamentos on any range of subjects seemed baffling. "A group of comrades . . . have asked me to give my opinion in the press on questions relating to the science of language," he wrote in *Pravda* on June 20, 1950, five days before the start of the Korean war. "I have therefore consented to answer a number of questions put by these comrades." No, it was "*not* true that language was a superstructure on the base"; yes, of course there was such a thing as "non-class language common and uniform to all people in a society." Indeed *Pravda* "*was* acting correctly in inaugurating this open discussion on linguistics," for the important reason that "the regime prevailing in linguistics cultivates irresponsibility and . . . conduct tantamount to sabotage." The discussion would "expose this regime" and "smash it to smithereens!" What was baffling in the abstract was thus murderous and stultifying in reality. Without intellectual creativity, the possibilities for sustained economic and social development were limited; without a modicum of free expression, even on such politically innocuous subjects as linguistics, the possibility of rational decision making in areas central to social well-being was limited in the extreme.

Thus the revolutionary process in Soviet Russia reached a stage where it could no longer involve the criticism of social elites (much less their dislodging), since it was Stalin's regime itself that held concentrated wealth and power and made criticism equivalent to subversion. Hierarchy had come to dominate social relations no less than under Nicholas II. Commitment to revolution ceased to mean commitment to change. Vital connections were severed even to the goals of October and to fundamental values of socialist social organization.

Such, in part, was Stalin's legacy, as much as industrial might and military power. And in such circumstances Soviet Russia endured the last years of his rule. Pressure built in the countryside and also within the party. Again, there was a dangerous enemy close at hand. Again new plan targets at the 1952 Congress demanded extraordinary efforts. There were also new purges, especially of the Leningrad party organization (as in 1925), and rumors of more to come. To many inside the party and out, the country's course must have seemed perilous, politically and economically. Whether Stalin appreciated this concern (or whether it finally led in fact, to the conspiracy against him he feared so intensely), his rule was now so distant from ordinary affairs that even the most accurate information would not have changed his views. Stalin "*knew*," and Soviet socialism in the last dismal years of his life had become entirely a function of his "knowledge."

CIVIL WAR IN CHINA

Meanwhile, as Stalinist socialism remained a "model" for those who wanted (or were forced to accept) the services of Soviet industrial and military strength, civil war raged in China. When the war in the Pacific ended on August 14, 1945, the territory governed by the Communists included nineteen base areas strung out across North, Central, and South China, with a total population of 100,000,000 and an army of one million regulars and two million militia. Expanding slowly from the original base area in Yanan, they had functioned as a legitimate government for almost a decade, and they had no intention of relinquishing power now.

Yet it is barely possible that civil war might have been avoided had the Communists, Nationalists, and the United States all negotiated in good faith. Uncertain of their strength nationally, long used to the strains of a united front, the Communists were ready—indeed eager—to join in a coalition government in which they would continue to govern the liberated areas, maintain their military force, and share power with the Nationalists in a reformed central government. It is hardly surprising that Chiang Kai-shek demurred. The coalition the Communists had in mind, essentially, would have made explicit the revolutionary situation itself—two contenders for state power claiming sovereignty over the same population—and, in fact, legitimized it. Mao and his comrades were confident that, in any purely political competition, they were bound to gain influence and power; Chiang agreed and therefore opted for a military contest. The United States, its actual policy muffled in the rhetoric of good will, did little to dissuade him.

It is not necessary to dwell here in detail on the political and military aspects of the struggle, which was fought from 1946 until the Communists' final assumption of state power in October 1949. In briefer compass, but with no less ferocity, the civil war recapitulated the history of the war against Japan. Well-equipped Nationalist troops, supplied by the United States at four times the level of the Pacific war years, collapsed in the face of the Communists, turned on the population for whose loyalty they presumably contended, and by their every act of omission and commission, ensured that the outcome of civil conflict would be total Communist victory.

During the war against Japan, military security had been, as Chen Yi explained to John Service, the precondition for rural reform; now the reverse was true. Class struggle was the ground on which troops were recruited into the People's Liberation Army (PLA), guerrilla struggle was sustained, and the revolutionary promise of the Communist party was fulfilled. Analyzing the impact of land reform directives formalized in 1946, Suzanne Pepper notes that its "key objectives were not just land-to-the-tiller, but the political and economic destruction of the existing rural elite, and the mobilization of peasant support for the creation of a new one."[6] China's October could not lie in the control of one or more major city; here, the countryside, its old ruling class destroyed, had to liberate the cities. The civil war thus returned the party to the tasks it had first undertaken in the Jiangxi years, enriched now by the experience of government and administration during the war. And in the course of leading social revolution in the countryside, itself inseparable from waging the civil war against the Nationalists, the early lineaments of a Chinese road to socialism could be discerned.

A central dimension was the relationship between poor peasant demands, local cadres, and party directives. In the Soviet Union, agrarian revolution in 1917 had proceeded unchecked by Bolshevik control, and the consequences redounded to their immediate benefit, whatever price had later to be paid. But the fact of ongoing civil war in China meant that the CCP, intent on forging as large an anti-KMT unity as the goals of social revolution allowed, had to control peasant actions from the outset. Moreover, the CCP vision was not the fulfillment of traditional peasant egalitarian yearnings, but the structural transformation of China's society and economy. Land reform was only a first step, though much depended on the way in which it was conducted.

By the time David and Isabel Crook arrived at the village of Ten Mile Inn in 1948, for example, there were no more landlords, nor even rich peasants.[7] Former members of both classes now held only one-sixth of the land they had possessed in the past. About one-third of all village families had become, as a result of earlier reform movements, "new middle peasants." One-third of Ten Mile Inn's people were still poor peasants, but they all owned land and "there was not a single person in Ten Mile Inn who lived by exploiting the labor of others." Who then were the exploiters? And if there were none, why were so many still so very poor? Attacks on middle peasants caused a serious decline in production. Fearing confiscation, the more prosperous peasants sold their farm animals, planted less, reaped less, and worked hard to give the impression of dire poverty, all of which seriously affected production. Work teams sent to the villages from county towns found that, in the words of one senior member, "whenever the peasants are mobilized to struggle they push on toward extreme egalitarianism and the cadres are apt to be swept along with them." Firm party directives attempted to stem this tide: "The Party must resolutely and by every means draw the middle peasants into the movement and see that they benefit from it. . . . The whole struggle must be conducted with the genuine consent and to the satisfaction of all peasant masses, well-to-do middle peasants included."

The method with which the CCP dealt with this problem was at the same time a substantive aspect of China's approach to socialism itself. The current stage of the revolution remained bourgeois-democratic; no immediate transition to socialized agriculture or nationalized industry was contemplated. Nevertheless, the elimination of feudal relations in the countryside had to be achieved in such a way as to make that later stage more, rather than less, possible. To that difficult end, the relationship between party and mass had to be one of trust, understanding, and intimacy. The mass line, as Mao Zedong had articulated it in Yanan, had to govern all party cadres: to the masses, from the masses, in an endless spiral of close investigation, education, and change. For Mao, unlike Stalin, revolution purely from above was unacceptable—tactically and theoretically. Tactically it would never yield the mobilization necessary to defeat the KMT; theoretically it violated his deep, passionate trust in the capacity of China's hundreds of millions of ordinary peasants for revolutionary change. Peasants had to act on their own, for their own liberation; but they had to be persuaded to do so within constraints established by the party, constraints whose necessity they would have to recognize.

In practice, in contrast to Soviet Russia, the mass line meant that the process of land distribution could not take place once and for all from above, but was subject to constant investigation, rectification, and redistribution. In Soviet villages and factories, workers and peasants murmured criticisms and were surprised if they went unpunished; bolder resisters took up weapons and were crushed. In China, local party members were the object of harsh mass criticism in public meetings. They themselves also engaged in public self-criticism, the better to encourage broad acceptance of the process. Although there was still some popular dissatisfaction ("Who can eat self-criticism?" peasants complained), this direct expression of control by the people over the party cadres was politically as massive a transformation as land reform was economically.

Yet here, too, the painful dialectic of concrete revolutionary change was evident. Public criticism of cadres frequently rendered them reluctant to exercise any leadership whatsoever. Passivity was safer by far. Criticism itself was often simply the expression of ancient village spites, fierce petty antagonisms that could (and did) erupt into brutal violence. And how, precisely, did one become a "student of the masses," as Mao so confidently instructed, when what the masses taught violated party directives?

Consider, for example, the task of mobilizing and emancipating village women, also a high party priority. It was held as almost religious conviction by most male peasants, including party members, that the "militant women weren't virtuous and the virtuous women weren't militant." It was one thing to pass legislation prohibiting forced marriages and allowing divorce; it was quite another to get poor peasant cadres, who were in charge of administering that law, to enforce it, especially when it went so directly against their own interests. Chinese peasant women, like peasant men, had to be directly engaged in the struggle for their own liberation.

Contrary to the fears of the Right, as well as the romanticism of some on the Left, oppression is not the best school for revolution. Peasant anger, deep, unforgiving, would not automatically express itself with the arrival of a county cadre or two. People had to be persuaded to speak up, convinced that in their unity there was the strength to resist efforts to force them back into silence. *Suku* ("speak bitterness") was both a technique for mobilizing peasant anger and a revolutionary act in itself. For a poor peasant to stand up and give voice to decades of rage against a rich peasant or landlord, for a woman to directly accuse her husband or parents-in-law of mistreatment, was an almost immeasurable break with the past.

One account of the *suku* process will perhaps illustrate its meaning and importance to the development of socialism in China more profoundly than any number of abstract descriptions. Jack Belden, following the course of the civil war in North China, spent some time in the village of Lijiazhuan, Hebei province, population 300, where for days he listened to the life history of a young woman named Jinhua (which Belden translates into English as Gold Flower).[8] Beaten and semi-starved by her father-in-law while her husband was away, by both of them when he was home, Gold Flower's initial response to news that a Women's Association had been formed in the village was skeptical. After much persuasion she confided the details of her ill-treatment to one of her friends in the association, who returned a few days later with four other members to speak with the father-in-law. Predictably he ordered them out of his house. To the total shock of both Gold Flower and the old man, the delegation responded by tying him up and leading him to a room in the Women's Association headquarters where he was held prisoner for two days. Then a general assembly of all the women in the village was called and addressed by a district cadre: "We stretch out our sisterly hands to the oppressed women, and hope that in our struggle against the dictatorship of Chiang Kai-shek and the landlords we shall find faithful allies among the village women. . . . Hand in hand we shall go into the struggle against those who have enslaved us for two thousand years. And any man, any husband, any father-in-law who opposes us we shall beat to the ground and treat without mercy." At this point Gold Flower's father-in-law was led into the meeting room and, overcoming a moment of total panic, Gold Flower began to speak the truth of her life, the truth of the lives of so many women in that room. As she did so the "crowd groaned" and pressed forward. "Let us spit in his face," shouted one woman and then did, followed by many others till the man stood trembling in the center of their rage. Promising to reform his ways, he was released, and Gold Flower herself joined one of the many small groups that had been established to investigate cases of abused women. The women had *acted* on their anger and at the same time moved profoundly against the entire system of female subordination. They had humiliated a man, an *old* man and a father-in-law—all the rules had been broken.

As the civil war drew closer to Lijiazhuan, the stake its women had in Communist victory was clear and immediate. When some protested against joining the men in field work, Gold Flower explained: "If we do not work, the fields will produce little; there will be no grain for soldiers at the front. Then we shall be threatened to death by Chiang Kai-shek's army and lose all we have gained. And again we will have to depend on our husbands." There remained the matter of her own husband. When he returned, his father at once informed him of the outrage that had occurred in his absence and he promised his wife an exemplary beating, one that would break her arms and legs: "Then you can't go to your meetings. On your broken legs, you won't even be able to crawl." Instead Gold Flower's husband was hauled before the Women's Association where, like his father before him, he faced Gold Flower's accusations. Dissatisfied with his response, their anger at high pitch, the women beat him thoroughly and extracted a written guarantee of future good behavior. When the shallowness of his resolve became clear, Gold Flower moved once more to call down the wrath of the Women's Association. Chased by forty women intent on beating him, Gold Flower's husband kept on running and did not return. At the time Belden spoke with her she was in the process of getting a divorce. "In the women of China," Belden concludes, "the Communists possessed, almost ready made, one of the greatest masses of disinherited human beings the world has ever seen. And because they found the key to the heart of these women, they also found one of the keys to victory over Chiang Kai-shek."[9]

Anger, articulated, organized, and acted upon, was thus at the heart of Communist mobilization during the civil war. But what is important about the Chinese revolutionary process, and a central point of comparison with Soviet Russia, is that even after the final defeat of the KMT, when the party had the power to impose its will on the countryside and the need to mobilize against the KMT was absent, the land revolution was conducted in much the same way. To be sure, the decentralized, frequently violent nature of land reform, valuable in terms of mobilization during the civil war, had now to be brought under firmer central control and "ultra-left excesses" were severely condemned. But, as a senior official insisted, it was not enough for the peasants to want land; the question was, from *whom* did they want it? "Giving them land when they merely want it from the government will provide the landlords with opportunities to ruin everything."[10] In provinces liberated by the PLA, as in the older base areas during the war against Japan and the civil war, land reform was never seen as simply an economic measure; it was to be quite consciously a social revolution, which meant the full and *conscious* participation of masses of peasants. The methods of revolutionary rule were to be modeled on the methods of revolutionary struggle.

Even after 1949, when the civil war had ended in Communist victory, land reform followed civil war patterns. It began with the classification of villagers into categories (landlord, rich peasant, middle peasant, poor peasant, landless laborer) for purposes of confiscation and distribution of land and property. The classification meetings were open and village-wide, a step toward overcoming peasant fear and the traditional organization of village power. In the public act of classification, the sheer numerical weight of poor, landless, and middle peasants was dramatically visible. The moment at which a poor or landless peasant stood up to defy publicly those who had held power over him was the moment he irrevocably joined the revolution, even if its broader course and substance remained unclear. And the moment at which, in public session, a peasant could criticize the way in which the new elite of cadres had conducted some aspect of reform, was the moment he learned the reality of an utterly new possibility of political expression and potential power. In all of this, the contrast with the Soviet Union could not be greater.

THE CCP ASSUMES STATE POWER

Facing the gates of the Forbidden City, where for centuries the Sons of Heaven ruled the Middle Kingdom, is a vast square whose dimensions fix the human observer firmly in an attitude of appropriate awe. There, in the Square of Heavenly Peace, Mao Zedong, chairman of the newly proclaimed People's Republic of China, ceremonially announced the foundation of the republic in October 1949.

Months before, with final victory certain, Mao had outlined the nature of the new regime in a long reflective essay commemorating the twenty-eighth anniversary of the founding of the party. The form of the state would be a "people's democratic dictatorship," which looked forward to the ultimate withering of both state and classes, and recognized the distance not only of that goal, but even of a quick transition to socialism. Imperialism had taught the Chinese people that "Western bourgeois civilization, bourgeois democracy and the plan for a bourgeois republic" in China were all "bankrupt." "Imperialist aggression," he reminded his readers, "shattered the fond dreams of the Chinese about learning from the West. It was very odd—why were the teachers always committing aggression against their pupil?" So China instead had learned from the people of Soviet Russia, who had given them an invaluable weapon: "This weapon is not a machine-gun, but Marxism-Leninism."[11]

Mao's conception of a "people's democratic dictatorship," however much it may have owed, in a general way, to the weapon proffered by the Soviet Union, was in fact uniquely his own; indeed its relationship to standard Marxist-Leninist formulations on state power seems remote. But it was shaped, as were so many other aspects of the Chinese revolution, to and by the particularities of China's social and historical situation. Ever since 1911, Mao argued, bourgeois and petty-bourgeois nationalists had attempted to lead revolutions that would establish an independent, economically developing Chinese state—and had failed: "In the epoch of imperialism the petty bourgeoisie and the national bourgeoisie cannot lead any genuine revolution to victory." Now, twenty-four years after Sun Yat-sen's death, the Communist party had succeeded because it had learned to "unite the working class, the peasantry, the urban petty bourgeoisie and the national bourgeoisie" in a "domestic united front under the leadership of the working class." People's democratic dictatorship meant democracy within this coalition, dictatorship over all who opposed it. The national bourgeoisie, although permanently disqualified as holders of state power, must nevertheless be encouraged and reassured. With the imperialist powers at China's back, a "most ferocious enemy" hoping for failure, all efforts had to be bent to the development of the national economy. "China must utilize all the factors of urban and rural capitalism that are beneficial and not harmful to the national economy and the people's livelihood."

In agriculture, the most serious problem was "the education of the peasantry." Socialized agriculture was essential, but it would "require a long time and painstaking work." Above all, Mao warned his comrades, they must be able to learn:

We must overcome difficulties, we must learn what we do not know. We must learn to do economic work from all who know how, no matter who they are. We must esteem them as teachers, learning from them respectfully and conscientiously. We must not pretend to know when we do not know. We must not put on bureaucratic airs. If we dig into a subject for several months, for a year or two, for three or five years, we shall eventually master it.[12]

In essence, the "new democracy" the party claimed to initiate in 1949 was a continuation of the united front policy it had used so creatively during the civil war. The point was, once again, "to unite with all those people who can be more or less united with." Such unity was limited and flexible; its components would shift as the social and political forces at play in the society shifted. Controlled and manipulated by the party, this course nevertheless allowed nonparty groups to cooperate for mutually agreed-upon goals that, once realized, might well mean a basic shift in the composition of the front itself. Everything about the conception was dynamic, fluid, and impermanent. Through struggle *and* unity, new social alliances would emerge, focused on the principal contradiction of that particular period. Thus, the national bourgeoisie would eventually fade from the scene, but for the moment, in the effort to begin the task of economic development, the party had to "struggle with them on the one hand and unite with them on the other."[13]

What the pace of change in China might have been had not the Korean War intervened is unclear. But only one year after its proclamation, the People's Republic of China was once more embattled—this time with the most powerful military force in world history. In September 1949, Mao had insisted: "Our nation will never again be an insulted nation. We have stood up." From 1950 to 1953 China made good that claim.

STALIN'S DEATH AND THE COMPARATIVE TASKS
OF NEW SOCIALIST DEVELOPMENT

Although fought by proxy, the Korean War was also Stalin's last direct engagement with the forces of the "bourgeois" world. The Soviet leader was exceptionally cautious about involving his own armed forces, and the war was essentially a North Korean undertaking. But Soviet Russia's industrial strength was now an arsenal for the Koreans and Chinese, as well as a base for building China's own industrial power. In fact, for many in the Chinese leadership, particularly Gao Gang, the head of the vast industrial region of Manchuria, the importance of closer ties with the USSR was now beyond question, as was the strength of Stalin's leadership.

In March 1953, Stalin died. Communist leaders everywhere were stunned. Russians themselves bewildered; the country was "like a horse which has pulled a heavy cart for twenty years, unable to understand when the yoke is finally removed."[14] The official announcement of his death was a remarkable document. Citizens were admonished to "avoid all confusion and panic" and assured that the Politburo had matters well in hand. The Kremlin was ringed with troops. Elite units of the secret police rumbled toward the center of Moscow in tanks and half-tracks, heavily armed, to "preserve order." At night throughout the city, one could hear the ominous sounds of engines warming in the distance.

However, Moscow was far from any thought of civil disturbance. The most serious "confusion and panic" was not in the streets, but inside the Kremlin. Beria's police evoked familiar anxieties. Just after the Nineteenth Party Congress in October 1952, Stalin had "discovered" a "Doctor's Plot" to murder him and other (unnamed) high party officials. A number of arrests had been made, others were promised. The similarity to Kirov's murder in 1934 after the Seventeenth Party Congress was all too apparent, and with it the prospects of a bloody new purge. There also may have been fears of disorders over lack of food and other essential goods. Those familiar with the countryside, like the Ukrainian party leader Nikita Khrushchev, also realized the extent of peasant resistance to high tax obligations and higher prices. If the Kremlin's fears were misplaced, it was only because Russia's political leadership had become so isolated from the people as to misperceive how effectively the personality cult had created real feelings of popular attachment to Stalin, and how the news of his death had evoked genuine feelings of loss, not because they failed to understand the likely causes of popular discontent.

Stalin's death was the beginning of a remarkable decade, one in which the contradictions of his era simply had to be faced and resolved, and the Soviet Union's socialist road redefined. In comparative terms, this necessarily affected China since even a marginal adjustment of Stalinist patterns implied the possibility of further weaknesses to be corrected, and hence the validity of questioning a wide variety of premises on which the process of revolutionary change under Stalin had been based. If one were to look comparatively at the transformation of Russia and China in terms of developmental stages, the early 1950s in China might best be likened to the late twenties in the Soviet Union. The tasks of industrialization and socialist construction lay ahead for the CCP, despite the party's relatively secure social base, and the problem of strategies and tactics was quite logically a question of adapting a Stalinist model. Although valuable in some ways, one weakness of such forms of analysis is that they tend to ignore the actual dynamics of interstate relations and the role such relations play developmentally. The fact that in terms of chronological comparison, the early 1950s was also a time of new definition in Moscow meant that the parallel developments of both societies became much more closely intertwined, as the resolution of issues in one country implicitly became a challenge and a model for the other.

At the same time, the dialectics of these complex relations between the two communist powers turned on the unfolding of several processes that might, at first glance, be considered autonomous and distinct. Within Soviet Russia itself, the post-Stalin leadership's goal was to restore what it regarded as a genuine socialism. First, there was the process of ending the flagrant abuses of Stalin's dictatorship, a course of "de-Stalinization" aimed in part at restoring some semblance of normalcy to ordinary political affairs. Second, there was an effort to improve dramatically Soviet Russia's economic performance and the material well-being of its people. Closely related was a third process, an effort to change the structure of party and state administration to both facilitate economic development and to assure that the "mistakes" of the Stalin era would not be repeated. And finally, there was a concomitant search for international security, involving at the same time a new posture of strength in international affairs. Each of these closely interrelated patterns was part of a general effort to establish a new political legitimacy for the CPSU, based in its leaders' eyes on secure, stable, and progressive economic and social development. The socialist road in Russia would gain new acceptance through performance. When others saw where it led, the place of communism (and its parties and leaders) would finally be secure.

If the death of Stalin thus led in Russia to an effort at resolving the contradictions flowing from twenty-five years of Stalinist socialism, in China the years immediately following his death saw the emergence of those very contradictions, largely as a result of China's effort to pursue the Stalinist model. China's goal, as Soviet Russia's had been, was to develop her industrial might. The Korean War clearly revealed the continuing dangers of weakness. There were also the tasks of further political consolidation and the completion of the agrarian revolution. Before 1953, Tito's experience in Yugoslavia revealed the costs of defying Stalin's wishes. Now, paradoxically, his death allowed Communist leadership in Peking to define on their own what a Stalinist road in China would actually be.

POLITICAL CONSOLIDATION IN CHINA

The tasks of political consolidation in China involved both the end of a period of repression and the further centralization of party control from Peking. The initial moderation of urban and rural policies was modified sharply during the war in Korea. The reality of external threat increased when President Harry Truman ordered the Seventh Fleet into the Taiwan Straits, relentlessly pursued a policy of international trade embargo against China, and through these and other policies, artificially prolonged the Chinese civil war. China may have "stood up," but internationally it was barred from the United Nations, at war with the hegemon of the bourgeois world, and subject to American-supported harassment, sabotage, and infiltration from the "Republic of China," its tiny island doppelgänger.

Repression had taken the form of a series of movements, some of which would probably have been conducted in any event though with what severity it is impossible to judge. In rapid succession throughout 1951 and 1952, campaigns were conducted first to suppress "counterrevolutionaries," next to control the relationship between state cadres and private business enterprises, and finally, in the "five anti" movement, to bring private industrial and commercial enterprises more firmly under state supervision.

Although the exact figure will never be known, most accounts estimate that some two million people were killed between 1945 and 1953 either by state judicial machinery or in semispontaneous executions in the course of land reform. Perhaps as many again were imprisoned for varying periods of time. No rhetoric can absolve such terror of its inhumanity. Violence, however, was not the main mechanism of political consolidation. State supervision of private industrial and commercial enterprise meant integration of personnel, not their elimination. Thought reform programs were instituted in schools at all levels, directed at an inner transformation of Chinese academics and intellectuals through small, intense study groups, criticism and self-criticism, and, in some cases, reeducation through manual labor in the countryside.

William Sewell, a British professor of chemistry at a small Sichuan university, has described the painful, yet exhilarating experience of these sessions, similar in many ways to what we would now call consciousness raising. Groups were given specific instructions on how to strip themselves down through the layers of Western-inspired values, elite arrogance, and indifference to the suffering of others. The attempt was to bring urban intellectuals to an awareness of how their lives had embodied privilege—how even their most minor acts reflected attitudes and ways of living that contradicted their own best hopes for themselves, and for China—and to encourage them to live out of the center of their new consciousness. For many, it worked:

> For the individual members there was never any feeling that ideas were being forced upon them. So skillful did many of the leaders become that ideas seemed to be separately born within the group and, even more subtly, that they were born in each individual mind. The feeling was fostered in each of us . . . that we, however humble we might be, had a real share in building China.[15]

For others, especially as the pressure of the movement increased with the Korean war, it was an intolerable experience. "The agony," Sewell wrote, "increased as the struggle became keener, as we were urged to come clean and then cleaner still." People broke under the strain and several committed suicide.[16]

Political consolidation, of course, was only one aspect of the broader task of socialist development. Despite the route the Chinese had taken to state power, their understanding of how to achieve socialism remained essentially Soviet. Industrialization was the major goal, with investments in heavy industry a high priority; and as in the Soviet Union, agriculture (supplemented by such aid as Russia could provide) would fund economic development. How to increase agricultural productivity to meet these needs remained an open question.

There is nothing surprising about the extent to which the Chinese took the Soviet Union as a model for industrial growth. The particular nature of Stalinist socialism seems not to have troubled, or even intruded on, the consciousness of Chinese leaders. Russia was *assumed* to be socialist and a reliable guide to drawing a backward, agrarian nation into the ranks of industrial strength. Also, the Soviet Union alone was ready to aid, advise, and assist China in areas of crucial need. And the need was extraordinary: of the 10,000 industrial workers (out of a prewar 120,000) who remained on the staff of the Anshan iron and steel works, for example, only 100 could be called skilled. China's tiny modern industrial base, far smaller than Russia's in 1917, had been largely built by, for, and with foreign imperialist funds and technology. Chinese agriculture, similarly, operated at a technological level much lower than Russia's at the time of the October revolution. Sino-Soviet aid agreements in 1950, 1953, and 1954 gave China access to Soviet technology, managerial approaches, and model industrial plants. Finally, in terms of national security, China's reliance on the Soviet Union was not one merely of current Cold War need, but one that arose from the very circumstances in which the CCP came to power. In 1917, alone in the bourgeois world, the Bolsheviks could look only to the receding hope of proletarian revolution in Europe. But, as Mao explained China's more fortunate circumstances:

> If the Soviet Union had not existed, if there had been no victory in the anti-fascist Second World War, if Japanese imperialism had not been defeated, if the People's Democracies had not come into being, . . . if not for all these in combination, the international reactionary forces bearing down upon us would certainly be many times greater than now. In such circumstances, could we have won victory? Obviously not. And even with victory, there could be no consolidation.[17]

By 1956, the nationalization of industry was virtually complete, although a small group of businessmen continued to receive remittances as compensation. As Carl Riskin observes, the regime had, within just a few years of taking power, succeeded in "establishing firm and honest control in the cities. . . . The complicated tasks of keeping alive and utilizing the private sector, while leading it into state-directed channels, had been handled on the whole successfully."[18]

Under the banner, "Let's Be Modern and Soviet," the core of China's First Five-Year Plan lay in some 156 Soviet-aided projects, aided by 14,000 Soviet technicians, while a total of 13,000 selected Chinese trained in Russian technical institutes and factories. The Plan, inaugurated in 1953, gave primacy to capital-intensive heavy industry, relied on the privately organized agrarian sector for food, resources, and capital supplies, and established nationally centralized, strictly hierarchical planning ministries. Factory organization followed the Soviet system of one-person management, and the movement away from the decentralized, self-reliant, "guerrilla mentality" of the Yanan approach to production and development seemed complete. Rationality, systematization, efficiency, technical expertise—the modern virtues of advanced industrial society—were, it seemed, revolutionary virtues as well, or at least, the virtues of the revolution in power.

But if the form of industrialization was to be Soviet, the Chinese leadership in Peking had no desire to allow intimate Soviet political domination of the process. Before Stalin's death, the relationship between Russia and Gao Gang, head of the State Planning Commission, political and economic "tsar" of Manchuria, caused Peking considerable concern. One of the founders of the Shaanxi base areas, Gao had been a guerrilla leader of prominence and power. In 1945 he became head of both party and government in what was then the Northeast Military Region, one of the five "Great Areas" into which China was then divided—an area in which Russia historically had had both special interests and privileges. It seems likely that Stalin regarded Gao as a particular favorite among the Chinese leaders, and in 1949, before Mao's own trip to Moscow, he had welcomed a visit from Gao and negotiated an economic agreement pertaining solely to Manchuria. Given China's dependency on the Soviet Union for economic aid and military security, the fear that the relationship between Gao and Stalin might develop in ways that vitally threatened China's integrity seemed reasonable.

But with Stalin's death, Peking felt free to move swiftly against Gao's "independent kingdom." The purge of Gao (and a host of his followers, real and alleged, including the head of the Shanghai industrial region, freed the leadership to pursue what remained a Stalinist model of development without fear of Stalin's control or interference.

There was one element in the Stalinist model, however, that the

Chinese were determined to avoid: the disasters of forced collectivization. By 1952, the revolution on the land, having brought land to the tiller, was over. The locus of further change was to be the cities, and the task of the countryside was to increase production whose surplus could be applied to the primary task of industrialization. In the absence of collectivization, understood as dependent upon mechanization, this necessarily meant relying primarily on rich and middle peasants, who were best able to produce a surplus, just as the Soviet Union had done during the 1920s. The peasantry may have been a force in making the revolution; they were not a force that could lead in the transition to socialism.

Peasant cadres were not unaware of the shift, and some complained bitterly that it was peasants, not workers, who had made the revolution; peasants who had liberated the workers, not the reverse. Why should workers be "elder brothers" to peasants when peasants outnumbered them many hundred thousand times over? A sharp decline in rank-and-file rural cadre morale was everywhere noticeable, reinforced by the stress on increased agricultural production through encouraging individual, and in particular rich peasant, production.

Yet, in terms of expanding production, the rich peasant proved a weak reed

> as a capitalist type, rich-peasant farming in China was still in a low stage of development. Their capitalist activities were mainly directed towards commercial speculation and usury; their management of farming in a capitalist way did not show any marked advance; and their production did not display much superiority over that of peasants working on their own.[19]

Not only did reliance on the rich peasants fail to yield the necessary increase in production, there was considerable danger of a repolarization of rural classes, especially when, as was often the case, rich peasants were themselves party cadres. The small and scattered holdings poor peasants and landless laborers had received in land reform were simply not feasible economic units. Moreover they lacked tools, animals, low interest credit, and seed. Many were falling dangerously into debt, selling their labor, their land, or both. In the abstract, it might make a great difference that a poor peasant now worked for, owed money to, was exploited by, a "new middle" or "new rich" peasant rather than a landlord. The new village elite could never hold the same power, politically or socially, as the old landlord class. But concretely, in the real lives of village peasants, the difference was less palpable. More disturbing to the leadership, peasants forced finally to sell their land were leaving the countryside for the cities, which could neither feed nor employ them.

CHINA'S NEW SOCIALIST ROAD

Out of this contradiction came elements of a new socialist road in China. In order to raise production, and reduce, or at least freeze, renewed class division, without recourse to forced collectivization, two forms of voluntary cooperation were encouraged. The first, mutual aid teams, were rooted in traditional modes of rural labor exchange. Although they remained seasonal in nature, as had been the case traditionally, they involved more formal exchanges of draft animals, tools, and labor, shared among some five neighboring households, with returns adjusted to the quality and quantity of inputs each household made. At the same time another, more highly developed, form of agricultural cooperative was promulgated. Lower-stage agricultural producer cooperatives allowed for individual ownership of the land, but all land and equipment were pooled. In time, it was hoped, membership in such cooperatives would be village-wide, thus contributing to the breakdown of vertical clan and lineage hierarchies within each village and allowing for an increasingly rational and specialized use of land, labor, and draft animals.

Moreover, the cooperatives might continue to develop, in smooth stages, to higher-stage cooperatives with land owned collectively and returns based solely on labor rather than, as remained the case in LAPCs, on the amount of land, equipment, and labor each household contributed. Semisocialist in nature, the lower-stage agricultural producer cooperatives quickly ran into the further contradictions such forms of organization engender: land could be, and often was, withdrawn at will from the cooperative; richer peasants found it far more profitable to pool land and equipment with each other and systematically excluded poor peasants; inexperienced cadres sometimes forced into cooperatives unwilling middle and well-off peasants, who retaliated by killing off their livestock and destroying other valuable agricultural property. While the pace was slow, by 1955, 15 percent of the population had organized as LAPCs, although production remained low and class differentiation grew.

As in the Soviet Union the questions of raising rural production and achieving socialism were intimately linked. But how to convey the link and implement the goal was another matter. Yet there was a more central issue: not only how to continue to make revolution, but *why?* For a substantial portion of the peasantry possession of land was itself fulfillment. Mutual aid teams and cooperatives (at higher or lower stages) were irrelevant, indeed outright interventions of a state authority that could quickly become as obnoxious as the old landlord order had been. Not surprisingly, because that is exactly who they were, local cadres as well as their new and old middle and rich peasant constituency embodied that "small producer mentality" that, Lenin insisted, would daily, hourly, and on a massive scale, reproduce capitalism. "After I make a little money," one cadre argued, "I'll become active again." "All my life I have suffered hardship," another complained, "now that I have been given land, I am completely satisfied, so why continue to make revolution?"[20] A popular short novel of the period catches the mood of these newly affluent peasants with precision. Accused of a "spontaneous tendency" toward capitalism, a hardworking peasant responds with understandable fury:

> Is there anything wrong with my way of doing things? To become rich through production, and the protection of private property! Didn't the cadres tell us this before? I never imagined that after all my toil and sufferings from cold and hunger I should be accused of taking the wrong road. Some people refuse to work hard and talk behind their back about others who have profited by their own labor. They say that I have a "spontaneous tendency." I say, "They are jealous and envious of me!"[21]

When the principle of cooperatives is explained, the old man is genuinely puzzled: "How can there be no difference between the rich and the poor? If nobody becomes poor, how can some become rich?"

There was simply no way to coerce the peasantry, even if the party had wished to do so, into an increase in production necessary for industrialization without weakening incentives to increase agricultural production, thereby reducing future surpluses.[22] Thus by 1955 the Chinese road to socialism, embracing the goals Stalin had set for Soviet Russia's economic development but rejecting his methods in the countryside, had reached an impasse.

NEW SOCIALIST ROADS IN THE USSR

Stalin's goals without Stalinist methods was also a critical problem for the new Soviet leadership. Within a few weeks after his death it was clear that radical changes were in the offing. Retail prices were cut sharply; wheat flour was placed on daily sale in government stores. Various articles appeared in *Pravda* and *Izvestiia* indicating that more consumer goods would soon be available. Shortly afterwards, the new chairman of the Council of Ministers, Georgy Malenkov, announced that clothing production would be expanded dramatically (240 percent), along with the production of meat (230 percent), butter (180 percent), and other essential items. At the same time, the system of procurements in the countryside was almost entirely overhauled. Taxes were reduced sharply, purchase prices increased, and special levies on livestock eliminated completely. In many places peasant debts were cancelled outright. In the summer of 1953, the new first secretary of the party, Nikita Khrushchev, put through a plan to replace taxes in kind in the countryside with monetary taxes, based on the number of people in an individual household. Agricultural surpluses would be *purchased* from peasants at relatively high prices, rather than taken almost entirely in the form of taxes, as before.

Such measures were readily understandable both in terms of the new party leadership's desire to appease a populace it feared was prone to panic and disorder and in terms of the patent weaknesses of Russia's agricultural system. Whether they had any deeper meaning for the process of communist development in Russia was, at first, quite uncertain. Also unclear was the meaning of a series of measures that, on the surface, at least, seemed to undermine radically Stalin's system of political controls. On March 27, a general amnesty was declared for all political prisoners serving terms of five years or less. One week later Lavrenti Beria, head of the secret police, released the doctors arrested in connection with the alleged plot on Stalin's life. *Pravda* announced that "all cases of official high-handedness" would be severely punished. Lydia Timashuk, whose denunciations had "unearthed" the plot, was told to surrender her Order of Lenin and was publicly disgraced. More quietly, Beria himself went to the railroad station to welcome back personally Molotov's wife from the prison camps.

To some in the West these steps seemed curious, even reckless given the party's "totalitarian" politics. Stalin's heirs, after all, were Stalin's men, individuals whose power depended heavily on the terrorist methods of the secret police. Indeed, when Beria himself was arrested shortly afterwards, and then summarily shot, it appeared the party leadership might be involved in a vicious cycle of cannibalization, as would-be "Leaders" jockeyed for control over the political levers Stalin had bequeathed.

In fact, something quite different was occurring—a process of metamorphosis, in which party leaders were beginning to seek a new basis of political legitimacy and to reassociate themselves with what would increasingly be defined as "basic socialist goals." These involved, in particular, increased material well-being and a genuine degree of security, both politically (in terms of popular support for the party and its programs) and personally (in terms of shedding the terrible fear of arbitrary arrest and disgrace that pervaded the party in Stalin's last years). Closely involved as well was a desire for international security, particularly an end to the Korean war, and a new degree of protection against a hostile West's nuclear might.

The problem of personal insecurity explains both the party's release of the "Doctors' Plot" figures and Beria's own subsequent arrest and execution. While denunciations and arbitrary arrests were "ordinary" police activities, the "Doctors' Plot" had been "discovered" by Stalin himself. Like Kirov's murder in 1934, it was announced in the press together with attacks on the police for "insufficient vigilance" and "incompetence." The police themselves, in all likelihood, were thus about to be purged. Releasing the doctors (and welcoming Molotov's wife) may thus have been an effort on both the party's and Beria's part to restore "normalcy," although Beria's own success in this regard may have made him too powerful in the eyes of his Politburo comrades, which increased *their* personal insecurity and led to his arrest. The police were now to be brought closely under party supervision, stripped of arbitrary power, and restored to a "rightful" (Leninist) role as an organ of state security.

To do this, however, Beria's henchmen had to be removed as well, the police apparatus reformed, and those clearly detained without reason released. Khrushchev and other Politburo figures undoubtedly hoped this could be done quietly and carefully. But the Gulag Archipelago presented Stalin's successors with a fearsome display of abuse, startling even to those who had helped contribute victims. Reports by unimpeachable Stalinists indicated hundreds of prominent national figures had been detained without discernible cause; as their cases were reviewed, thousands, and then tens of thousands of lesser figures came to light.

The process of investigation and rectification had a dynamic of its own. By the end of 1953 only about 4,000 of the estimated 13 million prisoners had been released, but each had many tales to tell. By 1954 the new leadership was left with little choice but to begin dismantling the Gulag system in its entirety. The full magnitude of the twentieth century's other holocaust was becoming more and more clear. So, consequently, was the need for relegitimizing the party politically.

Efforts to improve material welfare similarly may have started from concerns about party security in 1953, but here, too, the process had its own dynamic. Nikita Khrushchev, Stalin's successor as first secretary, was elected to that post by his Politburo comrades in part because he seemed an obvious lesser light (and thus unlikely to assume greater personal power than more prominent colleagues like Molotov, Mikoyan, Kaganovich, and especially Malenkov, who was forced to relinquish the secretary's position), but also because he was the only ranking party figure genuinely familiar with the countryside. Khrushchev began almost immediately to make new appointments. Within a year he had replaced more than half the party's provincial first secretaries. This undoubtedly helped secure his personal ascendancy in the party, but equally important, it brought into crucial party positions persons of recognized administrative and economic competence, appointed to correct Russia's chronic economic problems. And if *blat* ("influence peddling") had been "higher than Stalin," as popular wisdom had it, economic expertise now became more important than personal political loyalties. In the process, the party began to reidentify itself as an instrument of social progress, rather than simply of social control.

Some elements of this reidentification were easily articulated. The party opened vast new "virgin lands" in Central Asia to increase the cultivation of wheat. The March 1954 Central Committee plenum resolved to start cultivation on more than thirteen million hectares of

Central Asian grasslands, hoping to generate some twenty million tons of additional grain. Equipment was mobilized and a massive volunteer recruitment plan begun, reminiscent of the first months of Bolshevik rule and correspondingly publicized.

There were also new production campaigns, new production incentives, higher wage scales, new imports of foreign goods, and a series of similar measures directed, in Malenkov's words, "towards the quick rise in the standard of living of the working class, collective farmers, and the whole people."[23] Special attention was given to increasing livestock and the output of "private plots," a vast and important source of fresh foodstuffs on open, collective farm markets, despite the ideological difficulties of private property. New housing plans were announced for urban areas, and several major apartment developments for workers in Moscow and Leningrad were begun with great fanfare.

There were, however, serious problems here, both economically and politically. Assuaging popular discontent by making more foodstuffs and commodities immediately available was one thing; sustaining a rapid increase in material well-being without a fundamental shift in investment priorities, a relaxation of the international political climate (to allow for a reduction in military expenditures), and a rapid advance in technology and managerial know-how, was quite another. There were also chronic distribution problems, ingrained habits of understating production capacities and overstating resource needs (as protection against sanctions for not fulfilling plans), and above all, serious problems of generating capital to support ambitious new investments. Under Stalin, all deficiencies were "cured" by an intensification of labor, a course at odds with the new party leadership's political objectives.

For much of 1954, these issues were widely debated in party circles. Premier Malenkov took the lead in stressing the desirability of rapidly increasing the supply of consumer goods, but found himself opposed by hardliners who insisted Stalin's emphasis on heavy industrial development had to be maintained. The question of Russia's military posture increasingly became a matter of concern; and so, undoubtedly, did the question of whether the virgin lands project would actually increase agricultural production and hence be worth the enormous investment. In December 1954, *Izvestiia*, speaking for Malenkov, editorialized strongly in favor of consumer goods while *Pravda*, the party organ presumably reflecting Khrushchev's views, argued for rapid growth of heavy industry. Shortly afterwards, Malenkov resigned his post as premier.

The consolidation of Khrushchev's power within the party came about partly, of course, as a result of his authority to appoint new party officials, just as Stalin's had. But issues of policy were equally, if not more, important. The pace of consumer goods development could not outstrip the pace of capital goods investment without producing serious problems: already housing plans exceeded supplies of building materials, demands for foodstuffs exceeded the capacity of agricultural machinery, demands for transport exceeded both automotive production and highway construction. Khrushchev's own emphasis in the debates was on strengthening the chemical industry, a heavy industry crucial to capital goods production but also capable, through the manufacture of new plastics, fertilizers, and synthetics, of meeting increased consumer needs. While this strengthened his personal position within the Politburo, his close association with the virgin lands became problematic, especially after Malenkov's resignation in early 1955.

The first signs from the virgin land areas in 1954 were unclear. Production initially was good, but much of the increased ouput came from more intensive cultivation of existing grain areas. After an extremely hard winter, in which new settlers suffered from inadequate housing and insufficient supplies of food and other commodities, the weather in 1955 turned dry. Much of the newly sown spring wheat failed to ripen. As thousands of settlers who had moved "permanently" to the region began to leave, and several new large-scale collective farms were forced to shut down, Khrushchev and other supporters of the program were accused by Malenkov, Kaganovich, and especially Molotov of using reckless methods.[24] Again, concerns about popular disaffection must have surfaced among the leadership; again, these concerns must have been felt in terms both of party and personal security. In April and then in September 1955, a new range of prisoners were amnestied, including hundreds of thousands accused of "collaborating" with the Germans during World War II. Party control over the police was strengthened, and radical changes took place in Soviet foreign policy. In May, Khrushchev himself visited Yugoslavia to express "sincere regrets" over Russia's (Stalin's) past hostility.

Could a sense of security ever be achieved by Russia's political leadership, however, while it remained so strongly identified with Stalin's brutal methods of "resolving" differences and "correcting" failures? Weren't Khrushchev, Malenkov, and their Politburo comrades themselves responsible in some measure for the unjustified imprisonment of thousands now being released from the camps? And was it possible under these conditions to enlist active and enthusiastic support for new social programs and "great leaps forward" when such a heavy residue of cynicism, suspicion, and caution hung from the past? The irony of Stalin's inheritance lay in the contradiction between enormous achievement and incredible cost, a price exacted in the name of socialist transformation. In China, by 1955, party leaders had to resolve the contradiction that derived from following a pattern of industrialization whose price, in its distortion and violation of their own revolutionary history and method, was unacceptable. In the Soviet Union, Stalin's heirs had somehow to develop a mode of political behavior compatible with their new objectives.

8

GREAT LEAPS FORWARD:
Ironies and Contradictions,
1954-1964

The decade 1954 to 1964 was one of the most remarkable in the history of revolutionary Russia and China. Discussion concerning the direction of Soviet economic development, which occurred after Stalin's death, opened Russia to a period of experimentation and debate it had not experienced since the 1920s. The debate was not only possible, but necessary. Without an all-powerful *Vozhd'* to issue pronouncements and resolve disputes, party leaders were forced to come to grips with Soviet reality and the implications of various courses of action. Discussion led to debate, experimentation, brief successes, and acknowledged failure. Factions formed, maneuvered, and dissolved. Politics, in short, again became complex.

Such complexity had always existed in China, but the new level of discussion in Moscow implicitly called into question the very validity of the Stalinist industrialization model that the Chinese were pursuing. In Peking, too, party leaders were forced to look at the social consequences of economic policy rather than focus on its theoretical underpinnings. Was the First Five-Year Plan working? What was its impact on the development of the state and its bureaucratic apparatus, on mass initiative and a sense of revolutionary involvement, so crucial to Chinese success in the 1930s and 1940s? And what of the problem of agriculture? How could capital for industrialization be accumulated without either a dangerous and expensive dependence on the Soviet Union or swift collectivization?

Moreover, neither the Soviet Union nor China were free to work out their respective destinies in an international vacuum. Despite the end of the Korean War, the United States still seemed a direct military threat. Its imposition of an international trade embargo exacerbated China's already monumental problems of economic development. Washington had clear superiority in atomic weaponry, was constantly improving its technology, and often threatened its use. Although actual American policy in this period remained one of containment, the rhetoric of "rollback" and the tactics of brinkmanship obviously could not be discounted in Peking or Moscow.

Our study cannot hope to discuss in detail all the momentous changes that took place in China and the Soviet Union during this period. Our effort instead must be to examine the contours of change within the broad pattern of Russian and Chinese development as communist states, and to explore the relationship between these changes and the revolutionary process. With China, this means focusing first on what Mao called the "high tide of socialism" and its problematic consequences: the rapid and relatively peaceful collectivization of agriculture followed by a series of movements in both urban and rural society that heralded a great leap into the communist future. With the Soviet Union, it means examining Khrushchev's dramatic unveiling of the Stalinist past; the fitful but no less remarkable liberalization of Russian policies toward intellectuals; a leap forward to outstrip and overtake Western society in output and standard of living; and dramatic new initiatives in international affairs. The irony of the decade is that it ended not only with the total collapse of its opening promise both within Soviet Russia and China but with enduring enmity between the two communist powers that has profoundly shaped present world possibilities.

COLLECTIVIZATION IN CHINA

In its elimination of the landlord-gentry class, land reform in China had been a social revolution of vast importance. By 1953 it was complete. But reform alone achieved neither economic nor socialist transformation and to most of the party leadership this was only to be expected. The task of the peasantry was to produce for the cities, funding the industrial progress that would, in time, make possible the mechanization of agriculture and its collectivization. Peasants might fuel *social* revolution, in the sense of mobilizing for the overthrow of a traditional ruling class; but they were incapable of making *socialist* revolution, that move from individual to collective (and ultimately national) ownership of the means of production. (Indeed, even in rural Russia, with the exception of state farms, ownership of the means of production was collective and not by the "whole people.")

Modest trends toward the resurgence of a "rich peasant" economy —with an increase in the buying and selling of land, of money lending, of hired labor, and the persistence of individual peasant households working small, scattered plots—worried the Chinese leadership. But what disturbed them most was continued low productivity, not the way in which the land was worked. The *social* relations of production, who worked for or with whom and how surplus was distributed among households, would change only with the further development of the *forces* of production, the amalgamation of individual holdings that could then be worked by machines. Mutual aid teams and lower-stage agricultural cooperatives were being established, but the pace was slow and many of the cooperatives were dissolved by party branch leaders who felt they had been too hastily organized in the first place. Political, economic, and social backwardness were to blame, but in time a strong centralized state development plan would yield the material base necessary to move the countryside from individual to collective forms of agricultural labor. Meanwhile, fiscal mechanisms for encouraging peasant incentive and a modest plan for increasing the rate at which lower-stage cooperatives were formed would have to do. Or so most party leaders believed.

Making his own observations of the situation, however, Mao Zedong had, by 1955, come to radically different conclusions. As always in Mao's vision, China's backwardness did not seem to be an obstacle to socialist transformation but an advantage. Just as in the 1920s Mao had argued that China's semicolonial, semifeudal condition raised hitherto unforeseen possibilities for revolution, so now he insisted that "poor people want change, want to do things, want revolution. A clean sheet of paper has no blotches, so the newest and most beautiful words can be written on it, the newest and most beautiful pictures can be painted on it." China, "poor and blank," was capable of painting its own revolutionary epic. Above all, the Chinese revolution must not be "simply the stabilization of victory."[1]

The trouble with the First Five-Year Plan, in Mao's view, went well beyond its dependency on insufficient agrarian funds. It had produced some things in abundance: routinization, the growth of an indifferent bureaucracy, and increasing gaps between peasant and workers, between mental and manual labor. The party seemed to consider equilibrium the norm—struggle a sometime thing. However, for Mao, "disequilibrium is normal and absolute, whereas equilibrium is temporary and relative."[2] Worse, the party's approach separated socialist ends from socialist means, as if socialism were simply about raising living standards. (Years later he contemptuously referred to a similar Soviet notion: "Of course! And swimming is a way of putting on trunks.")[3]

In short, the problem in China lay not in backwardness but in a failure to proceed, with equal fervor, toward two goals at once: the development of socialist relations of production and the further growth of productive forces. There could be no resting place. "In making revolution," Mao argued, "one must strike while the iron is hot, one revolution following another; the revolution must advance without interruption." Peasants, as such, could take the socialist road, just as they had taken the revolutionary road. They did not need to wait until urban factories gave them the material means. Only 20 to 30 percent of the rural population was "well-to-do or comparatively well-to-do" and some of them were "trying hard to go the capitalist way." But the rest, the overwhelming majority of China's population, were not well off and for them, "socialism is the only way out."[4]

In July, 1955, Mao appealed over the head of the Central Committee directly to provincial and regional party representatives who were meeting in Peking for the National People's Congress (a breach of party discipline of the sort that preceded Trotsky's expulsion from the Bolshevik party in 1927). The modest agricultural plans of the central leadership—increased state assistance to individual farmers in hopes of raising their incentive to produce more and the organization of one-third of peasant households into lower-stage cooperatives by 1957—were utterly inadequate. *Look* at the countryside, Mao insisted. Class polarization was increasing daily. To wait for the development of appropriate technology before undertaking the transition to socialism would be to abandon the revolution voluntarily. Instead "socialist transformation of the whole of agriculture" must proceed "simultaneously with the gradual realization of socialist industrialization." Indeed, the social transformation of the countryside was the main task, technical transformation was secondary.[5]

In all of China in 1955, as in Hunan in 1927, Mao insisted that the villages possessed the energy, the imagination, and the deep desire for vast revolutionary change. In 1955, as in 1927, he ferociously attacked those who would moderate or trail behind that great force. "A new upsurge in the socialist mass movement is imminent throughout the countryside," he declared. "But some of our comrades are tottering along like a woman with bound feet and constantly complaining, 'You're going too fast.'" The movement needed "active, enthusiastic and systematic leadership" not cautious, distant, doubting bureaucrats. The pace of cooperatization should be increased, despite the errors acceleration would surely produce. Errors could always be corrected; the important thing was to act and through action learn: "Both cadres and peasants will remould themselves in the course of the struggles they themselves experience."[6] In just this way almost three decades before, Mao and Zhu De had learned how to forge an army out of peasants, rural laborers, secret society hangers-on, and outright bandits who scraped a living from the harsh soil of Jinggangshan; in just this way they had learned how to turn the blockaded, embattled Shaanxi base into a self-sufficient vanguard in a people's war of total resistance; in just this way they had taken revolution to the cities of China. Through struggle, experience, and connection with the power, potential, and knowledge of ordinary people (that is, through the mass line), the party could realize socialism in the countryside, provided only it had faith in its own capacity to lead and faith in the masses; the result would be the release of the immense productive energy that could move China forward.

Mao's speech also dealt concretely with the reluctance of more affluent peasants to join cooperatives and the "wait and see" attitude of poor peasants. He reiterated the need for a gradual and voluntary approach to cooperatization, one that would demonstrate to all that their immediate material interests lay in joining up. No one should be "dragged in against their will," but at the same time every sign of successful efforts to pool resources should be supported. To be sure, China had to learn from the "impetuosity and rashness" of

Soviet collectivization, but "on no account should we allow . . . comrades to use the Soviet experience as a cover for their idea of moving at a snail's pace."[7]

If we concentrate here on Mao, it is because he not only articulated alternatives most fully, but because his interventions now, as so often in the past, set the context for party politics. Mao's insistence that the pace of cooperatization could and should be increased (and even so, he expected full collectivization would be achieved only at the end of a third five-year plan) set him apart from the party majority, but in a tactical, not strategic sense. The major departure of the July speech, one that would be elaborated over the next several years, was his injection of the energy of genuine dialectics into the more linear mode of thought predominant in the party. Consciousness and material conditions, in Mao's thinking, were not dichotomous but were completely interactive. Of course, transformation in the material base was necessary for a change in consciousness, but equally consciousness could—must—create the conditions under which material life changed.

Mao's July speech was also intended to fortify, inspire, and expand a procedure that had been operating slowly and with great hesitation since 1953 and the end of land reform. Building on mutual aid teams already organized, county-level work teams now launched intensive political campaigns that urged the mutual benefit to all of cooperatization and trained selected poor peasants in methods of implementation. When, as Thomas Bernstein describes it, "a climate of enthusiasm for socialism and an acceptance of its inevitability" had been created, mass sign-up meetings were convened, followed by the organization of a committee to work out the details of property transfer from individual peasant household to collective ownership. Finally, a management committee was selected that would organize work units, make production decisions, and devise a system for distributing returns. Intended to take months to complete and perhaps years to consolidate, during 1955 and 1956, encouraged perhaps, by unexpected success, the entire procedure was sometimes completed in days or weeks and moved on to the organization of higher-stage cooperatives (or full collectives).[8] Relying on basic village-level cadres, hundreds of thousands of whom were given brief training courses, the need and desire of poorer peasants for forms of agricultural work that would overcome the disadvantages—in quality of land, level of skill, and possession of draft animals and tools—uncorrected by land reform was successfully channeled, and the fears of the more affluent peasants buried in an avalanche of changes they could not resist. When an entire village signed up, how could even the richest peasant continue to farm on his own? Whom could he hire to help farm his fields? Who would need to borrow his money at sufficiently profitable rates?

Response to the press for cooperativization astonished Mao himself. By the end of 1955, the target for the creation of lower-stage cooperatives had been exceeded by 50 percent; new targets were announced and then surpassed; lower-stage cooperatives already established were reorganized as full collectives. During 1956, 90 percent of the peasants joined full collectives and the remaining 10 percent were incorporated by spring planting of 1957. Mao had hoped only that LAPCs would encompass the entire peasantry by 1960. Now, three years ahead of schedule, higher-stage cooperatives—full collectives—were the norm, and a process that had brought Soviet agriculture to a virtual halt was accomplished with only incidental violence, on the part of peasants or cadres.

One can see the party's concern about this process in a collection of accounts on how collectivization proceeded, which Mao himself edited in the fall and early winter of 1955. The book, and his introductory notes to each article, was intended to give wide publicity to the actual, concrete experience of peasants all over China, illustrating mistakes and how they had been corrected, triumphs and how they had been achieved. It was a kind of critical manual, an anthology in which Mao's headnotes called attention to what was most salient in the essay that followed. (At times he allowed himself to complain about the style of some of the articles in the book itself: "Quite a number of the 170 articles selected for this book reeked heavily of stereotyped Party writing." They were dull, indifferent to syntax, employed a stylistic mix of the literary and colloquial that offered the worst of both, "at times verbose and rambling, at times elliptical and archaic, as though they were out to torment the reader." Even after heavy editing, some were simply hopeless and were included only for their content. "How much longer," Mao asked, "before we read less of this stereotyped Party writing which gives us such headaches?") The liveliness and vivacity so lacking in the bureaucratic rendering of village experience, however, was fully present in the work of villagers themselves: "The masses have unlimited creative power. They can organize themselves to take on all spheres and branches of work where they can give full play to their energy."[9]

While coercion was probably widespread, collectivization in China was thus intended to be, and largely was, a movement of poor peasants and local cadre, called forth by Mao and his supporters against comrades equally committed to communism but preferring a more gradual path. Reviewing the reportedly rapid pace of the movement, Mao asserted a basic dictum:

> The masses have a potentially inexhaustible enthusiasm for socialism. Those who can only follow the old routine in a revolutionary period are utterly incapable of seeing this enthusiasm. They are blind and all is dark ahead of them. . . . Let something new appear and they always disapprove and rush to oppose it. Afterwards, they have to admit defeat and do a little self-criticism. But the next time something new appears, they go through the same process all over again. . . . Such people are always passive, always fail to move forward at the critical moment, and always have to be given a shove in the back before they move a step. When will it be possible for such people to walk of their own accord and walk properly?[10]

But what Mao called walking on their own and properly, his critics saw as reckless, utopian, and anarchist, in spirit if not in theory. What he saw as their blindness, they saw as reasonable caution, based on a clear understanding of the requirements of economic development. Peasant willpower was all very well; but to his opponents, Mao seemed close to committing that worst of Marxian sins, sheer idealism, which held that the dialectic could run from consciousness to material base.

Collectivization alone, however, did not solve the problems of agricultural productivity. Apart from predictable difficulties in the early stages—inexperienced managers, questions of appropriate size, resistance by many of the more affluent peasants, administrative confusion, and inequities in distribution—the collectives could not make a perceptible impact on incentives to produce unless the state reduced its claim on the surplus. Yet more liberal policies of taxation and compulsory purchase, introduced in 1957, while they effectively encouraged an increase in production, reduced the amount of surplus available for investment in heavy industry. The economic dilemma posed by China's backwardness remained. Nevertheless, by the standards the Soviet Union had set, when the Eighth Party Congress of the CCP met in September of 1956, China's transition to socialism was complete: industry was nationalized and agriculture collectivized. As Maurice Meisner has put it, "If socialism is taken to mean the abolition of private property and the control of the means of production by a state in the hands of a socialist party, then China was no less socialist than the Soviet Union."[11]

THE SOVIET TWENTIETH PARTY CONGRESS
AND ITS AFTERMATH

While Mao and the Communist leadership in China thus struggled to define both the nature of the revolutionary process and the next stage of socialist development, Khrushchev in Moscow was redefining the past. Late one night in February 1956, toward the end of the Twentieth Party Congress, the Soviet first secretary called delegates back from their hotel rooms to the Congress hall in the Kremlin. Beginning a little before midnight, and then continuing for an incredible four hours, the newly confirmed Soviet party leader subjected leading party officials from across the country to a stunning series of revelations, the debasement of a man thought godlike in his power, and who had once commanded all of their lives. Building on data accumulated by the Politburo's own investigating committee, headed by a hard-line Stalinist, P. N. Pospelov, but without, apparently, the approval of his Politburo comrades, Khrushchev exposed a series of lies and crimes absolutely unimaginable for overwhelming numbers of Communists everywhere. By the time he was finished, many weeping delegates felt their sense of Russia's political past had been totally shattered, as well as the meaning of their own lives.

In retrospect, ironically, Khrushchev's redefinitions and Mao's new definitions were in many respects remarkably similar in their implications, although neither was ever to appreciate the efforts of the other. Both were assaulting bureaucratization, one in its very essence, the other in its fearsome consequences; both were assaulting the notion that powerful individuals, experts or otherwise, could presume control over revolutionary processes without fundamentally distorting their nature; both by implication were challenging their parties to reexamine values and confront revolutionary origins; and

both were recognizing the importance to further socialist development of exposing party cadre to the living realities of the societies
they ruled.

Thus Stalin's "cult of personality" had been a "grave perversion
of party principles, party democracy, and revolutionary legality."
Lenin himself had wanted Stalin removed from his powerful positions, but those who later joined Lenin in this belief were "doomed
to subsequent moral and physical annihilation." The "Trotskyites,
Zinovievites, Bukharinites," and others were, indeed, enemies of
Leninism; but long before Stalin had them killed, they were totally
defeated and their positions totally discredited. Their murders therefore were unnecessary.

But Stalin *did* have them killed. "It is clear," Khrushchev revealed, "that Stalin showed in a whole series of cases his intolerance,
his brutality, and his abuse of power. . . . Many 'enemies' were
actually never enemies, spies, wreckers, etc., at all, but were always
honest Communists. . . . It has been determined that of the 139
members and candidates of the party's Central Committee elected
to the Seventeenth Congress, 98 persons, i.e., 70 per cent, were arrested and shot. . . . (indignation in the hall)." The assassination of
Kirov in 1934, at the start of the great purges, was apparently on
Stalin's orders; scores of other leading party figures were "forced
under torture" to sign their confessions, and subjected to vile persecution. "Many thousands of honest and innocent Communists have
died as a result of monstrous falsification, . . . of slanderous confessions . . . as a result of the practice of forcing accusations against
oneself and others." Even Stalin's wartime role was attacked. Stalin's
unchecked power led to lack of preparations and the "grievous annihilation of many military commanders and political workers."

Khrushchev laced his speech throughout with poignant excerpts
from letters and appeals from tortured, imprisoned party comrades.
"I am calling to you for help from a gloomy cell," the old Communist Kedrov wrote to the Central Committee. "Let my cry of
horror reach your ears; do not remain deaf; take me under your protection; please, help remove the nightmare of interrogations and
show that this is all a mistake." But as if this itself was not enough
to move the delegates, Khrushchev also cited Stalin's letters and
notes in detail, indicating how the all-powerful leader ignored economic realities, scorned the peasants and the collective farms, and

even wrote his own biography in the *Short History of the Party*. The phrase "Stalin is the Lenin of today" was considered too weak an appreciation of Stalin's greatness; it had to be changed and amplified.

In the end, Khrushchev called his numbed colleagues to a reaffirmation of Leninism; to abolish the cult of the individual decisively, once and for all; to return to the Marxist-Leninist notion about the people as a creator of history; to correct the erroneous views connected with Stalin's personality cult in the areas of history, philosophy, economics, literature, fine arts, and elsewhere; to assure principles of collective leadership, observance of the statutory norms of party life, and widespread criticism and self-criticism; and finally, to end all violations of revolutionary socialist legality.[12]

As some have argued, there may well have been a number of motivations behind the decision to reveal Stalin's crimes: an effort to escape personally from charges of collusion; a desire to discredit fully potential political rivals, particularly Molotov; a desire to set a new independent course in foreign affairs; and even, perhaps, the wish to attack aggressively at the outset the possibility of broad popular reaction to the revelations of Pospelov's committee and those returning from the camps.

But it is essential to bear in mind that the Twentieth Congress had also boldly reaffirmed a dramatic leap forward for the Soviet Union in social and economic terms, an objective set first in the immediate aftermath of Stalin's death. The USSR was now to "overtake and surpass the most highly developed capitalist countries in per capita output," a staggering objective, if not totally unrealistic. And to do this, Khrushchev and the party had to try to disassociate themselves from crimes and excesses of the past and generate a new sense of confidence and commitment. For these reasons alone Khrushchev's revelations would have been necessary.

But such a course also robbed tens of thousands of party officials of any sense of their lives' coherence; however vital to Soviet Russia's new tasks of socialist construction, it could not help but have deep repercussions, inside the USSR and out, where Communists deeply believed in their past and owed their positions to Stalin and Stalinist policies. Within months, Khrushchev faced two assassination attempts; within a year and a half, Molotov, Kaganovich, and other Stalinists of the "antiparty bloc" made a concerted effort to strip him of power. But such resistance within Soviet Russia paled in comparison to reactions in the Bloc, particularly in Hungary and Poland. Before the year was out, it was clear that the leap toward parity with "the most highly developed capitalist countries" would involve not only expulsions and retrenchment at home, but a new wave of brutal repression abroad.

In Poland and Hungary difficulties stemmed essentially from the fact that de-Stalinization in Bloc affairs involved both a reconciliation with Tito, anathematized by Stalin after 1948, and the acknowledgement that under Stalin's aegis, scores of Titoist "national Communists" in countries more directly under Stalin's control had been cruelly slandered and killed. Although the "Spirit of Belgrade," as Tito and others labeled the Kremlin's new attitude toward Yugoslavia after Khrushchev's famous visit in June 1955, implicitly involved recognizing that there were "many roads to socialism," the concept was formalized by Khrushchev at the Twentieth Congress in his presentation of the Central Committee report. He now suggested, moreover, that diversity within the international communist movement was likely to increase, rather than contract, as "the forms of transition to socialism became more and more varied."[13]

In the aftermath of the Twentieth Congress, consequently, East European parties found themselves not only under the pressure of de-Stalinization, which involved painful rehabilitation campaigns and the removal of outspoken Stalinists from high party positions; they also felt growing popular demands for political and social liberalization along national communist lines. From Belgrade, Tito and his comrades seemed to take special pleasure in the discomfiture of old adversaries and urged their supporters on; from Moscow, the prestige (and power) of the new Khrushchev regime was now fully committed to exposing and correcting the abuses of personality cults and destroying Stalin's political legacy. Thousands of new prisoners were soon released from East European and Soviet jails; the number of confessed "mistakes" and rehabilitations stunned officials and ordinary citizens alike. In Hungary, pressure grew for the reinstatement of Imre Nagy, who had been expelled from the Politburo for excessively liberal views only the year before. In Poland, sentiment mounted in favor of Gomulka, recently released from five years of jail for "revisionism." Responding to domestic pressure, Hungarian leaders Kadar and Gero travelled to Moscow in early fall to secure Nagy's reinstatement in the party, but within weeks, Nagy's popularity had increased to such an extent that he replaced Rakosi himself as the party's head. A series of dramatic reforms was promised almost immediately. There were even rumors that Nagy would withdraw Hungary from the Warsaw Pact.

Thus began the remarkable series of events leading to the Hungarian rebellion in early November, the outbreak of anti-Soviet violence in Poland, and the eventual decision by Moscow to crush East European dissidence by force. It is not necessary here to rehearse that painful sequence, but only to indicate the broader consequences of de-Stalinization and the manner in which Khrushchev's "two steps forward" simultaneously necessitated "one step backward." If the Soviet Union was indeed to take a "great leap forward" in economic and social development after the death of Stalin, it was clearly necessary to reestablish the party as a viable, legitimate organ of management, to reset the party firmly "from bottom to top," as Khrushchev declared in his secret speech, on "Leninist principles of party leadership." For this, thousands of officials who owed their positions not to personal ability or ideological commitment, but to Stalinist whim, had to be removed. Between 1956 and 1961, Khrushchev later reported, more than 200,000 party members were dismissed from their posts. Reliable Western estimates place that figure much higher.[14] One might argue, as Khrushchev's own successors were to do later, that the problems of 1956 were largely the result of style, that a less dramatic, less flamboyant disclosure of Stalin's crimes might have minimized subsequent problems. One must recognize, however, that Khrushchev's break with the Stalinist past involved precisely the establishment of a new legitimacy for the CPSU, a revitalization of the party apparatus, and an effort to move the Soviet Union rapidly forward on the basis of new political foundations. "Overtaking and surpassing the most highly developed capitalist countries" was no mere rhetoric. It was a goal for development that would at once vindicate Soviet Russia's socialist commitment, validate a Marxist conception of world historical process, and demonstrate the ideological rectitude of Leninism, whose probity Stalin had implicitly brought into question, and which remained the legitimizing ideological underpinning of the Soviet state. If Khrushchev had acted on impulse (and even recklessly in terms of continued Stalinist domination of most East European regimes), it was still true, as Lenin might have argued, that the Stalinist egg could not be broken gently. And once the Polish and Hungarian dissidents had been contained, dissidents whose rebellion threatened briefly to tear the whole Soviet Bloc apart, destroying the Warsaw Pact, undermining Soviet defense, disrupting economic relations, and perhaps even overthrowing Communist party regimes, it was also true that the limits of Khrushchevian liberalism were more clearly defined. In June of 1958, in a crass and most cruel reminder of these limits, Imre Nagy was put to death. Still, a clear break with the past had been made and legitimacy (and party position) tied to communist achievement. The ground was thus prepared for rapid economic development in the Soviet Union, just as socialization and the completion of collectivization had cleared the way for a "great leap forward" in China.

THE PROBLEM OF THE INTELLECTUALS

There was still, however, the problem of making better use of the energy, if not the political commitment, of intellectuals and professionals in both countries. Although never fully articulated in Khrushchev's speech or elsewhere, Stalin's successors must at some level have understood the penalties Soviet Russia had paid for insisting upon a slavish acceptance of party dicta by professionals and other experts who, however much enlisted in the tasks of Soviet development, might otherwise had made much more significant contributions. In China too, even before Khrushchev's speech, the party leadership had contemplated a policy of liberalization looking toward an end to what Zhou Enlai called the "estrangement" between itself and intellectuals. But here, as in the Eastern European countries, liberalization in one realm was intimately connected to a larger understanding of social, economic, and political systems.

The issue in its simplest terms had to do with the nature and degree of intellectual freedom in societies that remained politically authoritarian, whatever their social goals. There is an interesting dialectic associated with Khrushchev's speech. In revealing Stalin's lies, Khrushchev implicitly called for the truth. But how much, about what, and to whom should it be disseminated? Events in Poland and Hungary soon demonstrated how quickly political systems could unravel when the "truth" contradicted the basis of power. But if imagination, innovation, and broad cultural freedom were essential to rapid, successful, and humane social transformation, could limits be placed on how intellectuals used their minds?

In calling for liberalization in January 1956, Zhou, Liu Shaoqi, and the majority of the CCP hoped to enlist the technological expertise of the Chinese intelligentsia in pursuit of a rational and efficient Second Five-Year Plan. Khrushchev similarly hoped that ridding the party of its Stalinist past would encourage a like enlistment of Russian professionals to the new cause of overtaking and outstripping the West. In both cases this assumed that intellectuals would not violate politically acceptable limits of criticism.

Mao's approach, however, was somewhat different. Liberalization had less to do with hitching technical and intellectual energy to the cart of the Second Chinese Five-Year Plan than to its potential for reviving the party itself, exposing bureaucrats to the cleansing wind of outside criticism. In May 1956 Mao, in what came to be known as the "Hundred Flowers campaign," vigorously supported the call for "one hundred schools of thought to contend" and "a hundred flowers to blossom."

These contradictions and ambiguities in the approach of both the Soviet and Chinese leadership to the issues of intellectual liberalization would soon penetrate all major social undertakings in both societies. In China, a brief period of intellectual openness was followed by harsh repression, complex intraparty maneuvering, and the explosion of a uniquely Maoist path to communism: the Great Leap Forward. In the Soviet Union, repression in Poland and Hungary was followed by the ouster and disgrace of Khrushchev's own opponents, the scrapping of carefully laid plans for orderly growth under the Sixth Five-Year Plan, and the dramatic announcement of a new Seven-Year Plan designed to "bury the West" in unprecedented Soviet socialist achievements. The irony of these apparently parallel processes is not only that they failed, but that in the course of conflict and failure they became each other's negative image.

NEW DIRECTIONS IN CHINA

Although the Chinese were insulted, like others in the Bloc, at the lack of warning, their response to Khrushchev's speech was positive. "We did not agree with demolishing [Stalin] at one blow," Mao remarked later, but it was "completely necessary to remove the lid, to break down blind faith, to release the pressure, and to emancipate thought."[15]

A month after Khrushchev's speech, Mao addressed himself directly to the issue of "blind faith." Speaking at length to the Politburo, he asked his comrades to confront current Chinese problems in the light of recent Soviet revelations so that the "detours" the Russians had taken could be better avoided. Reading through reports on the state of industry and agriculture, Mao had isolated ten problems: the relationship between heavy and light industry and agriculture; between coastal and interior industry; between economic construction and defense; between the state, units of production in agriculture and industry, and the workers in each; between central and local authorities; between Han Chinese and the national minorities; between party and nonparty people; between revolution and counterrevolution; between right and wrong; and between China and other countries. It is a speech of enormous richness, not in its theoretical but in its practical aspects, and, as its title "On the Ten Great Relationships" indicates, its understanding is thoroughly dialectical. Indeed Mao attempted to articulate, in the most concrete way, how the dialectic can be made flesh, how the party could continue to make revolution rather than stabilize victory. With patience, humor, references to recent and ancient Chinese history and literature, at times with great lyricism, and always clearly and succinctly, Mao criticized blind faith in any foreign model. "What we must study is all that is universally true and we must make sure that this study is *linked with Chinese reality*. It would lead to a mess if every single sentence, even of Marx's, was followed."[16] One brief example illustrates both tone and message. It was wrong, Mao argued, to keep factories too closely controlled by central, provincial, or municipal authorities. They needed to have room for independent action; centralization and independence were a "unity of opposites." The idea is abstract, and Mao immediately offers a concrete picture:

For instance, we are now having a meeting, which is centralization; after the meeting, some of us will go for a walk, some will read books, some will go to eat, which is independence. If we don't adjourn the meeting and give everyone some independence but let it go on and on, wouldn't it be the death of us all? This is true of individuals, and no less true of factories and other units of production. Every unit of production must enjoy independence as the correlative of centralization if it is to develop more vigorously.[17]

Everyone agreed, Mao acknowledged, that heavy industry was essential to further Chinese economic development. But the way to satisfactorily strengthen heavy industry was to increase investments in light industry and agriculture, creating the skills, the market, and the capital for further heavy industrial development. Effective centralization was obviously desirable, but the way to achieve it was to strengthen local units, permitting local economic initiative to be vigorously exercised and then fed back into more centralized planning. In agriculture, production would rise only by the most careful attention to the welfare of the peasantry. "The Soviet Union has adopted measures which squeeze the peasants very hard." That, according to Mao, was logically absurd. "You want the hen to lay more eggs and yet you don't feed it, you want the horse to run fast and yet you don't let it graze."[18]

The speech amounts to an overwhelming indictment both of Soviet approaches to building socialism and of those Chinese who clung to the literal example of those approaches. Delivered while others were working on a conventional Second Five-Year Plan, "On the Ten Great Relationships" is an appeal to the party to move in a new direction, one born out of their experiences as revolutionaries in the countryside.

The "blind faith" Mao referred to in praising Khrushchev's speech was not the issue in the Hundred Flowers campaign, but a "release of pressure" and "emancipation of thought" were. Burned by earlier thought-reform campaigns, intellectuals were at first wary of accepting the invitation to "bloom" and contend. Still, by the summer of 1956, people were beginning to speak their grievances and, as Mao had suspected and party bureaucrats had feared, their focus was on the arbitrary, indifferent, and commandist behavior of party cadres themselves. Poland and Hungary provided the party leadership with a ready excuse to call off the campaign altogether, and its revival in the spring of 1957 was linked to another stage in what was becoming a major struggle at the center over the direction in which China should proceed.

At the Eighth Party Congress, in September 1956, the role Mao was permitted to play in formulating policy was clearly restricted. Liu Shaoqi and Deng Xiaoping gave the main political reports, the new party constitution eliminated all references to the "thought of Mao Zedong," and the old post of party general secretary was revived and given to Deng. Whatever his personal prestige, Mao's direct political power was much reduced. And however welcome Mao might have found Khrushchev's speech on general grounds, its attack on the cult of personality served his opponents' interests all too well. Two years later Mao went to some pains to point out that there were "two kinds of cult of the individual. One is correct, such as that of Marx, Engels, Lenin, and the correct side of Stalin. These we ought to revere and continue to revere for ever. . . . As they held truth in their hands, why should we not revere them?"[19]

The truth Mao felt he himself held in his hands he revealed in a major speech in February 1957. As in 1955, he made an end run around a recalcitrant Central Committee, delivering the talk, "On Contradictions," to the Supreme State Conference. The September party Congress held that the struggle between capitalism and socialism in China had ended in a clear victory for socialism. Wrong, Mao declared. Class struggle, in the ideological realm, continued to exist; the choice between socialism and capitalism was still open, and by implication, the struggle was not confined to remnant bourgeois elements, but could exist within the ranks of the party itself. Once more Mao invited one hundred schools of thought to contend, one hundred flowers to blossom: "Marxism can develop only through struggle, and not only is this true of the past and the present, it is necessarily true of the future as well." Ideological struggle was crucial, although "the only method to be used . . . is that of painstaking reasoning and not crude coercion." Party bureaucrats must learn to listen to criticism from all quarters; they must "temper and develop themselves and win new positions in the teeth of criticism and in the storm and stress of struggle." Confident that it was possible to engage the overwhelming majority of the population in the process of building socialism, Mao was convinced that a rectification campaign confined to party ranks would only reinforce the growing separation between leaders and led.[20]

The response of intellectuals, like the response to the agricultural cooperative movement two years earlier, exceeded Mao's expectations. However, just as party bureaucrats feared, criticism was not confined to the manner of party rule, but to its very existence. On university campuses the mood resembled the glory days of the May Fourth movement (and the comparison was specifically made). One professor said he had received many letters from parents asking him to restrain their impetuous offspring. He could not, he insisted, just as "we would not accept the advice of our parents when we were students." Mao, deeply disturbed by the reaction, remarked that "with a people like this it is necessary to observe certain limits."[21] In June a student riot in Hanyang city led to outright repression, and its leaders were executed.

Quickly the direction of the campaign was reversed, from an invitation to criticize the party to a call for an all-out attack on "rightists." Fighting a rearguard action, Mao opposed a witch-hunt and argued for some moderation in the punishment meted out. But recent evidence suggests that some 100,000 people were sentenced to lengthy terms for "counterrevolutionary" and "rightist" activity, and it is hard to see this as moderation.

The significance of the Hundred Flowers movement and its disastrous aftermath lies in the different lessons learned from it by Mao and his opponents. The latter, concerned by the degree of disaffection that had been uncovered, were reconfirmed in their view of the necessity for party discipline and party control. Intraparty rectification might be necessary periodically. But opening the doors to the people at large was both dangerous and foolish. At all costs the party's monopoly on political power must be maintained; experiments in wider forms of democracy led only to anarchy.

For Mao, on the other hand, the lessons lay elsewhere. Urban professionals and intellectuals had proved themselves untrustworthy, unable to understand the relationship between democracy and centralism, and blind to the fundamental difference between bourgeois liberalism and the necessities of a socialist state. They could not serve as the "organic intellectuals" of a worker-peasant society. Instead, workers and peasants would have to develop, out of their own ranks, their own intellectuals. The results of the movement in no way dissuaded him from the conviction that the ideological struggle between socialism and capitalism remained ongoing. If anything, it strengthened his views. An increasingly bureaucratic state structure, a professional and intellectual class still mired in bourgeois thinking, a party leadership unresponsive to bold departures threatened the revolution as severely as any external enemy.

Moreover, Mao was able to take political advantage of the anti-rightist campaign that ended the Hundred Flowers movement. His opponents had used the campaign to punish critics of the party; Mao and his supporters used it to "cleanse" the ranks of the party itself. In the name of the mass line, state and party officials were, in large numbers, "sent down" (*xiafang*) to the countryside to learn, through labor, from the peasants. "By the time the purge had run its course," one observer writes, "over a million party members had been expelled, put on probation, or officially reprimanded. In the process, Maoists regained control of the party apparatus."[22]

CHINA'S GREAT LEAP FORWARD

By late 1957, early 1958, the Second Five-Year Plan, adopted only the year before, was essentially junked in favor of what must now be called a Maoist plan for economic development. The Great Leap Forward was a campaign designed to carry China directly from socialism to communism with no stops in between. China would not only outproduce the West, as Khrushchev had assured the Twentieth Party Congress Soviet Russia would do; it would also beat the Soviet Union itself to communism.

The focus of the Great Leap was on production, but its approach to increased production was a radical shift from the basic policies that had thus far guided the country. The fundamental economic problem facing China remained the harsh reality that production growth was reaching its natural limits. Given continued population increases and a respectable but still entirely inadequate industrial base, the prospects ahead were grim unless some breakthrough occurred. There was only one arena in which to maneuver: the mobilization and organization of the Chinese people into new patterns of work, which would yield higher output without capital investment, without new machinery.

Toil, Mao insisted, can be transformed into dreams, dreams into toil. How shall we go about building socialism, he asked, "coldly and deliberately, or boldly and joyously?" Even that ancient sin, "revolutionary romanticism" was not spurned; on the contrary, it is a "good thing" so long as practical measures give it life. Above all, the heart of the universe is struggle and transformation: "If there were no contradictions and no struggle, there would be no world, no progress, no life, there would be nothing at all." It was time to leave behind, forever, the dead hand of an irrelevant revolutionary experience.[23]

Reviewing the history of China from 1950 to 1957 Mao also hammered away at the dogmatism that viewed Soviet models with total awe. Study should have been directed at the party's own experience; instead, in almost all areas, Soviet example ruled, with the result, Mao complained, that "I couldn't have eggs or chicken soup for three years because an article appeared in the Soviet Union which said that one shouldn't eat them. Later they said one could eat them. It didn't matter whether the article was correct or not, the Chinese listened all the same and respectfully obeyed." Later in the same talk, Mao voiced what must have been an old grudge: Chinese artists always painted him "a little bit shorter" than Stalin, "thus blindly knuckling under to the moral pressure exerted by the Soviet Union."[24] Chicken soup and height sensitivity aside, Mao's declaration of independence from the Soviet path had major implications for every institution in Chinese society.

In industry, the Soviet system of one-person management, already modified in the mid-1950s, was thoroughly transformed. Factories would now be run by a "triple combination" of workers, technicians, and administrative cadres working in teams at every level from the shop floor to the central office. Cadres would, on a regular basis, engage in the actual productive work of the factory; technological innovations would flow from workers themselves, with the help and advice of technicians. Politics, not economics, was to command the style and content of industrial work. Experts had to be "Red," workers (their "Redness" presumably guaranteed) had to become expert. Experimentation, innovation, self-reliance—these were to be the watchwords. In both country and city, people were encouraged to try small-scale manufacturing, including the production of pig-iron, so that they could produce their own tools and reduce their reliance on inadequate state supplies. There was to be a breaking down of walls, of divisions. Once, in the mountains of North China, Communists had understood how much they had to learn from ordinary peasants, how close the relationship between party and mass had to be if the revolution was to succeed. It was a lesson they had to learn again in the cities.

In the countryside, the changes envisioned were of even greater magnitude. Given the level of industry, the cities could not employ peasants who, underemployed at home, were drawn to them in search of work. The solution was now to bring industry to the countryside, to organize the peasantry for forms of industrial labor that would *simultaneously* solve a range of problems: labor could be fully employed in rural areas, local small-scale industry would directly serve agricultural needs and generate funds for further capital investment in heavy industry, peasants would be able to bridge the terrifying gap between themselves and more advanced technology—all in an unending upward spiral of development whose roots, resources, and control would be located where people actually lived and worked.

Building on spontaneous experiments in economies of scale employed by some collectives in Henan, the move to establish communes was encouraged, financed in part by the party's willingness to leave at least some surplus in the collective for investment rather than being scooped up entirely by the state. By amalgamating several collectives, a fundamental reorganization of work patterns was possible—with no capital investment, with no new machinery. Large-scale tasks (irrigation, land reclamation, repair shops for tractors the commune could now purchase rather than rent) could be relegated to specialized brigades drawing on a labor pool much larger than the traditional village. Within production brigades (roughly corresponding to higher-stage producer cooperatives and thus to the natural village itself) work could be further divided so that the most rational, specialized division of labor would be possible. Private plots were largely eliminated; all work would now be collective. Moreover, earnings would be distributed largely on the basis of need, at commune, rather than brigade or team level. In this way, incomes within the commune would be more or less equalized, although differences between communes themselves would remain.

Drawing on the full labor potential of the countryside, a vast mobilization of women for agricultural work was also undertaken, which, in turn, brought about tremendous changes in family life. Communal dining, child care, and socialization of specific household tasks were all experimented with. A revival of the people's militia accompanied the drive for communalization, not so much as an active element in national security but, as an editorial in the journal *Red Flag* put it, "for the purpose of carrying on the struggle with nature."[25] As in similar campaigns in other developing socialist countries, military metaphors were intended to invoke an earlier period of united struggle. The key was struggle, the result was to be unity, a holistic onslaught against the fetters, human and natural, that kept China poor, class divided, and endangered.

Briefly the commune movement held out another hope, a promise central to Marxism, unrealized anywhere in the world: the withering away of the state. Throughout the country, communes became the smallest units of government, merging with the *xiang*, so that local administration was also a unit of production, directed from above but also operating autonomously with its own funds. State and society were thus, at this lowest rung of the governmental hierarchy, merged.

Decentralization had been policy in both the Soviet Union and Eastern Europe in the 1950s—but it was nothing like the bold leap toward local autonomy China experienced in 1958. "A great spiritual force," Mao insisted, "becomes a great material force." Cadres must believe not only in their own capacity but in the masses. In a series of talks remarkable for their informality, their wide ranging through history, philosophy, current politics, evolution, and the universe itself, Mao urged party activists to take a long view.

> There is nothing in the world that does not arise, develop, and disappear. Monkeys turned into men, mankind arose; in the end, the whole human race will disappear, it may turn into something else.[26]

The family, which remained important as a unit of consumption and distribution under socialism, would also change with the achievement of communism. "After maybe a few thousand years, or at the very least several hundred years, the family will disappear. Many of our comrades do not dare to think about these things." As for intellectuals, Mao warned, it was necessary to face one's own fear of them:

> Professors—we have been afraid of them ever since we came into the towns. We did not despise them, we were terrified of them.

When confronted by people with piles of learning we felt that we were good for nothing. For Marxists to fear bourgeois intellectuals . . . is strange indeed. . . . We must not tolerate it any longer. Naturally we cannot go out tomorrow and beat them up. We have to make contact with them, educate them and make friends with them. They may have studied more natural science than we have, but they do not necessarily know more social science. They may have studied more Marxism-Leninism but they are incapable of entering into the spirit of it, or really understanding it.[27]

Education was not about schools as such, but about "whether your direction is correct or not and whether you come to grips with your studies. Learning has to be grasped." He recalled that he and his comrades had been in their twenties when they began their life in revolution—their elders "had more learning, but we had more truth."

RUSSIA'S "GREAT LEAP" UNDER KHRUSHCHEV

While the Chinese were smashing the Soviet model, Khrushchev and the new Russian leadership were reshaping it. If the Great Leap Forward was an effort by Mao and his supporters to translate truth into a new communist reality, the ambitious plan for new Soviet development was an effort to reassociate reality with communist ideals. The contours of this new development were laid dramatically in 1957. They involved, first, a thorough restructuring of the Soviet economic apparatus, designed to facilitate in administrative terms the achievement of higher economic goals; and second, just as in China, a forceful effort to tune the party itself closely to economic achievement, identifying party officials with the specifics of economic performance and bridging the great chasm that had long existed between the activities, ideas, and interests of the party elite, and those of ordinary citizens. In terms of revolutionary process in Russia, this latter effort was more interesting than the former. It included mass involvement, if not participation, in significant party decisions and led eventually to "production principle" as a new basis of party organization, radically revising (at least theoretically) the party's social role. Initially, however, it was the economic reforms, along with some spectacular economic and technological achievements, that captured world attention.

One must recognize that 1957 was the fortieth anniversary of the

1917 Revolution, and hence a special, "jubilee year" in which singular achievements were to be expected. Soviet citizens could not have been very surprised in late January when *Pravda* and *Izvestiia* both heralded the "spectacular achievements" of the Soviet people in "greatly overfulfilling" the 1956 goals of the Sixth Five-Year Plan; nor could they have been surprised by the reiteration of "catching up with and surpassing the most developed countries in per capita production" as the "main task" of the immediate future. But shortly afterwards the Central Committee was summoned to a special plenary session in Moscow and presented with a dramatic plan for the reorganization of industrial management. It was now necessary, Chairman Khrushchev told the Committee members, in terms that now sound rather like Mao, to transfer the centers of industrial management away from Moscow to the localities of industry and construction themselves. Centralized ministerial guidance was remote, often ineffective. Bureaucracy tended to supplant managerial competence. The only way economic problems could be solved efficiently was to involve those directly engaged in production and tackle issues "on the spot."[28]

Russia was to have a new system of regional economic councils (*Sovnarkhozy*). These would take over the "main tasks" of managing industrial production and construction. Such councils had been organized before in Soviet Russia, shortly after the Bolsheviks came to power, and hence could be considered (and were presented as) genuinely Leninist institutions. Approximately one hundred *Sovnarkhozy* were to be set up, each given general control over all industrial enterprises in its region. Only the areas of military armament, electricity, and chemicals were left to direction from Moscow.

For those directly involved, the *Sovnarkhozy* reform was stunning, not so much for what it promised in terms of future production, but for what it meant in terms of administrative (and personal) dislocation and, not incidentally, the consolidation of Khrushchev's political power. Massive numbers of state officials had to move from the cosmopolitan centers of Moscow and Leningrad out into the provinces—"hinterland" in the view of many used to the capital's amenities. More than 140 All-Union, Union Republic, and Republic ministries were abolished when the economic councils came into being in May 1957, a spectacular administrative decentralization that involved, among other things, the abolition of more than 50,000 government jobs and the simultaneous strengthening of regional and local authorities, who were now becoming, presumably, Khrushchev's principal base of support. "The creation of a powerful socialist economy in the USSR is a triumph of the Leninist party line!" Khrushchev later declared in celebrating the change. There would soon be no limits to the possibilities of Soviet economic growth.[29]

Such exuberance soon found new expression. In Leningrad in May, Khrushchev suddenly announced spectacular new goals in the production of milk, dairy products, and meat. Within three years the Soviet Union was to overtake and surpass the United States in each of these areas, which meant in the case of meat more than doubling current production. Khrushchev apparently hoped to rely on new livestock feed production to support such ambitious plans, but even so, his dramatic announcement apparently came as a complete surprise not only to those directly involved in agricultural production, but also to his comrades in the Politburo and the Central Committee.

In retrospect it seems likely that Khrushchev's enthusiasm on this issue was a precipitating factor in an effort shortly afterwards to strip him of his post—a move in July of the so-called antiparty bloc, which led after three days' discussion in the Politburo to his dismissal from the first secretary's position by an eight to four vote. Khrushchev had little support in the ministries or the presidium of the Supreme Soviet for his program of administrative decentralization; many in the party's top leadership resented his growing power and worried about his ambition and the grandiosity of his plans. Khrushchev weathered this storm by calling the Central Committee urgently to Moscow and by securing a vote of confidence in this larger body, to which the Politburo was responsible. In the aftermath, the members of the Politburo majority (Kaganovich, Molotov, Malenkov, Voroshilov, and others) not only lost their positions, but the policies of the reinstated first secretary secured firm political endorsement. Soviet Russia's "great leap" could now proceed full speed.

In September, Russia learned that the Sixth Five-Year Plan would be scrapped altogether and replaced by a much more grandiose and ambitious Seven-Year Plan, beginning in 1959. By 1965 the United States and other advanced capitalist countries would be "buried" in an avalanche of socialist achievement. Agricultural output, as we shall see, was to be the highest in the world, both in gross and per capita terms; Russia's industrial growth rate would be five times that of the United States; and by 1970—the date was clearly specified—the Soviet Union would have the "world's highest" standard of living.[30] When the *Sputnik I*, the first earth satellite, was launched in October 1957, it appeared to some a fitting symbol not only of Soviet technological accomplishment, but of the boundless potential of the Russian socialist future.

There were other significant aspects of the Seven-Year Plan. In the countryside, compulsory deliveries of agricultural products were discontinued and new, "correct" procurement prices set to replace them. Machine tractor stations, for years the centers not only of agricultural machinery (and hence production control) for collective farms, but also political surveillance, were reduced to the status of repair stations, their machinery (and authority) sold to the collective farms themselves. *Khozraschet*, a system of economic accountability, was introduced in a number of sectors. This effectively changed the system of measuring economic performance by factoring into success indicators such considerations as labor and materials costs, delivery time, and capital expenditures. There was also a dramatic announcement about reducing the work day. By the end of 1960, *Pravda* declared, a seven-hour day was to be "universal," and a further transition to a thirty- and thirty-five-hour week was to begin.[31]

But accompanying all this was another dramatic set of changes, designed in some measure to reassociate party and people, or at least make the party and state bureaucracies more responsive and effective. As new economic goals were suggested, and plans laid out for administrative decentralization, the party urged massive discussion of issues, problems, and objectives. According to Khrushchev, more than 514,000 public meetings were held between March and May 1957 in conjunction with the introduction of the regional economic councils. More than 40,820,000 persons were said to have attended these sessions, at which more than 2,300,000, apparently, had something to say![32] When control figures for the Seven-Year Plan were proposed, 968,000 meetings were held. Now more than 70,000,000 participated actively.[33] All over the Soviet Union, in other words, workers and peasants were being mobilized to support far-reaching achievements and reforms. "Volunteer Work Saturdays" (*Subbotniki*) were also brought back in a massive way, recreating the "revolutionary atmosphere" of the early Bolshevik period when "contributed" labor had important economic significance. Hundreds of thousands of work hours were donated to special projects, often municipal construction, in a (reported) holiday atmosphere.

Stalin, of course, had also used volunteer workdays and mass discussions, but Khrushchev's mobilization was different. However cynically many may have viewed this "involvement of the masses," state and party officials were now specifically enjoined to use the discussions as a means to develop workable production strategies and techniques. There was implicit recognition that many not formally involved in the policy or strategy-making process had valuable experience and expertise to share, that the party could, in fact, learn from the public, or at least from the experts among them. The clue that this was not mere showboating came with the flowering in various public and scholarly journals of significant differences of opinion on major issues. The use of profits as economic indicators soon became a subject of heated debate, and so did such issues as material incentives, plan orientation to output goals, economic accountability, agricultural sales, marketing techniques, and even the terms by which collective farm organizations were to purchase equipment from the machine tractor stations.

Spirited debate soon flowered in other areas as well. Lawyers began to discuss criminal law reform, educational changes were debated, Lysenko's genetics theory came under public attack, and even groups like the Writers' Union, a conservative bastion of party orthodoxy, opened its forums to discussion of such critical volumes as Vladimir Dudintsev's *Not by Bread Alone*. Historians were condemned for "dogmatism" and "talmudism" and exhorted to "eliminate completely" the harmful consequences of the personality cult (although the "excessive" liberalism of some "politically inexperienced people" immediately after the Twentieth Party Congress was also condemned, and the editorial board of *Voprosy Istorii* was shaken up for publishing new material on 1917).

In the area of morals and public order, there were extensive discussions of proposed "parasite laws," the plan to establish quasijudicial comrades' courts in all public institutions, and the desirability of forming citizens' *druzhiny*, police auxiliary patrols that had been widely used in the Red Guard era of the civil war. In large measure, extensive public involvement in such institutions as comrades' courts (which could censure, levy fines, and even exile citizens without approval of formal judicial authorities) was a means of developing public sanctions to supplant the discredited secret police, using social coercion, in other words, and an intensive degree of public pressure, directed by local party officials, to maintain social discipline. But the net effect remained a degree of public discussion and mobilization unprecedented in Russia since the early days of Bolshevik power.

The most important area, however, in which the party encouraged discussion after 1956 remained the economy. And here, although mass mobilization aspects of the debate in its initial stages undoubtedly contributed to increased productivity, the more significant consequences of public involvement soon proved to be pointed criticisms both of Soviet economic procedures and of Khrushchev's vaunted development goals. The question of Western rates of production, for example, and especially the availability of investment capital and the potential for future growth, pressed one economics journal to sound a note of caution as early as 1959 on the prospects of overtaking the United States.[34] *Voprosy Ekonomiki* officially applauded Khrushchev's decision to shorten the Russian workday to seven hours, but warned in its January 1960 issue that such a conversion implied a sharp rise in labor productivity if the volume of industrial output was to increase as planned.[35] Difficulties in agricultural production were attacked even more sharply. Public discussion of the proposal to abolish the machine tractor stations and have collective farms purchase the machinery evoked hundreds of essays and editorials pointing in part to serious problems of collective farm management, capital allocation, transport difficulties, problems of wages, and even serious issues concerning the availability of resources necessary to manage the purchases. Similar complaints emerged in connection with the regional economic councils. By 1959 the power of these units to allocate capital resources had been restricted, and one year later new councils at the republic level were set up for the RSFSR, the Ukraine, and Kazakhstan to supervise and coordinate lower agencies. Complaints about inefficiency and even outright administrative confusion increased.

In the summer of 1960, and again in early 1961, the Central Committee itself took up these issues in special plenary sessions, which were remarkable in several ways. There was intensive dialogue between Khrushchev and Committee members giving reports, amounting, in effect, to a form of direct accountability. The plenums were open in their admission of failures and weaknesses, even to the point of some embarrassment. According to official resolutions, economic deficiencies were to be met by "comprehensively increasing labor productivity as the decisive source of expanded socialist production"; the campaign against "parasites" and "idlers" was also to be stepped up markedly.

Shortly afterwards, following a review of the party's role in future communist development and the adoption of a new party program at the Twenty-Second Party Congress in October 1961, Khrushchev embarked on yet another series of administrative reforms, this time attacking the party's own organizational structure directly. From top to bottom, the "production principle" was now to replace territorial division as the primary basis of party organization. Within the limits of existing regions, separate party committees and hierarchies were to be established for industry and for agriculture—in effect, two independent organizations. In Moscow province, for example, a Provincial Party Committee for Industrial Production was formed to unite some 4,000 primary party organizations located in industrial enterprises, construction, transport, and communications, involving some 220,000 party members and some 32 provincial city and town organizations. At the same time, the Moscow Provincial Party Committee for Agricultural Production organized to unite more than 1,000 primary party organizations on collective farms, state farms, and other agricultural units. More than 50,000 party members were to be joined organizationally here, each of whom was directly involved in and had direct responsibility for some form of agricultural production.

Again, as with the earlier ministerial reform, one effect of these radical new party reforms was to push party officials out of their administrative "nests" and back into rural and industrial production tasks. Much more important, however, the reform also firmly established specific competence in one or another sector of production as the most significant criterion of party office, marking, in theoretical terms at least, the final transition of the CPSU from a Stalinist satrapy to a functional, managerial organization, the energy of all of whose members went toward production. Expertise in the area of economic and technological development would hopefully provide party leaders themselves with the ability to settle practical problems.

Innovation would be speeded, reserves and other economic resources more effectively utilized. Officially, moreover, party leaders would be better able to select their own committee personnel, since those with proven economic ability and special knowledge would be needed for local and provincial production committees to perform effectively. In sum, the "production principle" theoretically allowed the integration of party and mass, the identification of politics with practical achievement, and the integration of "redness" and "expertise" that Khrushchev hoped might finally lift Soviet Russia into world leadership in production and material standard of living. If these changes were successful, communism in the near future was assured.

REVOLUTIONARY PROCESS AND THE SINO-SOVIET SPLIT

Whether or not the Soviet Union and the Peoples' Republic achieved the transition to communism their "great leaps" promised, it was clear by late 1958 that they were not going to do it together. Three factors underlay their rapidly deteriorating relationship; two central to the internal policies pursued by each, and a third, personality, which exacerbated the other two. First was the fact that both Khrushchev and Mao had achieved the power to experiment and make changes through constant political maneuvering, a process requiring continual consolidation through negotiation and success. Each had dealt hard, sometimes ruthlessly, in the political arena, and each remained vulnerable. Each, in order to succeed, had to persuade and carry with them their respective parties and populations, which circumscribed their range of actions toward the other. Second, the successes for each, politically and in terms of economic development, required different, indeed opposite, international climates. The personality factor laced these two more primary structural features with tactlessness, lack of understanding, mutual ignorance, and finally open dislike, which at times transformed even minor incidents into major events.

As laid out during the formal sessions of the Twentieth Party Congress and then elaborated in 1957 and the Seven-Year Plan, Khrushchev's grandiose objectives for Soviet development were premised on peaceful coexistence between communist states and the West. "Certain" of ultimate communist victory in competition with capitalist states, Khrushchev advanced the "fundamental principle" that war was "not a fatalistic inevitability." "Either peaceful coexistence or the most destructive war in history," Khrushchev said, "there is no third way."[36] For some this was clearly a revision of orthodox Marxist-Leninist theory, but its impetus was more practical than theoretical. In order to invest heavily in improving Soviet conditions, a peaceful international environment was essential. Expanded trade was required if the CPSU was to learn from the best in Western goods and services. The more that could safely be diverted from military and defense expenditures, the better the possibility of reaching the advanced objectives of the Seven-Year Plan. Many in the West suspected Khrushchev's intentions, but between 1955 and 1958, Soviet troop strength was reduced by more than two million men, producing substantial savings. Above-ground nuclear testing was also suspended.

Many in the Soviet Union were suspicious as well, whether for their own personal political reasons or because they maintained an honest distrust of Western intentions. The benevolence of Eisenhower and Dulles seemed a weak reed upon which to rest any part of the Soviet future. Administrative changes and the decentralization of party and state bureaucracies provoked opposition to Khrushchev's leadership on the part of old Stalinists and new technocrats alike, who were unconvinced, each for their own reasons, of the merits of Khrushchev's national and international departures.

At the same time, Khrushchev's conciliatory tone to the West could not help but be unpopular in Peking. Peaceful coexistence was at odds with the rhetoric of, and more importantly the instrumental necessity for, Great Leap Forward mobilization. Certainly there were also real dangers from Chiang Kai-shek and American militarists. By shutting the door to improved Sino-American relations in 1957, the Chinese leadership was naturally and legitimately threatened by apparent American intentions underlying improved relations with Moscow.

It was also unclear that peaceful coexistence was necessary given Chinese perceptions of Russian military strength. The successful launching of *Sputnik* was the occasion for a major speech by Mao applauding a great turning point in history: the East wind now prevailed over the West wind; the forces of socialism were certain to overtake imperialism in the near future. In such a context, appeasement of the West could only be demobilizing, destructive of those very popular forces that made for revolutionary strength.[37]

Moreover, the only way a third world war could be avoided, Mao had argued as early as 1947, was through the unity of struggle of "all countries menaced by U.S. aggression." The United States was the leader of the forces of imperialism: "Our socialist camp must also have a leader, and that leader is the Soviet Union. If we do not have a leader our forces might disintegrate!" Finally, in a phrase that cannot have been pleasant reading in Moscow, Mao pointed out that, should fighting break out, although China only had "hand grenades and not atomic bombs . . . the Soviet Union has them." If worst came to worst and imperialist "war maniacs" unleashed a nuclear war, one half of mankind might well die, but "the other half would remain, while imperialism would be razed to the ground and the whole world would become socialist."[38] The Chinese thus expected the Soviet Union not only to be a forceful, even militant, leader of an ongoing global revolutionary process, but also to be willing to use its actual military strength.

In sum, it was not necessary in Peking to accommodate in order to be secure; in fact, it was positively counterproductive. China's revolutionary experience had demonstrated time after time that peaceful coexistence destroyed revolutionary movements unless backed by independent political and military strength *and* the readiness to use it. From this perspective, Khrushchev's motives seemed obscure, particularly in the light of his obvious reluctance to either share nuclear capability with the Chinese or commit himself to its use in the event of a Sino-American conflict in the Taiwan Straits.

Chinese anxieties culminated in the summer of 1959. The Great Leap itself, as we shall see, was in trouble; a Chinese military mission to Moscow learned that an apparent agreement on nuclear sharing would not be acted upon; and Moscow announced that Khrushchev would become the first Soviet premier to visit the United States and have direct consultations with an American president at his summer retreat. Although Camp David produced more in the way of atmospherics than substantive change, and Khrushchev himself visited Peking soon after to reassure the Chinese, these anxieties were not eased. Commitment to socialist revolution was being dampened at precisely the moment it was needed for China's own transition to communism.

Coincidentally, Khrushchev's policies were also encountering difficulties, which may have contributed to an angry defensiveness on the part of the Soviet premier. Both Khrushchev's personal power and the success of his policies now depended increasingly on the acceptance of the "spirit of Camp David" by his own associates and other Bloc parties. Antagonisms on the periphery, whether the Taiwan Straits, the Sino-Indian border, or Southeast Asia, were intolerable and unnecessary provocations. In effect, having abandoned Stalinist politics as a necessary condition to leading Soviet Russia forward, Khrushchev found himself hostage of forces in and outside the USSR he could no longer control or repress.

In May 1960, eleven days before a new summit conference was scheduled to open in Paris, Soviet armed forces brought down an American U-2 spy plane piloted by Gary Powers. Wherever the decision was made (and in all likelihood it was not made in the Politburo), the episode was highly embarrassing to Khrushchev and grist for the mill of antirevisionists everywhere. The Russians withdrew from the Paris summit, but Khrushchev simultaneously went on the offensive against his enemies both within Russia and abroad. At the Bucharest conference of Communist parties in June 1960, the "erroneous and wrongheaded views" of the Chinese were attacked head-on, and the Chinese responded in kind. Shortly thereafter Khrushchev precipitously ordered the immediate withdrawal of all Soviet technicians from China.

Over the next fifteen years Soviet and Chinese ideologues would develop elaborate theoretical explanations of the break for domestic and international use. The debate became a major part of the fabric of domestic political life in China and, at an international level, would play an increasingly significant role in the lives of Koreans, Vietnamese, Laotians, Cambodians, the peoples of Chile and Cuba, and Communist parties everywhere, fractioning in tune with the centrifugal pull of the split. For Chinese especially, the Soviet Union, in its alleged double-time march toward "capitalism" (even "fascism"), became the antithesis of communist thesis and praxis. And the Soviet Union, in perhaps surprising accord with American analysts, saw in Chinese developments only madness.

It is not necessary here to follow the course of this further division. By the summer of 1960, for all intents and purposes, the split was complete, despite a brief period of accord. By the end of the decade major military installations and perhaps as many as two million troops lined the Sino-Soviet border on both sides. Bloody armed clashes occurred along the Ussuri River, and there was genuine fear of war. For our purposes, it is important only to emphasize the degree to which this remarkable antagonism originated in the demands made by the leadership of each country in the name of new roads to socialism, demands that were made both on a wary and at times overtly hostile outside world, and on the Chinese and Soviet societies themselves. The rupture was thus paradoxically an integral part of the revolutionary process in both countries, as each pressed (or was pressed) toward its own vision of the communist ideal. And its intensity symbolically reflected both the enormous efforts of "great leaps forward" and, as we shall see, their failures.

9

CULTURAL REVOLUTION
AND THE
QUESTION OF STABILIZATION

The "great leaps forward" proved to be phases of instability in the revolutionary processes of Soviet Russia and China, but their radical nature and the conscious efforts of party leaders to tie them to the revolutionary origins of both societies made them important phases in the overall pattern of development. In China, the reversal was well underway by the summer of 1961, while Khrushchev in Moscow was experiencing severe problems in terms both of his personal political position and the goals of the Seven-Year Plan. The question in both countries was whether radical change was still an appropriate mode of social transformation, whether drastic changes in the structure and role of the party were suited to situations in which the issue of the party's political control itself was no longer in doubt.

As we shall see, difficulties in the USSR pressed Khrushchev to still more changes and to strategies of party reorganization that appear in retrospect, paradoxically, to have remarkable Maoist overtones. The "arch-revisionist" and "capitalist roader" assaulted "entrenched officialdom" with what many regarded as reckless abandon, "banging his shoe on every table," and driving the country toward communism with unstinting enthusiasm. "I am convinced more than ever," he insisted to reporters during his trip to the United States, "that the best man can create, the holiest of holies, is socialist society, the

Communist system."[1] But if his colleagues agreed that Marxist-Leninist teachings could be "spread with a piece of butter," that "with good housing, with a better and more abundant life, with good schools, we will win all the peoples for socialism and communism,"[2] they became increasingly convinced that stability, rather than rapid or drastic change, was both desirable and necessary.

In China, the struggle between those committed to the revolutionary mentality and radical methods of the Great Leap and those favoring stabilization continued until Mao's death in 1976. Here, however, the tasks of development remained staggering, comparable in Mao's view to the tasks of survival during the 1930s and the Long March. The split with Moscow greatly complicated technological development and industrial growth, while the problems of state security increased with Soviet belligerence. In China, consequently, a brief period of stability after 1961 was followed by new and even more radical upheavals. While the Soviet Union returned to "normalcy," the Great Proletarian Cultural Revolution committed Chinese society in the mid-1960s to the Maoist vision of ongoing radical transformation—a vision that equated the establishment of egalitarian communism with the revolutionary process of total social mobilization and constant change, and that saw ultimate social security in the absence of permanent, hierarchical social structures. But here, too, with hindsight, it seems apparent that the pressures for stabilization were ultimately stronger and that China's commitment to uninterrupted revolution, like Soviet Russia's, would come to an end.

RETRENCHMENT IN CHINA

The Great Leap had begun in China in the summer of 1958, a time of exceptionally good harvests. By fall there were already signs of serious difficulties. The movement to rapidly expand communal organization in China had economic consequences similar to Soviet collectivization. The hasty establishment of huge communes (750,000 collectives had merged into 26,578 communes with an average membership of 20,000 to 25,000 people) created a variety of organizational problems of increasing seriousness: there was a widespread lack of managerial skills capable of meeting the needs of such large economic units; decentralization led to chaos in planning at the national level, with shortages of raw materials, an overtaxed transport system and inefficiencies in production and distribution, which plagued both cities and countryside; local cadres, out of enthusiasm, opportunism, or both, grossly inflated production statistics, adding to difficulties of rational planning at the national level; commandist cadre techniques alienated peasants drafted for large-scale communal projects without appropriate remuneration; efforts to fully utilize female labor ran aground on the lack of funds for collective facilities for child care and other supportive services. Everywhere there were complaints and, on the part of party bureaucrats, a growing concern that Mao's radical vision would destroy the steady modest gains made possible by successive five-year plans of a Soviet type.

Reaching into an apparently bottomless store of peasant proverbs, Mao once compared the process of the Great Leap to Hunanese sandalmaking: "There is no pattern for straw sandals, they take shape as you work on them." The touchstone of Mao's revolutionary praxis lay in his deep belief in the creative power of ordinary Chinese to shape the revolution. The ultimate goal—a sandal, an equitable society—was clear. To reach it one must trust the shoemaker. Mistakes would be made, struggle was inevitable, unity was desirable—though not at any cost. For Mao the economic and social crisis that seemed to flow directly from the "utopian" effort of the Great Leap could not imply abandonment of the revolutionary process it encompassed. To others in the party, however, like Liu Shaoqi and Deng Xiaoping, it was clearly time to call a halt. A nation as close to the edge of subsistence as China could not afford the luxury of peasant metaphors. Besides, what was needed was large-scale manufacture of leather shoes, not sandals at all.

Peng Dehuai, commander of the People's Liberation Army, Mao's comrade in arms from the earliest days in Jiangxi, challenged the entire Great Leap strategy head-on. It was, he argued, an example of petty-bourgeois fanaticism that threatened to delay the urgent tasks of industrialization and modernization. Peng's attack, which he had discussed on his recent trip to the Soviet Union and Eastern Europe, was publicly echoed by Khrushchev in a manner certain to arouse suspicion in China. At a meeting preparing for the Eighth Plenum of the Central Committee in 1959, Mao met the challenge in a startling way. Yes, the Great Leap had run into problems causing chaos for which he personally took responsibility. But if its overall strategy were abandoned, he would "go to the countryside to lead the peasants to overthrow the government. If those of you in the Liberation Army won't follow me, then I will go and find a Red Army, and organize another Liberation Army."[3] Given his record, it was hardly a dare the party relished accepting, and, when the Plenum met in August, Peng Dehuai was denounced and dismissed. But this affirmation of the Great Leap was truncated to begin with and short-lived in its outcome. Private plots, widely eliminated in the first thrust of enthusiastic communal organization, were restored and granted explicit protection; private ownership of homes, small farm tools, poultry, and pigs was sanctioned; the organization of production and distribution, already reduced from commune to brigade level, dropped one step further, and the team (often coinciding with the old mutual aid units) became the basic unit of accounting on communes throughout the countryside.

To the disruption in production caused by organizational failure was now added the strain of a series of extraordinary natural disasters. Drought and flooding had reduced harvests in 1959. By 1960 the situation was critical. Typhoons in Central and Northeast China combined with drought in the Yellow River basin, battering fully 60 percent of China's total cultivated area with severe drought or flooding. At the same time, as we have seen, Khrushchev recalled every single Russian technical adviser in China—and ordered them to take their blueprints with them, adding considerably to the desperate economic situation.

Only fifteen years earlier, such a series of setbacks would have resulted in widespread famine, epidemic disease, and death. If objective proof of the success of the revolution was necessary, the manner in which China survived these years of bad weather and poor harvests would be enough: people were hungry and there were certainly deaths from malnutrition, but there was no massive famine, no recourse to traditional means of coping—sale of wives and children, infanticide, waves of refugees. Through rationing and the fair distribution of imported grain, China pulled through. To hundreds of millions of Chinese, the revolution they had made saved them from the horror of remembered famine, an experience still endemic in large parts of the world.

Reluctantly, Mao acknowledged that the Great Leap campaign was over and withdrew from participation in the day-to-day politics of China. And yet, when the dust had settled, it seemed clear that the Chinese had broken from the Soviet model of development.

CONTRADICTIONS OF REVITALIZATION IN THE USSR

As in China, poor weather also played a role in undermining Khrushchev's determined effort to "overtake and outstrip the West," but other factors were far more important. The Seven-Year Plan targets were set in 1957–58 against a background of favorable conditions and rising agricultural output. A grain harvest of 105 million metric tons in 1957 had grown by 1958 to 141.2 million tons, a remarkable increase indeed, particularly when compared to the harvests of 82.5 and 85.6 million tons in 1953 and 1954.[4] Khrushchev expected enormous potential growth in other areas as well, enough, in fact, so that great increases were targeted throughout the economy. Iron ore was to increase from 88.8 million tons to between 150 and 160 million by 1965; steel from 54.9 to as much as 86 million tons; gas from 29.9 billion cubic meters to 150; electricity from 235 to 500 billion kwh. The consumer sector was to develop just as rapidly. A grain harvest of 180 million tons was targeted for 1965. Wool fabrics were to increase at a threefold rate from 303 million square meters to 1,485; housing from 71.2 to 650 million square meters, an incredible ninefold increase; and meat, an all-important index of consumer prosperity, from 3.37 to 6.13 million tons, almost twice the output of 1958.[5] "In the immediate foreseeable future," Khrushchev proclaimed with a somewhat redundant exuberance, "our country will ensure such living and cultural standards for working people of town and countryside as are inaccessible to any capitalist country, even the richest!"[6]

Favorable conditions, however, can be a very poor basis for planning, and exuberance a distorter of reality. The grain harvest in 1959 dropped considerably over 1958 and remained below 1958 levels in 1960 and 1961. Khrushchev's government was unable to build reserves, and doubts developed about its ability not only to support the vast new construction projects envisioned by the plan, but even to maintain supplies, particularly if weather conditions turned unfavorable (as they were to do in 1963 and 1965). As early as July 1960, *Pravda* reported rather ponderously that "the rates of growth of capital investments allocated for the construction industry and building materials industry do not assure that the development of these branches will stay ahead of needs."[7] Translated, this meant that development in all economic sectors dependent on new construction was in difficulty.

Khrushchev's response, again, was to lash out at those he thought responsible (just as he lashed out at this time at the Chinese by withdrawing Soviet technicians). Workers had to work harder ("increasing social labor productivity [is] the decisive source of expanded socialist reproduction"); incompetent managers had to be replaced ("Some comrades do not yet have an inculcated pride, an inner dignity. A self-respecting leader would have sent in his resignation!").[8] But the problems he faced were much more complex. The very mechanism of Soviet state planning remained ill-suited to rapid and dramatic increases in output and even less able to control quality and product mix. In the best of circumstances planners needed hard data in order even to approximate balances between the myriad of inputs and outputs in what was now a complex, industrialized society. The very feature of rapid growth implied the obsolescence of past output statistics, the planners' most reliable guides. Khrushchev had hoped decentralization through the 104 new regional economic councils would make economic administrators more knowledgeable and more responsive, but while this may have been so on a regional level, the effect nationwide was to isolate individual regions from activities elsewhere, an isolation intensified by the concurrent abolition of centralized state ministries. Simply put, surpluses and shortages became more difficult to match as real levels of output became more uncertain.

In the countryside, similar problems followed Khrushchev's well-intentioned decision to abolish the machine tractor stations (MTS), hated bastions of Stalinist political control. The party leadership had hoped to make collective farms more autonomous and self-sufficient by having them purchase MTS machinery outright, but the acquisition costs were too high, there were too few mechanics on the farms to keep the equipment running, and replacement parts were scarce or nonexistent, particularly for older machinery that the government, in its wisdom, priced the same as new. Other important capital-intensive projects (the modernization of dairy equipment, for example, necessary to outproduce the United States in the production of butter, milk, and eggs) had to be deferred or cancelled. Building up the collective farms also involved pressure against private plots and privately held livestock (through taxes, limited pasture rights, and restrictions on fodder). Despite real improvements in their material welfare, consequently, peasant resentments also grew, even somewhat more rapidly, no doubt, because of higher expectations.

Khrushchev's bombastic attacks on party and state officials who refused to "dirty their hands" with the day-to-day problems of management made excellent copy in Western and Soviet newspapers alike, but many failed to appreciate the insecurities the attacks engendered, or the possible consequences. When Khrushchev angrily demanded an increase in the Seven-Year Plan of some 60 to 70 percent in the output of meat, the ambitious first secretary of the Riazan *oblast* ("regional") committee, A. N. Larionov, promised his district would more than double the output of meat in one year alone, from 48,000 tons to 150,000! Promises piled on promises, as did the rewards and incentives. After initial successes in Riazan, Khrushchev himself went to the region in February 1959 to confer on it the Order of Lenin. The extraordinary targets, however, were being met by an extraordinarily profligate system of slaughtering, which in some Riazan districts extended to milk cows and breeding stock. Larionov, now a Hero of Socialist Labor and decorated with the Order of Lenin, worked himself and the region into an untenable position, emulated of course by others. "Thoroughly carried away with their own charlatinism," as Roy and Zhores Medvedev report, he promised the *oblast* would sell even more to the state in 1960. The result was disastrous. Desperate efforts were made throughout the region to meet the impossible goal; meat was purchased and stolen from other areas, private stocks were decimated. In all, only 30,000 tons could be delivered in 1960, and only 50 percent of the region's grain quota could be met, so decimated were the collective farms. Larionov himself committed suicide.[9]

Such "storming" techniques (and such disastrous consequences in many areas) recalled the gross distortions of the Stalinist period and reflected not only patterns of deeply rooted socioeconomic behavior, but persistent structural difficulties. Planners tried to tinker with reward and incentive systems, and new debates took place in leading economic journals about possible measures to remedy what were, in effect, the defects of planning and economic management systems more appropriate to periods of scarcity than the relative abundance of the early 1960s. There remained, for example, no charge on capital which enterprises received from the state. All sorts of urgent requests were consequently made for funds without proper attention to their relative costs or utility. As a result, the allocation of capital led frequently to waste and inefficiency. And again, the decentralization of ministries and other economic institutions only made matters worse.

Economic experts also recognized that intensification of labor was not the remedy now that it had been to a large degree in the 1930s. Further reforms were needed to assure the most rational allocation of scarce capital resources (particularly in terms of "rate of return" or profit), prices functionally related to real cost, an effective incentive system (eliminating such retardants to growth as the "rachet" mechanism), and effective real-wage allocations (appropriate to manpower needs, technological requirements, and the like). From the standpoint of those directly involved in economic management, such revisionism was the necessary consequence of an increasingly complex and technologically sophisticated economic structure.

In response to all this and also, no doubt, in response to the increasing criticism economic shortcomings must have engendered within official circles, Khrushchev pressed even further with new administrative reforms, some moving back in the direction of re-centralization (such as the decision in early 1963 to merge regional economic councils together and reduce their total number from 104 to 47), and some in the direction of pressing officials further into everyday production tasks (such as the splitting of party organizations into agricultural and industrial sections in 1962). But the very confusion engendered by such shuffling and reshuffling took its own toll. On crucial issues of economic administration, Khrushchev's government seemed to lack resolution and direction. Some even feared the party might have to ration essential foodstuffs after the drought and poor harvest of 1963.

Still, Khrushchev persevered, deeply committed to the rapid achievement of communism, as intense and trenchant as ever. Party plenums followed party plenums; tongue-lashings, public scoldings, and reassignments followed new commitments and a new insistence that officials either get even closer to ordinary work and production problems or resign their positions. In one move, regarded by many bureaucrats and administrators as particularly "hare-brained," Khrushchev had the entire USSR Ministry of Agriculture moved out of Moscow to a state farm some 100 kilometers away. (The Agricultural Department of the Russian Republic—RSFSR—was similarly moved.)

> Shifting the ministries to the countryside took place overnight—no time was allowed to construct the necessary office buildings or housing. . . . The Ministry's staff had to commute daily from Moscow in special buses over poor roads. Usually the trip took two to three hours each way. Visitors from other cities or delegates invited to various conferences also had to make the trip, staying at hotels in Moscow. In addition, all the staff members, from administrative heads down to cafeteria workers, had to devote some time to working in the fields, testing new types of equipment, and often performing the most basic chores, such as weeding, or digging potatoes. For the middle- and upper-level executive, this was quite an ordeal!
>
> Within a year, more than 1,700 of the 2,200 staff members had given notice.[10]

If sugar beets grew in the Ukraine, Khrushchev reasoned, or potatoes in the Russian countryside, there was no reason for scientists and officials engaged in agricultural work to be "nestled comfortably around the Bolshoi theater as if it were their chief station."[11]

Khrushchev's radicalism found other expressions as well, some relatively trivial, some of enormous global importance. After suppressing *Doctor Zhivago* in 1957 and castigating Boris Pasternak without mercy when it earned him the Nobel Prize, Khrushchev permitted the publication of Alexander Solzhenitsyn's *One Day in the Life of Ivan Denisovich*, a deeply moving account of Stalin's camps, and *Pravda* published a stunning Yevgeny Yevtushenko poem, "Stalin's Heirs," ironically dedicated to Enver Hoxha and referring to Khrushchev's decision at the extraordinary Twenty-Second Party Congress in 1961 to remove Stalin's body from the mausoleum on Red Square:

> And I turn to our government
> > with a request:
> to double
> > to triple
> > > the guards over that gravestone

So that Stalin cannot rise
                    and with Stalin—
                                    the past . . .
     To Enver Hoxha
                    Stalin transmits his latest edicts.
     To what other places is that direct line linked up?
     No Stalin did not surrender.
                                    Death's to him
                                        a mistake to be corrected.
     With determination
                    we took him out of the Mausoleum
     But how out of the heirs of Stalin
                                    do we take Stalin?[12]

Yet two months later Khrushchev visited an art exhibition in Moscow that included a small selection of abstract sculpture and painting, and exploded with indignation. "I would say that this is just a mess," he declared in front of one modernistic painting:

> I will probably be told that I am not sophisticated enough to appreciate such works . . . but if you excuse me [such painting] looks as though a child has done his business on the canvas when his mother was away and then spread it around him with his hands. . . . We are going to take these blotches with us into communism, are we? If state funds have been paid for this picture, the person who authorized it will have the sum deducted from his salary. . . . Judging by these experiments, I think you are parasites, and for that you can get 10 years. You've gone out of your minds and now you want to deflect us from the proper course. You won't get away with it.[13]

Such differences on art and literature were not really a reflection of inconsistency on Khrushchev's part, as they were frequently regarded both in the Soviet Union and abroad, since the first secretary remained unwavering in his insistence that all art and all literature serve the party and the tasks of building communism, even if the content of those tasks themselves changed frequently in response to his own impulsive views. Yet frequent change was unnerving to officials and ordinary citizens alike. It seemed too much like a revolutionary atmosphere at a time when Russians liked to think of the Soviet Union as a mature state system. Banging one's shoe on the desk at the United Nations, as Khrushchev did in 1959, was undignified and inappropriate; favoring university applicants with "production training" over those without recalled the 1920s and early 1930s, which most established professionals were ready to consider "history"; and installing missiles in Cuba was an unnecessary and clearly a poorly planned strategy, which failed to consider properly the likely American response. Kennedy's triumph was Khrushchev's embarrassment, a dismal failure. "A self-respecting leader would send in his resignation," those around him must have muttered.

Enthusiastic, petulant, committed to a radical revitalization of Soviet Russia's state and social structure and to enormous material progress, Khrushchev in a paradoxical sense was rapidly becoming a victim of his own success. In the area of producers goods, as opposed to foodstuffs and other consumers goods, the actual results of the Seven-Year Plan were impressive (a 96 percent increase over 1958 levels, and some 8 to 12 percent over plan),[14] but queues at the food stores grew longer, particularly in 1963, and people's patience shrank. Artists and writers, who had appreciated the remarkable liberalization underlying the publication of "Stalin's Heirs" and *Ivan Denisovich*, suffered frightening abuse and even arrest. Party and state officials publicly cheered their enthusiastic first secretary, but the changes he imposed rankled deeply; having been brought into responsible positions precisely because of their expertise and managerial ability, many opposed his reforms precisely because they recognized consequent distortions. Others simply rejected his style and the threat he posed to their comfort and personal security. If it was true that sugar beets did not grow in Moscow, it was equally the case that the Bolshoi did not play in Ukrainian fields. Finally, there was, perhaps, for some, a real feeling that Khrushchev's impetuous style would lead to disaster. China was a concern, if not yet a genuine fear, Vietnam was a worry, and the Cuban missile crisis a real fright. Angry, dissatisfied consumers threatened social stability. Stalin *was* safely interred, but the questions of heirs and inheritance remained. In sum, performance *had* become the key; on the terms he himself had established, Khrushchev was found wanting. On October 13–14, 1964, the Presidium of the Central Committee unanimously resolved to terminate his appointments as first secretary of the party and chairman of the Council of Ministers, as well as his membership in the Central Committee, and he agreed to resign.

CONTRADICTIONS OF STABILIZATION IN CHINA

Meanwhile, key elements of the Great Leap strategy, however modified, continued to mark Chinese society. The per capita income of Chinese peasants was low, and like peasants in all developing agrarian societies, they paid a disproportionate share of development costs. Yet the communal organization of agriculture, with its remarkable flexibility in terms of the mobilization and use of labor, its capacity to fund and direct self-sustaining local industries, and its potential for expanding distribution of income at ever higher levels of collectivity remains China's unique contribution to the possibilities of revolutionary modernization elsewhere in the Third World.

While many of the structural features of the Great Leap endured, however, other crucial aspects of the Maoist road were buried. After 1961 primary emphasis on agriculture over heavy industry remained policy, but Mao's "guerrilla" tactics, his reliance on the spontaneity of the masses, was firmly rejected. The values and modes of operation of a top-down Leninist party became increasingly dominant. For Mao, the Communist party remained a necessary core organization (although late in the 1960s he was to express total indifference to what such an organization was called). Yet he felt the party was not *automatically* in a position to lead the masses by tautological definition; on the contrary, there was nothing sacred about the party as such. It was not immune to any social ill; indeed it might itself become the breeding ground for hierarchy and new oppression. To Mao's opponents, however, now safely in control of a revived party apparatus, any return to the disorganized spontaneity of the Great Leap had to be avoided at all costs. Order, stability, discipline—these were the watchwords of the mid-1960s. The first task of the leadership was to restore production in both industry and agriculture. No less than Mao, its goal was socialist development; that the means they took to achieve it might, in time, distort the end they sought was a necessary risk, but one far more acceptable than those Mao insisted on taking. It is precisely because the goal was shared that the antagonism between the tactics of stabilization and renewed revolution was so intense, ultimately violent, and still unresolved in the early 1980s.

The first step on the path to restabilization was to reassert the authority of centralized institutions in all areas of the society. Local rural cadres were blamed for the failures of the Great Leap and purged; regional party bureaus were established with clear lines of authority to the Central Committee; formal cadre ranks were introduced for both party and state functionaries; cadre duties were defined as the implementation of directives from superior levels of the hierarchy. In the countryside, control over the educational system was removed from the commune and restored to county government; communes were administered by full-time salaried officials responsible for supervising action on centrally defined policies; control of commerce, finance, and tax collection reverted to the county government.

We can observe the change more closely by considering the shift in policy on tractor stations. In 1953–54 an emissary of Mao's had investigated Soviet tractor stations and concluded, as Khrushchev himself was to do, that they were simply tax collecting units that "held the peasants to ransom and were divorced from the people."[15] During the Great Leap, accordingly, the stations were dismantled and tractors distributed directly to communes. Local committees of technicians, artisans, and peasants were formed to experiment with the invention and improvement of farm machinery at every level of mechanization, including "animal-power farm tools."

In direct contrast, in 1962 Liu Shaoqi switched to a scheme that would push for full-scale mechanization in a number of selected districts. This would have involved the creation of centrally controlled tractor stations run on a profit-making basis, despite the fact that in conditions of undermechanization, such stations, as the Soviet experience demonstrated, were necessarily centers of great power, subject to abuse. Also, where Mao had called for the "various localities [to] pay attention to their particular conditions and . . . never do things in the same way," Liu proposed state corporations to ensure standardization of farm machinery production. "In rejecting Mao's road to mechanization," as Jack Gray points out, "his opponents were rejecting the whole of his economic strategy," and with it, the whole of his road to socialism.[16]

In industry, while some degree of economic autonomy at the

enterprise level was retained, centralized planning returned in full measure, and the central economic ministries once more became principally responsible for the general direction of economic development. The power of factory managers, much reduced during the period of experimentation with more radical forms of organization, was restored. Consonant with the stress on hierarchy, organization, order, and stability was a range of economic policy designed to increase production as rapidly as possible within an orderly framework. Communal constraints on individual peasant enterprise were discouraged and private plots allowed to increase to 12 percent of the tillable land in any one commune. Untilled land was open to individual peasant reclamation, private peasant markets were permitted to flourish, as in the Soviet Union, and, though frowned upon, the tendency in many areas was for collective labor to decline as peasants increasingly, literally, tended their own gardens. By 1962, some estimates indicate, private grain harvests in the province of Yunnan were larger than those made by collectives and privately cultivated land had risen to 50 percent of the total. Essentially, a modified version of the Soviet economic pattern of development was emerging.[17]

We can follow the many forms of decollectivization in one county, Lianjiang, for which we have detailed information.[18] Here, production was contracted out to individual households and those with plenty of labor prospered. Labor-poor households were forced to rent their land or even hire themselves out to richer neighbors. Collective sources of fertilizer were commandeered for use on private plots, collective land usurped for purposes of private home construction; in fishing collectives, state-owned oyster and clam beds were fished by individual households for their own profit; and the contract system produced new forms of sharecropping arrangements.

Along with this resurgence of old forms of economic relations came a revival of old social customs. Extravagant banquets, gambling, usury, and traditional forms of ancestor worship and marriage practices reappeared. The ready participation of local cadres in the full range of abuses was particularly disturbing. One investigation revealed that 48 percent of the cadres in one brigade had committed errors of "capitalism, feudalism and extravagance." A careful reading of the cases indicates that most of their crimes were on small claims court scale, but the tendency was clear. The political privilege of cadres, once it became linked to a resurgent rich peasant economy, represented precisely what Maoists most feared: a reversal of revolution, the first steps on the slippery road to "capitalism."

Yet some of the choices made by teams and cadres must have reflected the most immediate desires of their constituency. In Lianjiang, for example, teams of women apparently used collective funds to organize "large-scale play companies" and buy "ancient-style opera costumes. They have even taken young people to study acting. Some teams, in order to maintain play companies, have even asked counter-revolutionaries to direct them. Others have hired play companies from distant places and have continually put on performances."[19]

What did the masses really want? An investigation of a team in which the move toward individual enterprise had reached alarming proportions revealed that, of the fourteen households involved, only four (classified as "affluent middle peasants") were firmly in favor of the move, six were "confused," and the remaining four, all poor and lower-middle peasants, "resolutely opposed." If individual enterprise was really the way to get rich, the authors of the report point out, "how come our ancestors did it for thousands of years and only a handful got rich?"[20] Mao's hopes for revolutionary transformation rested precisely on the ability of cadres to communicate this fundamental fact to the "confused" middle group and, building on the resolution of the poorest, forge a majority capable of overcoming the desire of more affluent peasants to go their own way. In the absence of such leadership, effective collectivization and equitable economic development were impossible.

If there were growing income differentials in rural counties like Lianjiang, the same was true for the cities. Material incentives, in the form of individual bonuses, rewards, and piece rates, were reinstated, again reflecting Soviet patterns. The power and prestige of technical experts and managers divorced from the shop floor increased. Between the countryside and the cities and within each sector, differences widened, reinforced by a refurbished educational system that amounted to tracking, giving urban children of professional or bourgeois background decided advantages.

Yet by most economic indicators, Liu Shaoqi's policies, endorsed by the party majority, were a great success. Industrial and agricultural production both increased substantially; the hard years were over. Nor was the policy a complete reversion to the Stalinist model. Agriculture, not heavy industry, remained the acknowledged foundation of the economy, and capital investments to it increased from 1960 through 1965 at the same time urban industrial facilities were redirected toward the production of chemical fertilizers, small tractors, and other agricultural necessities. Rural electrification was widely expanded, and, while pricing policy continued to favor industry over agriculture, nothing like the 1920s Soviet "scissors" crisis developed.

The ruling party faction recognized and deplored many aspects of decollectivization, but what separated them from Mao and his allies was their willingness to countenance a greater degree of social inequality as the necessary price for China's flourishing statistical indices and their bureaucratic approach to correcting the abuses such inequality produced.

A Socialist Education Movement, launched by Mao in May 1963, was intended to deal with the danger to the whole structure of collective agriculture represented by the system of individual household contracts. Those who posed the danger were defined as local cadres who, in collusion with remnant "bad class elements," exploited the masses. Investigation into how cadres determined work points, kept account books, distributed supplies, and supervised communal granaries was to be undertaken. But who was responsible for conducting investigations and disciplining cadres remained an issue of contention and helped define the different approaches of major leadership groups.

Both Liu and Deng Xiaoping favored the use of work teams, sometimes operating secretly, sent into the countryside from higher party levels. Offenders were to be dealt with harshly through official channels. Mao, on the contrary, urged the reestablishment of poor and lower-middle peasant associations, mass organizations that would be responsible for investigation and appropriate discipline. For him, the problem lay not in individuals, but in the party itself; cadre corruption could not be solved from within. It was not a momentary lapse, Mao believed, but the expression of ongoing class struggle, the growth of a new class faction, in collusion with remnant bourgeois elements perhaps, but with its own stake in preserving the status quo. As in the past, the solution was direct exercise of political power by the masses of people. Unless cadres became "red again," unless they merged with the masses in China's three great struggles—"class struggle, production struggle, and scientific experiment"—the party of Marx and Lenin would "turn into a party of revisionism, of fascism. The whole of China would then change color."[21]

Mao's notion of the party changing color was absurd within the framework of orthodox Marxism-Leninism, which held that, by definition, the Communist party was the vanguard of the revolution. It could no more change color than the proletariat could "become" capitalist. Shaped by its relationship to the revolutionary class, the party, whatever troubles might befall it, remained the consciousness of that class. Liu and others joined Mao in noting various tendencies with alarm. Certainly there seemed to be a developing elite sector—based in the party and the state bureaucracy—that mediated between state and people, interpreted for them the dominant ideology, and received that range of deference that accompanies high status, and some of its minor material rewards as well. Opportunities for corruption were clear. The solution was to *improve* the elite through inner party rectification campaigns, moral exhortation, stints of productive labor, and so on. Dedication, discipline, regulation, and clear lines of authority would ensure a responsible functioning elite able to devote its full energies toward the urgent tasks of development. Moreover, if the task was to "serve the people," if one must in good Maoist fashion seek "truth from facts" and not give way to infantile leftism or anarchist egalitarianism, then surely all had to agree that what people wanted above all was an improvement in their actual material situation. The wild experimentation of the Great Leap, its radical effort to institute communism by sheer willpower had led to economic disaster on every front.

In 1963 Mao warned that the Communist party of China could become not merely revisionist in nature, but even "fascist." By 1965 he was ready to name the struggle in its starkest terms. In a speech before a national work conference, he declared that the struggle between capitalism and socialism had been resolved neither in China, as a society, nor in its governing party. "Those people in positions of authority within the Party who take the capitalist road" must be struggled against—and Mao did not mean local rural cadres. Somewhat later in the year he told André Malraux that he felt himself to be "alone with the masses, waiting."[22] It was not a long wait.

Before the year was out, the Great Proletarian Cultural Revolution had begun.

THE GREAT PROLETARIAN CULTURAL REVOLUTION

Given his reduced state of political power in the early 1960s, it is somewhat surprising that Mao was able to launch the Cultural Revolution at all. His earlier efforts at mass mobilization, such as the Socialist Education Movement, had been quickly contained and channeled by the party leadership. The Cultural Revolution might have suffered the same fate but for two crucial factors: the nature of the People's Liberation Army (PLA) under Lin Biao's leadership, and the depth of discontent among significant urban groups.

Lin Biao, veteran of the Long March, civil war hero, took command of the PLA when Peng Dehuai was ousted in August 1959. His decisive alliance with Mao on the major issues of the Great Leap Forward included a shared perspective on military policy. Lin's design for the PLA was no less "modern" in terms of equipment and training than Peng Dehuai's had been. What separated them was the political nature of that force. To Lin, a PLA increasingly dominated by a professional officer corps and dependent on the Soviet Union for technology could not possibly serve the needs of the ongoing Chinese revolution. Instead, the PLA had to become a model of what was possible in the society at large: an agency for the creation, through consciousness, of new socialist men and women (though far more men than women, to be sure). As the perfect embodiment of communist values, of a proletarian outlook, the PLA would be a "school for society." Transformation was dependent on how successfully the individual could grasp and apply the thought of Mao Zedong. In May 1964 the army published and widely distributed a collection of Mao's thoughts appropriately bound in bright red.

Although claims for the power of the *Quotations From Chairman Mao* became more and more extravagant, it was in fact more than just an artifact in the growing cult of Mao. Western observers who disparagingly referred to it as a pocket Bible missed the point. It *was* a kind of vernacular bible, putting into the hands of hundreds of millions of people the means by which they could analyze their situation, think through solutions to problems, and argue with party bureaucrats who hitherto alone possessed the sacred canon of Marxism-Leninism-Mao Zedong Thought. The "little red book," in a sense, destroyed the elite's ownership of the "mode of knowledge." If the grounds of argumentation were genuinely communized, made available to the whole people, then, in some considerable measure, the gap between mental and manual labor would begin to be bridged. The compactness of the book, the clear common sense of the quotations were in line with Mao's own distaste for excessive "book learning." "One must not read too much," Mao advised in 1964. "Books by Marx should be read but not too many of them. A few dozen volumes will do. Too much reading will lead you to the opposite of what you expect to be, a bookworm, a dogmatist, a revisionist."[23]

Armed with the *Quotations*, PLA cadres spread a growing cult of Mao, which he more than tolerated. Through it, and the continued support of the army, Mao could begin to make headway against an entrenched party leadership. The Great Leap, after all, had proceeded because Mao was able to appeal to a larger constituency over the heads of the Central Committee. The Cultural Revolution followed the same course.

It began quietly enough and in a most academic way. In the fall of 1965, Yao Wenyuan, a young Shanghai journalist and theoretician close to Mao, published a scathing critique of a play written years earlier by Wu Han, the vice-mayor of Peking. *Dismissal of Hai Rui from Office* had been a thinly veiled attack on the Great Leap, and on Mao. Yao's attack was similarly a thinly veiled attack on party policies from 1961 to 1965. For almost a year, the debate was confined to the realm of literature and culture. Although Mao had managed to win Politburo consent to the launching of a "cultural revolution," its five-man committee was led by Peng Zhen, mayor of Peking and a close ally of Wu Han. It was not until the spring of 1966 that the movement really got underway. Backed by Lin Biao, Mao drafted a directive in mid-May that condemned Peng Zhen, charged that the party was infiltrated at all levels by the bourgeoisie, and established an ad hoc Cultural Revolution Group that superseded the Central Committee. It was the sort of move Trotsky was never able to make, though his own "new course" could have succeeded in no other way.

The result was an explosion of popular expression. Less than ten days after the May sixteenth directive, Peking University was swept up in an all-out attack by students on the faculty and administration. By June, all university entrance examinations were postponed, awaiting a promised total restructuring of the entire educational system. In the summer the student movement organized itself into Red Guard units dedicated to the pursuit of the twin tasks announced earlier by the Cultural Revolution Group: to overthrow those in authority taking the capitalist road and to destroy the "four olds"— the old ideas, culture, customs, and habits that, presumably, continued to hold China back from full socialist transformation. The cities of China were wallpapered with popular expressions of opinion, passion, and discontent; on August 5, Mao himself posted a "big character poster" on the door of the Central Committee meeting room. It was brief and powerful: bombard the headquarters.

Two weeks later, at the Eleventh Plenum of the Central Committee, a "Declaration in Sixteen Points" defined guidelines for the movement already underway. The Cultural Revolution's objective was to "struggle against and crush those in authority who are taking the capitalist road, to criticize and repudiate the reactionary bourgeois academic 'authorities' and the ideology of the bourgeoisie and all other exploiting classes and to transform education, literature, and art and all other parts of the superstructure that do not correspond to the socialist economic base, so as to facilitate the consolidation and development of the socialist system."[24] The statement was a full expression of the Maoist line: China's problem was not its backward "productive forces," as Stalin thought Russia's had been, but its backward ideology. The persistence of bourgeois thinking in art, literature, and education expressed itself politically in a proliferating, indifferent bureaucracy that commanded people rather than led them, that honored mental over manual work, that feared the masses and no longer knew how to merge with them. The method of the Cultural Revolution, point four of the sixteen points made clear, was for the "masses to liberate themselves, and any method of doing things on their behalf must not be used." The effort of Liu Shaoqi and Deng Xiaoping to use work teams to control mass criticism was thus explicitly rejected. "Cast out fear," point four insisted, "Don't be afraid of disorder." But this disorder should not interfere with production. Indeed, the "aim of the Great Proletarian Cultural

Revolution is to revolutionize people's ideology and *as a consequence* to achieve greater, faster, better, and more economical results in all fields of work."[25]

The Declaration specifically praised new political forms that were emerging spontaneously in the course of the movement. Cultural revolutionary groups, committees, and congresses in schools and other units were "excellent new forms of organization" that were still, however, to operate "under the leadership of the Communist Party." They were a "bridge to keep our party in close contact with the masses." As "permanent, standing mass organizations" they were useful not only in schools and government bureaus but also in factories, mines, cities, and villages. "It is necessary to institute a system of general elections, like that of the Paris Commune, for electing members to the cultural revolutionary groups and committees and delegates to the cultural revolutionary congresses."[26] Although suggestive of wider possibilities (and acted upon in unexpected ways in Shanghai, as we shall see), neither this point nor the Declaration as a whole looked to an end to party rule. General elections were to apply to cultural revolutionary groups within established units, not to replace the structure of party and government themselves.

Somewhat more firmly structured, Red Guard units now rapidly organized throughout the country, and financed by the state, students began to travel on simulated (and rather more comfortable) "long marches." For millions of Chinese who had grown up entirely within the revolution it was an opportunity to see the country for the first time, to learn directly from each other in an "exchange of revolutionary experience," and to learn from the peasants and workers they met on the way. Encouraged to "dare to struggle," they did so in vast numbers, and on August 18, one million passed before the reviewing stand in Tiananmen Square to see the "greatest Marxist-Leninist of [the] era," Mao Zedong, wearing a Red Guard armband, wave them genially on their way.[27]

Yet precisely what made the Red Guards attractive to their youthful emulators in the West was terrifying even to those "elders" in China sympathetic to the Cultural Revolution's objectives: the students' apparent taste for direct, often violent, confrontation with party and school authorities, and the humiliating and punitive nature of the public self-criticism sessions they organized for erring party cadres. At a party work conference in Peking in October 1966, Mao tried to be reassuring. "When you have had more contact" with the students, he told assembled provincial and municipal party leaders, "you realize there is nothing to be afraid of; instead you think they are quite lovable." At the same time he confessed surprise at the speed with which events had turned since the summer: "One big character poster, the Red Guards, the great exchange of revolutionary experience, and nobody—not even I—expected that all the provinces and cities would be thrown into confusion."[28] He urged them to be open to the assault of the students, no matter how painful: "I think that there are advantages in being assailed. For so many years you had not thought about such things, but as soon as they burst upon you, you began to think." No one wanted to overthrow them, he insisted. "Undoubtedly you have made some mistakes . . . but they can be corrected and that will be that!"[29] Finally, he confessed that he, too, shared their anxiety, and with good reason. Violence was extensive and wanton. Although the evidence is unsatisfactory and incomplete, there is little doubt that thousands, possibly tens of thousands, were beaten, even tortured to death, and that millions suffered exile, imprisonment, and horrifying personal privations.

To the outside world at the time, Soviet and Western, the years of the Cultural Revolution were years of madness, as mass organizations formed, split, reformed, and violently fought each other. The current official assessment is even harsher. The "ten long years" of the Cultural Revolution "spelt calamity for our people and constituted the most severe reversal of our socialist cause since the founding of the People's Republic."[30]

Despite the urging of Mao and other members of the Cultural Revolution Group that contradictions among the people had to be settled peacefully, that those who had been reeducated should be reenlisted, and that force should not be employed or production in any way halted, the movement grew increasingly confused, incoherent, and factionalized. How, after all, was one to discriminate between capitalist and socialist roaders when all quoted expertly from the Chairman himself? If a cadre had a "good style of work" but espoused "incorrect ideas" (or the reverse, for that matter), how was one to judge him? Was it possible, after all, to merge the task of rectification and ideological purification with a movement described as a revolution? It was one thing to have clear enemies: landlords, warlords, imperialists. It was quite another when the enemies turned out to be the very people who had led the revolution itself for the past thirty odd years.

In an effort to control the mass movement, some party leaders tried to narrow its focus to criticism of China's "first and second Khrushchevs," Liu Shoaqi and Deng Xiaoping. But there was a corresponding narrowing in another and more disturbing direction: rather than the masses of people possessing the power of definition through their understanding of the way Mao approached a problem, that power increasingly lodged in the person of Mao himself. He became the final arbiter of which ideas were correct, which incorrect. Objective means of distinguishing Left from Right disappeared. Mao labelled himself a "center leftist," but he alone defined where the center was. The more factionalized the movement became, the greater the stress on Mao's person rather than his "thought." Statues, of the sort that beg to be toppled, were erected; Mao's calligraphy and his aphorisms adorned every public building; Mao buttons, of all sizes, were produced in the millions. In the morning, his plaster statue would receive pledges of loyalty; in the evening, a report on the day's activities.

Without doubt, this cult of Mao was a corruption, indeed a parody of mass line politics. "To the masses" went not policy but homilies; "from the masses" came endless repetition of "revolutionary" determination. Mao explained it to Edgar Snow as the consequence of three thousand years of Emperor worship, which could not be expected to disappear overnight. But his encouragement, or at the very least, his failure to discourage the development of the cult, reinforced that tradition. It belied everything he had earlier argued about the way in which consciousness develops and transforms reality, a process in which hero worship was to have no place.

However, the cult had its uses. Politically, it was a powerful weapon in the struggle against Mao's opponents within the party: an implicit threat against any who thought the Cultural Revolution had gone too far. Yet despite obvious and disturbing similarities, it did not carry the same meaning as Stalin's cult of personality. In Soviet Russia, the cult was largely a glorification and distortion of past achievements, a consequence of unbridled political power concentrated in Stalin's hands. In China, it emerged essentially as an instrument to correct past abuses of power and set the revolution back on the right track. In both countries, of course, cult politics degenerated rapidly and inevitably into abusive, meaningless personal attacks and individual persecution, a reflection of the revolution in power, with its full potential for the exercise of total state authority over society.

The promise, and the ultimate tragedy, of the Cultural Revolution can be seen by a brief look at Shanghai. Initially, instructions from Peking had ordered the Red Guards not to interfere with production—either agricultural or industrial. For workers, cultural revolutionary activity was to be strictly an after-hours affair. Nevertheless, by November 1966, workers' groups were forming spontaneously, making direct demands upon the municipal party leadership, insisting that they be recognized. Anxious to keep order and perhaps following what he assumed was official policy, the mayor of Shanghai firmly opposed them. Defiantly, the central rebel group, the Headquarters of the Revolutionary Revolt of Shanghai Workers, commandeered a train to take their representatives to Peking, only to have it halted by the municipal authorities. The Cultural Revolutionary Group in Peking authorized Zhang Chunqiao, an early supporter of the Cultural Revolution and head of the Shanghai party's propaganda department, to investigate the dispute. To the consternation of the mayor, Zhang at once took the part of the Workers' Headquarters. But the Shanghai leadership did not give way at once. In a complex series of moves, in which the interests of the regular party leadership coincided with the interests of a considerable portion of Shanghai's permanent and senior work force, the Scarlet Guards, a rival organization said to represent some 800,000 workers, was organized. Conflict between Scarlet Guards and Workers' Headquarters quickly became violent.

Whether in direct collusion with the Scarlet Guards or out of their shared self-interest, factory managers and party authorities launched a campaign against Workers' Headquarters that involved, first, a generous distribution of bonuses and other material rewards and, second, a general strike. It was an astonishing action: the city government itself calling on workers to lay down their tools—there cannot have been another general strike like it in all of labor history.

Workers' Headquarters responded by rallying its forces to restore production and run the factories. By early January the strike was broken, leftists took over the Shanghai media, a new leading governmental body was organized, and the Shanghai Commune, explicitly modelled on the Paris Commune of 1871, was proclaimed in February, with Zhang Chunqiao elected as first secretary.[31]

The Cultural Revolution in Shanghai thus developed from a movement among students criticizing established party, educational, and cultural authority to a genuine class struggle, a revolution, in which disadvantaged groups of workers (many of them seasonally recruited from the countryside) combined with dissident students and younger party cadres to challenge the local government and seize political power. Unable to respond to the real social turmoil in Shanghai, and anxious to protect its own position, the municipal party committee had sought instead to stay as close as possible to what it assumed to be Peking's wishes. In this it violated the first premise of the Cultural Revolution itself, which was not to *control* the mass movement, but to learn from and lead it on the basis of the deepest understanding of the mass line.

In Peking, Mao at first greeted events in Shanghai with enthusiasm: "Internal rebellions are fine. . . . This is one class overthrowing another. This is a great revolution."[32] On January 16, 1967, a call to "Resolutely seize power from the handful of people within the Party who are in authority and are taking the capitalist road!" was even published in *Red Flag*.[33] But the direct democracy reflected in the Commune carried with it a serious threat of further disorder, disruption of production, and factionalization. The form of power seizure Mao seemed to prefer was exemplified in Shanxi province where, at around the same time Shanghai was experimenting with the Commune, a revolutionary committee had been established, consisting of a "three-way alliance": representatives of mass organizations, the PLA, and state and party cadres. By late February 1967, Shanghai was called upon to transform its Commune into the new approved form of revolutionary committee. "Communes," Mao pointed out, "are too weak when it comes to suppressing counter-revolution."[34] Although revolutionary committees held the possibility of greater mass participation, they quickly devolved in most places, whether at provincial, factory, rural commune, or university level, into new organs of bureaucratic control, dominated by "reeducated" party officials.

Bringing Shanghai to heel did not, however, end the deep and bitter struggle there or elsewhere in China. Concerned by the extent of the disorder, Mao denounced those who raised the slogan "Doubt everything and overthrow everything." It was reactionary, he insisted, "extreme anarchism." "In reality," he instructed the two leading Shanghai radicals, Zhang Chunqiao and Yao Wenyuan, "there will still always be 'heads.' "[35] "If everything became Commune," Zhang reports him as saying, "what about the Party? . . . There certainly must be a Party! There must be a nucleus, no matter what it is called."[36]

Increasingly, the PLA was called upon to restore order, at first with instructions to support the "Left" side in factional disputes. But the Left was difficult to define, and order could often best be brought by siding with more conservative and experienced power-holders. Nor was the PLA monolithic. A mutiny by a PLA unit in the major industrial city of Wuhan was only barely brought under control. Thousands may have died in the process. By late August 1967, the possibility of all-out civil war could not be ignored. Relieved of their obligation to lean to the Left, the PLA, in September, was simply ordered to restore order; by early fall they had, in the main, achieved that goal. Blame for the chaos of the summer was attributed to a mysterious May Sixteenth group, whose politics, "ultra-left in form, but ultra-right in essence," were now condemned. Its membership turned out to be a substantial portion of the original Cultural Revolution group.

Here, precisely, one can perceive the social and political matrix that spawned the astonishing casualty figures later reported with such ill-disguised satisfaction by opponents of Mao and by Western critics: the victimization of 100 million, the death of 3 million. Mao's ideological prescription "Bombard the Headquarters!" had become a literal battle cry. Orders to the PLA to "repress mutiny" and "restore order" could simply not be carried out without pitched battle and the consequent loss of life. The struggle between two strategies for Chinese development, between permanently implanting revolutionary experience and process, as Mao insisted, and building on revolutionary foundations in as orderly and stable a way as resources and international circumstances permitted, as Deng, Liu, and Mao's opponents argued, had become in Shanghai, Wuhan, and elsewhere the basis for fratricidal military action. In the process, as in civil conflict everywhere, legitimate differences of political opinion became the rationale for brutal resolution of countless private and petty grievances and even broader, residual social animosities.

One is tempted, in reviewing this process, to draw comparisons to the Soviet experience: to Kronstadt, in 1921, when Red Army men repressed mutinous communist sailors more radical and revolutionary than Bolshevik politics could sustain; to collectivization and the early 1930s, when conflicting Soviet development strategies became the basis for lethal party conflicts; and even to the purges. In China's case, however, even if one can see parallels in both circumstance and cause, the longer range issues were quite different, and so was the influence of the Cultural Revolution as a whole on the Chinese revolutionary process.

The evidence is not yet fully before us, but it seems possible that the longer range issues in China had as much to do with the recrudescence of traditional, hierarchical institutions and values as they did with immediate strategies of development. The spectacular triumph of Chinese communism clearly had been only *endured* by millions of the nation's professional and intellectual elite, however loosely committed they were to the idea of social betterment and material progress. Conditions of relative political stability, genuine commitment to China's welfare as a nation, and the structural needs of a transitional, developing society all came together during the post-1950 period to provide special opportunities to those members of the elite who were needed, and were willing to accept them. In the process, it was hardly unnatural that traditional values and social patterns also reemerged, or that radicals and revolutionary fighters should develop resentments. It was even logical that these resentments should become fierce, given their ideological overlays.

What was particular about the Chinese revolutionary process, however, was the manner in which those resisting postrevolutionary tendencies toward stabilization found a leader in Mao. The tendencies toward political centralization we have discussed at length in connection with the Soviet Union were also, of course, implicit in the Chinese experience, but this had the consequence of giving extraordinary energy to the opponents of stabilization, not its advocates. Given communist intolerance for party pluralism, it was inevitable that the political struggles of China's Cultural Revolution were waged by all sides in the party's name. In comparative terms, moreover, it is perhaps not so surprising that ultimately, the "stabilizers" purged the "radicals," as indeed the Stalinist "Right" purged Trotskyist "ultra leftists" in the mid-1930s, even if comparison becomes almost hopelessly confused in the association between Deng Xiaoping and Stalin. For however much the Cultural Revolution represented a profound effort to maintain the ethos of Chinese revolutionary accomplishment, and however much this ethos was, together with Maoist strategy, a critical factor in the CCP's ability to "dare to struggle, dare to win," the revolution *had* come to power in China, and the pressures for social stability and orderly development had become an intrinsic and overwhelming aspect of the revolutionary process.

When the Ninth Congress of the CCP met in April 1969, the Cultural Revolution came to a more or less official halt. Lin Biao was named Mao's "successor," the need to rebuild the party was given top priority, and no one seemed to echo Mao's admonition that "after a few years maybe we shall have to carry out another revolution."

FURTHER ASPECTS OF CULTURAL CHANGE

The Cultural Revolution must be also seen in the context of Mao's effort to pursue policies first undertaken in the Great Leap Forward and then abandoned, in the aftermath of its failure, by a party leadership intent on pursuing a different road to socialism. Like the earlier movement, the Cultural Revolution was aimed initially at reducing the "three great differences" whose unchecked growth, even in a context of increasing material progress, threatened to transform and distort the revolution. These "differences"—the separation between mental and manual labor, between peasant and worker, between agriculture and industry—are, in fact, the salient characteristics of developing Third World countries everywhere and, in the eyes of some economists, the regrettable but necessary price of what they call "modernization." It was not, however, a price Maoists felt China should pay. "Revolutionary modernization" was the alternative, bourgeois ideology within the party was the main enemy, and mass mobilization was the chosen instrument of continued revolutionary process. In 1962 Mao had spoken frankly with 7,000 cadres from various levels of the party:

> Those of you who shirk responsibility or who are afraid of taking responsibility, who do not allow people to speak, who think you are tigers, and that nobody will dare to touch your arse, whoever has this attitude, ten out of ten of you will fail. People will talk anyway. You think that nobody will really dare to touch the arse of tigers like you? They damn well will![37]

From 1966 to late 1968 the "arse of the tiger" was not merely touched but solidly whacked. In the process, policies that Maoists had urged on a variety of fronts in the past were also acted upon.

In public health, for example, Mao had complained as early as 1965 that the countryside was neglected in favor of the cities:

> Tell the Ministry of Public Health that it only works for fifteen percent of the total population of the country and that this fifteen percent is mainly composed of gentlemen, while the broad masses of the peasants do not get any medical treatment. . . . The Ministry of Public Health is not a Ministry of Public Health for the people, so why not change its name to the . . . Ministry of Urban Gentlemen's Health?[38]

Doctors concentrated on "rare, profound and difficult diseases" that, given China's population, should properly get only a "small quantity of manpower and material . . . while a great deal of manpower and material should be spent on the problems to which the masses most need solutions." During the Cultural Revolution and in its aftermath, medical education and health care were both radically reformed. Medical schools experimented with innovative curricula that could graduate a large number of doctors; doctors rotated to the countryside for extended stints during which they participated in the training of a corps of "barefoot doctors"—ordinary peasants selected by their local units for training in preventive health care and paramedical techniques. Paid in work points and continuing to work with their production teams in agriculture, the barefoot doctors brought basic medical skills within reach of hundreds of millions of peasants.

Similar efforts were made to remedy "deficiencies" in the educational system, although many now argue the remedies did more harm than good.[39] "The school years are too long, courses too many," Mao insisted in 1964:

The children learn textbooks and concepts which remain [merely] textbooks and concepts; they know nothing else. . . . the method of teaching is by injection instead of through the imagination. The method of examination is to treat candidates as enemies and ambush them.[40]

According to Mao, the situation was less severe in engineering schools because those students were, of necessity, in touch with reality, and efforts were being made to attach factories to various faculties of science and engineering. "But we cannot set up factories for arts faculties . . . these faculties should regard the whole of society as their factory. Their teachers and students should make contact with the peasants and urban workers." "Do not," Mao warned a visiting Nepalese delegation, "entertain any blind faith in the Chinese educational system. Do not regard it as a good system. Any drastic change is difficult, [as] many people would oppose it."[41]

As schools slowly reopened during 1967 and 1968, the drastic changes Mao advocated began to be implemented: entrance examinations were abolished; all middle-school graduates were required to work for at least two years in factories or communes; candidates for university were nominated by their work units on the basis of ideological as well as intellectual criteria; an enormous variety of work-study programs were instituted in factories; and, in addition to schools becoming associated with factories, factories themselves established schools that could teach workers relevant technological skills. Most important, there was an absolute emphasis on increasing educational facilities in rural areas, and the establishment of primary schools in every rural brigade, controlled by that brigade (with middle schools at the commune level), became a national goal.[42]

In both agriculture and industry, approaches advocated by Mao and his allies in the mid-1960s also became national policy. Poor and lower-middle peasant associations were revived, and their delegates joined militia representatives or demobilized soldiers and party cadres to form the revolutionary committee that administered the commune. Private plots were strictly limited to 5 percent of the available land area within any given commune, free markets were discouraged, and, above all, rural industrialization was forcefully pursued. Local industries, run by the commune and recruiting workers from its membership, produced an enormous variety of products for local consumption as well as sale on a wider market: chemical fertilizer, consumer items, small-scale farm machinery, farm tools, drugs, cement and other construction material. Untapped raw materials and surplus farm labor were combined in hopes of yielding the benefits the Great Leap had promised: a solution to rural underemployment, a closing of the gap between peasants and workers, a rise in rural living standards and purchasing power, which itself produced new capital for further investments. Rural self-sufficiency held out the real possibility of industrialization without the brutality and dislocation of rapid urbanization. Moreover, it was intended to free resources for state investment in medium and heavy industry.

Although recent evidence suggests an enormous amount of factual distortion, Dazhai Brigade, a small village in the hard-scrabble Shanxi mountains, was promoted as an "advanced model" as early as 1964. During and after the Cultural Revolution, the injunction to "learn from Dazhai" became far more insistent, and the village received thousands of visitors from all over China. Through the fullest mobilization of its small labor force, inspired by a charismatic brigade leader, the eighty-eight households of Dazhai were said to have transformed barren, eroded mountain sides into arable terraces, dug a four-mile canal to supply the village with water, established several local industries, made radical egalitarian innovations in the distribution of work points and income, and eliminated private plots entirely. Dazhai's innovations were intended not to be imitated, but to teach and inspire. Accounting at the brigade level (a step down from the equalization of income that commune-level distribution during the Great Leap attempted) remained beyond the ability of most brigades, but the widely publicized example of Dazhai in this and other areas was an important educational tool, whatever the reality.[43]

In heavy industry another model, Daqing, received similar publicity. A huge oil field in the northeastern province of Heilongjiang, Daqing's system of management maximized worker participation in all aspects of production, innovation, and experimentation. As significantly, the organization of this giant enterprise was consciously designed for integration with the surrounding countryside. Rather than build a concentrated urban center, housing was scattered and self-sufficiency in food supply sought through enabling workers' families to engage in agriculture and sideline production.

A more complicated aspect of the way in which the Cultural Revolution was intended to reduce the "three great differences" was the policy toward urban-educated young people. The new educational requirement that all middle school graduates spend at least two years in productive labor on farm or factory had a clear ideological justification. The intellectual elite fostered by the earlier educational system could survive neither this system nor a university admissions procedure that stressed correct politics and selectively discriminated in favor of the children of peasants and workers. Insofar as urban-educated youth received a higher quality of education, their transfer to the countryside represented another instance of enriching rural, as compared to urban, resources. Presumably these more skilled young people would bring to the communes and brigades rare talents and strengths, even as they learned from the peasants what only life on the land could teach.

But the program had other, less attractive, aspects. The transfer of urban youth to the countryside, which had been going on at low levels since the 1950s, was radically expanded during the Cultural Revolution and thereafter. From 1968 to 1975 some twelve million people were "sent down," amounting to fully 10 percent of the urban population. Whatever its ideological underpinnings, this system was also a convenient way both of dealing with problems of unemployment and politically demobilizing the Red Guards. Those youth who found themselves permanently assigned to the countryside—often thousands of miles away from family and friends and among hostile or indifferent peasants who frequently had no idea what to do with them—took cold comfort in Maoist aphorisms. When and however they could, many made their way back to the city.

Other issues which had concerned Mao were also acted upon. Like the "sent down youth" program, they carried contradictions within them that a genuine dialectician like Mao might have welcomed and even used imaginatively, but to which his less-creative comrades took a formalistic approach. The importance of cadres engaging in productive labor, for example, was institutionalized in the form of May Seventh Cadre Schools, established in 1968. Usually attached to a nearby brigade, cadres were expected to clear land and grow their own food, as well as engage in intense political study for periods varying from a few weeks to one or two years. As a form of bringing vanguard and mass closer together, the schools faced certain inherent problems: they were physically separated from villages themselves, cadres continued to receive their office salaries, and there was an inescapable sense in which labor on the land retained a certain punitive flavor. By the mid-1970s, at any rate, the schools seemed superficial and ritualized, more like a diorama of one of Mao's quotations rather than a lived reality. At their best, the schools gave urban cadres a chance for a few healthy weeks in the countryside working with their hands. This probably had a salutary effect on many; at their worst, they were endured by cadres in ways that can only have increased their cynicism about revolutionary politics and that of any peasants with whom they came in contact.

In art and literature, the impact of the Cultural Revolution was similarly enormous. Mao's 1963 criticism of the Department of Cultural Affairs as a "department of emperors and generals, useless scholars and sickly maidens"[44] was swiftly acted upon by his wife, Jiang Qing, during and after the Cultural Revolution. Taking a leading role in cultural affairs, Jiang, a former actress, worked closely with theatre groups in Peking and Shanghai to produce a set of "model" operas that, transferred to screen and ballet, comprised Chinese theatre for almost ten years. Traditional dramatic forms were banned, peasant poetry and painting encouraged, and the effort to create proletarian culture by fiat was pursued in a variety of ways, including the absolute repression of artists in all fields deemed insufficiently revolutionary.

At the same time, however, writing and painting workshops were established in factories and communes (as they had briefly been during the Great Leap Forward as well). Here, guided by professional writers and artists, ordinary people began to express, in media closed to them before, the shape and meaning of their daily lives. "An illiterate like me takes pen to write poetry," a peasant wrote in 1958,

> Joy fills my heart as water fills the river.
> For a thousand years the tip of my pen never talked,
> Now I have more to say than I can ever finish.[45]

The intent was to give voice to the pens of peasants and workers. In the early 1970s, Hsu Kai-yu reported,

> writers' workshops for writing teams in factories and communes are sponsored by the teams of paid professional writers and artists permanently attached to the Bureau of Cultural Affairs in each country, district and city. It is the duty of the professionals to uncover, encourage, and assist new talent. Anyone can submit a plan of his creative work, and if it is approved, the amateur writer is entitled to an appropriate amount of release time to complete his project.

At the same time, professional writers and artists submitted their work to the scrutiny of peasants and workers, accepting criticism and suggestions for revision. Such criticisms ranged from "wanting a single word changed in a speech to make it more authentically peasant, to altering the plot to make a character more heroic."[46]

What disturbed many observers at the time, and continues to cause unease (though from the opposite political pole), is the choice Chinese seemed to be making between a liberation of the creative energies of ordinary people and the full exercise of those same energies by an urban, educated elite. Here, parallels with Stalinist Russia are both compelling and misleading. The overt control of art, literature, and music, exercised directly and with coercive power for narrow political ends, is clearly comparable, and the social impact equally devastating. It is a form of social malignancy that imagines that a living proletarian culture can be created through the mechanistic suppression of "incorrect" ideas and the encouragement of "correct" ones. That necessary component for the solution of social problems—the creative innovation and imaginative energy of a nation's artists and intellectuals—is not simply an "input" that can be automatically increased or decreased. But the differences between Maoist China and Stalinist Russia must also be kept in mind, however similar the effects seem to have been. In China, the goal of policy was to enable masses of people to become artists and intellectuals organically related to the proletariat. Everywhere the individual artist was to be subject to the collective intelligence; everywhere the peasant and worker were to be preferred to the urban professional. It was not a question, as it was in Stalin's Russia, of which party hack would rise to the top of a preordained hierarchy, but one, however brutally pursued, of toppling the hierarchy altogether.

Some aspects of policy during the Cultural Revolution have been subject to particular scorn abroad, such as the prohibition on Western music, art, and literature. Beethoven, we insist, is universal in his appeal. To ban his music is mindless philistinism. And yet it is worth considering the reasons for such rejection of Western culture. The effort in China was not only to create proletarian culture, but *Chinese* proletarian culture. The poet Guo Moruo posed the issue as early as 1963: "We must make our poetry more 'Chinese' so it may be better enjoyed by the Chinese people." After May 4, 1919, Guo argued, there was a revolution in Chinese literature led by "intellectuals who turned to the Western world for inspiration. As a result, the new poetry since the May Fourth movement has remained remote from the broad masses of China, leaving the revolution in Chinese poetry incomplete." Closing the door to Western influence was one way of dealing with the issue, along with the insistence that poets must merge with the "laboring people, study society without ceasing, study Marxism-Leninism and Mao Tse-tung's thought without ceasing."[47]

What is tragic, and confusing, is the conviction, which underlay cultural policy in these years, that there was a *necessary* choice between the freedom of artists and intellectuals and the free flourishing of a people's culture.

AFTERMATH

The political aftermath of the Cultural Revolution was, if possible, even more confused and confusing than the movement itself. A rendering by a sympathetic Westerner, in its deceptively low-key phrasing, indicates just how Byzantine Peking politics had become:

> To simplify matters, what was called "Lin Biao's antiparty clique" was made up of elements who had a common interest in opposing the line established by the Ninth Congress; these included Lin Biao, who knew that he was no longer Mao Tsetung's official successor even though the official documents designated him as such, Chen Bo-da and the others who saw the end of the Cultural Revo-

lution's ultra-left radicalism coming, and some regional military leaders who had had de facto political power since the Cultural Revolution and saw this power coming to an end with the reconstruction of the party.[48]

In September 1971 Lin Biao simply disappeared from sight. One year later, details of his death during an alleged escape to the Soviet Union were widely published. Mao's "close comrade in arms" had apparently plotted Mao's assassination, in a scenario that rivalled Le Carré's wildest inventions. The motivation was declared to be Lin's ultraleftism. By 1973, however, Lin was being attacked as a rightist—and not merely a rightist, but a Confucianist to boot. A campaign to "criticize Lin Biao, criticize Confucius" was launched in 1973 and ran a somewhat erratic course until it quietly died out in 1975. Meanwhile, and in conjunction with these events, Chinese foreign policy elevated the Soviet Union to the prize spot of principal enemy, made its peace with the United States, and, in consequence, the People's Republic was finally accorded justice when it assumed its rightful place among the United Nations.

In April 1973, Deng Xiaoping, the "second leading person in authority taking the capitalist road," was rehabilitated as vice-premier. For the next three years, until its final resolution in October 1976, power at the top seemed to be divided between Deng (who rose and fell from grace one more full cycle before again assuming a current preeminent position) and a group of cultural revolutionary radicals (excoriated as the Gang of Four after their overthrow), which included Jiang Qing, Wang Hongwen (a Shanghai labor leader), Zhang Chunqiao, and Yao Wenyuan. Premier Zhou Enlai, whose skills at negotiating, moderating, and persuading had been vital to such balance as Peking politics had enjoyed at the top, continued to serve as a fulcrum until his death in January 1976. A brief struggle for power ensued thereafter but was quickly resolved once Mao died in September 1976, and the Gang of Four found themselves without the prestige Mao's support had given them in the past. In October 1976 they were arrested, and in the fall of 1980 they were put on trial for their lives.

Yet Mao's vision of protracted revolutionary struggle, however distorted in the actual historical working out of the Cultural Revolution, was nonetheless widely shared. There is no other way to understand the depth of the upheaval China experienced from 1966 to 1969. It would be absurd to imagine that Deng could permanently halt it—as it was absurd for Mao to dream that he could permanently orchestrate it. History, Marx wrote, is masses of people in motion. The straw sandals are still being woven.

10

STRAW SANDALS:
The Ambiguities of Power

I have, let's see
that I've learned to read, to count,
I have that I've learned to write
and to think
and to laugh.

I have that I now have
a place to work
and a place to earn
what I have to have to eat.

I have, let's see,
I have what I had to have.

Nicolás Guillén

"REVISIONISM" IN THE EARLY 1970s

Soviet and Chinese perspectives on each other's development as communist societies had never been marked with particular sympathy or understanding, but nothing quite matched Mao's scathing assault on the "phoney communism" of Khrushchev and his successors, or Moscow's mass attack on Maoism, "a confused mixture of ideas hostile to Marxism-Leninism . . . leading to chaos."[1] The attacks continued even after Mao's death in 1976. Soviet Russia remained "a social-imperialist country, not a socialist country . . . [which] bullies, enslaves, and exploits." China was an arch-enemy to peace and the development of scientific socialism.[2] The historical irony of this continued mutual vituperation is not so much the way it recapitulates past ignorance or grievance, however, as the way it masks real and growing similarities and hence perpetuates misunderstanding. And in an age where nuclear proliferation and the dangers of global destruction are increasing daily, the willingness of political figures anywhere to prey on this difference for their own advantage seems far greater folly than the occasional efforts of radicals elsewhere to transport wholesale the Chinese or Soviet revolutionary experience, as if it could be lifted from its historical context.

The Maoist attack on "Khrushchevism" and the Soviets' "capitalist road" focused essentially on the principles and practices of Soviet economic administration, but also connected these with a counterrevolutionary state of political consciousness that eschewed class struggle in favor of stability. By implication, stability meant increasing social differentiation, bureaucratism, administrative commandism, and the emergence of "bourgeois social relations." Mao may not have understood Khrushchev's own revolutionary enthusiasm or his efforts to break up bureaucratic nests around the Bolshoi theatre, "sending down" officials in his own version of what would later be seen as a core element of Maoist politics, but the Great Helmsman rightly sensed the conservatism of Khrushchev's successors.[3] Brezhnev, Kosygin, and the post-1964 Soviet leadership displayed none of Khrushchev's revolutionary élan, none of his penchant for radical change, for shaking established institutions and attempting boldly to make them more responsive, more adaptive to goals of rapid development. But while repudiating his "hare-brained schemes," they retained his objective of material advancement and his association of socialism with prosperity and security.

Within two months of Khrushchev's ouster in October 1964, his successors reunited the industrial and agricultural branches of the party into single organizations, terminating the 1962 reforms and returning the party apparatus to its traditional structure. Collective farm debts, largely incurred through the forced purchase of machinery from the state, were cancelled, and procurement prices were increased. New controls were placed on capital allocations, and new incentive mechanisms were introduced in an effort to regulate the quality and distribution of output. In September 1965, the party largely restored the system of industrial ministries, which had existed prior to the regional economic council (*Sovnarkhozy*) reform of 1957. These changes were marked by efforts to stabilize Soviet foreign relations, particularly through the development of new bilateral relations with Western Europe, and by a studied refusal to use the dramatic escalation in Vietnam as cause for new conflict. Collective leadership—i.e., management—became both an ideological commitment and an operational reality, despite the emergence of Aleksei Kosygin and Leonid Brezhnev into positions of clear dominance. In a phrase, orderly economic progress and political stability became the touchstones of a new era.

From China, Maoists decried orderliness as a further revisionist deviation from the socialist path, a view echoed by radical Communists elsewhere. Conflict, not stability, was the essence both of socialist reality and the dialectics of progress; materialism—the gratification of individual over collective interests, and particularly the use of such expedients as material incentives, market forces, profit indicators in industry, and even limited private ownership in agriculture—was precisely what would engender petty-bourgeois mentalities and the restoration of capitalist structures. Borrowing from Western management systems was equally fraught with dangers, epitomized in open admiration of American ideas and styles. Yet experimentation with such practices characterized a new succession of Soviet five-year plans, either emphasizing consumer needs (1965–75), or seeking balanced growth (1975–80) through increased productivity, foreign trade, and further efforts at rational accounting and capital allocation. As labor reserves have become less important and technological innovation more central to the tasks of its economic progress, the pace of growth in the Soviet Union has slowed markedly, but the government's response has been to seek improvements by extending Western methods within established patterns of sociopolitical relationships, rather than to consider radical readjustments. Massive imports of Western grain have served to blunt whatever latent impulses may have existed for radical change in the countryside (still a source of enormous economic and social weakness); the use of European construction crews and the wholesale importation of Western technicians (in hotel construction, for example, or the decision to meet consumer automotive need by producing a Russian version of the Fiat) have been preferable to radical effort at overhauling Soviet practices. At the same time, use of Western abilities and techniques has given unprecedented practical foundations to the ideological components of détente.

Meanwhile, in marked contrast to Maoist insistence on the importance of struggle, a rather remarkable degree of internal consistency has characterized Soviet party leadership. Eighty-three percent of the Central Committee elected at the Twenty-third Party Congress in 1961 was reelected in 1966 despite Khrushchev's ouster. In 1971, 81 percent of the living full members of the 1966 Central Committee were reelected; and 89 percent of the 1971 Committee was reelected in 1976.[4] The trend continued at the Twenty-sixth Party Congress in February, 1981. Although the party faced serious internal problems and moments of grave international tension under the leadership of Brezhnev, he remained respected and generally admired, if not the object of any special attachment. A "universally accepted leader" (*obshchepriznannyi lider*), as he has often been officially called, is perhaps one of the most appropriate designations in the history of Soviet political propaganda.

Technology and technological innovation, with their implicit requirements for intellectual creativity, have remained serious problems in the pattern of Soviet development since 1964, even as the regime has allowed a substantial expansion of cultural interchange with nonsocialist societies. Domestic political dissidence has become more visible and vocal, and contained with greater or lesser degrees of repression, but always in ways to maximize the insecurity of those tempted to act on their beliefs. Still, what is most remarkable about the Brezhnev era is not the degree of overt dissent, but the relatively consistent pace of liberalization that has developed in tandem with continued repression. At one time or another a very large portion of the Soviet population, perhaps as much as 40 percent, has heard Voice of America broadcasts, even as censorship remains a powerful political instrument. Several hundred thousand Jews have emigrated to the West (many for reasons having little to do with religious beliefs), though other Jews and dissident nationals despair at restrictions on their movements. Blue jeans purchased from Western tourists, once objects of official scorn, have become tolerable, if not officially approved; and since the late 1960s, increasing hordes of Western tourists have pressed a truly prodigious quantity of ballpoint pens and bubblegum on eager Soviet children.

For Maoists, such vulgar lassitude only reflects deeper patterns of capitalist deviation. Right through the mid-1970s, Mao and his supporters continued to exhort their comrades to "study well the theory of proletarian dictatorship" and "guard against the expansion of bourgeois right," the formal end of the cultural revolution notwithstanding. "Bourgeois right" was a catch phrase to describe those persistent elements of inequality that would mark China until communism itself was achieved. Defined as a product of an economic system in which small-commodity production, exchange through money, and limited modes of collective ownership, particularly in agriculture, characterized the economy, bourgeois right could not be entirely eliminated, but its toleration had to be accompanied by constant vigilance against its expansion.[5]

Most important, bourgeois right meant the growth of "the three great differences"—between workers and peasants, between town and country, and between mental and manual labor—precisely the trend of events in the Soviet Union. "If these differences are not reduced but extended without limit," warned an essay in *Peking Review*, "the worker-peasant alliance will inevitably be undermined, town and country will be seriously opposed to each other, the working class will lose its reliable ally, and a handful of bourgeois intellectual aristocrats will be engendered, monopolizing the cultural, educational and other undertakings in society whereby they proceed to look for economic and political privileges."[6] "Concerned workers" echoed these views in the Chinese press. "If bourgeois rights were not restricted, things like 'material incentives,' 'putting profit in command,' and 'free trade' would grow, and that would lead to capitalist restoration," a veteran worker from Lanzhou Chemical Company reportedly insisted; workers at a Tianjin water supply company "held that analysis of the phenomenon of class struggle . . . will help increase [our] ability to resist corrosion by bourgeois ideology, do away with the bourgeois style of work, and uphold the new way of the proletariat."[7] To those unnamed people who charged that a "wind of 'communization' " was being stirred up, one of Mao's closest supporters, Zhang Chunqiao, replied that "another kind of wind . . . is now blowing—the 'bourgeois wind!' This is the bourgeois style of life Chairman Mao has pointed to, an evil wind stirred up by those 'parts' of the people who have degenerated into bourgeois elements.

The 'bourgeois wind' blowing from among those Communists, particularly leading cadres . . . does us the greatest of harm."[8]

These persistent arguments in favor of a Maoist approach to Chinese development, which had so crucially shaped its history from the mid-1950s on, were laid out with renewed insistence in the late winter and spring of 1975, perhaps for the last time. In January, Zhou Enlai, already seriously ill with cancer, announced what would soon become the new underlying theme of Chinese development: the drive to achieve "four modernizations" by the year 2000 (in industry, agriculture, science and technology, and defense). Shortly afterward, Deng Xiaoping, vice-chairman and first vice-premier, drew up a series of draft programs intended to implement these modernizations, in which the named enemy was not a "capitalist roader" in or out of the party, but one who pays insufficient attention to production, indulging instead in "metaphysics"; who says that "a certain place or work unit is carrying out revolution very well when production is fouled up"; who separates "politics from economics and revolution from production," "talking only about politics and revolution and labelling anyone who discusses economic construction as a revisionist."[9] Indifferent to the larger significance of Deng's new line, and concerned above all with the continued anti-Soviet thrust of his foreign policy, Russian "revisionists" and "capitalist roaders" continued to visualize China as largely bound by Maoist practice, and read the Chairman's assaults themselves as testimony to the dangers of "personality cults." Precisely the type of devastating power struggle that mature Soviet socialism had outgrown seemed about to engulf Peking, just as it had during the Cultural Revolution. According to Moscow, the Maoist leadership was in an "unprincipled struggle for power," determined at all costs, and perhaps again by means of the Red Army, to consolidate its political hold, purge its opposition, and "open the gates to anarchy and chaos."[10]

It is possible such thoughts occurred to the once-disgraced Deng, and to others, who could hardly forget the fate of Liu Shaoqi. Several months after Zhou Enlai died in January 1976, thousands of people intent on laying funeral wreaths gathered in Tiananmen Square in what has since been memoralized as a "great revolutionary event." They were met first with astonishment and then with violence by security forces. Accused of having organized the demonstration,

Deng Xiaoping was once again dismissed from all party posts; when Mao died in September 1976, Hua Guofeng, a former Hunanese provincial party official who had become acting premier after Zhou's death, included Deng's name in the list of "revisionists" over whom Mao had triumphed. Yet Mao's successors, the Gang of Four, remained a minority faction with little of the Chairman's power or prestige. Within months, Deng Xiaoping was once again rehabilitated and on his way to becoming the People's Republic's most powerful political figure.[11]

There can be little question that the Maoists' fall (although not necessarily the rise of Deng) was greeted with rejoicing by many ordinary Chinese people, perhaps even a majority. The language with which the campaign against "bourgeois right" had been launched was only a moderated version of the language of the Cultural Revolution; and the dislocations of that period, its violence, and the degeneration of politics, were too recent for most people to welcome its return. It was, no doubt, a positive relief *not* to have to "study well" the theory of the proletarian dictatorship; *not* to worry lest one's response to moral incentives was somewhat lax; *not* to feel that such consumer pleasures as China offered violated canons of "plain and simple living"; *not*, if you were a cadre, to constantly fear criticism for actions taken or (out of that same fear) not taken; *not* to be fed a constant diet of revolutionary uplift in story, song, and art when your own eyes told you reality was not nearly so glorious. For a time, cities once more exploded with wall posters, now, however, violently criticizing Maoists, not revisionists. There was an unauthorized flow of "sent down youth" back to their home towns; literary figures long suppressed reappeared for welcome home ceremonies and extensive interviews; intellectuals and professionals began to speak *their* bitterness, as peasants had in the past. They recalled in painful detail the ways they had been shamed, the deaths of their friends and relatives, the often brutal conditions under which they had lived in prison, and perhaps most of all, the waste of their talent. Deng Xiaoping never made a "secret speech," but the pages of China's journals began to fill with critiques of just about every phase of Maoist theory and practice. The Cultural Revolution, the "decade of turmoil," was bitterly denounced, as was the Great Leap Forward. The importance of "protracted, repeated, tortuous and complex class struggle," a touchstone of Mao Zedong thought, was ignored.

If the Soviet Union in the 1970s retained Khrushchev's vision of socialism while eschewing his radical and often ambiguous methods (as well, one should add, as his sense of urgency), and if the Soviet leadership offered instead as proof of its abilities the fact that average wages for workers and employees have increased more than 60 percent since 1964, along with vast increases in the number of automobiles, refrigerators, and other indices of material betterment, "Khrushchevism without Khrushchev"—or at least what Mao had emphatically denounced as Khrushchev's "phoney communism"—also became the policy of the People's Republic after 1976. The new confluence is as strong as it is unacknowledged. In place of uninterrupted revolution in China there emerged an uninterrupted drive to achieve the "four modernizations." In agriculture, this meant retention of the communal system as the basic organizational form but, as in the Soviet Union, relaxed restrictions on the amount of land devoted to private plots, free rural markets, and numerous programs to increase peasant incentives (including a significant cut in taxes and a rise in state procurement prices, precisely the steps taken by Brezhnev and Kosygin after Khrushchev's ouster). The notion that a desire for material gain is "antisocialist" was denounced as a Gang of Four ultraleftist absurdity.

In industry, modernization similarly meant not only an increase in wages and other material incentives, but also large-scale efforts to import foreign technology, including the purchase of foreign plants from Western international corporations. Factory revolutionary committees were abolished. Management was thoroughly critiqued and efforts made to decentralize planning and increase autonomy, an approach Soviet commentators themselves affirmed as "that of planned construction of the foundations of socialism taking into account the laws of socialist construction confirmed by the experience of other socialist countries."[12] Worker participation in management was limited to expressing opinions at meetings and, according to Stephen Andors, all efforts to break down the division of labor between workers and managers, in fact ended. There was great interest in Western systems of industrial management, as Deng's visit to the United States, like Khrushchev's in the late 1950s, amply testified; and not too surprisingly, profit became an acceptable index of industrial efficiency. Just as in the Soviet Union, publicly announced pay increases generally favored those at the bottom of the wage scale, and the regime remained officially concerned about levels of income inequality. But those who "work hard and make a greater contribution should get more and be well off, ahead of the others," a *Beijing* [Peking] *Review* article asserted in 1980.[13]

Finally in the modernization of science and technology, and in defense, the new Chinese leadership revamped the entire educational system and emphasized the rapid development of advanced weapons systems. Entrance examinations were reinstituted and resources poured into upgrading "key" schools at all levels, primarily in urban areas. Experts now mattered. It became many times more likely for the graduate of an urban key school to get into university than for graduates of rural schools, a situation comparable to that in the Soviet Union. Rural education, work-study programs, and such institutions as factory-run schools still received official attention, but the main thrust of policy was on the rapid and thorough training of experts. Those who worked with their minds (the "laboring intelligentsia," in Soviet parlance) were now to be accorded as much respect as those workers and peasants who built socialism in other ways. (In the past, one senior professor noted, he was very depressed and confused. Were intellectuals "masters of the country, friends or guests, or enemies of the people?" Now he was sure that intellectuals "too are masters of the country, and together with the workers and peasants," could press forward with the "four modernizations.")[14]

In short, struggle between classes, as part of the ongoing fabric of socialist political life, condemned as a fundamental Gang of Four heresy in China, just as it no longer had any operational relevance in the Soviet Union.

THE AMBIGUITIES OF POWER

In important ways the Brezhnev era and the post-Mao leadership may be said to signal the end of revolutionary process in Soviet Russia and China. In both societies, the idealized goals of revolutionary achievement have become broadly accepted as the legitimizing ideological underpinning of well-established, powerful authoritarian political systems. Communism, in the Soviet Union for some time, in China only since Mao's death, has come above all to mean unchallenged party control, international security, internal social security, stability, and the promise of continually improving material well-being. The state apparatus, established by means of massive social upheaval, has gained maximum control over the allocation of capital and an unprecedented capacity to regulate the means of production and the distribution of income. In both societies, a vanguard party governs in the name of ultimate social and economic equality, and with the responsibility of maintaining the welfare of all, but how (and whether) it does this is its business.

In neither China nor the Soviet Union, moreover, are there actual or potential contenders for state power, real or imagined. The organization of state power by Communist parties in both ended the exercise of political power by a ruling class rooted in its ownership of land, the primary means of production. The expropriation of propertied classes was the signal social revolutionary change that, in time, guaranteed to Communist parties their unique and total political hegemony. The processes of radical change and restructuring that both societies underwent in obtaining this control has logically, and perhaps even necessarily, given way to efforts at improving the way the governing apparatus functions. Efficient and orderly governance and growth are now perhaps the primary social commitment of each.

While it is not necessary here to recapitulate the comparable points of revolutionary transformation each society has undergone, several broadly determinative aspects of the revolutionary experience in each country do deserve particular notice by way of conclusion, in terms of their intrinsic significance, and in terms of the way Soviet Russia and China, each in its own fashion, continue to remain global models of revolutionary transformation while themselves maturing into conditions of stability and order.[15]

First is the fact that the consolidation of radical political power in both Russia and China occurred in essentially agrarian societies characterized by economies of scarcity, rather than abundance. In both, a small prerevolutionary social elite monopolized political power and controlled agrarian surpluses. Whatever the rhetorical commitments of tsarist or mandarin officials, or even those of the Provisional Government and the Kuomintang, worker and peasant welfare (and hence the welfare of the overwhelming majority of ordinary Russians and Chinese) was inextricably linked in a subordinate fashion to an elaborate sociopolitical structure whose maintenance perpetuated vast social and economic inequities. In good times, inequities could be tolerated, even respected through the prisms of ideology and belief with which both official structures surrounded themselves. In bad times, the iconoclastic reality of want superceded all.

The need under such circumstances for powerful political authorities committed first and foremost to meeting popular need rather than maintaining traditional institutions and values, and able both to control the allocation of scarce resources and determine a more or less equitable distribution of scarce commodities, facilitated mass support for relatively centralized authoritarian political organizations. That Marxist-Leninist parties could emerge in China and Russia was due to their willingness and ultimate ability to meet these needs, whatever distortions occurred in the process. This willingness, in turn, was itself conditioned by a convincing ideological explanation of the origins and nature of mass deprivation, and a political ability derived essentially from a readiness to utilize the vast power of mobilized workers and peasants to destroy traditional social and political structures, however awesome and brutal this power sometimes was. In the process, each Communist party created a popular (mass) foundation that their political rivals could not match.

The agrarian nature of prerevolutionary Russia and China had further significant consequences. Whatever its other objectives, communism in both societies held out the promise not only of social security for ordinary workers and peasants, but for conditions of material well-being and, eventually, abundance.[16] Revolution was the means to industrial might, the end of Russia being "beaten for her backwardness," of China's being "sliced up like a melon." Yet expropriating gentry and bourgeois elites meant destroying both a primary source of investment capital and the class repository of technical expertise. Barring massive aid from more developed Western societies, which became both the desperate hope and despairing failure of revolutionary internationalism, capital for industrial construction and growth had somehow to come from the countryside, from those least able to provide it; technical expertise had to be borrowed from "class enemies" or developed anew.

This created both opportunity and risk. Opportunity stemmed from simultaneous conditions of cultural and material deprivation. Modern, technologically advanced communist societies could only emerge with the disappearance of superstition, ignorance, and primitive methods of production. If progress here could be directly linked to material betterment, the implicit bond between popular aspirations and the political goals of revolutionary Communist parties, which characterized the period of revolutionary upheaval and civil war in both countries, could become a firm basis for postrevolutionary political legitimacy and stability. Risk stemmed from the very need to penetrate and control the countryside required by these tasks. In Soviet Russia, as we have seen, the Bolsheviks' ability to secure state power *before* establishing a firm basis of support and trust among the peasantry led to a deepening of peasant withdrawal and an intensification, rather than mitigation, of the political tasks of penetration and control. As agrarian surpluses dwindled, as peasants became more resistent to taxation and the need for investment capital became more intense, as grain procurements and ultimately the welfare of the city populations seemed to be threatened, the Bolshevik party under Stalin moved logically, if ambiguously, toward a second social revolution. There were alternatives. Some involved securing peasant support with economic rewards, others with making rural cultural and social welfare improvements a genuine party priority. While forced draft collectivization, with all its attendant horrors, did, in the end, secure the party's control over all social and economic sectors, it also left deep residues of suspicion, hostility, economic dislocation, and continued material deprivation that were only finally addressed directly by Stalin's heirs. It is this aspect of Khrushchev's administration that prompts us to consider the 1956–64 period in the Soviet Union as a final stage of revolutionary process, a "great leap forward" that had as its objective the realization of Russia's revolutionary goals of relative prosperity, security, and social equity for all.

In China, conversely, the party's failure in the 1920s to obtain political power led to the necessity of building a mass peasant base in order to survive. In the process, the tasks of overcoming material and cultural deprivation in the countryside could be identified with, and become an integral part of, the very process of struggling for political power. The "mass line" was never simply rhetoric. It was a profoundly original—and politically necessary—means of rooting the Chinese Communist party in the countryside. As an armed party (rather than, as in the Soviet Union after 1917, a party-state with an army) the Chinese Communists became the governing authority of a population in excess of ninety million people by 1945; they then successfully fought a civil war, assuming responsibility for the unification and reorganization of China's state and society. The Bolsheviks, on the other hand, fought a civil war to defend power already gained. The deep identification of party and peasant majority was thus for the Chinese both a means to national power and a revolutionary end in itself. For the Bolsheviks, *control* over the peasantry was a means toward objectives that peasants themselves never accepted as their own.

Once in power, then, China's leadership faced the task not of securing peasant support, but of finding patterns of industrial development appropriate to China's demography and natural resources. As shown, there was, on the part of Mao and others, a deep fear that historic (and structural) tendencies toward social stratification and bureaucratic elitism in China would shape the process of development in ways that belied the revolution's promise of equity—and ultimately equality—for all. And there was, as well, a recognition of the ways in which new stratifications might be generated by the socialist system itself. Mao's death hardly changed the continuing reality of those tendencies; it did mean the loss of a powerful political force urging that the elimination of these tendencies must remain a primary focus of party concern.

Different internal strategies and conditions profoundly shaped the historical development of revolutionary Russia and China, but a fundamental and comparable determinant for each remained its agrarian condition, compounded in the Chinese case by its semicolonial status. In both cases, the forms of state socialism pursued by the ruling party have yielded much of what they promised: noncapitalist economic development, the abolition of private property, the institutionalization of collective and state ownership of the means of production, the elimination of traditional ruling classes, and the firm establishment of national sovereignty and independence.

Here we must also mention briefly the importance of particular *collective* historical experiences for the people of both societies. Part of the social revolutionary appeal of communism and Communist parties has been their explicit ideological opposition to the hegemony of individualism and individual rights, perspectives that characterize most "bourgeois democratic" parties and underlie the socioeconomic principles of liberal corporate capitalism. The realization of self *through* the collective (rather than the notion that the self can be eliminated entirely) is at the heart of communist morality. The identification of private with public good, however, cannot be achieved by rote preaching of the principle by party cadres, anymore than by Christian ministers. If it occurs at all, it is as a result of a constant interplay between consciousness and action. In the early days of the Russian revolution, and in China with varying emphasis up to the present, the effort to change consciousness through education, persuasion, and the creation of contexts for collective action has been constant. "You Christians are not very clever," a Chinese cadre told a foreign professor. "You set before people an ideal which they cannot possibly reach. . . . We, on the other hand, never suggest . . . any thought too advanced for the groups to grasp, or any action too difficult for them to take. . . . Time is no object as long as even the smallest movement takes place and the direction is right."[17] By understanding where people were and then pushing slowly outward from that point, the Chinese were able to accomplish the collectivization of agriculture relatively peacefully. It is, perhaps, a particularly striking historical irony that the time the Chinese were able to take was won for them, in part, by the Soviet peoples' very different revolutionary experience. Forced collectivization, and the survival of the particular form of socialism that engendered, provided the support and security that gave China the space to attempt change from the bottom up.

For both Russians and Chinese, the necessity of living for and through a collectivity larger than self or family was most vividly experienced at times of deep social crisis or national emergency. The Russian social revolution in 1917 was possible only because workers and peasants mobilized and acted collectively, understanding the benefits each would achieve through such collective action. Chinese peasants united behind the Eighth Route Army for similar reasons, knowing the impossibility of uncoordinated, individualized opposition to landlord oppression or Japanese aggression. Both Bolsheviks and Chinese Communists were attuned ideologically to the spontaneous efforts of groups of ordinary people to liberate themselves from exploitation and oppression, through their acceptance of Marxist conceptions of class struggle and imperialism and their ability to direct spontaneous and often self-defeating rebellion into revolutionary movements that attacked the very foundation and structures of the exploiting societies. Both parties, as well, tapped into deep long-ings for a society that could realize mutuality, rather than rapacious-ness, connection rather than alienation, equality rather than hierarchy —in short, the "great harmony" of traditional Chinese philosophy.

More prosaically, to be a member of a collective entity in both of these postrevolutionary societies ensured one's share in the distribu-tion of social benefits, as well as the actual distribution of goods and services. To be classified a worker or a poor or lower-middle peasant meant dignity, not contempt, and whatever benefits were accorded the general social category redounded to each individual in it.

One consequence of the development toward communism in both Soviet Russia and China, however, has been the gradual inversion of the collective/individual relationship. Economic prosperity and political security have brought an end to emergency and the safe guarantee of at least elemental needs. As members of collectives become more prosperous, the benefits of collective membership diminish, particularly if desired goods and services can be obtained outside collective boundaries by individuals acting on their own.

This can be seen most clearly in the Soviet Union, and perhaps it will become increasingly the case for China as well. When goods were scarce, consumers bought whatever the state provided—and gratefully. Black markets always functioned, but inequitably and in a manner that bred corruption and despair. As goods became more abundant, consumers could exercise discretion, purchasing only what they actually wanted. The state's task, therefore, became to satisfy not so much collective need as individual desire. The very conditions of relative economic prosperity—relative, it must be stressed, to Rus-sia and China's past, not to the present noncommunist West—make it more difficult for officials to reach decisions concerning the distri-bution of goods on the basis of collective, rather than individual interests. In the Soviet Union, this tentative degree of "consumer sovereignty," however limited, has led to the development, since 1964, of what is now commonly called the "second economy," a pattern of goods distribution outside official networks that operates virtually like the capitalist marketplace.[18] China remains some dis-tance from such a development, but given current policies, it would not be surprising if a similar phenomenon occurs in the future.

Mao's vision of uninterrupted revolution has, for the moment, faded from the Chinese scene and was absent from Soviet Russia

almost from the start. What may be most significant about it, however, is less its lasting impact on Chinese political reality, than its
influence on the consciousness of those still struggling to achieve
the goals of social justice, equality, and material well-being for all,
imbedded in the fundamental goals of both the Chinese and Russian
revolutions. For many, stabilization and even the end of the revolutionary process in Soviet Russia and China does not necessarily lessen
the significance or attractiveness of either as models for radical social
change. Quite the opposite, in fact, may be true, since both histories
demonstrate the possibilities not only of successful social revolution,
but of the eventual stabilization of new social relationships in secure,
relatively prosperous state systems. Revolutionaries in other societies
may or may not find Leninist vanguard parties to be a source of
inspiration or emulation, but the actual coming to power of groups
organized to overthrow all that seemed most oppressive in traditional
societies is a rare historical occurrence, of obvious importance to
dissident groups everywhere.

Even more remarkable, however, and undoubtedly an even greater
source of inspiration to revolutionaries in the developing world, is
the fact that both revolutions occurred almost entirely outside the
world capitalist system, in direct and fervent opposition to its institutions, values, and power. The appeal of Western material well-
being and power was never in itself (and is not now) the issue. But
the alienation, exploitation, social dislocation, and brutality of capitalist industrialization, seen by some Western analysts as a necessary
component of "modernization," is.

In the Soviet Union and China, egalitarian goals remain an ideal
yet to be fully realized, but they remain important values in those
societies. Elitism, officiousness, intolerance, and repression also exist,
but they remain objects of struggle for those genuinely committed
to the historical objectives of both revolutions. Does this mean the
revolutions considered here should be judged "successful"? This, of
course, depends on one's commitments and perspectives, as well as
the range of one's historical vision. The difficulty of the question for
most Western students lies in the groups with whom they tend to
identify: dissident intellectuals, a displaced bourgeoisie, the tragic
inhabitants of Solzhenitsyn's *Gulag*, the youth "sent down" to the
Chinese countryside. These are proper, indeed crucial connections
to make in moral terms, even for—especially for—communist revolu-

tionaries themselves. Yet one must also be able to identify with "Juan Without Anything," and make judgments on this basis as well. For the fact remains that for a majority of the global population, Juan's world is the sole reality. The question of radical alternatives is not one of desirability but of necessity. And China and Soviet Russia continue to represent the possibility of having what one has to have.

The question remains, what *is* it one has to have? How to write and think and laugh, Guillén reminds us, as well as a place to work and enough to eat. The *promise* of the October Revolution for the working people of the world went beyond material gains and a relatively relaxed bureaucratic authoritarian state. There was to be an end to exploitation of all kinds, a dramatic shift in the way people might live with each other—as fellow workers, as family members, as citizens. There was to be the creation of a new culture, one that, in Trotsky's vision, possessed the past, absorbed it, touched it up, rearranged it, and built on it further, in directions still unimaginable.[19] To what extent has the promise of new socialist men and women been realized in either Russia or China? In some respects, the lineaments of a new culture seem clear. Revolutionary struggle has made possible the realization of a range of civil rights—although obviously not including the civil liberties bourgeois revolutions achieved in the West. Legal equality between women and men, for example, although hardly equivalent to the full emancipation of the socialist ideal, has profoundly changed the lives of Russian and Chinese women as well as the nature of family relationships. Patriarchal attitudes and practices remain, but their material and ideological foundation have suffered a massive assault. At the same time, the question of whether revolutionary promises will ever be fully realized is not one that can be answered now. Bourgeois culture and the shape of its human relationships evolved over several centuries; we simply do not know, logically cannot know, what the ultimate historical legacy of social revolution and postrevolutionary stabilization will be.

It is, however, difficult to see what the sources of further radical change might be in either country. Communism, that realization of a society in which each person contributes to the public good according to her or his ability and receives from society what she or he needs, in Marx's original formulation, was to be accompanied by the withering away of the state and the fullest participation by all citizens in their own governance. It is as difficult to see by what mechanisms the Soviet or Chinese state will wither away as it is to imagine how, without violent struggle, it might happen in the advanced capitalist countries. Bourgeois state forms have been crushed in Soviet Russia and the People's Republic, but the party-state has proved to be capable, in its own way, of great oppression and exploitation, and it is most unlikely to dissolve itself. Moreover, the gap between vanguard party and mass is no less, and many would argue much greater, than it is in the formal democracies of the advanced capitalist world.

Thus, in addition to the realization of economies of abundance, there remain revolutionary tasks in both China and the Soviet Union. If there are groups of people in either country who are convinced that these tasks are not only desirable and necessary, but also possible of achievement, then the revolutionary process may well not have ended, but only paused.

Notes

PREFACE: REVOLUTION AS PROCESS

1. With some major exceptions, current social science analysis reinforces these popular conceptions. See, e.g., Seymour M. Lipset, *Revolution and Counter-Revolution: Change and Persistence in Social Structures* (Garden City, N.Y.: Doubleday Anchor, 1970); Chalmers Johnson, *Revolutionary Change* (Boston: Little, Brown, 1966); Ted R. Gurr, *Why Men Rebel* (Princeton: Princeton Univ. Press, 1969); Samuel Huntington, *Political Order in Changing Societies* (New Haven: Yale Univ. Press, 1968); James C. Davies, "Toward a Theory of Revolution," *American Sociological Review*, 27 (1962): 5–19; and esp. Peter Calvert, *A Study of Revolution* (London: Oxford Univ. Press, 1970), and H. Seton-Watson, "Twentieth Century Revolution," *Political Quarterly*, XXII (July 1951): 251–65. A good analysis of the issue is by S. Wolin, "Politics of the Study of Revolution," *Comparative Politics*, 5:3 (April 1973): 343–58.
2. On this, see the very useful contributions by Charles Tilly, *From Mobilization to Revolution* (Reading, Mass.: Addison-Wesley, 1978), and "Does Modernization Breed Revolution?" *Comparative Politics*, 5:3 (April 1973): 425–47; "Revolutions and Collective Violence," in *Handbook of Political Science*, eds. F. I. Greenstein and Nelson Polsby (Reading, Mass.: Addison-Wesley, 1975); and "Collective Violence in European Perspective," in *The History of Violence in America: Historical and Comparative Perspectives*, eds. Hugh D. Graham and Ted R. Gurr (New York: Praeger, 1969), pp. 4–44.

3. See, e.g., L. Pye, "Roots of Insurgency," in *Internal War*, ed. H. Eckstein (Glencoe, Ill.: Free Press, 1964), pp. 157–58.
4. On this, see esp. Tilly, *From Mobilization*, p. 191, and the discussion in Theda Skocpol, *States and Social Revolutions* (London: Cambridge Univ. Press, 1979), chap. 1.

CHAPTER 1: REVOLUTIONARY RUSSIA
AND THE DILEMMAS OF SOCIAL DEMOCRACY

1. A. I. Shingarev, *The Dying Village* (St. Petersburg, 1907), p. 23 [in Russian].
2. D. Mackenzie Wallace, *Russia on the Eve of War and Revolution* [orig. pub. 1912] (New York: Vintage, 1961), p. 344.
3. Quoted in F. Venturi, *Roots of Revolution* (New York: Knopf, 1961), pp. 295–96.
4. S. M. Stepniak-Kravchinskii, "Underground Russia," in *Collected Works*, ed. S. Vengerov (St. Petersburg, 1906–8), vol. I, p. 380 [in Russian].
5. O. V. Aptekman, *The 'Land and Freedom' Society of the 1870s* (Petrograd, 1924), note 192 [in Russian].
6. See the "Letter from the Executive Committee" of the People's Will published on March 10, 1881, and then widely circulated, as quoted by Venturi, *Roots of Revolution*, p. 716.
7. See K. Pobedonostsev, *Reflections of a Russian Statesman* (London: Grant, Richards, 1898), pp. 26–58, and R. Byrnes, *Pobedonostsev: His Life and Thought* (Bloomington: Indiana Univ. Press, 1968), esp. pp. 74–92, 154–56.
8. See the description by Lev Deutsch cited in S. Baron, *Plekhanov, The Father of Russian Marxism* (Stanford: Stanford Univ. Press, 1963), p. 17.
9. Karl Marx and Frederick Engels, *Selected Correspondence* (Moscow: Foreign Languages Publ. House, 1953), pp. 411–12.
10. N. Valentinov (N. V. Volski), *The Early Years of Lenin* (Ann Arbor: Univ. of Michigan Press, 1969), pp. 195–96.
11. V. Shelgunov, "Workers on the Road to Marxism," *Staryi Bol'shevik*, 2 (5) (1933): 99–100 [in Russian].
12. N. Krupskaia, *Memories of Lenin* (New York, 1930), vol. I, pp. 3–4.
13. V. I. Lenin, "Our Program" (1899), in *Complete Collected Works* (Moscow, 1959), 5th ed., vol. IV, pp. 182–83 [in Russian].
14. Ibid., "Our Immediate Task," pp. 188–89.
15. Ibid., "Our Program," p. 184.
16. Ibid., "Our Immediate Task," pp. 189–90.
17. Ibid., pp. 189–91.
18. Ibid., "Draft Program of Our Party," pp. 211–39.
19. V. I. Lenin, *What Is to Be Done?* (New York: International Publishers, 1929), pp. 166–68.

20. V. I. Lenin, "Draft Program of Our Party," op. cit., p. 242.
21. See the discussion in L. Haimson's superb monograph, *The Russian Marxists and the Origins of Bolshevism* (Cambridge: Harvard Univ. Press, 1955), part III.
22. L. Trotsky, *1905* [orig. pub. 1909] (New York: Vintage, 1971).
23. *Osvobozhdenie*, Jan. 12/25, 1905 [in Russian].
24. As cited in Laura Engelstein, "Moscow in the 1905 Revolution: A Study in Class Conflict and Political Organization," (Ph.D. dissertation, Stanford Univ., 1976), p. 174.
25. The name "Menshevik" was applied by Lenin after the Second Congress of the Russian Social Democratic Party in 1903 to the "minority" faction of the party that opposed "Bolshevik" ("majority") insistence on the directive role of party professionals, who, through tight control of the party newspapers and organizations, would work to bring consciousness" to Russian workers. Mensheviks on the whole worried about the authoritarian tendencies in such a position and envisioned a more open, democratic, mass labor movement in Russia; Lenin and his supporters were convinced such a mass movement would lose its revolutionary commitments and vitality, as seemed to have happened in Western Europe. At the Second Congress, and afterwards, particularly in pamphlets and the party press, Mensheviks like Pavel Akselrod, Vera Zasulich, Iulii Martov, and others argued in favor of a broadly based workers' party open to all who accepted its goals and were willing to cooperate in its efforts, rather than a more restricted organization of revolutionary professionals. As the dispute was elaborated between 1903 and 1917, Bolsheviks came increasingly to represent a party-directed revolutionary uprising (with mass support), while Mensheviks were generally wary of "premature" socialism, before the proletariat had become fully "conscious" and capable of self-government, but lines between the factions were often quite indistinct and, before 1917, frequently had more polemical than practical significance. See Haimson, *Russian Marxists*, esp. part III, and Leonard Schapiro, *The Communist Party of the Soviet Union* (New York: Random House, 1959), part I.

CHAPTER 2: 1917: THE PARADOX OF VICTORY

1. *Izvestiia Revoliutsionnoi Nedeli*, 1 (Feb. 27, 1927) [in Russian]. Many important documents of the 1917 revolution are translated in R. Browder and A. Kerensky, eds., *The Russian Provisional Government 1917*, 3 vols. (Stanford: Stanford Univ. Press, 1961).
2. M. V. Rodzianko, "The State Duma and the February 1917 Revolution," *Arkhiv Russkoi Revoliutsii*, VI (1922): 56–57 [in Russian].
3. N. N. Sukhanov, *The Russian Revolution 1917, Eyewitness Account*, ed. J. Carmichael (New York: Harper & Brothers, 1962), vol. I, p. 61.
4. Ibid., p. 60.

5. The new government included Prince G. L. Lvov (Minister-President and Minister of the Interior), P. N. Miliukov (Minister of Foreign Affairs), A. I. Guchkov (Minister of War and Navy), N. V. Nekrasov (Minister of Transport), A. I. Konovalov (Minister of Trade and Industry), M. I. Tereshchenko (Minister of Finance), A. A. Manuilov (Minister of Education), V. Lvov (Ober-procurator of the Holy Synod), A. I. Shingarev (Minister of Agriculture), and A. K. Kerensky (Minister of Justice). See William G. Rosenberg, *Liberals in the Russian Revolution* (Princeton: Princeton Univ. Press, 1974), chap. 3. A superb study of the February revolution by the Soviet historian E. N. Burdzhalov appears in translation in *Soviet Studies in History*, XVIII: 1 (Summer 1979): 11–96.

6. V. V. Shulgin, *Days* (Belgrade, 1925), p. 178 [in Russian].

7. P. Miliukov, "Constantinople and the Straits," *Vestnik Evropy*, 1 (1917): 355–65 [in Russian]. See the discussion in Rosenberg, *Liberals*, pp. 67–133, and Rex A. Wade, *The Russian Search for Peace, 1917* (Stanford: Stanford Univ. Press, 1969), chap. 3.

8. Sukhanov, *The Russian Revolution*, vol. I, pp. 269–70.

9. *Pravda*, April 7, 1917.

10. *Vestnik Vremennago Pravitel'stva*, 40 (April 26, 1917). The incident is told in some detail by I. Tsereteli, *Memoirs of the February Revolution*, 2 vols. (Paris, 1963) [in Russian], partly translated in the *Russian Review*, 14 (April-Oct. 1955): 93–108, 184–200, 301–21; 15 (Jan. 1956): 37–48.

11. See A. Kerensky, *The Catastrophe* (New York, 1927), pp. 195, 207.

12. *Izvestiia*, March 29, 1917.

13. D. A. Chugaev et al., eds., *The Revolutionary Movement in Russia in May-June 1917. The June Demonstrations* (Moscow, 1959), pp. 494–95 [in Russian].

14. *Rech'*, July 19, 1917. The July Days incident is told in considerable detail by A. Rabinowitch, *Prelude to Revolution* (Bloomington: Indiana Univ. Press, 1968).

15. Browder and Kerensky, vol. III, p. 1573. See the discussion in Rosenberg, *Liberals*, chap. 7.

16. Cited in D. Mitchell, *1919: Red Mirage* (London: Jonathan Cape, 1970), p. 44.

17. *Sotsial Demokrat*, Feb. 28, 1918.

18. The fullest treatment in English of the Constituent Assembly Elections is O. Radkey, *The Elections to the Russian Constituent Assembly of 1917* (Cambridge: Harvard Univ. Press, 1950).

19. A. Kollontai, *The Workers' Opposition in the Russian Communist Party* (Chicago: Kerr, 1921), p. 15. For an excellent discussion of the oppositionist Bolsheviks, see R. V. Daniels, *Conscience of the Revolution* (Cambridge: Harvard Univ. Press, 1965), esp. chaps. 3–6.

20. Daniels, *Conscience*, pp. 144–45.

CHAPTER 3: CHINA AND THE MEANINGS
OF RUSSIA'S REVOLUTION

1. See, for example, A. Nathan, "Imperialism's Effects on China," J. Esherick, "Harvard on China: The Apologetics of Imperialism," in *Bulletin of Concerned Asian Scholars*, 4:4 (Dec. 1972): 3–16; J. K. Fairbank, J. Esherick, and M. Young, "Imperialism in China—an Exchange," *Bulletin of Concerned Asian Scholars*, 5:2 (Sep. 1973): 32–35; R. F. Dernberger, "The Role of the Foreigner in China's Economic Development, 1840–1949," in *China's Modern Economy in Historical Perspective*, ed. Dwight H. Perkins (Stanford: Stanford Univ. Press, 1975), pp. 19–48; perhaps the most interesting recent theoretical contribution to the debate is Frances V. Moulder, *Japan, China and the Modern World Economy: Toward a Reinterpretation of East Asian Development ca. 1600 to ca. 1918* (London: Cambridge Univ. Press, 1977).

2. Quoted in E. P. Young, "Problems of a Late Ch'ing Revolutionary: Ch'en T'ien-hua," in *Revolutionary Leaders of Modern China*, ed. Chün-tu Hsüeh, (New York: Oxford Univ. Press, 1971), p. 220.

3. See John Lust, "Secret Societies, Popular Movements, and the 1911 Revolution," in *Popular Movements and Secret Societies in China, 1840–1950*, ed. Jean Chesneaux (Stanford: Stanford Univ. Press, 1972), p. 167.

4. The most interesting and sophisticated study of this period is Joseph W. Esherick, *Reform and Revolution in China: The 1911 Revolution in Hunan and Hubei* (Berkeley: Univ. of California Press, 1976). The single best interpretive essay on the forces that contributed to the making and shaping of the revolution of 1911 is Ernest P. Young, "Nationalism, Reform, and Republican Revolution: China in the Early Twentieth Century," in *Modern East Asia: Essays in Interpretation*, ed. James B. Crowley (New York: Harcourt, Brace & World, 1970), pp. 151–79. Mary C. Wright, ed., *China in Revolution: The First Phase, 1900–1913* (New Haven: Yale Univ. Press, 1968) is an excellent collection of monographic essays. For Sun Yat-sen see Harold Z. Schiffren, *Sun Yat-sen and the Origins of the Chinese Revolution* (Berkeley: Univ. of California Press, 1968). A valuable symposium on 1911 appears in *Modern China*, 2:2 (April 1976).

5. Lu Xun, "The True Story of Ah Q," in *Silent China*, ed. and trans. Gladys Yang (New York: Oxford Univ. Press, 1973), pp. 14–58.

6. Lu Xun, "A Madman's Diary," ibid., p. 13. The best account of the Yuan Shikai presidency is Ernest P. Young, *The Presidency of Yuan Shih-k'ai: Liberalism and Dictatorship in Early Republican China* (Ann Arbor: Univ. of Michigan Press, 1977). An intriguing analysis of renewed revolutionary efforts in the aftermath of the failure of 1911

is Edward Friedman's *Backward Toward Revolution: The Chinese Revolutionary Party* (Berkeley: Univ. of California Press, 1974).

7. Quoted in Chow Tse-tung, *The May Fourth Movement: Intellectual Revolution in Modern China* (Cambridge: Harvard Univ. Press, 1960).

8. Pa Chin [Ba Jin], *Family* (New York: Doubleday Anchor, 1972), pp. 195–96.

9. Chow Tse-tung, *May Fourth*, p. 57.

10. Qu Qubai, quoted by Paul G. Pickowicz, "Qu Qubai's Critique of the May Fourth Generation: Early Chinese Marxist Literary Criticism," in *Chinese Literature in the May Fourth Era*, ed. Merle Goldman (Cambridge: Harvard Univ. Press, 1972), p. 373. See also Perry Link's fascinating analysis of popular literature, "Traditional-Style Popular Urban Fiction in the Twenties and Thirties," pp. 327–50.

11. Chow Tse-tung, *May Fourth*, p. 57.

12. Maurice Meisner's *Li Ta-chao and the Origins of Chinese Marxism* (Cambridge: Harvard Univ. Press, 1967) is a sensitive and immensely rich account of Li's life, thought, and role in the founding of the Chinest Communist party. The best scholarly account of the early Chinest socialist movement is Martin Bernal, *Chinese Socialism to 1907* (Ithaca: Cornell Univ. Press, 1976).

13. Meisner, *Li Ta-chao*, p. 96. Disillusion was general and deep. See Chow, *May Fourth*, pp. 92 ff.

14. Chow, *May Fourth*, p. 173.

15. Ibid., p. 196.

16. The most detailed account of worker participation is Joseph T. Chen, *The May Fourth Movement in Shanghai: The Making of a Social Movement in Modern China* (Leiden: Brill, 1971). See also Jean Chesneaux, *The Chinese Labor Movement, 1919–1927* (Stanford: Stanford Univ. Press, 1968).

17. Quoted by Jean Chesneaux, *China from the 1911 Revolution to Liberation* (New York: Pantheon, 1977), p. 97.

18. Meisner, *Li Ta-chao*, p. 87.

19. Shen Ts'ung-wen, "A Bandit Chief," in *Anthology of Chinese Literature*, ed. Cyril Birch (New York: Grove, 1965), vol. 2, p. 283. The best accounts of the warlord period are those that focus on particular warlords or warlord cliques: James E. Sheridan, *Chinese Warlord: The Career of Feng Yu-hsiang* (Stanford: Stanford Univ. Press, 1966); Diana Lary, *Region and Nation: The Kwangsi Clique in Chinese Politics, 1925–1927* (London, New York: Cambridge Univ. Press, 1974); and Gavan McCormack, *Chang Tso-lin in Northeast China, 1911–1928: China, Japan and the Manchurian Idea* (Stanford: Stanford Univ. Press, 1977).

20. Chow, *May Fourth*, p. 219.

21. Meisner, *Li Ta-chao*, p. 107.

22. Chen Duxiu, "The Monument to von Kettler," and "Two Mistaken

Ideas That We Have About the Boxers," in *Marxism and Asia: An Introduction with Readings*, eds. Hélène Carrère d'Encausse and Stuart R. Schram (London: Allen Lane/Penguin, 1969), pp. 210, 223.

23. Extracts from Lenin's and Roy's reports at the Second Congress of the Communist International can be found in d'Encausse and Schram, pp. 149 ff.

24. Bertolt Brecht, "The Measures Taken," in *The Jewish Wife and Other Short Plays*, trans. Eric Bentley (New York: Grove, 1965), p. 82. Benjamin Schwartz, *Chinese Communism and the Rise of Mao* (Cambridge, Mass.: Harvard University Press, 1951) continues to remain an extremely useful work on the early history of the party and its relationship to the Comintern.

CHAPTER 4: SHANGHAI: THE PARADOX OF DEFEAT

1. There is a fairly rich literature on the subject, including translations of two primary sources: Vera Vladimirovna Vishnyakova-Akimova, *Two Years in Revolutionary China, 1925–1927* (Cambridge: East Asian Research Center of Harvard University, 1971), an exciting account of the experiences of a very junior Soviet advisor; and *Documents on Communism, Nationalism and Soviet Advisers in China, 1924–1927*, eds. C. Martin Wilbur and Julie Lien-ying How, (New York: Columbia Univ. Press, 1956). See also Conrad Brandt, *Stalin's Failure in China, 1924–1927* (Cambridge: Harvard Univ. Press, 1958); Robert C. North and Xenia J. Eudin, *M. N. Roy's Mission to China: The Communist-Kuomintang Split of 1927* (with documents trans. by Helen I. Powers) (Berkeley: Univ. of California Press, 1963). Harold Isaacs, *The Tragedy of the Chinese Revolution* (Stanford: Stanford Univ. Press, 1961) is a vividly rendered account from an explicitly Trotskyist position; Angus W. McDonald, Jr., *The Urban Origins of Rural Revolution: Elites and the Masses in Hunan Province, 1911–1927* (Berkeley: Univ. of California Press, 1978) covers a longer time period and focuses on a single province in a way that greatly illuminates the issues; S. Bernard Thomas's monograph, *"Proletarian Hegemony" in the Chinese Revolution and the Canton Commune in 1927* (Ann Arbor: Center for Chinese Studies, Univ. of Michigan Papers in Chinese Studies, No. 23, 1975) reviews the way the commune has been interpreted by Chinese and Russian commentators; and Hsiao Tso-liang's *Chinese Communism in 1927: City vs. Countryside* (Hong Kong: The Chinese Univ. of Hong Kong, 1970) is a detailed account of the commune itself and the policies related to urban and rural insurrection at the time.

2. V. I. Lenin, "State and Revolution," *Collected Works* (Moscow, 1964), vol. 25, pp. 387–88, 403–4, 466–68, (our italics).

3. Quoted in Maurice Meisner, *Li Ta-chao and the Origins of Chinese Marxism* (Cambridge: Harvard Univ. Press, 1967), p. 107.

4. James Pinckney Harrison, *The Long March to Power: A History of the Chinese Communist Party, 1921–1972* (New York: Praeger, 1972), p. 103.

5. Cited in McDonald, *Urban Origins*, p. 261.

6. Meisner, *Li Ta-chao,* discusses the relationship between Wu and Li, pp. 211–12.

7. See Roy Hofheinz, *The Broken Wave: the Chinese Communist Peasant Movement, 1922–1928* (Cambridge: Harvard Univ. Press, 1977) and Yong-pil Pang, "Peng Pai: From Landlord to Revolutionary," *Modern China,* 1:3 (July 1975): 297–322.

8. Jean Chesneaux, *The Chinese Labor Movement, 1919–1927* (Stanford Univ. Press, 1968), has two superb chapters on these events, "The May Thirtieth Movement," pp. 262–89 and "The Canton-Hong Kong Strike," pp. 290–318.

9. Borodin is quoted in Louis Fischer, *The Soviets in World Affairs,* (London, 1930), vol. 2, p. 647. The documents in Part IV, "Friction and Reconciliation in the Revolutionary Camp, July 1925, to July 1926," 206 ff. in Wilbur and How, *Documents on Communism, Nationalism and Soviet Advisers,* are particularly illuminating.

10. Mao Zedong, "Report on an Investigation of the Peasant Movement in Hunan," *Selected Works* (Peking: Foreign Languages Press, 1965), vol. I, p. 23.

11. McDonald, *Urban Origins,* p. 306.

12. Hsieh Ping-ying, *Girl Rebel* (New York: John Day, 1940), pp. 81–82.

13. Vincent Sheean, *Personal History* (New York: Modern Library, 1940), p. 219, brilliantly captures the mood of Wuhan.

14. McDonald, *Urban Origins,* p. 250; Chesneaux, *Chinese Labor Movement,* p. 322.

15. Cited in Leon Trotsky, *Problems of the Chinese Revolution* (Ann Arbor: Univ. of Michigan Press, 1967), pp. 383–84.

16. Isaacs, *Tragedy,* p. 231. The most moving account of the Shanghai massacre is André Malraux's *Man's Fate* (New York: Random House, 1961).

17. Harrison, *Long March,* pp. 98 ff. summarizes the debates at this crucial meeting.

18. North and Eudin, *M. N. Roy's Mission,* p. 120.

19. Isaacs, *Tragedy,* p. 251.

20. Hsieh, *Girl Rebel,* p. 111.

21. See Elizabeth Croll, *Feminism and Socialism in China* (London: Routledge & Kegan Paul, 1978).

22. Isaacs, *Tragedy,* p. 220.

23. Mao, "Report on an Investigation," pp. 24, 28. Among the most interesting analyses of the failure of the first united front is A. Neuberg, *Armed Insurrection* (London: New Left Books, 1970). Neuberg

is a pseudonym for a Comintern committee that, under the editorship of the Italian Communist, Togliatti, put together a series of Red Army staff reports on various insurrections including Shanghai and Canton. Ho Chi Minh's contribution, "The Party's Military Work among the Peasants," is particularly important both in terms of Ho's later revolutionary activities in Vietnam and the similarities and differences between his approach and Mao's.

CHAPTER 5: VANGUARDS: THE PARTIES AND PARTY-MASS
RELATIONS IN THE 1930s

1. *Documents de l'Opposition et la Réponse du Parti* (Paris, 1927), p. 65.
2. I. V. Stalin, *Works* (Moscow, 1946–52), vol. IX, pp. 225–27 [in Russian].
3. L. Trotsky, *Problems of the Chinese Revolution* [orig. pub. 1932] (Ann Arbor: Univ. of Michigan Press, 1967), pp. 37, 44.
4. William Hinton, *Fanshen: A Documentary of Revolution in a Chinese Village* (New York: Monthly Review, 1966), p. 39.
5. Benjamin Schwartz, *Chinese Communism and the Rise of Mao* (Cambridge: Harvard Univ. Press, 1951), p. 137.
6. Mao Zedong, "Report on an Investigation of the Peasant Movement in Hunan, March 1927," *Selected Works of Mao Tse-tung* (Peking: Foreign Languages Press, 1965), vol. I, p. 27. For a detailed discussion of Mao's early categories of analysis, see Philip C. C. Huang, "Mao Tse-tung and the Middle Peasants, 1925–1928," *Modern China*, 1:3 (July 1975): 271–98; on the peasant movement in Hunan, see Yokoyama Suguru, "The Peasant Movement in Hunan," in ibid., 1:2 (April 1975): 204–38, and A. W. McDonald, Jr., *The Urban Origins of Rural Revolution: Elites and Masses in Hunan Province, 1911–1927* (Berkeley: Univ. of California Press, 1978), chap. 6.
7. *Thirteenth Congress of the RCP(b). May 1924. Stenographic Report* (Moscow, 1963), pp. 165–66 [in Russian]. For the best analysis of Trotsky's views, and particularly his behavior during this period, see I. Deutscher, *The Prophet Unarmed, Trotsky: 1921–1929* (London: Oxford Univ. Press, 1959), chap. II.
8. Trotsky, *Problems*, p. 13.
9. See the discussion in T. H. Rigby, *Communist Party Membership in the U.S.S.R. 1917–1967* (Princeton: Princeton Univ. Press, 1968), pp. 97–100.
10. The quotations are from A. Kollontai, *The Workers' Opposition in the Russian Communist Party* (Chicago: Kerr, 1921), p. 44; and the "Declaration of the Twenty-two," signed by Kollontai, Shliapnikov, and other Workers' Opposition leaders and submitted to a Comintern conference discussing questions of a "united front" of various workers' groups, published in *Izvestiia* March 22, 1922.

11. A particularly good discussion of the scissors crisis appears in M. Dobb, *Soviet Economic Development Since 1917* (New York: International Publishers, 1948), chap. 7.

12. L. Trotsky, *The New Course* [orig. pub. 1923] (Ann Arbor: Univ. of Michigan Press, 1965), esp. pp. 106–13, from which the quotations are taken.

13. Ibid., p. 28.

14. See the discussion in M. Lewin, *Lenin's Last Struggle* (New York: Pantheon, 1968), pp. 77–90.

15. *14th Congress of the All-Union Communist Party (b). December 18–31, 1925. Stenographic Report* (Moscow, 1926), esp. pp. 220–23, 521–25 [in Russian]. After the congress, Molotov, Voroshilov, and Kalinin were elected to the Politburo, becoming Stalin's closest supporters and the so-called "Stalinist center." Kamenev was removed from most of his posts, holding only that of commissar of trade, which he lost shortly afterwards to Mikoyan. For a time, Zinoviev remained a Politburo member, Kamenev a candidate.

16. See A. G. Meyer, "The War Scare of 1927," *Soviet Union*, 5 (1978): 1–25.

17. Mao Zedong, "The Struggle in the Chingkang Mountains," *Selected Works*, vol. I, p. 73.

18. Ibid., "On Correcting Mistaken Ideas in the Party," p. 106; "Struggle in the Chingkang Mountains," p. 83; "On Correcting Mistaken Ideas in the Party," p. 113. The full category of mistakes Mao discusses in this important essay are: the purely military point of view, ultra-democracy, disregard of organizational discipline, absolute equalitarianism, subjectivism, individualism, and the "ideology of roving rebel bands." Hinton, *Fanshen*, pp. 55–57, uses the essay to discuss peasant "weaknesses" as such and their relationship to the peasant mode of production.

19. Mao Zedong, "A Single Spark Can Start a Prairie Fire," *Selected Works*, vol. I, p. 127.

20. Cited in Dick Wilson, *The Long March, 1935: The Epic of Chinese Communism's Survival* (New York: Avon ed., 1973), pp. 76–77.

21. Mao Zedong, "A Single Spark Can Start a Prairie Fire," *Selected Works*, vol. I, pp. 122, 123.

22. Mao Zedong, "Oppose Book Worship," *Selected Readings from the Works of Mao Tse-tung* (Peking: Foreign Languages Press, 1971), pp. 41, 45.

23. Conrad Brandt, Benjamin Schwartz, and John K. Fairbank, eds., *A Documentary History of Chinese Communism* (New York: Atheneum, 1967), p. 225. Two recent books on the Jiangxi period have greatly expanded our knowledge of how the first Soviet government in China functioned: Trygve Lötveit, *Chinese Communism, 1931–1934: Experience in Civil Government* (Scandinavian Institute of Asian Studies Monograph Series No. 16, 1973), and Ilpyong J. Kim,

The Politics of Chinese Communism: Kiangsi under the Soviets (Berkeley: Univ. of California Press, 1973). John E. Rue, *Mao Tse-tung in Opposition, 1927–1935* (Stanford: Stanford Univ. Press, 1966) is an intensive examination of policy issues that divided the party at this time.

24. Mao Zedong, "Struggle in the Chingkang Mountains," *Selected Readings*, p. 89.
25. Mao Zedong, "Oppose Book Worship," *Selected Readings*, p. 47.
26. Mao Zedong, "Be Concerned with the Well-being of the Masses, Pay Attention to Methods of Work," *Selected Works*, vol. I, pp. 147, 149.
27. The third campaign was cut short due to the Japanese attack on Mukden, but a new assault was launched as soon as Chiang Kai-shek reached a compromise agreement with the Japanese in the spring of 1932.
28. Dick Wilson, *Long March*, p. 91. See also Edgar Snow's classic recounting of the march in *Red Star over China* (New York: Random House, 1938), and Jerome Ch'en, *Mao and the Chinese Revolution* (London: Oxford Univ. Press, 1965).
29. Translated by Michael Bullock and Jerome Ch'en in *Mao and the Chinese Revolution*, p. 337.
30. Cited in Maurice Meisner, "Yenan Communism and the People's Republic," in *Modern East Asia*, ed. J. Crowley, p. 274.
31. Quoted in Agnes Smedley, *The Great Road: The Life and Times of Chu Teh* (London: Calder, 1958), pp. 320, 322. Smedley's biography of Zhu is a magnificent work, combining the passion of its author with that of its subject.
32. Mao Zedong, "On Tactics Against Japanese Imperialism," *Selected Works*, vol. I, p. 160.
33. See Mark Selden's excellent study, *The Yenan Way in Revolutionary China* (Cambridge: Harvard Univ. Press, 1971).
34. *History of the Socialist Economy of the USSR* (Moscow, 1976), vol. II, pp. 384–86 [in Russian]. See also R. W. Davies, *The Socialist Offensive: Collectivization of Agriculture 1929–30* (London, 1980), pp. 419–20.
35. *History*, vol. III, pp. 326–33.
36. See the discussion of these problems in Lewin, *Russian Peasants*, esp. part II, and Davies, *Socialist Offensive*, pp. 41–51, 106–7. Bread rationing was introduced in the winter of 1928–29, sugar and tea in the summer of 1929, meat and other goods in the fall and winter of 1929–30.
37. Evidence comes from the Smolensk Region party archive, captured by the Germans in World War II and now available to Western scholars on microfilm. See the full discussion of these issues in W. Rosenberg, "Party-Worker Relations and the 'Vanguard Problem'," *Russian Review*, 36:2 (April 1977), pp. 127–50.

38. *Fifteeth Congress of the ACP(b). December 1917. Stenographic Report* (Moscow, 1961–62), vol. II, pp. 1229–35 [in Russian].
39. Quoted by M. Lewin, "The Immediate Background to Soviet Collectivization," *Soviet Studies*, 17:2 (1965), p. 165, n. 7.
40. J. Karcz, "Thoughts on the Grain Problem," *Soviet Studies*, 18: 4 (1967), pp. 399–434.
41. See T. Shanin, *The Awkward Class* (London, 1972), and D. J. Male, *Russian Peasant Organization before Collectivization* (Cambridge, England, 1971).
42. See the discussion in R. Medvedev, *Let History Judge* (New York: Knopf, 1971), pp. 71–82.
43. Davies, *Socialist Offensive*, pp. 25–27.
44. M. Sholokhov, *Virgin Soil Upturned* (Moscow: Foreign Languages Pub. House, n.d.), pp. 23–24.
45. *Pravda*, November 7, 1929.
46. *Collectivization of Agriculture* (Moscow, 1957), esp. chap. 5, pp. 101–2 [in Russian]. See also V. P. Danilov, ed., *Essays in the History of the Collectivization of Agriculture in the USSR in the Period of Reconstruction* (Moscow, 1960) [in Russian].
47. Krupskaia's views were published in a *Pravda* article entitled "Lenin and Kolkhoz Construction," Jan. 20, 1929. Bukharin's views were also still published in *Pravda* at this time, but see esp. *Sotsialisticheskii Vestnik*, 9 (1929), p. 10, where Bukharin's comment is recorded, and Stephen F. Cohen, *Bukharin and the Bolshevik Revolution* (New York: Knopf, 1973), chap. IX.
48. Stalin, *Collected Works*, vol. XI, pp. 41–63, and passim. [in Russian].
49. J. Karcz, *The Economics of Communist Agriculture: Selected Papers* Bloomington, Ind., 1979), p. 320.
50. James Millar calls the collectivization campaign an "unmitigated economic policy disaster." See his "Mass Collectivization and the Contribution of Soviet Agriculture to the First Five Year Plan," *Slavic Review*, 33:4 (Dec. 1974): 764–65. See also the discussion in Karcz, ibid., pp. 309–31.
51. The proportion of the peasantry organized in collective farms may have fallen by as much as half between March and June 1930. Stalin's strictures against becoming "dizzy with success" apparently demoralized and confused many local officials, some of whom clearly regarded it as surrendering to the peasants. See the discussion by M. L. Bogdenko, "Collective Farm Construction in the Spring and Summer of 1930," *Istoricheskie Zapiski*, 76 (1965), pp. 17–41 [in Russian].
52. John Scott, *Behind the Urals: An American Worker in Russia's City of Steel* (Bloomington, Ind., 1973). Written in 1941.
53. Karcz, *Economics of Communist Agriculture*, pp. 452–57. By 1931, grain exports had jumped some forty times that of 1926–27, but so irrationally was grain dumped on the foreign market that British im-

port prices fell almost 50 percent, and the value of exports in terms of purchasing foreign machinery may even have been smaller in 1931 than it had been in 1926–27.

54. J. Stalin, *Problems of Leninism* (Moscow, 1945), pp. 355–56.
55. Sholokhov, *Virgin Soil Upturned*, p. 167.
56. Ibid.
57. V. Tendriakov, "Death," *Moskva*, 3 (1968): 37 [in Russian].
58. The estimate of deportees is from Lewin, *Russian Peasants*, p. 508.
59. F. Belov, *The History of a Soviet Collective Farm* (New York, 1955), pp. 12–14. The famine is discussed carefully and in detail by D. G. Dalrymple, "The Soviet Famine of 1932–34," *Soviet Studies*, 15:3 (1964), pp. 250–84.
60. See, e.g., P. H. Solomon, Jr., "Soviet Penal Policy, 1917–1934: A Reinterpretation," *Slavic Review*, 39:2 (1980), pp. 195–217.
61. E. Pashukanis, *The Soviet State and Revolutionary Law* (Moscow, 1930), as translated in *Soviet Legal Philosophy* (Cambridge: Harvard Univ. Press, 1951), pp. 237–80.
62. See the discussion in Medvedev, pp. 139–46.
63. B. Nikolaevsky, *Power and the Soviet Elite. "The Letter of an Old Bolshevik" and Other Essays* (New York: Praeger, 1965), p. 11.
64. See the figures from *Socialist Construction* (Moscow, 1934) [in Russian] cited by A. Nove, *An Economic History of the U.S.S.R.* (New York: Penguin, 1976), p. 191, and the discussion in Dobb, *Soviet Economic Development*, pp. 254–89, esp. on the problem of Soviet industrial statistics.
65. According to Medvedev (p. 156) the chairman of the Elections Commission, V. P. Zatonskii, called in L. M. Kaganovich, who ordered the destruction of many ballots on which Stalin's name had been crossed out. The Congress was told that only three votes had been cast against both Kirov and Stalin. See also Nicolaevsky's essay "Stalin and Kirov" in *Power and the Soviet Elite*, pp. 69–104.
66. S. Volkov, ed. and trans., *Testimony: The Memoirs of Dmitri Shostakovich* (New York: Harper & Row, 1979), p. 81. On the memoir itself, see the discussion by Laurel E. Fay, "Shostakovich versus Volkov: Whose Testimony?" *Russian Review*, 39:4 (1980), pp. 484–93.
67. E. Ginzburg, *Into the Whirlwind* (London: Collins/Harvill, 1967).
68. Nove, *Economic History*, p. 225, citing plan documents and *Industry of the USSR* (Moscow, 1957) [in Russian].

CHAPTER 6: GREAT PATRIOTIC STRUGGLES:
THE SOVIET UNION AND CHINA IN WORLD WAR II

1. Chalmers Johnson, *Revolutionary Change* (Boston: Little, Brown, 1966), pp. 169–70.
2. Donald Gillin, "Peasant Nationalism in the History of Chinese Communism," *Journal of Asian Studies*, 23:2 (Feb. 1964): 269–89.

3. Mao Zedong, "On Tactics Against Japanese Imperialism," *Selected Works of Mao Tse-tung* (Peking: Foreign Languages Press, 1965), vol. I, pp. 164, 165.
4. Ibid., pp. 166, 167, 168, 170.
5. Ibid., p. 167.
6. Cited in Tien-wei Wu, *The Sian Incident: A Pivotal Point in Modern Chinese History* (Ann Arbor: Center for Chinese Studies, Univ. of Michigan, 1976), p. 101. Wu's monograph is the most detailed account of the incident available. See also Lyman Van Slyke, *Enemies and Friends: the United Front in Chinese Communist History* (Stanford: Stanford Univ. Press, 1967).
7. Chen Yi, "Guerrilla Fighting in Southern Kiangsi," *Chinese Literature*, 8 (1961): 34. See also the August 1937 poem cited in Gregor Benton, "Communist Guerrilla Bases in Southeast China, after the start of the Long March," (paper presented at Harvard University Conference on Communist Rural Bases, August, 1978); for Wang Ming's policy see Gregar Benton, "The Second Wang Ming Line," *China Quarterly* 61 (March 1975): 61–94, and Richard C. Thornton, *China: The Struggle for Power 1917–1972* (Bloomington: Indiana Univ. Press, 1973), chaps. 4 and 5. For a rather muted statement of the hesitation many guerrillas in Jiangxi must have felt about the new policy, see the essay by Tuan Huan-ching, "Hold onto the Struggle in the Hunan-Kiangsi Border Region," in *The Unquenchable Spark* (Peking: Foreign Languages Press, 1964), esp. pp. 54–55.
8. Mao Zedong, "The Role of the Chinese Communist Party in the National War," *Selected Works*, vol. 2, p. 200.
9. Ibid., "Urgent Tasks Following KMT-CCP Co-operation," p. 39.
10. Ibid., "The Situation and Tasks in the Anti-Japanese War after the Fall of Shanghai and Taiyuan," pp. 61, 62.
11. Ibid., "On Protracted War," p. 155.
12. Ibid., "The Role of the Communist Party in the National War," p. 100. (Our italics.) For an informative discussion of early policies on class struggle and mobilization, see Carl E. Dorris, "Peasant Mobilization in North China and the Origins of Yenan Communism," *China Quarterly* 68 (Dec. 1976): 697–719.
13. Cited in Jane Price, *Cadres, Commanders, and Commissars; the Training of the Chinese Communist Leadership, 1920–1945* (New York: Westview Press, 1976), p. 143.
14. Cited in S. Bernard Thomas, "Party Policy and Labor: Yenan and the North China Bases, 1936–1945," (paper presented at Harvard University Conference on Communist Rural Bases, August, 1978).
15. Suzanne Pepper, *Civil War in China: the Political Struggle, 1945–1949* (Berkeley: Univ. of California Press, 1978), p. 231.
16. Ibid., p. 434.
17. Mark Selden, *The Yenan Way in Revolutionary China* (Cambridge: Harvard Univ. Press, 1971), p. 252.

18. Pepper, *Civil War*, pp. 261 ff. describes rent reduction in Shandong province during the war against Japan.

19. Mao Zedong, "On Tactics against Japanese Imperialism," *Selected Works*, vol. I, p. 160.

20. Mao Zedong, "Rectify the Party's Style of Work," *Selected Readings from the Works of Mao Tse-tung* (Peking: Foreign Languages Press, 1971), p. 218; "On New Democracy," *Selected Works*, vol. II, p. 381; "Yenan Forum on Literature and Art," and "Concerning Methods of Leadership," *Selected Readings*, pp. 284, 290.

21. For popular responses to the Red Army see contemporary accounts by Edgar Snow, *Red Star over China* (New York: Grove, 1961); Jack Belden, *China Shakes the World* (New York: Harper & Brothers, 1949); and esp. Agnes Smedley, *Battle Hymn of China* (New York: Knopf, 1943).

22. Chen Yi, "Guerrilla Fighting in Southern Kiangsi," p. 36.

23. Cited in Michael R. Schaller, "The United States and China" (Ph. D. dissertation, Univ. of Michigan, 1974), pp. 100–101.

24. Theodore H. White and Annalee Jacoby, *Thunder out of China* (New York: Sloane, 1946), pp. 170–71.

25. Joseph W. Esherick, ed., *Lost Chance in China: The World War II Dispatches of John S. Service* (New York: Random House, 1974), p. 12.

26. White and Jacoby, *Thunder*, p. 176.

27. Esherick, *Lost Chance*, p. 13.

28. Ibid., p. 14.

29. Ibid., pp. 14–15.

30. Isabel and David Crook, *Ten Mile Inn: Mass Movement in a Chinese Village* (New York: Pantheon, 1979), p. 10.

31. Esherick, *Lost Chance*, pp. 193–98, passim.

32. Smedley, *Battle Hymn of China*, p. 179.

33. Esherick, *Lost Chance*, p. 221.

34. Ibid., p. 222.

35. Ibid., p. 223.

36. Ibid., p. 224.

37. Jack Belden, *Still Time to Die* (New York: Harper & Brothers, 1943), pp. 311–12.

38. On the distinction between rhetoric and working (or operational) creeds, see esp. the discussion by H. Zinn, *Postwar America: 1945–1971* (Indianapolis: Bobbs Merrill, 1973).

39. It should be noted, however, that despite these diatribes, first articulated in a comprehensive argument in *Mein Kampf*, and then endlessly repeated, Hitler did ratify an agreement between the Soviet Union and Germany in May 1933, which had been worked out two years earlier and was ostensibly the foundation for normal relations. Stalin and others may therefore have been inclined to dismiss much of Hitler's bombast as political rhetoric.

40. *History of the Great Patriotic War of the Soviet Union, 1941–45* (Moscow, 1965), vol. VI, pp. 123–24 [in Russian].

41. Chamberlain's views were based in part on the fact that for the Soviet Union to come to the aid of Czechoslovakia, the Red Army needed permission to cross either Polish or Rumanian territory, which was quite unlikely to be given. Stalin's indignation was consequently "safe" in that he was unlikely in any event to be able to honor his treaty commitments. See the discussion in J. W. Wheeler-Bennett, *Munich: Prologue to Tragedy* (New York: Viking, 1964), esp. part II. Chamberlain's diary is quoted by K. Feiling, *The Life of Neville Chamberlain* (London, 1946), pp. 402–3.

42. See the discussion by R. Tucker, "The Emergence of Stalin's Foreign Policy," *Slavic Review*, 36: 4 (Dec. 1977: 563–89).

43. Marshal R. Ia. Malinovskii, "On the Twentieth Anniversary of the Beginning of the Great Fatherland War," *Voenno-Istoricheskii Zhurnal*, 6 (1961): 6.

44. A. M. Nekrich, *June 22, 1941* (Moscow, 1965), trans. in *June 22, 1941: Soviet Historians and the German Invasion*, ed. V. Petrov, (Columbia, S.C., 1968), pp. 112–13.

45. R. Medvedev, *Let History Judge* (New York: Knopf, 1971), p. 217; Nekrich, *June 22, 1941*, pp. 173–74.

46. Nekrich, *June 22, 1941*, p. 448.

47. A. Clark, *Barbarossa: The Russian German Conflict, 1941–45* (New York: Morrow, 1965), pp. 50–51.

48. Ibid., p. 55.

49. A. Seaton, *The Russo-German War 1941–45* (New York: Praeger, 1971), p. 110.

50. Clark, *Barbarossa*, p. 56.

51. Ibid.

52. F. Halder, *War Diary* (Stuttgart: W. Kohlhammer, 1962), vol. 3, p. 220 [in German]. General Halder was chief of staff of the German army.

53. I. V. Stalin, *Works* (Stanford: Hoover Institution Press, 1967), vol. 2 (XV: 1941–45), pp. 32–35 [in Russian]. A. Werth, *Russia at War* (New York: Dutton, 1964) is far and away the best book in English on the war.

54. See the discussion in the English-language volume, *Great Patriotic Struggle of the Soviet Union, 1941–1945* (Moscow, 1974), pp. 448–50, an abridgement from the six-volume Russian edition.

55. See Milovan Djilas, *Conversations with Stalin* (New York: Harcourt Brace, 1962), esp. pp. 87–124. There is abundant Soviet material on Stalin as a military commander and the horrendous consequences of many of his orders, much of it published in the 1960s in an attempt to rehabilitate Red Army men unfairly purged and disgraced. In English, see, e.g., G. K. Zhukov, *The Memoirs of Marshal Zhukov* (New York: Delacorte, 1971). A good summary of the literature,

including unpublished materials, appears in Medvedev, *Let History Judge*, chap. 12.

56. W. Churchill, *Hinge of Fate* (Boston: Houghton-Mifflin, 1950), p. 268. See also esp. pp. 313–44, 472–502.
57. Ibid., p. 271.
58. Ibid., pp. 478–83.
59. Ibid.
60. *Great Patriotic Struggle*, p. 334.

CHAPTER 7: SOCIALIST ROADS AND THE
VARIETIES OF RECOVERY

1. I. V. Stalin, *Works* (Stanford: Hoover Institution Press, 1967), vol. 3 (XVII, 1946–53), pp. 1–22 [in Russian].
2. Cited by Georges Bortoli, *The Death of Stalin* (New York: Praeger, 1975), p. 3.
3. See the discussion in Walter LaFeber, *America, Russia, and the Cold War, 1945–1966* (New York: Wiley, 1967), pp. 21–23, and Gabriel Kolko, *The Politics of War* (New York: Vintage, 1968), pp. 389–427. According to LaFeber (p. 22), Stalin's request for a loan was found only after the failure of the Foreign Ministers' Conference in December.
4. See the discussion by Naum Jasny, "Kolkhozy, the Achilles' Heel of the Soviet Regime," *Soviet Studies*, III: 2 (Oct. 1951): 150–62.
5. A. Nove, *An Economic History of the U.S.S.R.* [orig. pub. 1969] (New York: Penguin, 1976), p. 300. See also A. Nove, "Rural Taxation in the USSR," *Soviet Studies*, V: 2 (Oct. 1953): 159–66.
6. Suzanne Pepper, *Civil War in China: The Political Struggle, 1945–1949* (Berkeley: Univ. of California Press, 1978), p. 274.
7. Isabel and David Crook, *Ten Mile Inn: Mass Movement in a Chinese Village* (New York: Pantheon, 1979), p. 11.
8. Jack Belden, *China Shakes the World* (New York: Harper & Brothers, 1949), pp. 275–307.
9. Ibid., p. 317.
10. Cited in Vivian Shue, "Personal Power and Village Politics: Hunan Peasants During Land Reform" (paper presented at Univ. of Michigan conference on Political Interest Groups in China, August, 1977).
11. Mao Zedong, "On the People's Democratic Dictatorship," *Selected Works of Mao-Tse-tung* (Peking: Foreign Language Press, 1961), vol. 4, pp. 412, 413.
12. Ibid., p. 423.
13. Mao Zedong, "Don't Hit Out in All Directions," *Selected Works*, p. 35.
14. The image is Yevtushenko's. See his *A Precocious Autobiography* (New York: Dutton, 1963), esp. pp. 84, 89.

15. William Sewell, *I Stayed in China* (London: Allen & Unwin, 1966), p. 98.
16. Ibid., p. 191.
17. Mao Zedong, "On the People's Democratic Dictatorship," *Selected Works*, vol. 5, p. 416.
18. See Carl Riskin, "State Power and the Foundations of Socialism," in his forthcoming study of the economic history of modern China.
19. Ibid., "Mobilization and Social Transformation, 1949–55."
20. Cited in Thomas P. Bernstein, "Problems of Village Leadership after Land Reform," *China Quarterly*, 36 (Oct.-Dec. 1968): 2, 8.
21. Liu Shu-teh, *We Crossed the Bridge Together* (Peking: Foreign Languages Press, 1963), pp. 39, 118.
22. Riskin, "Mobilization and Social Transformation, 1949–55."
23. See, e.g. Malenkov,'s speech to the Supreme Soviet in August, 1953 (*Pravda*, Aug. 9), and the October 28 announcement of new plans for increasing the output in consumer goods.
24. See the discussion in R. and Z. Medvedev, *Khrushchev, the Years in Power* (New York: Columbia Univ. Press, 1976), esp. pp. 58–65.

CHAPTER 8: GREAT LEAPS FORWARD:
IRONIES AND CONTRADICTIONS, 1954–1964

1. Stuart R. Schram, *The Political Thought of Mao Tse-tung* (New York: Praeger, 1963), p. 253.
2. Mao Zedong, "Sixty Points on Working Methods," in Jerome Ch'en, *Mao Papers: Anthology and Bibliography* (London: Oxford Univ. Press, 1970), p. 66.
3. Conversation with André Malraux, *Antimémoires* (Paris: Gallimard, 1967), p. 550.
4. Mao Zedong, "Cooperative Transformation of Agriculture," *Selected Works* (Peking: Foreign Languages Press, 1977), vol. 5, pp. 194–95.
5. Ibid., p. 197.
6. Ibid., pp. 184–85.
7. Ibid., p. 198. See also Jack Gray's excellent discussion, "The Two Roads: Alternative Strategies of Social Change and Economic Growth in China," in *Authority, Participation and Cultural Change in China*, ed. Stuart R. Schram (Cambridge: Cambridge Univ. Press, 1973), pp. 109–58.
8. Thomas Bernstein, "Leadership and Mass Mobilization in the Soviet and Chinese Collectivization Campaigns of 1929–30 and 1955–56: A Comparison," *China Quarterly*, 31 (July-Sep. 1967): 14. See also Kenneth R. Walker, "Collectivization in Retrospect: The 'Socialist High Tide' of Autumn 1955–Spring 1956," *China Quarterly*, (April-June 1966): 1–43.
9. Mao Zedong, "Notes from 'Socialist Upsurge in China's Countryside,' " *Selected Works*, vol. 5, p. 265.
10. Mao Zedong, "Selections from the Introductory Notes in 'The Social-

ist Upsurge in China's Countryside,' " *Selected Readings from the Works of Mao Tse-tung* (Peking: Foreign Languages Press, 1971), p. 421. Volume 5 of the *Selected Works* has a less vivid translation on p. 246.

11. Maurice Meisner, *Mao's China. A History of the People's Republic* (New York: Free Press, 1977), p. 167.

12. The most informative presentation of Khrushchev's secret speech is B. Nicolaevsky, ed., *Crimes of the Stalin Era* (New York: New Leader, 1962).

13. See Khrushchev's report in *Current Soviet Policies II: Documentary Record of the 20th Party Congress and Its Aftermath* (New York: Praeger, 1957), esp. pp. 39–46.

14. Sec T. H. Rigby, *Communist Party Membership in the U.S.S.R., 1917–1967* (Princeton: Princeton Univ. Press, 1968), pp. 309–14.

15. Mao Zedong, "Talks at Chengtu," in *Chairman Mao Talks to the People, Talks and Letters: 1956–1971*, ed. Stuart R. Schram (New York: Pantheon, 1974), p. 101.

16. Mao Zedong, "On the Ten Major Relationships," *Selected Works*, vol. 5, p. 304. (Our italics.) Schram, *Mao Talks to the People*, has a slightly different translation of this text: "On the Ten Great Relationships," pp. 61–83.

17. Mao Zedong, "On the Ten Major Relationships," *Selected Works*, vol. 5, p. 290.

18. Ibid., p. 291.

19. Mao Zedong, "Talks at Chengtu," in Schram, *Mao Talks to the People*, p. 99.

20. Mao Zedong, "On the Correct Handling of Contradictions Among the People," *Selected Works*, vol. 5, pp. 409, 410, 411.

21. Roderick MacFarquhar, *The Origins of the Cultural Revolution* (New York: Columbia Univ. Press, 1974), pp. 222, 223.

22. Meisner, *Mao's China*, p. 200.

23. Mao Zedong, "Talks at Chengtu," in Schram, *Mao Talks to the People*, p. 107.

24. Ibid., pp. 98, 99.

25. Cited in Meisner, *Mao's China*, pp. 239–40.

26. Mao Zedong, "Talks at Chengtu," in Schram, *Mao Talks to the People*, p. 110.

27. Ibid., p. 116.

28. See *Pravda*, Feb. 16, 1957.

29. Ibid., April 5, 1958.

30. Ibid., July 9, 1958.

31. Ibid., Sep. 20, 1959.

32. Ibid., May 8, 1957.

33. Ibid., Feb. 8, 1959.

34. See e.g. Mikoyan's discussion in the journal *Mirovaia Ekonomika i Mezhdunarodnye Otnosheniia*, 9 (1958), pp. 1–8.

35. Ia. Feig'in, "On Studying Contemporary Problems of the Distribution of Productive Forces," *Voprosy Ekonomiki*, 1 (Jan. 1960): pp. 59–68 [in Russian]. See also pp. 134–38.
36. See e.g. Khrushchev's report to the Twentieth Party Congress in *Current Soviet Policies II*, pp. 36–37, as well as his *For Peaceful Competition and Cooperation* (New York: International Arts and Sciences Press, 1959), and *For Victory in Peaceful Competition with Capitalism* (New York: Dutton, 1960).
37. Mao Zedong, "East Wind Prevails over the West Wind," in Schram, *Political Thought*, p. 283.
38. Ibid., "Reactionaries and Atom Bombs are Paper Tigers," and "East Wind Prevails," pp. 279–83.

CHAPTER 9: CULTURAL REVOLUTION AND
THE QUESTION OF STABILIZATION

1. *Let Us Live in Peace and Friendship—The Visit of N. S. Khrushchev to the U.S.A.* (Moscow: Foreign Languages Publ. House, 1959), p. 338.
2. Thomas P. Whitney, *Khrushchev Speaks* (Ann Arbor: Univ. of Michigan Press, 1963), p. 4.
3. Mao Zedong, "Speech at the Lushan Conference," in Stuart R. Schram, *Mao Talks to the People, Talks and Letters: 1956–1971* (New York: Pantheon, 1974), p. 139.
4. *Agriculture in the USSR* (Moscow, 1960), pp. 90–92, 226–29 [in Russian].
5. The figures, from the journal *Narodnoe Khoziaistvo* (1960), are given in A. Nove, *An Economic History of the U.S.S.R.* [orig. pub. 1969] (New York: Penguin, 1976), pp. 352–53. See also N. S. Khrushchev, *Target Figures for the Economic Development of the Soviet Union 1959–1965* (London: Soviet Booklet No. 47, 1959), a report to the 21st Congress of the CPSU.
6. *Pravda*, July 9, 1958.
7. Ibid., July 14, 1960.
8. Ibid., Jan. 11, 1961.
9. R. and Z. Medvedev, *Khrushchev, The Years in Power* (New York: Columbia Univ. Press, 1976), pp. 94–101.
10. Ibid., p. 112.
11. *Pravda*, January 14, 1961.
12. *Yevtushenko Poems—Bilingual Edition* (New York: Dutton, 1966), pp. 110, 112.
13. Cited in P. Johnson, *Khrushchev and the Arts* (Cambridge: MIT Press, 1965), pp. 101–5.
14. See Nove, *An Economic History*, p. 353.
15. Jack Gray, "The Two Roads: Alternative Strategies of Social Change

and Economic Growth in China," in *Authority, Participation and Social Change in China,* ed. Stuart R. Schram (Cambridge: Cambridge Univ. Press, 1974), p. 143.

16. Ibid., pp. 141, 144.
17. See Gray's discussion in ibid., pp. 136 ff.
18. C. S. Chen and C. P. Ridley, *Rural People's Communes in Lien-chiang* (Stanford: Hoover Institution Press, 1969), doc. 5.
19. Ibid.
20. Ibid.
21. Cited in S. Schram, "The Cultural Revolution in Historical Perspective," in Schram, ed., *Authority, Participation and Social Change,* p. 76. The essay is a thorough historical review of the two lines of struggle. See also Richard Baum and Frederick C. Teiwes, *Ssu-Ch'ing: The Socialist Education Movement of 1962–1966* (Berkeley: Univ. of California Press, 1968).
22. André Malraux, *Antimémoires* (Paris: Gallimard, 1967), p. 551.
23. Mao Zedong, "Spring Festival Day on Education," in *Mao Papers, Anthology and Bibliography,* ed. Jerome Ch'en (New York: Oxford Univ. Press, 1970), p. 96. See also the longer version in Schram, *Mao Talks to the People,* pp. 197–211.
24. Text of the "Sixteen Points: Guidelines for the Great Proletarian Cultural Revolution," in *The People's Republic of China: A Documentary History of Revolutionary Change,* ed. Mark Selden (New York: Monthly Review Press, 1979), p. 550.
25. Ibid., p. 555.
26. Ibid., p. 554.
27. Lin Biao, "Foreword to the Second Edition of 'Quotations from Chairman Mao Tse-tung,'" in *Quotations from Chairman Mao Tse-tung* (Peking: Foreign Language Press, 1966). For an intriguing personal account of the Red Guards see Gordon A. Bennett and Ronald H. Montaperto, *Red Guard: the Political Biography of Dai Hsiao-ai* (New York: Doubleday, 1971). Among the best accounts of the Cultural Revolution is Nancy and David Milton, *The Wind Will Not Subside: Years in Revolutionary China—1964–1969* (New York: Pantheon, 1976). Neale Hunter's *Shanghai Journal* (Boston: Beacon, 1971) conveys the extraordinary excitement and confusion of that city during the Cultural Revolution, and William Hinton's, *Hundred Day War: The Cultural Revolution at Tsinghua University* (New York: Monthly Review, 1972) is essential to understanding the movement in the universities. On the Cultural Revolution in the countryside, see Richard Baum, "The Cultural Revolution in the Countryside: Anatomy of a Limited Revolution," *The Cultural Revolution in China,* ed. Thomas W. Robinson (Berkeley: Univ. of California Press, 1971). For a complex interpretation of the Cultural Revolution in the context of American and Russian responses to it see James

Peck, "Revolution versus Modernization and Revisionism," in *China's Uninterrupted Revolution from 1840 to the Present*, eds., James Peck and Victor Nee (New York: Pantheon, 1975).

28. Mao Zedong, "Talk at the Report Meeting," in Schram, *Mao Talks to the People*, pp. 264–65.

29. Ibid., p. 273.

30. Speech by Comrade Ye Jianying, chairman of the NPC Standing Committee in celebration of the thirtieth anniversary of the founding of the PRC, in *Beijing Review*, 40 (Oct. 5, 1979), p. 15.

31. For two very different approaches to Shanghai during the Cultural Revolution, see Maurice Meisner, *Mao's China. A History of the People's Republic* (New York: Free Press, 1977), pp. 317–24, 354; and Andrew G. Walder, *Chang Ch'un Ch'iao and Shanghai's January Revolution* (Ann Arbor: Center for Chinese Studios, The Univ. of Michigan, 1978).

32. Mao Zedong, "Talk at the Meeting of the Central Cultural Revolutionary Group," in Schram, *Mao Talks to the People*, p. 275.

33. Cited in Schram, "Historical Perspective," in *Authority, Participation and Cultural Change*, p. 92.

34. Mao Zedong, "Talks at Three Meetings with Comrades Chang Ch'un-ch'iao and Yao Wen-yuan," in Schram, *Mao Talks to the People*, p. 278.

35. Ibid., p. 277.

36. Cited in Graham Young, "Vanguard Leadership and Cultural Revolution Activism," *Australian Journal of Chinese Affairs*, 3 (Jan. 1980): 43.

37. Mao Zedong, "Talk at the Enlarged Central Work Conference," in Schram, *Mao Talks to the People*, p. 167.

38. Ibid., "Directive on Public Health," p. 233.

39. The most interesting reassessment of Maoist educational policy and the post-Mao "pragmatic" reform argues that the simple rejection of cultural revolutionary policies is neither desirable nor possible. See Suzanne Pepper, "Chinese Education After Mao: Two Steps Forward, Two Steps Back and Begin Again?" *China Quarterly*, 81 (March 1980): 1–65.

40. Mao Zedong, "Conversation with the Nepalese Delegation of Educationists," in Ch'en, *Mao Papers*, p. 22.

41. Ibid., p. 23.

42. To be sure, there are other ways of looking at this effort. Whatever the ideological justification, commune and brigade level schools shifted the cost of education from the state onto peasant communities themselves. Quality also left much to be desired, though here, as in the case of open enrollment or community control of schools in the United States, the issues are complex and definitions of "quality" become important.

43. Judgments about Dazhai have undergone radical revisions since the

fall of the Gang of Four. Among other charges, brigade production figures are said to have been wildly falsified.

44. Cited in Kai-yu Hsu, *The Chinese Literary Scene: A Writer's Visit to the People's Republic* (New York: Vintage, 1975), p. 51.

45. Translated by Kai-yu Hsu, *Twentieth Century Chinese Poetry: An Anthology* (Ithaca, N.Y.: Cornell Univ. Press, 1970), p. 440.

46. Kai-yu Hsu, *Chinese Literary Scene*, p. 95.

47. Ibid., pp. 32–33.

48. Jean Chesneaux et al., *China: The People's Republic, 1949–1976* (New York: Pantheon, 1979), p. 175. See also Jean Daubier, *A History of the Cultural Revolution* (New York: Vintage, 174), pp. 265 ff. On the policy of "rusticating" urban youth, see Thomas P. Bernstein's *Up to the Mountains and Down to the Villages: The Transfer of Youth from Urban to Rural China* (New Haven: Yale Univ. Press, 1977). On rural industrialization, see Jon Sigurdson, *Rural Industrialization in China* (Cambridge: Council on East Asian Studies, Harvard Univ., 1977). On health policy, see Victor W. and Ruth Sidel, *Serve the People: Observations on Medicine in the People's Republic of China* (New York: Macy, 1973). On changes in industrial management, see Stephen Andors, *China's Industrial Revolution: Politics, Planning and Management, 1949 to the Present* (New York: Pantheon, 1977).

CHAPTER 10: STRAW SANDALS:
THE AMBIGUITIES OF POWER

1. V. Glebov, *Maoism: Slogans and Practice* (Moscow: Novosti, 1978), pp. 8–9 [in Russian]. See also Mao Zedong, *On Khrushchev's Phoney Communism* (Peking: Foreign Languages Press, 1964), and F. Burlatsky, *Mao Tse-tung: An Ideological and Psychological Portrait* (Moscow: Progress, 1980).

2. E.g., *Beijing Review*, 20 (May 19, 1980): 5; and *Pravda*, August 27, 1977, an analysis of the Eleventh CPC Congress.

3. On the meaning of "conservatism" in the Soviet context, however, see the thoughtful discussion by J. Hough, *How the Soviet Union Is Governed* (Cambridge: Harvard Univ. Press, 1979), pp. 264–66.

4. J. Hough, "The Brezhnev Era," *Problems of Communism*, 25: 2 (March-April 1976): 4.

5. A parallel and connected campaign, to criticize Lin Biao and Confucius, had as a primary focus the position of women in China. See Elizabeth Croll, "The Movement to Criticize Confucius and Lin Piao," *Signs: Journal of Women in Culture and Society*, 2:3 (Spring 1977): 721–26.

6. *Peking Review*, 22 (May 30, 1975): 10.

7. "The Nation Studies Theory of Dictatorship of the Proletariat," *Peking Review*, 8 (Feb. 21, 1975): 3–4.

8. Zhang Chunqiao, "On Exercising All-Around Dictatorship over the Bourgeoisie," in *And Mao Makes 5: Mao Tse-tung's Last Great Battle*, ed. Raymond Lotta (Chicago: Banner Press, 1978), p. 219.

9. Ibid., pp. 439, 441.

10. Glebov, *Maoism*, pp. 14–16, 114–17, 120–21.

11. For a particularly interesting discussion of the differences between Deng and Zhou see John Bryan Starr, "From the 10th Party Congress to the Premiership of Hua Kuo-feng: The Significance of the Colour of the Cat," *China Quarterly*, 67 (Sep., 1976): 457–88.

12. Glebov, *Maoism*, p. 114.

13. *Beijing Review*, 6 (June 2, 1980): 6. The harshest assessment of Deng's policies is Charles Bettleheim's lengthy, "The Great Leap Backward," *Monthly Review*, 30 (July–Aug. 1978): 37–130. A more generous and tentative critique is Mark Selden's comments in his introduction to *The People's Republic of China: A Documentary History of Revolutionary Change*, pp. 147–61. See also David M. Lampton's judicious essay, "New 'Revolution' in China's Social Policy," *Problems of Communism*, 28: 5–6 (Sep.-Dec., 1979): 16–33. For Stephen Andor's excellent assessment of the impact of the new economic policies, see S. Andors, "The Political and Organizational Implications of China's New Economic Policies, 1976–1979," *Bulletin of Concerned Asian Scholars*, 12: 2 (April-June 1980): 44–57.

14. *Beijing Review*, 28 (July 13, 1979): 19.

15. Readers might also like to examine, however, two studies that do catalog in topical fashion the differences between Chinese and Soviet communism: Donald W. Treadgold, ed., *Soviet and Chinese Communism: Similarities and Differences* (Seattle: Univ. of Washington Press, 1967), and Kurt London, ed., *Unity and Contradiction: Major Aspects of Sino-Soviet Relations* (New York: Praeger, 1962). See also John G. Gurley, "Dialectics of Development: USSR vs. China," *China Quarterly*, 4:2 (April 1978): 123–55, and esp. Bernard M. Frolic, "Comparing China and the Soviet Union," *Contemporary China*, 2:2 (Summer 1978): 24–42.

16. James C. Scott argues, however, that peasants may have maintained these goals as part of their own rebellious tradition whose relationship to the "great tradition" of communist revolution in China was complex and often in conflict. See "Revolution in the Revolution: Peasants and Commissars," *Theory and Society*, 7: 1–2 (Jan.-March 1979).

17. William Sewell, *I Stayed in China* (London: Allen & Unwin, 1966), p. 98.

18. On the "second economy" see esp. G. Grossman, "The 'Second Economy' of the USSR," *Problems of Communism*, 26: 5 (Sep-Oct. 1977): 25–40.

19. Leon Trotsky, *Literature and Revolution* [orig. pub. 1924] (Ann Arbor: Univ. of Michigan Press, 1960), esp. chap. 8.

Chronology of Major Events

1613–1917: Romanov rule in Russia

1644–1911: Rule of the Qing dynasty in China

1870: Lenin born in Simbirsk (April 10)

1893: Mao born in Hunan province (Dec. 26)

1898: First Congress of the Russian Social Democratic Labor party (March 1–3)

The Hundred Days of Reform in China (June 11–Sept. 16)

1898–1900: Boxer Rebellion

1902: Publication of Lenin's "What is to be Done?"

1903: Formation of the Bolshevik faction at the Second Congress of the Russian Social Democratic Labor party (July 30–Aug. 23)

1904–05: Russo-Japanese War

1905: Revolution in Russia, called by Lenin and others a "dress rehearsal" for 1917

Examination system abolished in China

Formation of Tongmenghui

1912: National Assembly elects Yuan Shikai provisional president of the Chinese Republic (Feb. 15)

1914: Russia enters the First World War (Aug. 1)

1915: Publication of *New Youth* magazine and the beginning of the New Culture movement in China

1916–28: "Warlord" period in China

1917: Overthrow of Tsar Nicholas II (Feb.–March)
Formation of the Provisional Government (March 2)
Lenin Returns to Russia (April 3)
Spontaneous occupation of factories and expropriation of gentry land (spring through late fall)
Overthrow of the Provisional Government and establishment of Bolshevik rule (Oct. 25–26)
Land Decree issued in Russia, formally abolishing landowners right to own land. (Oct. 27)
1918: Treaty of Brest-Litovsk between Soviet Russia and Germany (March 3)
Beginning of Russian civil war
1919: May Fourth movement begins in Peking
1921: Kronstadt Rebellion (March 2–17) and the end of civil war in Russia
Tenth Party Congress in Moscow (March 8–16) and beginning of NEP
Founding and First Congress of the Chinese Communist party (CCP) (July 1)
1922: Stalin becomes first secretary of the Russian Communist party (CPSU) (April 3)
Fourth Congress of the Communist International (Comintern) calls for an alliance between the CCP and the Kuomintang (KMT) (Nov. 5–Dec. 5)
Lenin has his second stroke and prepares his "Testament" (Dec. 16–25)
1923–24: Reorganization of the KMT and first united front with the CCP
1924: Death of Lenin (Jan. 21)
1925: May Thirtieth movement spreads from Shanghai
Mao and others organize Hunan peasant movement
1926: Beginning of Northern Expedition to unify China against warlords and imperialists (July)
1927: Chiang Kai-shek strikes against the CCP in Shanghai (April 12)
Execution of CCP leaders in Peking by Zhang-Zuolin (April 28)
Comintern Eighth Plenum at which Stalin defends his position on China against attacks by Trotsky (May 20–26)
Autumn Harvest Uprising led by Mao in Hunan (Sept. 5–18)
Mao establishes small base at Jinggangshan, on Hunan/Jiangxi border (October)
Trotsky and Zinoviev expelled from the CPSU (Nov. 15)
Canton Commune insurrection (Dec. 11–14); end of first united front; and massive "White" terror throughout China (1927–28)
1928: Grain procurement crisis in the Soviet Union

1930–34: Jiangxi Soviet established by CCP
Collectivization of agriculture and the First Five-Year Plan in the USSR
1930: First KMT annihilation campaign against CCP
1931–32: Japanese occupation of Manchuria
1932–33: Famine in the Russian countryside
1934: Seventeenth Congress of the CPSU (Jan. 30–Feb. 4) (Congress of the "Victors")
Assassination of Kirov (Dec. 1)
1935: Trial of Zinoviev, Kamenev, and others (Jan. 15–17); beginning purges
Long March of the CCP from Jiangxi to Shaanxi
1936: Moscow trials continue; execution of Kamenev and Zinoviev
1937: Trial and execution of Marshal Tukhachevskii begins massive purge of the Red Army (June)
1937–45: Full-scale war between Japan and China; second KMT-CCP united front
1937–38: High period of the Stalinist purges
1939: Nonaggression pact between USSR and Germany (Aug. 23)
Outbreak of World War II in Europe (Sept. 1)
1941: Germany invades Soviet Union (June 22)
1942: Party rectification movement (*zhengfeng*) in China
1942–43: Battle of Stalingrad (Nov.–Feb.); turning point on the Eastern Front
1945: Battle of Berlin and German surrender (May 1–8)
Japanese surrender to US (Sept. 2) and Chiang K'ai-shek (Sept. 9)
1946–49: Full-scale civil war in China
1949: CCP victory and establishment of People's Republic in Peking (Oct. 1)
1950–53: Korean War
1953: Death of Stalin (Mar. 5); Khrushchev becomes first secretary of the party; Malenkov becomes chairman of the Council of Ministers
1955–56: Collectivization of Chinese agriculture
1956: Twentieth Party Congress (Feb. 14–25) and Khrushchev's secret speech
1956–57: One Hundred Flowers Campaign
1958–60: Great Leap Forward in China
1958: Khrushchev becomes chairman of the Council of Ministers (Mar. 27)
1959: Beginning of Khrushchev's Seven-Year Plan in the USSR
Khrushchev's first visit to the US (Sept.), followed by visit to Peking
1960: Withdrawal of all Soviet aid and technicians from China (July–Aug.)

1962: Cuban missile crisis (October)
Chinese border clash with India (Oct.–Nov.)
Start of the Socialist Education movement in China
1964: First Chinese A-bomb exploded (Oct. 16)
Khrushchev removed from all official responsibilities (Oct. 16); period of Brezhnev-Kosygin joint leadership begins
1966–69: Great Proletarian Cultural Revolution in China
1969: Armed clashes on Sino-Soviet border
1971: China enters the United Nations (Oct. 25)
1976–80: Period of the Fifth Chinese Five-Year Plan ("four modernizations")
1976: Death of Zhou Enlai (Jan. 8) and Mao Zedong (Sept. 9)
1980: Trial of the Gang of Four and associates

Suggestions for Further Reading

The following suggestions for further reading are by no means a comprehensive guide to the available literature, which is vast. We wish only to call attention here to major secondary studies, most of which contain extensive bibliographies. Footnotes to each chapter also contain suggestions for pursuing particular points. Some of the most important work appears in periodicals. See especially *Asian Survey, Bulletin of Concerned Asian Scholars, China Quarterly, Far Eastern Economic Review, Journal of Asian Studies, Journal of Modern History, Modern Asian Survey, Modern China, Pacific Affairs, Russian History, Russian Review, Slavic Review, Soviet Studies,* and *Soviet Union*. Excellent articles on comparative history and issues of comparative historical development may also be found in *Comparative Studies in Society and History, Journal of Economic History, Journal of Social History, Past and Present,* and *Social History*. For convenience, our suggestions are arranged by chapter heading.

PREFACE: REVOLUTION AS PROCESS

We wish to reemphasize the importance of Charles Tilly, *From Mobilization to Revolution*, and Theda Skocpol, *States and Social Revolutions*, as well as the essays noted in Footnote 2. Tilly contains a very extensive bibliography on collective action, interest groups, revolutionary mobilization, and revolution in general, while Skocpol has comprehensive bibliographies on Russia, China, France, and revolutionary theory. A particularly sensitive essay on the politics of scholarly analyses of revolution is Sheldon Wolin, "Politics and the Study of Revolution," *Comparative Politics*, V:3 (April 1973), 343–58. Bernard M. Frolic, "Comparing China and the Soviet Union," *Contemporary China*, II:2 (Summer 1978), 24–42, discusses various efforts at comparing the revolutionary processes in Russia and China, and Donald W. Treadgold, ed., *Soviet and Chinese Communism* (Seattle: University of Washington Press, 1967), offers a number of topic by topic comparisons written by various specialists in the field.

CHAPTER 1: REVOLUTIONARY RUSSIA
AND THE DILEMMAS OF SOCIAL DEMOCRACY

Unfortunately, there is no good single study of prerevolutionary Russian society. Readers might avoid popularistic regime studies in favor of such contemporary analyses as Sir Donald Mackenzie Wallace, *Russia on the Eve of War and Revolution*, first published in 1871 and extensively rewritten in 1912 (New York: Vintage Books, 1961); the liberal leader Paul Miliukov's *Russia and Its Crisis* (New York: Collier Books, 1962), from a lecture series given in the United States in 1903 and 1904; or the classic study of the British journalist historian, Sir Bernard Pares, *The Fall of the Russian Monarchy* (New York: Alfred Knopf, 1939), based on extended research and personal contacts during the years 1904–19. An interesting, brief description of the prerevolutionary Russian countryside can be found in J. Rickman's essay in J. Rickman and G. Gorer, *People of Great Russia* (New York: Norton, 1962); a somewhat more detailed and comprehensive study is John Maynard, *The Russian Peasant* (New York: Collier Books, 1962), first published in 1942. The best analysis of early Russian Marxism is Leopold Haimson, *The Russian Marxists and the Origins of Bolshevism* (Cambridge: Harvard Univ. Press, 1955). See also Allan Wildman, *The Making of a Workers' Revolution: Russian Social Democracy, 1891–1903* (Chicago: Univ. of Chicago Press, 1967). On the failure of Russia's experiment with parliamentary monarchy see especially Geoffrey A. Hosking, *The Russian Constitutional Experiment: Government and Duma, 1907–1914* (London: Cambridge Univ. Press, 1973). There are a number of excellent biographies of early Russian Marxists. Among the best are Samuel Baron, *Plekhanov* (Stanford: Stanford Univ. Press, 1963); Israel Getzler, *Martov: A Political Biography of a Russian Social Democrat* (London: Cambridge Univ. Press, 1967) and Abraham Ascher, *Pavel Axelrod and the Development of Menshevism* (Cambridge: Harvard Univ. Press, 1972). See also Isaac Deutscher's definitive three-volume biography of *Trotsky* (New York: Oxford Univ. Press, 1954–63), his *Stalin: A Political Biography* (New York: Oxford Univ. Press, 1961), and Bertram Wolfe's lively but somewhat dated *Three Who Made a Revolution* (Boston: Beacon Press, 1948), on Lenin, Trotsky, and Stalin. A superb study is Stephen F. Cohen, *Bukharin and the Bolshevik Revolution* (New York: Alfred A. Knopf, 1973), republished with new material in 1979 (New York: Oxford Univ. Press).

CHAPTER 2: 1917: THE PARADOX OF VICTORY

The best general history of the Russian Revolution and civil war remains William H. Chamberlin, *The Russian Revolution*, 2 vols. (New York: Macmillan, 1935), despite the publication in recent years of several excellent specialized studies. E.H. Carr, *The Bolshevik Revolution* (New York: Macmillan, 1951–53), is a thorough, if somewhat idiosyncratic analysis of Bolshevik theory, practices, and foreign policy. The political parties have been treated by Oliver H. Radkey, *Agrarian Foes of Bolshevism* (New York: Columbia Univ. Press, 1958), Alexander Rabinowitch, *The Bolsheviks Come to Power: The Revolution of 1917 in Petrograd* (New York: Norton, 1976), and William G. Rosenberg, *Liberals in the Russian Revolution* (Princeton: Princeton Univ. Press, 1974). A superb new study of Moscow workers in 1917 is Diane Koenker, *Moscow Workers and the 1917 Revolution* (Princeton: Princeton Univ. Press, 1981). John Keep, *The Russian Revolution: A Study in Mass Mobilization* (New York: Norton, 1976) has good material on the Russian countryside, as well as an analysis of workers' committees and other elements of the mobilization process. The issues of committee organization and revolutionary mobilization are also the focus of the excellent study by Allan Wildman, *The End of the Russian Imperial Army* (Princeton: Princeton Univ. Press, 1980).

Much work remains to be done on Russian civil war. Robert V. Daniels, *The Conscience of the Revolution* (Cambridge: Harvard Univ. Press, 1965) has several good chapters on Bolshevik policy formation in the 1917–21 period, concentrating on oppositional elements; Leonard Schapiro, *The Origin of the Communist Autocracy* (London: G. Bell, 1955) surveys the repression of oppositional parties. Two good new studies of Bolshevik administration, one concentrating on Bolshevik government in Moscow and one focusing on the provinces, are T.H. Rigby, *Lenin's Government: Sovnarkom 1917–1922* (Cambridge: Cambridge Univ. Press, 1979), and Robert Service, *The Bolshevik Party in Revolution, 1917–1923* (New York: Barnes and Noble, 1979). Both contain good bibliographies. On the Kronstadt rebellion in 1921, see especially Paul Avrich, *Kronstadt 1921* (Princeton: Princeton Univ. Press, 1970). There is also a vast memoir literature on the revolutionary period. See in particular N.N. Sukhanov, *The Russian Revolution 1917*, 2 vols. (New York: Oxford Univ. Press, 1955), and John Reed's classic *Ten Days that Shook the World* (New York: Signet Books, 1967).

CHAPTER 3: CHINA AND THE MEANINGS
OF RUSSIA'S REVOLUTION

As noted in Footnote 4, the most interesting and sophisticated local study of this period is Joseph W. Esherick, *Reform and Revolution in China: The 1911 Revolution in Hunan and Hubei* (Berkeley: Univ. of California Press, 1976). In addition to the other works cited in the notes, the following books have added to our knowledge of the revolution of 1911 and the early Republic: Mary Backus Rankin, *Early Chinese Revolutionaries: Radical Intellectuals in Shanghai and Chekiang, 1902–1911* (Cambridge: Cambridge Univ. Press, 1971); Hsueh Chun-tu, *Huang Hsing and the Chinese Revolution* (Stanford: Stanford University Press, 1961); K. S. Liew, *Struggle for Democracy: Sung Chiao-jen and the 1911 Chinese Revolution* (Berkeley: Univ. of California Press, 1971); Ernest P. Young, *The Presidency of Yuan Shih-kai: Liberalism and Dictatorship in Early Republican China* (Ann Arbor: Univ. of Michigan Press, 1977); and Edward Rhoads, *China's Republican Revolution: The Case of Kwangtung, 1895–1913* (Cambridge: Harvard Univ. Press, 1975) all of which have good bibliographies. A good collection of essays reflecting recent research in the field has been edited by Charlotte Furth, *The Limits of Change: Essays in Conservative Alternatives in Republican China* (Cambridge: Harvard Univ. Press, 1976). Several biographies deepen our understanding of the May Fourth period and its impact on Chinese intellectuals. See especially Jerome B. Grieder, *Hu Shih and the Chinese Renaissance: Liberalism in the Chinese Revolution, 1917–1937* (Cambridge: Harvard Univ. Press, 1970); David Tod Roy, *Kuo Mo-jo: The Early Years* (Cambridge: Harvard Univ. Press, 1971); Charlotte Furth, *Ting Wen-chiang: Science and China's New Culture* (Cambridge: Harvard Univ. Press, 1970); Lawrence Schneider, *Ku Chieh-kang and China's New History: Nationalism and the Quest for Alternative Traditions* (Berkeley: Univ. of California Press, 1971). Benjamin I. Schwartz has edited a brief but provocative collection drawn from a conference on the subject: *Reflections on the May Fourth Movement: A Symposium* (Cambridge: East Asian Research Center of Harvard University, 1972). The standard text is by Chow Tse-tung, *The May Fourth Movement: Intellectual Revolution in Modern China* (Stanford: Stanford Univ. Press, 1967). On the influence of Marxist thought on Chinese revolutionaries, see especially Maurice Meisner's excellent study *Li Ta-chao and the Origins of Chinese Marxism* (Cambridge: Harvard Univ. Press, 1967). Don C. Price, *Russia and the Roots of the Chinese Revolution 1896–1911* (Cambridge: Harvard Univ. Press, 1974) is a useful monograph on the earliest ties between Chinese and Russian revolutionary developments, and Arif Dirlik, *Revolution and History: Origins of Marxist Historiography in China, 1919–1937* (Berkeley: Univ. of California Press, 1978) is a fascinating essay in the intellectual history of Chinese Marxism.

Lucien Bianco's *Origins of the Chinese Revolution, 1915–1949* (Stanford: Stanford Univ. Press, 1971) remains the best general history of the revolution in these years, which can be usefully supplemented by the chronologically organized treatment in Jean Chesneaux et al., *China: From the 1911 Revolution to Liberation* (New York: Pantheon Books, 1977). The best biography of Mao remains Stuart Schram, *Mao Tse-tung* (New York: Simon and Schuster, 1967).

CHAPTER 4: SHANGHAI: THE PARADOX OF DEFEAT

A number of important studies of this period are listed in the notes to Chapter 4, and need not be repeated here. In addition, Donald A. Jordan, *The Northern Expedition: China's National Revolution of 1926–1928* (Honolulu: Univ. Press of Hawaii, 1976) is a detailed treatment of the central event in China's "second" revolution and contains additional references. An important study of Soviet-Chinese relations in this period, in addition to the works of Isaacs and Brandt referred to in the chapter notes, is Robert C. North, *Moscow and Chinese Communists*, rev. ed. (Stanford: Stanford Univ. Press, 1963). See also Allen Whiting's detailed study *Soviet Policies in China, 1917–1924* (New York: Columbia Univ. Press, 1954). Jerome Ch'en, *Mao and the Chinese Revolution* (New York: Oxford Univ. Press, 1967) is an important history of the entire revolutionary period to 1949. See also Roy Hofheinz, *The Broken Wave: The Chinese Communist Peasant Movement, 1922–1928* (Cambridge: Harvard Univ. Press, 1977); Jean Chesneaux, *The Chinese Labor Movement, 1919–1927* (Stanford: Stanford Univ. Press, 1968); and Benjamin I. Schwartz, *Chinese Communism and the Rise of Mao* (Cambridge: Harvard Univ. Press, 1951), esp. chaps. 1–8. The classic treatment of the human tragedy at Shanghai in 1927 remains André Malraux, *Man's Fate* (New York: Random House, 1961).

CHAPTER 5: VANGUARDS: THE PARTIES AND PARTY-MASS RELATIONS IN THE 1930s

This enormously complex and difficult subject has been treated in many different ways by a host of books and articles, most focusing on one or another of its specific aspects. Perhaps the most comprehensive study of Soviet Russia in this period, and certainly the most interesting, is Roy Medvedev, *Let History Judge* (New York: Alfred A. Knopf, 1971). Its rough counterpart is the classic treatment by Edgar Snow, *Red Star Over China* (New York: Random House, 1938). In addition to the many studies referred to in the chapter notes, readers might also examine an interesting source on the Jiangxi period, the foreign service reports of O. Edmund Clubb, *Communism in China as Reported from Hankow in 1932* (New York: Columbia Univ. Press, 1968), and the important monograph by Derek J. Waller, *The Kiangsi Soviet Republic: Mao and the National Congresses of 1931 and 1934* (Berkeley: Univ. of California Press, 1973). See also Richard C. Thornton, *The Comintern and the Chinese Communists, 1928–1931* (Seattle: Univ. of Washington Press, 1969).

Moshe Lewin has contributed a superb monograph to the study of collectivization in Russia, *Russian Peasants and Soviet Power* (Evanston, Ill.: Northwestern Univ. Press, 1968), as well as a number of important essays on the 1920s, especially *Lenin's Last Struggle* (New York: Pantheon, 1968) and *Political Undercurrents in Soviet Economic Debates* (Princeton Univ. Press, 1974). See also Alexander Erlich, *The Soviet Industrialization Debate, 1924–1928* (Cambridge: Harvard Univ. Press, 1967), and the essays in Robert C. Tucker, ed., *Stalinism: Essays in Historical Interpretation* (New York: Norton, 1977). In addition to Evgenia Ginzburg, *Into the Whirlwind* (London: Collins/Harvill, 1967), a powerful and poignant memoir of the purges referred to in the text, readers might examine memoirs and recollections by Lydia Chukovskaia, *The Deserted House* (New York: Dutton, 1967), and Nadezhda Mandelstam, *Hope Against Hope* (New York: Atheneum, 1970), as well as, of course, Alexander Solzhenitsyn's classic treatment *Gulag Archipelago*, 3 vols. (New York: Harper and Row, 1973–76).

CHAPTER 6: GREAT PATRIOTIC STRUGGLES:
THE SOVIET UNION AND CHINA IN WORLD WAR II

An extraordinary group of Americans in China have recorded for us what Yanan was like at the time. In addition to the studies referred to in the chapter notes, see James Bertram, *Unconquered: Journal of a Year's Adventures Among the Fighting Peasants of North China* (New York: John Day, 1939); Harrison Forman, *Report from Red China* (New York: Da Capo, 1975); David Barrett, *Dixie Mission: The United States Army Observor Group in Yenan, 1944* (Berkeley: Univ. of California Press, 1970); and Nym Wales, *Red Dust* (Stanford: Stanford Univ. Press, 1962).

Tetsuo Kataoka, *Resistance and Revolution in China: The Communists and the Second United Front* (Berkeley: Univ. of California Press, 1974), is a provocative reinterpretation of the period. Chalmers A. Johnson, *Peasant Nationalism and Communist Power: The Emergence of Revolutionary China, 1937–1945* (Stanford: Stanford Univ. Press, 1961) first conceptualized "peasant nationalism" as a significant factor in communist victory and remains a standard interpretation acknowledged, if much disputed, by all later works. Essential to an understanding of Yanan communism are key documents of the period, which can be found in Boyd Compton's *Mao's China: Party Reform Documents, 1942–1944* (Seattle: Univ. of Washington Press, 1952), as well as the materials listed in the bibliography provided by Mark Selden in his *The Yenan Way in Revolutionary China* (Cambridge: Harvard Univ. Press, 1971). A major new work, published too late to be consulted, puts the communist movement in North China in a much larger time frame: Elizabeth J. Perry, *Rebels and Revolutionaries in North China, 1845–1945* (Stanford: Stanford Univ. Press, 1980).

For the Soviet Union, the best general study remains Alexander Werth, *Russia at War, 1941–1945* (New York: Dutton, 1964), although this analysis by the London Sunday Times correspondent is essentially a memoir, rather than a comprehensive history. A good scholarly treatment of the war from the Soviet perspective remains to be written, in part because of the difficulty in obtaining necessary primary materials. An important study based on German materials is Alexander Dallin, *German Rule in Russia* (London: Macmillan, 1957). See also Leon Goure and Herbert S. Dinerstein, *Moscow in Crisis* (Glencoe, Ill.: The Free Press, 1955) and Harrison E. Salisbury, *The 900 Days* (New York: Harper and Row, 1969), based extensively on Soviet memoir literature.

CHAPTER 7: SOCIALIST ROADS AND THE
VARIETIES OF RECOVERY

The literature on the impact of World War II on Russian society and the problems of Soviet reconstruction is surprisingly thin, again in part due to the difficulty in obtaining good data. The best material can be found in current journals, particularly *Soviet Studies*, and in chapters of more comprehensive works, such as Leonard Schapiro, *The Communist Party of the Soviet Union* (New York: Vintage Books, 1960), or Merle Fainsod, *How Russia is Ruled* (Cambridge: Harvard Univ. Press, 1953), revised in 1963, and again, in a controversial fashion, by Jerry Hough under the title *How the Soviet Union is Governed* (Cambridge: Harvard Univ. Press, 1979). English translations of proceedings at the Nineteenth (1952) and Twentieth (1956) Congresses of the CPSU, which contain much material on the postwar period as well as Khrushchev's analysis of the "cult of personality" have been edited by Leo Gruliow as *Current Soviet Policies* (New York: Current Digest of the Soviet Press, 1953–56). See also the interesting material in Alex Inkeles and Raymond Bauer, *The Soviet Citizen* (Cambridge: Harvard Univ. Press, 1959) and in their collaborative work with Clyde Kluckholn, *How the Soviet System Works* (Cambridge: Harvard Univ. Press, 1956), which derived from interviews with Soviet refugees in the early 1950s. The cult of personality has been discussed in an extended essay by Roy Medvedev, *On Stalin and Stalinism* (New York: Oxford Univ. Press, 1979), as well as his other writings. See also Barrington Moore, Jr., *Terror and Progress—USSR* (Cambridge: Harvard Univ. Press, 1954).

In addition to Suzanne Pepper, *Civil War in China: The Political Struggle 1945–1949* (Berkeley: Univ. of California Press, 1978), referred to in the text, Lionel Max Chassin's *Communist Conquest of China: A History of the Civil War, 1945–1949* (Cambridge: Harvard Univ. Press, 1965) is a useful military history of the civil war. See also, William Whitson, *A History of Chinese Communist Military Politics* (New York: Praeger, 1973). Two local studies examine the early period of Communist consolidation: Ezra Vogel, *Canton under Communism* (Cambridge: Harvard Univ. Press, 1969) and Kenneth G. Lieberthal, *Revolution and Tradition in Tientsin, 1945–1952* (Stanford: Stanford Univ. Press, 1980). Direct accounts by two very different Americans in China at the time are Derk Bodde, *Peking Diary: A Year of Revolution* ((New York: Henry Schuman, 1950) and A. Doak Barnett, *China on the Eve of Communist Takeover* (New York: Praeger, 1963).

CHAPTER 8: GREAT LEAPS FORWARD:
IRONIES AND CONTRADICTIONS, 1954–1964

David and Isabel Crook report on the transformation during the Great Leap of the village they knew intimately in the late 1940s in *The First Years of the Yangyi Commune* (London: Routledge and Kegan Paul, 1966). Jan Myrdal, *Report from a Chinese Village* (New York: Pantheon, 1965) has much useful information on village life in the aftermath of the Leap. Although focusing on a later period, E.L. Wheelwright and Bruce McFarlane, *The Chinese Road to Socialism: Economics of Cultural Revolution* (New York: Monthly Review Press, 1970) is an important analysis of the Great Leap as well. For a general treatment of this period, we recommend again Maurice Meisner, *Mao's China* (New York: The Free Press, 1977). Robert Bowie and John K. Fairbank, eds., *Communist*

China 1955–1959 Policy Documents with Analysis (Cambridge: Harvard Univ. Press, 1962), offers important primary material on this period. For the Sino-Soviet split see John Gittings, *Survey of the Sino-Soviet Dispute, 1963–1967* (London: Oxford Univ. Press, 1968) as well as Donald S. Zagoria, *The Sino-Soviet Conflict, 1956–1961* (Princeton: Princeton Univ. Press, 1962), which contain additional references.

The Khrushchev years in the USSR await thorough study. Roy and Zhores Medvedev, *Khrushchev: The Years in Power* (New York: Columbia University Press, 1976) is an extremely interesting and informative study, focused primarily on agricultural policies. Carl A. Linden, *Khrushchev and the Soviet Leadership, 1957–1964* (Baltimore: Johns Hopkins, 1966) examines high party politics in this period, and there are several interesting essays in Stephen F. Cohen et al., eds., *The Soviet Union Since Stalin* (Bloomington: Indiana Univ. Press, 1980). Abraham Brumberg, ed., *Russia Under Khrushchev* (New York: Praeger, 1962) brings together a large number of informative articles first published in the journal *Problems of Communism*. See also Sidney Ploss, *Conflict and Decision-Making in Soviet Russia, A Case Study of Agricultural Policy 1953–1963* (Princeton: Princeton Univ. Press, 1965), Mary McAuley, *Labor Disputes in Soviet Russia, 1957–1965* (Oxford: Clarendon Press, 1969), and Deming Brown's sensitive and informative study *Soviet Russian Literature since Stalin* (Cambridge: Cambridge Univ. Press, 1978). Khrushchev's tape-recorded memoirs, published as *Khrushchev Remembers* (Boston: Little, Brown, 1970), while suspect, make interesting reading.

CHAPTER 9: CULTURAL REVOLUTION AND
THE QUESTION OF STABILIZATION

In addition to the studies referred to in the chapter notes (esp. notes 27 and 48), see K.S. Karol, *The Second Chinese Revolution* (New York: Hill and Wang, 1974), a critical yet sympathetic acount of the cultural revolution by an acute observor whose earlier book, *China, The Other Communism* (New York: Hill & Wang, 1967), should also be read. Lowell Dittmer examines Liu Shaoqi's side of the struggle in *Liu Shao-ch'i and the Chinese Cultural Revolution: The Politics of Mass Criticism* (Berkeley: Univ. of California Press, 1974). An interesting structural interpretation is Byung-joon Ahn, *Chinese Politics and the Cultural Revolution: Dynamics of Policy Processes* (Seattle: Univ. of Washington Press, 1977). See also Edward Rice, *Mao's Way* (Berkeley: Univ. of California Press, 1972). Two more general works on the nature of ideology in China are also of interest: John B. Starr, *Ideology and Culture: An Introduction* to the *Dialectic of Contemporary Chinese Politics* (New York: Harper and Row, 1973), and Donald J. Munro, *The Concept of Man in Contemporary China* (Ann Arbor: Univ. of Michigan Press, 1977). Moss Roberts has translated a document of major importance to our understanding of Mao's critique of the Soviet Union: *Mao Tsetung: A Critique of Soviet Economics* (New York and London: Monthly Review Press, 1977). There is a small but growing body of literature on the subject of women in China. See especially Elizabeth Croll, *Feminism and Socialism in China* (New York: Schocken Books, 1980), and Delia Davin, *Woman-Work: Women and the Party in Revolutionary China* (London: Oxford Univ. Press, 1976), as well as Marilyn B. Young, ed., *Women in China: Studies in Social Change and Feminism* (Ann Arbor: Michigan Papers in Chinese Studies, 1973).

The transition in Soviet Russia from Khrushchev to Brezhnev, including analysis of the Twenty-second Party Congress, the Cuban crisis, and the events immediately preceding Khrushchev's ouster, is well covered in Michel Tatu, *Power in the Kremlin: From Khrushchev to Kosygin* (New York: Viking, 1969). For discussion of events in the mid- and late sixties, see Alexander Dallin and Thomas B. Larson, eds., *Soviet Politics Since Khrushchev* (Englewood Cliffs, N.J.: Prentice Hall, 1968). Two useful collections on the Brezhnev era are Henry W. Morton and Rudolf L. Tokes, eds., *Soviet Politics and Society in the 1970s* (New York: Free Press, 1974), and Archie Brown and Michael Kaser, eds., *The Soviet Union since the Fall of Khrushchev* (London: Macmillan, 1975). See also the very informative study by Alexander Yanov, *The Russian New Right* (Berkeley: Institute of International Studies, Univ. of California, 1978), and the recent analysis of the leadership cohort by Jerry F. Hough, *Soviet Leadership in Transition* (Washington:Brookings, 1980).

CHAPTER 10: STRAW SANDALS:
THE AMBIGUITIES OF POWER

On China post-Mao, Dick Wilson has assembled an interesting collection of essays in *Mao Tse-tung on the Scales of History: A Preliminary Assessment* (New York: Cambridge Univ. Press, 1977), which includes bibliography. See also Bill Brugger's anthology, *China Since the Gang of Four* (New York: St. Martin's Press, 1980). Of the many retrospective analyses of Soviet development, one of the most perceptive is Isaac Deutscher, *The Unfinished Revolution* (New York: Oxford Univ. Press, 1969).

Index
(With Brief Biographical Notations)

DATE DUE

FEB 4 1985			

GAYLORD

PRINTED IN U.S.A.